A NATURAL HISTORY OF THE SOUL

C. Flammarion (1888)

A NATURAL HISTORY OF THE SOUL

Who are we anyway?
What does our future hold?

Arnold M. Lund, PhD

Örn Press

Images in the book are owned by the author, provided by Wikimedia Commons, or are in the public domain. Web sources are as of the publication of this book and may change. Philosophical positions and schools of theological thought are inherently subject to interpretation, although a sincere attempt has been made to capture the broad, relevant themes.

First paperback edition August 2021

ISBN 978-1-7368742-0-2 (paperback)
ISBN 978-1-7368742-1-9 (ebook)

Library of Congress Control Number: 2021905348

Örn Press
437 5th Ave S, #3B
Edmonds, WA 98020
Ornpress.com

We have lost many family, friends, and colleagues during these stressful times. One form of existing beyond this part of our journey is how we live on in the hearts and memories of loved ones. For those of us who remain, it is comforting to know we are still connected with the souls who have gone ahead. This book is dedicated to the spirits who were crowding around my shoulders as I wrote this book, and they include:

Rev. Douglas Meland
Doris Meland
Dianne Hoover
Tim Johnson
Rev. William Bostrom
Ted Griffiths
Dean Mohr

"People say that what we're all seeking is a meaning for life...I think that what we're seeking is an experience of being alive, so that our life experiences on the purely physical plane will have resonances with our own innermost being and reality, so that we actually feel the rapture of being alive."
– Joseph Campbell

"There are no ordinary people...It is immortals whom we joke with, work with, marry, snub, and exploit— immortal horrors or everlasting splendours."
– C. S. Lewis

CONTENTS

ACKNOWLEDGMENTS

I should begin with the person who has been with me from well before this project began, my wife, Marlene. She probably thought, "Oh, oh!" when I returned from that fateful walk excited by my idea. She has listened patiently to me as I have discovered things I did not know and was a source of insights as we discussed questions that I was uncovering. She provided a wealth of experiences ranging from her time in Brazil to her recent work with moms of LGBTQ+ kids. I especially appreciate her willingness to invest so much of her time to provide the final editing pass on my book, and the book is far better for her valuable critique. Despite recently losing so many in her family, she continues to be a rock for all of us during these pandemic times. This book would not have happened without her support.

As a seminary student in the chaplaincy program at The Seattle School of Theology & Psychology, my daughter Sonja has carried a unique burden. She patiently responded to all my questions about Greek and Hebrew words. She naturally was roped into discussions about my questions and ideas. As an English major from Mills College, she also was my lifeline for questions like how to format a quote within a quote within a quote.

My other daughter Anna, the vampirologist and expert on esoterica, was a critical source as I worked on the section on popular culture, the history of the dead and the undead, and many other areas that captured my interest. She was a valuable voice when I was trying to decide on fonts, phrases, images, and further details that needed to be nailed down. Her storytelling expertise from her film degree and her gaming have been the source of hours of discussion.

My sister Christine Griffiths is the fourth partner in this journey. In some ways, this book was written for her. When I shared things I was thinking about, I knew I was on the right track if they caught her attention. She has also been the source of some of the particularly fascinating stories from our family shared in the book. Given her recent loss of her husband, Ted Griffiths, I am doubly thankful for her help. Ted, who was also my good friend, is one of those to whom the book is dedicated.

I have been fortunate to have had several professors who have shaped my thinking. Dr. Richard Lindley was my mentor when I started graduate school and helped get me on the path to my career. It did not hurt that he introduced Marlene and me to serious gourmet cooking. I was fortunate to have Dr. B. J. Underwood as my PhD professor, a true mentor, and I believe, a friend. A bonus, of course, is that I discovered gin and tonics as his student. When I was in seminary, I grew both in my critical thinking and spiritually studying under Dr. Clark Pinnock (systematic theology), Dr. Murray Harris (New Testament critical interpretation), and John Stott, CBE.

Finally, I am grateful to the University of Washington, Bothell School of Science, Technology, Engineering & Mathematics, and the Division of Computing & Software Systems, in particular, for letting me adjust my schedule to work on this book. I also need to give a shout-out to the Walnut Coffee Shop in Edmonds, WA, which kept me going with lattes and enthusiastic support as the book progressed.

A NATURAL HISTORY OF THE SOUL

INTRODUCTION

"It was a pretty place to die...Had you been visiting the Consumptives' Home in April 1901, you might have been witness to a curious undertaking."
— Mary Roach

L et's begin this natural history with a story, the story of the man who tried to weigh the soul in The Cullis Consumptives' Home in Dorchester, MA. Dr. Duncan MacDougall was a physician from Haverhill, MA. The events happened in the early 1900s. Dr. MacDougall was born in 1866 in Glasgow, Scotland, and was well into his career. He was starting to reflect the maturity of age a bit, with the stresses of practice just showing up in his hairline and around his waist. He was well respected and lived in a lovely home. Dr. Mac-Dougall received his medical degree from the Boston University School of Medicine. As a student, he had been quite successful there. He was the class president and class orator. *The Haverhill Evening Gazette* described him as "hard-headed and practical."

Mary Roach (Roach, 2005) wrote a delightful article on the MacDougall experiments, including descriptions of work inspired by the research. She says that Greg Laing (a historian for the local Public Library) visited the MacDougall household after Dr. MacDougall's death. He observed, "They were such grim, straitlaced people. Really and truly, they were

1

not esoterically inclined." Dr. MacDougall was not a man that his peers viewed as beyond the pale.

Dr. MacDougall was seeing enough of life, or rather of death, that he was beginning to wonder what exactly happens when we die. He had been thinking about this for some time, and an opportunity arose that let him test a unique hypothesis. As it happens, he knew the attending physician at the Consumptive's Home and had been volunteering there. The home was a kind of hospice for late-stage tuberculosis patients. Dr. MacDougall reasoned if people are a combination of a body and a soul, you could imagine the soul occupies space. If it occupies space, it might have substance. Most importantly, if the soul has substance, it must have weight. As we will see, there has been speculation and debate about this idea back to the Egyptians.

It seemed reasonable to Dr. MacDougall to hypothesize that the body should get lighter when the soul leaves the body. As a scientist, he realized that if the body does get lighter, that would not necessarily mean a soul has left the body; but a prediction from the theory would be that it would have less weight. If there is no change, that would be evidence against the hypothesis, and if it does get lighter, the next step would be to eliminate other explanations. He decided to conduct what today we would consider a pilot experiment. It would be a quick test to see if there might be any evidence that could be measured and to refine the methods and the apparatus used.

How might we begin to explore whether the soul has weight? You could start with a bed on a flat surface, and the bed would sit on a scale. Today we have excellent digital scales for delicate industrial work. You would probably work with hospice providers and families to identify a set of terminally ill people who would be willing to participate for the sake of science. In addition to weight, today, we would monitor brain and cardiovascular activity and the chemical composition of the breath and blood. You would observe changes over time, especially at the moment of death. Finally, you would be trying to rule out every possible explanation for your observations other than the hypothesis you are proposing.

Dr. MacDougall, with access to the Consumptive's Home through his friend, had exactly what he needed. He used the technologies of the day to see whether it might be possible to observe a change that can only be explained by assuming that something leaves the body at the point of death. He set up a cot on a "very light" wooden framework. The cot and frame were placed on a Fairbanks standard industrial scale, and the scale was accurate to two-tenths of an ounce. Fairbanks scales are still manufactured today, and they continue to take great pride in their accuracy. The linens were arranged so that they did not interfere with the scale.

Consumptive patients were selected because he observed that as they neared death after a long illness, they hardly moved, and the patients often knew that it would only be hours before they would die. As Dr. MacDougall noted (MacDougall, 1907), "A consumptive dying after a long illness wasting his energies, dies with scarcely a movement to disturb the beam, their bodies are also very light, and we can be forewarned for hours that a consumptive is dying." There are times when my doctor sounds a little like this. Roach does note that he had secured his patients' consent well beforehand.

Drs. Sproull and Grant assisted Dr. MacDougall. Dr. MacDougall took measurements to observe how the subjects' weight changed every fifteen minutes up to the moment they died, he measured at the point of death, and he measured afterward. He says that his first patient was a male of regular build and "standard American temperament." The patient was wheeled into the ward, and the physicians sat and watched the man for three hours and forty minutes. They took measurements until he died. Overall, he was able to work with six cases, although he could not keep all of them due to problems he identified during his measurements.

He ruled out the explanation of moisture loss through respiration or sweat by careful minute-by-minute measurements before and after death. He eliminated the explanation of the air's weight leaving the lungs by sitting on the apparatus himself and completely exhaling all of his air, and measuring the change. He also took measurements from a group of fifteen dogs as they died, reasoning that they did not have souls. We will see this assumption is a subject of some debate. Still, in general, he did not find that the dogs lost weight when they died.

In 1907, Dr. MacDougall published the article summarizing his work simultaneously in *American Medicine* (a private published-for-profit journal) and the *Journal of the American Society of Psychical Research* (MacDougall, 1907). To Dr. MacDougall's chagrin, the *New York Times* broke the story about his experiment under the headline "Soul has weight, physician thinks." The figure that entered popular culture through that article is that the soul weighs twenty-one grams (which sounded better in print than the

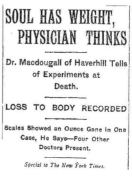

SOUL HAS WEIGHT, PHYSICIAN THINKS

Dr. Macdougall of Haverhill Tells of Experiments at Death.

LOSS TO BODY RECORDED

Scales Showed an Ounce Gone in One Case, He Says—Four Other Doctors Present.

Special to The New York Times.

BOSTON, March 10.—That the human soul has a definite weight, which can be determined when it passes from the body, is the belief of Dr. Duncan Macdougall, a reputable physician of Haverhill. He is at the head of a Research Society which for six years has been experimenting in this field. With him, he says, have been associated four other physicians.

three-fourths of an ounce that he reported in his article). The scientific criticism that arose from the *Times* article pushed the work into what today we might refer to as fringe science.

Dr. MacDougall wrote to a colleague, Dr. Hyslop, "I am well aware that these few experiments do not prove the matter any more than a few swallows make a summer, but yet the results should at least provide further experiments." It is clear from his article and the letters he exchanged about the work that he was conducting a pilot study to see if the method would work, identify relevant issues, and test whether he might find any evidence of a change at death. He never claimed the soul weighed twenty-one grams, but instead, he did find a range of weight loss in those he tested and that he felt produced reliable data between three-eighths of an ounce up to one and one-half ounces.

A more recent study by a physicist named Lewis E. Hollander Jr. (Hollander, 2001) looked at sheep and goats at the moment of death, and none lost weight. Instead, several gained weight as they died. Interestingly, as we will see later, some philosophers have posited that animals have at least some kind of soul. My daughter has reminded me that the sheep and goats study does bring to mind the Matthew 25:31-32's (NIV) description of judgment in the afterlife, "When the Son of Man comes in his glory, and all the angels with him, he will sit on his glorious throne. All the nations will be gathered before him, and he will separate the people one from another as a shepherd separates the sheep from the goats." However, I suspect not by weighing them at death.

How *out there* was the idea of looking at religious concepts like the soul from a scientific perspective? The early 1900s were an exciting time. The American Medical Association (AMA) began in 1848, but up until 1900, it had been a relatively weak organization. By the 1900s, though, the discipline had started an aggressive effort to enhance its reputation. At that time, there was a distinct lack of hospitals, labs, and medical libraries; and most surgeries were performed in homes. Part of the AMA's efforts were in response to a flood of tonics and patent medicines being promoted by charlatans and quacks. Diseases like pneumonia, tuberculosis, and diarrhea were the third-largest causes of death (including a forty percent death rate among children five years old or less). According to Roach, about half the medical schools in the United States taught the homeopathic approach to healing.

At around that same time, William James (1842 to 1910) was teaching the first psychology courses in the United States. He was one of the most influential philosophers in the United

States at the time, and he is considered the father of American psychology.[1] As it turns out, James also considered himself a psychical researcher and incorporated exploring some of the reported experiences involving mediums and telepathy into his thinking and research. Admittedly, those who cast their net widely in what they were studying were battling with those who wanted to expel psychical research from the emerging field of psychology. The purists felt it would cast a bad light on the field's scientific reputation (a battle similar to the AMA's fight to establish its reputation).

When Dr. MacDougall was doing his experiments, it was a tipping point in history. 1907 was at the tail of the Victorian era in many countries worldwide and the Gilded Age here in the United States. The détente between science and faith was breaking down. Many scientists maintained that science is about understanding the laws created by a supreme being in the natural world. But a growing number of scientists argued that science's goal is to continue uncovering the truth through the scientific method. They believed faith should live in the shrinking domain of the unexplained, and they argued philosophers and theologians should stay in their lane.

At the same time, Pasteur and others were making breakthroughs in vaccines, electrocardiography was invented, and many other breakthroughs were happening in medicine. The Wright brothers were flying, Marconi received radio signals over the Atlantic, and electricity and telephone networks spread across the country. Darwin's *Origin of the Species* was published in 1859. By the 1940s, most evangelicals were willing to accept a non-literal interpretation of Genesis informed by discoveries in geology and astronomy. Sigmund Freud had published the *Interpretation of Dreams*, and it transformed the way people thought about personality and culture. Nothing seemed out of bounds for science to explore.

In popular culture, the boundaries were also getting a little blurry. There were many magazines treating science and faith as a continuum. The number of science journals had increased from ten in 1700 to ten thousand in 1900. *Popular Science*, which is still around today, was founded in 1872. *Scientific American* started publication in 1845, and *National Geographic* began in 1888. Against this naturalistic and materialistic movement, there was also widespread interest in spiritualism and a world beyond the reach of the headlong advance of science. Dr. Mac-Dougall was well situated in a growing tradition of citizen scientists applying the scientific method to whatever caught their interest.

We are living through the same kind of revolutionary moment as Dr. MacDougall. The Digital Age has witnessed not only the ubiquity of computers, but we have created a world that adapts to us. We actively discuss the challenges and new ways of living brought on by the rapid evolution of artificial intelligence and empathy, machine learning, and the *Internet of Things* as we fill our homes with intelligent devices. We are pushing human augmentation boundaries to integrate our bodies with computers, sensors, and robotic devices. We are manipulating our DNA, combining it with that of animals, and working on biological computers built from living tissue. We are out in the universe searching for life that did not start here. With these changes, ethics, philosophy, and theology are trying to keep up. We live in a time when many are again wrestling with the fundamental questions about the nature of life, death, and moral responsibility.

This is a time when it is worth stepping back like Dr. Mac-Dougall did and thinking about who we are and how we define the soul, who we will be, and what it means in the context of the world in which we find ourselves. Later in this book, there will be some reflection about the implications of ideas about the soul and the afterlife for these developments and the policy decisions facing us. We will also be testing some of the ideas against the edge cases arising at this turning point in human history.

HOW THIS JOURNEY BEGAN

I should explain how I came to sit down to write this natural history and explore who we are and our ultimate destiny.

There was an immediate trigger that started my research. When I began, we were still in the middle of the coronavirus pandemic. One day in the summer, I walked through a nearby forest while being socially distanced. As I listened to my playlist, a song came up about life versus the afterlife. That started me thinking. Yes, I felt I had a soul and would end up in a good place. But if pressed for details, I realized I would have to mumble and look at my feet in embarrassment.

My wife and I are in that *highly vulnerable* category discussed in the press, so we have been thinking and talking more than usual about mortality. Our reflections have become personal as my wife's father died just a year ago, her sister died a few months ago, and her mom has now passed away from rapidly progressing dementia. More recently, I lost my brother-in-law, who had been a good friend and hiking partner. However, my interest in the topic has been building for a while. Over the arc of my life, mortality began to feel like death was walking in the shadows when I *started* losing friends and family.

The sister of a high school friend died unexpectedly in a small plane crash over the Great Lakes. One of our friends died in a plane crash not many years later while on a business trip, leaving his young family behind. There was the first high school reunion with the list of friends who would not be attending because they had passed. One by one, the older family members that I looked up to as a kid started going. Then friends and colleagues died in 9/11, cancer began to touch more and more, and as we know, death has been hovering closer during this recent pandemic. As each week goes by, it seems like I learn of another good friend who has died from COVID-19. Every time I leave our house, the act of picking up a mask makes me feel like I am about to enter a war zone that might be terminal not just for me but also for my family should I unknowingly bring something back. On a more positive note, every time I wake up in the morning with my cat massaging my stomach, I am incredibly thankful for another day. But it is true that the longer we live, the more we need to manage grief. If I might adapt an insight from a friend, "If you haven't lost a loved one, you haven't lived long enough."

On my walk, it occurred to me that I do have a vague, comforting idea of where those who have left this veil of tears have gone and that I will someday join them. But what does it mean to say I have a soul, and what will it be like in the afterlife? My fuzzy, happy hope of an eternity in Paradise with those I love is just that, fuzzy. As I thought about it, I realized I have a set of ideas absorbed from our culture, but they have not been tested critically. We often talk about how we imagine heaven and where we will be with those we love. It gives us comfort. However, when you think about it, *forever* is quite a long time. I certainly hope it will be interesting, compelling, and worthwhile. Frankly, by the time I got home from my walk, I was ready to annoy my family with whatever I could discover on the internet.

A rich set of influences shapes our selves, assumptions, and perhaps our souls. We are composed of the bits of our families, culture, knowledge, experiences, and stories we have absorbed. For me, one theme has been the religious tradition in which I grew up and how my faith journey has evolved as it has been forged in the furnace of life. My story also includes how I have changed and matured in reflecting on and living out my values while integrating them into my more data-oriented, hard-nosed choice of a career in science and technology.

Growing Up with the Afterlife

For those of us who grew up in a family where much of life was grounded in the community of a local church, synagogue, mosque, temple, or other religious institution, many of our beliefs come from or are a reaction to what we were taught. As we will see, the formal religious traditions that provide our culture's language have a lot to say about our views of who we are and the afterlife.

For myself, my family attended a small, non-denominational conservative Christian church. It was the kind of church where the Scandinavian pastor would sometimes lapse into Swedish in the middle of a sermon. When I was about to leave for college at the University of Chicago, the pastor called me up in front of the church to pray for my soul. He associated Chicago with Dr. Thomas Altizer, a seminal thinker in the "death of God" movement who was in the press a lot back then. The demonstrations at the Democratic National Convention in Chicago that summer did not help. Furthermore, while my peers were training for the ministry, I was studying to become a scientist.

It was also the kind of church that regularly held "the call" for people to come to salvation, which often seemed strange since the same people attended almost all the services (Sunday morning, Sunday evening, and Wednesday evening). At summer camp, towards the end of the week, there would always be a campfire, everyone would sing "Just As I Am," and there would be another call. Heaven and hell featured prominently, of course. The inspiring stories were often about those in crisis: alcoholics, criminals, sailors drowning after Pearl Harbor, and that kind of thing. The stories were about people who were transformed after they *saw the light*.[2] Even as a child, I noticed that some of the other kids seemed to get saved a lot, and you could wonder about their personal crises. For me, though, even though there were issues with my father's PTSD from WWII, my life growing up in a working-class neighborhood in a suburb of Seattle did not feel quite like those tragic stories. Still, this was the ground in which the seeds of my faith were planted.

My memories from back then are filled with stories of the afterlife. Some were presented on something called a flannel board. We saw pictures of lions and lambs lying around together and people walking through a garden with Jesus. Of course, there would only be a few people with Jesus and not the hundreds of millions that you would think might be there. That would take too much flannel. There were also images we would see of the new Jerusalem floating down from the sky, sometimes represented as a strange walled cube and sometimes as an ancient, glowing two-thousand-year-old Middle Eastern city. This new Jerusalem for those of you who have not heard of it is described quite colorfully in Revelation 21:17-25 (KJV)[3]:

"He measured the wall thereof, a hundred and forty and four cubits, according to the measure of a man, that is, of the angel. And the building of the wall of it was of jasper: and the city was pure gold, like unto clear glass. And the foundations of the wall of the city were garnished with all manner of precious stones. The first foundation was jasper; the second, sapphire; the third, a chalcedony; the fourth, an emerald; The fifth, sardonyx; the sixth, sardius; the seventh, chrysolite; the eighth, beryl; the ninth, a topaz; the tenth, a chrysoprase; the eleventh, a jacinth; the twelfth, an amethyst. And the twelve gates were twelve pearls: every several gate was of one pearl: and the street of the city was pure gold, as it were transparent glass.

"And I saw no temple therein: for the Lord God Almighty and the Lamb are the temple of it. And the city had no need of the sun, neither of the moon, to shine in it: for the glory of God did lighten it, and the Lamb is the light thereof. And the nations of them which are saved shall walk in the light of it: and the kings of the earth do bring their glory and honour into it. And the gates of it shall not be shut at all by day: for there shall be no night there."

Neither the rural nor the Middle Eastern urban depiction seemed to capture the kinds of places where some of us would like to spend eternity. Often, we were assured that as 1 Corinthians 2:9 (NIV) says, "'What no eye has seen, what no ear has heard, and what no human mind has conceived—the things God has prepared for those who love him." The idea was that we should not worry too much about the details. Furthermore, as 1 John 3:2 (NIV) says, there is no way we can even imagine it since "[W]hat we will be has not yet been made known."

The hope we had, and that many still have whatever their religious tradition, is expressed in Revelation 21: 4 (NIV), "He will wipe every tear from their eyes. There will be no more death or mourning or crying or pain, for the old order of things has passed away." Sometimes heaven was described as bringing back the original plan for the Garden of Eden, without the temptations, of course, and possibly with white robes instead of being naked. However, we were generally left to fill in a vision of heaven constructed from our hopes of what we delight in or hope for here on this physical plane. As will be discussed, the idea that "whatever heaven is, we'll love it" has been known to be used by some pastors as a rationale for seeing our loved ones and even our pets in heaven.

On the other hand, John the Seer's description of hell in Revelation was typically taken more literally. Revelation 20:10 and 21:14-15 (KJV) painted a clear picture, even if we were not sure we knew anyone who qualified other than Hitler.

> *"And the devil that deceived them was cast into the lake of fire and brimstone, where the beast and the false prophet are, and shall be tormented day and night for ever and ever....But as for the cowardly, the faithless, the detestable, as for murderers, the*

> *sexually immoral, sorcerers, idolaters, and all liars,*
> *their portion will be in the lake that burns with fire*
> *and sulfur, which is the second death."*

We wanted to avoid that! For some, like one of my grand-mothers, there was a fear that a tiny mistake just before dying would cause you to end up in the lake instead of the pasture. My church assured us that once saved, always saved (known as the doctrine of eternal security). However, there was a persistent irritation for others that someone who had spent their life being wicked could make a last-minute decision before dying and escape hell and get into heaven. That, somehow, did not seem fair.

Things That Go Bump in the Night

I must admit that baked into my experience are the stories passed down through our family, in the strange way that a family can have very conservative religious beliefs and yet also have a less orthodox thread that is very personal and real. As we will see later, there are formal theological and philosophical debates, but then there are the soul and the afterlife as they are experienced and made meaningful by regular people. Both interact to shape our ideas of the soul and the afterlife in our culture, which in turn influences our behavior and how we relate to one another.

Bill Locke

When my grandfather Locke was young, his mother had died. His dad was a farmer, and having far too many children to care for, he placed several of them in a Catholic orphanage and left them. My grandfather, his two brothers, and his sisters were there and remembered being poorly treated. They attributed the hostility to their not being Catholic, but they may just have not been very compliant.

According to the family stories, they had to eat oatmeal three times a day, his sisters got rickets, and they were "whipped" a lot. My grandfather and another little boy decided to run away, and they set a date. As he lay in his bed crying the night before, his mother appeared to him in a ghostly form. She came to him and said everything would be all right. The next day, his father showed up and removed them from the orphanage.

Later, when he was seventeen, he lied about his age to enlist in the Army to fight in WWI. He was part of the division known as the Sunset Division from here in the Northwest. They shipped out to France in 1917 and arrived on December 31st. A few months later, the night before they were going to the Front, he said his mother showed up in the dark of night and again said everything would be all right and not to worry. The next day the Armistice was signed.

Of course, various research studies have suggested these kinds of experiences can be created by the mind itself in response to deep personal needs. Research also shows that these experiences can be highly comforting and help many people cope with stress in essential ways. Joseph Campbell has said that "Myths are clues to the spiritual potentialities of the human life." In this sense, whatever the cause of the original experiences, these stories became a family *myth*. These stories help make *the other side* real and give emotional assurance that our loved ones are there. The stories get passed on across generations and bind us together as a family. In our culture (like all cultures), we use our stories and myths to transmit and shape our beliefs about the soul and the afterlife.

My father died when I was in college. It was sudden, and it was unexpected. It is now years later, and while I do not know if he is aware of my wonderful wife and amazing daughters, I want to believe that he is. I cannot help but feel that he is there, in a heavenly place, without all he suffered from his PTSD. My mom died a few years ago from Alzheimer's. Towards the end, we felt that somehow *she* had already left her body, and her body was just continuing to live. When she eventually died, searching within myself, I find the firm belief that she is with my dad. We buried her ashes in a hand-blown urn which she would have loved as an artist, along with her favorite chocolates, and it gave us great comfort.

My grandmother lived to be a hundred and four, and it is inspiring to think about everything she saw in her life. I remember when she was in her nineties and called to tell me how excited she was to be surfing the Net. Towards the end, there was a feeling that the veil between this life and the hereafter was getting thinner. While I was not able to be there at the end, my two sisters were. Their observations are interesting:

> *"Grandma was dying from congestive heart disease. She was fighting hard to stay alive so she could go to her great granddaughter's wedding. Jeanne and I knew it wasn't happening, but I did commit to bringing a video that we would share along with the wedding cake. Grandma started to fade, and then she would look intently out in front of her. She would say, 'Mama…Esther.' Esther was her sister who died at age 21. We started quietly telling her it was ok. We would all be fine, and it was time to go towards Jesus. She continued to move and moan.*

> *"As Jeanne and I were holding her hands, all of a sudden, a mist—I tend to call it a cloud, but it was more of a mist—floated up from her chest. From that moment, Grandma did not move again. Other*

*than her heart continuing to beat, she did not moan
or flinch…nothing. We looked at each other. We
both slowly looked up as if we were afraid to admit
what just happened. I think we both whispered,
'Did you see that?' and whispered 'Yes.' It took
several more days before Grandma's heart stopped.
We knew something special just happened."*

We will look later in this book at other observations from
people going through the process of death. It turns out my
family's experiences are similar to those many have had. The
ubiquity of these experiences has probably shaped the way humans across history have defined themselves and the beliefs
about the afterlife that have worked their way into people's
daily lives.

My Approach to the Journey

I am coming at this as a person of faith who believes that
whatever essentially is *me* (i.e., me as a soul) will have an afterlife. Research suggests that while we may differ in the details,
most of us today are similar in this fundamental belief. These
are my assumptions and the lens that I will tend to use in this
cross-disciplinary survey, although we will be looking at diverse
views and their implications as well. While I grew up in a very
conservative church, my faith has continued to evolve and be
refined as it has been tested through life and as I reflect on the
diverse sets of beliefs and insights expressed by fellow travel-
ers. But I also have spent much of my career as a scientist
working in emerging technologies, and I recognize that the assumptions of that part of my life for many tend to be grounded
in the faith that the physical world's properties can explain everything. Anything that is not subject to empirical analysis at
best is often dismissed as irrelevant.

For myself, I do resonate with the spirit of Goetz and
Taliaferro's (Goetz, 2011) observation that "The problem facing naturalism lies in accounting for the reality of 'conscious
experience, thought, value, and so forth' in a cosmos that is

ultimately void of purpose, thought, and value. We believe that the difficulties facing naturalism count as reasons for exploring an alternative, non-naturalist philosophy, including theism, which is more receptive to the existence of the soul." We will see this tension throughout this journey as theology, philosophy, and science slice and dice our experiences to understand the component elements and sometimes leave the whole behind. In this natural history, we will explore how people experience death, and we will approach the soul and the journey to the afterlife as topics worthy of study. How do these beliefs come to be? Why have they evolved? If they provide value, how might they develop in the future as the world itself changes ever more rapidly, and how should they influence the decisions we make individually and as a society?

I do see myself as a scientist. As a scientist, I also know that just because many people believe something does not mean it is true. Indeed, part of what we will find on this journey is that what people believe has evolved considerably across human history. The beliefs are as diverse and as rich as the human family itself, yet some common themes appear repeatedly. Much of what I found surprised me. Exploring this natural history of the soul has helped me better understand what is in store after I leave this mortal coil, and the ideas and questions provide an excellent excuse to have some fascinating conversations with friends and family.

I am the first to admit that despite my interests, I am not a theologian. I am not a philosopher. Fundamentally, I am just another person wandering through the forest of life, wondering about the ultimate question of what will happen to us after we die. I am a person of faith in a world of science and engineering, and that will inevitably influence some of my questions and reflections.

Nevertheless, I am attempting to approach this natural history with some naiveté and wonder. I am going to ask questions that I suspect many of us would ask on this journey. I am sure that I will get some details wrong, mostly when summarizing areas not in my expertise. What I will attempt to do, though, is to identify the big ideas, the big themes, that seem worth wrestling with as each of us comes to our own conclusions about what we believe about the destination. We will not know the answers for sure until we get there. I will tee up some possible ideas that may seem a little fringe, but rest assured, I am not proposing doctrine. Some are tests to make sure our ideas will scale as our society and culture evolve.

Through this natural history, I will be reviewing what people have believed across history and how and possibly why it has changed. But we will also see the shape of some of the gaps in what we believe where the best we can do is to reason, make inferences, and even speculate based on what we do know across disciplines and as we are guided by the larger principles we may hold. I hope to stimulate questions and discussion given these changing times to help refine our beliefs and better prepare us for the future we may face.

NAVIGATING THIS NATURAL HISTORY

When exploring this natural history of the soul, a good starting point is how we in our culture think of the soul and the afterlife today. Chapter 1 surveys how we talk about the soul and the afterlife. We will see how the ideas emerge, and how they are reinforced and extended in popular culture, as the afterlife appears in our movies, songs, books, and other art. We will touch on the evolution of the ideas through history. I will set a working definition of the concept of the soul as a framework for the other perspectives we will use in this journey.

Given the history of our species, it is worth understanding the evolution of the attributes that we associate with the soul. Some religious leaders (incl. some Jewish and Christian theologians) and philosophers have even argued either that animals' souls are identical to ours or that they have unique types of souls. The idea of the theory of mind in psychology is about what leads us to attribute mental states to ourselves and others. Adopting this approach to think about a theory of the soul suggests some novel ways of thinking about the nature of animals and what it tells us about ourselves. Chapter 2 explores the animal kingdom, especially social species that can communicate with each other and with us, that have cognitive abilities and exhibit emotions similar to ours.

Chapter 3 spends some time with our distant ancestors as they climbed down from the trees and managed to populate the Earth. Their emerging religious beliefs fill in the early chapters of our history. As our cognitive and social abilities developed, the evidence shows how we started to treat our families and friends differently in death. We began to think symbolically, language developed, and we created and passed on culture through storytelling. We told stories about the afterlife, and we represented the afterlife and attempted to control it in our art. Over time, our burial practices became richer, and as our social structures became more sophisticated, so did the religious beliefs and practices that emerged.

Maturing as a species, we grew beyond Maslow's idea of physiological and safety needs to societies and cultures that could support love and belonging. We could eventually think more deeply about esteem and self-actualization. Part of that rise was the emergence of philosophy. In Chapter 4, we will summarize a few of the significant philosophers. Their thoughts about the soul and the afterlife influenced contemporary Western religious thinking (especially early Jewish and Christian theologians) and have shaped our popular beliefs. These ideas have left their DNA in ethical discussions around current trends in medicine and technology today.

In Chapter 5, we will dig into several of the major religions in the world. While each speaks most directly to how we live our lives day to day, it is also true that part of the justification for why we should live in a particular way are their ideas about the afterlife. The afterlife and the nature of our souls help motivate the meaning in our lives. Furthermore, each religion's view is associated with rituals that give rhythm to the cycle of our lives, structure to our communities, and comfort at the end of physical life. While each has unique perspectives, it is also possible to see common ideas that have arisen from their followers' experiences and the messages of their prophets.

Over more recent history, views of the soul have increasingly aligned with the emerging understanding of conscious experience, personality, the theory of the mind, and moral behavior and ethics. During that time, the discipline of psychology began to diverge from theology and philosophy. An important focus has been on rational consciousness and the connection between the mind and the body. Psychology (including its various branches and related fields) applies the scientific method and more empirical approaches to understand how our experiences and the patterns in the behaviors that define us have emerged.

Interestingly, the Greek word psyche[4] means soul or breath. So while we think of psychology as the study of the mind, linguistically, you might think of it as the study of the soul. That is one of my excuses, as a psychologist, for writing this book. In Chapter 6, while I will not exhaust all of the interesting threads in contemporary cognitive science, neuroscience, and so on, I will highlight some of the emerging findings relevant to our experiences of the soul and ideas about the afterlife.

This period in which we live is likely to be even more revolutionary and transformative than the 1900s˙ when Dr. MacDougall lived. We have significant social issues that divide our country, like abortion, sexual orientation and gender identity, global warming, and our responsibility for the planet. We are at the beginning of incredible advances in areas like genetic engineering, cryogenics[5], medicine, biological computing, artificial intelligence, and robotics. We are amping up the search for life within and beyond our solar system and thinking about interacting with that life. How we define ourselves is central to how we address the ethical issues we are increasingly facing. How we determine our purpose for living in this physical world and envision the afterlife should inform our policy positions. Chapter 7 will frame some of these questions by speculating about the soul and the afterlife in the context of technological and medical trends. I will also be sharing my own conclusions as I have reflected on what I have found.

As you will see, I have not attempted to be exhaustive in each area. Instead, I am trying to provide an overview of this natural history that paints a picture of the general trends uncovered in my exploration. I can personally confirm that it is easy to get lost in all the fascinating detail in many of these areas. Much of what I am doing is curating examples to illustrate the big themes that I believe are relevant.

A final comment is that dates, interpretation, and evolving research and analysis are often somewhat contradictory across the literature in many of these areas. Furthermore, as mentioned, while I have had some broad exposure across these areas before starting this journey, I know that I am not an expert in many. As the naïve, curious observer, I admit I may be interpreting what I find with less nuance than a guru in any one of the areas might. Furthermore, while I believe I have captured the broad strokes, you may quarrel with individual points or arguments. Despite that, one of my goals for this book is to motivate you to go deeper in areas that catch *your* interest. The bibliography and footnotes should be a good place to start. I want to help you figure out for yourself how you want to think about your soul, about your future, and about how you can apply your reflections to create that future both here and in the afterlife. After all, a natural history is not defined by one person's interpretation and does not stop in the here and now.

---

[1] My PhD professor, Dr. B. J. Underwood, was a student of a student of William James; so James is a kind of academic ancestor of mine.

[2] We will see that given the research on near-death experiences, this phrase is even more apt than I realized at the time.

[3] Through this natural history, there are quite a few references to Hebrew and Christian scriptures. In general, I will be using a version of the Tanakh translated into English by the Jewish Publication Society (JPS). They use the Maerica Version that was the first version created by a committee of rabbis and other scholars. The Hebrew Tanakh and the later Septuagint (the Greek translation) are also the sources for the Old Testament in the Christian Bible. The English translation is available through the Jewish Virtual Library (jewishvirtuallibrary.com). For the New Testament, there are many

translations and versions. In a few places, I will use the King James Version (KJV) to give a sense of what we read and discussed when I was a child. Most of the time, I will be using the New International Version (NIV). The NIV was being translated with the earliest available texts and the latest scholarship when I was in seminary. Two of my professors were involved in the process. It can be valuable to compare translations coming from different points of view. Many of these are available at biblehub.com.

[4] The Greek Ψυχή is sometimes written psyche and sometimes psuche. I will be using psyche through this natural history.

[5] As you start to stretch your imagination, if the body (or the head) is preserved, is the soul? And if so, what is the state of the soul and consciousness? Is it asleep or is it in a waiting room for the afterlife and will return if the body is resuscitated? What can the neuroscience of near-death experiences tell us?

Chapter 1

THE SOUL
IN POPULAR CULTURE

"The soul comes from without into the human body, as into a temporary abode, and [as] it goes out of it anew it passes into other habitations, for the soul is immortal."
– Ralph Waldo Emerson

"Death is nothing else but going home to God, the bond of love will be unbroken for eternity."
– Mother Teresa

"I am confident that there truly is such a thing as living again, that the living spring from the dead, and that the souls of the dead are in existence."
– Socrates

An internet search on the word *soul* yields more than 1,610,000,000 hits on Google. In contrast, a search for the word Bing on Google only yields 389,000,000, and the Kardashians result in a mere 234,000,000 hits. The soul has social mindshare. Even removing hits on "soul music" (14,700,000) and "soul food" (23,100,000), soul as a concept is well embedded in our culture. If you included all the ways we describe the soul's journey into the afterlife to make it feel less painful, there would be even more.

Simon Davis (Davis, 2016) investigated this vocabulary cleverly. Recognizing that we have probably heard and used a wide array of words and phrases for death, Davis reached out to Legacy.com, an online provider of paid death notices. In

2015 there were 2,408,142 obituaries across the United States. Across this set, 1,341,870 included one of the ten most common euphemisms. He says, "The top term is unsurprising. 'Passed away' was used in 32.5 percent of all obituaries and topped the national list. In every single state, it was either 'passed away' or 'died' (20.6 percent nationwide at #2) that was used most often." Davis then looked at the most common term used that distinguishes each state. "Died" was the most popular in eleven states, "entered eternal rest" was next as the most popular in eight states, and these were followed up by "departed" (six states), "succumbed" (five states), and "left this world" and "went home" (each in four states).

When you look under the surface, the range of words and phrases we use is even richer. Daniel Szczesniak (Szczesniak, 2019) collected a list in "Euphemisms for Death: 200+ Ways to Describe Death & Dying." There are variations on being asleep, at rest, or at peace. In some cultures, this could mean "…and don't come back and haunt us!" There are ideas like going home, moving to a better place, or being in heaven. Some phrases like "being called" express the sense of a larger plan. They include "their hour came," or "taken." Some expressions recognize all of us are destined for death, such as "came to an end," "finished," "reached the finish line," and "breathed their last." Some point to the bigger picture (e.g., "returned to the earth"). There are phrases expressing variations of Dylan Thomas' "Do not go gentle into that good night." They cast the end as a battle. These ideas include bravely fought, lost, didn't make it, and succumbed. Some phrases speak to the idea of giving up the spirit or the ghost (speaking from the perspective of the body). Others take a slightly different pivot on the process and describe easing out of this life by slipping away quietly or passing away. In addition to the phrases mentioned earlier that offer the hope of an afterlife, some recognize another perspective on existing beyond this world. There are variations on living in the hearts of those who remain, for example, and being remembered by loved ones. Other expressions may try to ease the pain or personal fears by making light of the process (e.g., "kicked the bucket").

The richness of this language is probably not too surprising. After all, while the question of what happens next is not top of mind as we live most of our lives, we all face it at some point. It could begin with the loss of a pet, but as I mentioned in my case, it can eventually hit us with the loss of family and friends. In discussing the five stages of grief, Elizabeth Kübler-Ross (Kübler-Ross, 1969) says the immediate response is typically denial, and we need words to manage those feelings. If we live long enough, we may even contemplate the words we would like applied to ourselves when the time comes.

It does not take a lot of searching online to find amusing epitaphs people have written for themselves. Billy Wilder's epitaph says, "I'm A Writer, But Then Nobody's Perfect." Mel Blanc's says, "That's All Folks." Rodney Dangerfield's says, "There Goes The Neighborhood." Robert Lee Frost's reads "I Had a Lover's Quarrel With the World," Jack Lemmon's epitaph is a simple "In," and Merv Griffin's is "I Will Not Be Right Back After This Message." Finally, Dee Ramone's last words are "OK... I Gotta Go Now." They are not always trying to comfort their loved ones, but they are sharing something about themselves that they hope will live on within the memories of those left behind.

When our art is not about birth and relationships, it is often about dealing with death. Given the human grief associated with death, much of our emotional energy is invested in conveying empathy and helping others working through their grief. Somehow, intuitively, we know that it may not be comforting to say, "Your loved one is dead." "Your loved one is at peace" or "Your loved one is in heaven" is what we know we want to hear and what psychologically we often need for our healing. In essence, this is the power of our language that Joseph Campbell examines in the stories we tell and the myths we create. There is truth in how we in the Western world tend to think about facts, but there is also a constructed and shaped reality because we need it, and the truth is less in the facts than in the underlying meaning and intent.

DEFINING THE SOUL

> *"SOUL, n. A spiritual entity concerning which*
> *there hath been brave disputation. Plato held that*
> *those souls which in a previous state of existence*
> *(antedating Athens) had obtained the clearest*
> *glimpses of eternal truth entered into the bodies of*
> *persons who became philosophers. Plato himself*
> *was a philosopher. The souls that had least*
> *contemplated divine truth animated the bodies of*
> *usurpers and despots. Dionysius I, who had*
> *threatened to decapitate the broad-browed*
> *philosopher, was a usurper and a despot. Plato,*
> *doubtless, was not the first to construct a system of*
> *philosophy that could be quoted against his*
> *enemies; certainly he was not the last."*
> – Ambrose Bierce

Before we get to a review of the soul in culture, let's put a stake down on what we mean by the word *soul*. Part of why being clear in our language is important is because the language emerges from how we interact with each other, and it has a way of shaping our culture. We need to spend a little time considering some of the fiddly definitional bits before looking at how the concepts appear and change within our artistic heritage.

The first thing to do is to remind ourselves that the soul as a thing separate from the body is only one way we use the word. Using it, we take advantage of a broad range of meanings that we associate with the core concept as we imagine what it is and who we are. As the ancient Greeks and Jews did, we also regularly apply the word to convey new meanings and emphasize different aspects of the idea. Like any important word in our language, in experimenting with usage and applying it to a rich set of expressive needs, we, in essence, are exploring new sources of truth in different contexts. As we use a word like soul, it grows to fill the space that feels useful and right.

There is a hypothesis that is still debated called *linguistic relativity*. This idea is sometimes known as the Sapir-Whorf hypothesis, based on the two linguists who popularized the idea in the 1940s (Sapir-Whorf Hypothesis, n.d.). There is a lot of research that culture shapes language. Language evolves through our need to make sense of the world and communicate with those around us. We pass on and align around our stories. The linguistic relativity hypothesis argues that language also shapes thought and influences our decisions and actions. The movie *Arrival* (2016) uses this idea to tell the story of a human-alien meeting and suggests one of the character's brains can become *rewired* as she learns the alien language. While some are skeptical about this idea, research continues to explore this cyclical relationship between how we think and culture as our evolving language mediates it.

A typical example that usually gets teed up is the number of words the Inuit have for snow. Benjamin Whorf (Whorf, 1949) argued, "We [English speakers] have the same word for falling snow, snow on the ground, snow hard-packed like ice, slushy snow, wind-driven snow – whatever the situation may be. To an Eskimo, this all-inclusive word would be almost unthinkable." People who visit the Seattle area, where I live, find the dozens of words we have for rain in our weather reports amazing (e.g., rain, showers, mist, drizzle, downpour, cats and dogs, sprinkle, freezing rain, and so on). Over time this language often shapes how mentally and emotionally we come to terms with our winter season.

My wife has shared a variety of stories that illustrate this. Her parents were with a mission group called Wycliffe Bible Translators. Part of what they do is to go to parts of the world where languages are going extinct. A language goes extinct somewhere in the world roughly every two weeks. Her family lived in a remote village in Brazil that had a language that was disappearing as the young people began to migrate to the big cities and learned Portuguese. Living there and being a part of the day-to-day life of the village, they absorbed as much of the culture as possible. Her dad learned their language in that context, and then he created a written form to capture it and ensure it could pass from one generation to the next.

A clear challenge was to learn the native language well enough to identify a correspondence between their words and expressions and the English equivalent (e.g., including concepts like God, the soul, and the afterlife). Anyone who has tried to do this with Google translate knows how hard this is to do well. We know from the history of translation in the Judeo-Christian tradition that going from Hebrew to Aramaic to Greek to English across different cultures has inevitably caused some concepts to evolve in ways that were not intended or envisioned by the original writers. Tom Kelley (Kelley, 2001), a founder of IDEO—one of the more creative and iconic consultancies in the technology industry—wrote, "If you're not in the jungle, you're not going to know the tiger." Most anthropologists and linguists will agree that you need to immerse yourself in the real-world cultural context if you want to understand a language and a people.

Living in the Tribe, Brazil

The village itself believed in a universal God, but village life revolved around ancestor worship rituals, spirits, and a sacred tree through which the spirits spoke to the villagers. Many of the sacred concepts were not supposed to be shared with outsiders, especially not with children. This restriction included the beliefs and rituals around death and the afterlife. Some could be inferred, however, because they so clearly shaped the culture of the village.

For example, when my wife would travel with kids in the village, they would sometimes stop because they all simultaneously would see a spirit ahead. Her friends would describe it in detail, but my wife would not see it. At one point, members of the village came to their house and asked if they had seen the spirit the night before. They said it was an old, disabled man who crawled through the town screaming and knocking on people's doors. The whole town had experienced it, except for my wife's family.

Another story my wife shared was from a family staying with a Brazilian tribe that was nomadic, again, to help them turn their language into a written form. For this tribe, they believed that if someone died in a house, the spirit stayed in the house. Therefore, it was critical to burn the house down so the spirit could leave and begin its journey to the afterlife. If the house was not burned, the spirit was bound to the house and would cause great misfortune to the entire tribe. You could imagine the experiences through generations of a nomadic tribe that might lead to this belief. Picture the feelings of the family who could not yet speak the language when a villager died in their home.

My wife spent the years when she was developing her language skills as a young girl in that village where her parents were working with the tribe. She became fluent in the Portuguese they were speaking and in the village culture as she experienced it through the children she grew up with and through observing the adults. Reflecting on it, she remembers that while Americans have many euphemisms to avoid saying someone died, death happened all the time in the village.

When people talked about it, they just said people died. In that culture, when people died, they stepped into the other side, and their spirits might continue to walk among the living. By using appropriate rituals, the living could easily commune with the dead. Death was more of a change of state than the crossing of a chasm. My wife eventually became an emergency room and critical care nurse. She has noticed that the way she experiences and thinks about death is different from most Americans. It may be the result of these early formative years. It may be the unique culture of nurses who regularly deal with death and how they talk about dying to manage their own emotional states, but whatever it is, something feels different to her.

So how has our culture shaped the concept of the soul, and how is it reflected in how we talk about it and use it to communicate and tell stories? How is the idea of the soul itself influencing our culture? *The Merriam-Webster Dictionary* makes headlines each year based on the words it has added to reflect what is going on in our society. Since the 1880s, *Merriam-Webster* has grown a set of 15.7 million citations, examples of words and usage, and bibliographic information. Words get added to the dictionary based on the number and range of citations, and they make sure they capture changes as meanings evolve. A *Merriam-Webster* definition, then, is an editor's view of the most common meanings for a word in our culture.

Merriam-Webster defines the *soul* (Merriam-Webster, n.d.) as the "immaterial essence, animating principle, or actuating cause" of our lives. This definition is how most of us feel about our souls. Also, it includes the idea of the soul being the "spiritual principle embodied in human beings." This principle might be part of other rational and spiritual beings or even the universe itself. Other uses of the word soul include aspects like "a person's total self," "a moving spirit," "the moral and emotional nature of human beings," and "the quality that arouses emotion and sentiment." The word extends, as we know, to refer to individuals (as in "not a soul in sight"), an essential property (e.g., "she is the soul of integrity"), and to include references and categories like "having soul," soul music, soul food, and soul brother. These latter uses capture something shared among a community that defines their essence.

In the category of "possibly more information than you could ever want to know," but always a source of fascination for those wanting to explore the English language, is the *Oxford English Dictionary (OED)*. The *Dictionary* began in 1884, and in its second edition, the *OED* now consists of 21,728 pages in twenty volumes. It is somewhat different from, say, the *Merriam-Webster Dictionary* in that it attempts to trace the history of how the English language has developed and is continuing to evolve. A recent movie entitled *The Professor and the Madman* provides an insightful view into James Murray, the first primary editor, and the *Dictionary*'s creation. Given its goal, the *OED* is a comprehensive resource for researchers trying to understand how a word like *soul* has acquired the meanings we give it. I love the *OED* definition of the word *soul* because it informs the key concepts with quotes that help capture the definitions' nuances (OED, 2020).

James A. H. Murray and his Dictionary

For example, it defines the soul as "The principle of intelligence, thought, or action in a person (or occasionally an animal), typically regarded as an entity distinct from the body; the essential, immaterial, or spiritual part of a person or animal, as opposed to the physical." Then it supports the definition with examples such as: "It [sc. Death] must be dreadful, since it is sufficient to separate the soul from the body" (O. Goldsmith *His. Earth II.* 207), "The absence of the soul is far more terrible in a living man than in a dead one" (C. Dickens *Barnaby Rudge iii.* 251), and "Body and mind serve only as environment agencies to soul, which has no need of them beyond this life" (H. Holley *Mod. Social Relig.* vi 192). A quote that is relevant to a discussion we will have later is, "Insofar as we still dream of re-engineering humanity, we do so in terms of the body not the soul" (C. Coker *Human Warfare* viii. 147). One example of the essence of this first part of the definition that made me smile was, "I know many people have doubts as to the existence of souls in small boys of this class" (M. Kingsley *Trav. W. Afr.* 441).

The *OED* also includes the use of soul as "Contrasting with the body, life, with reference to the separation between a person's immaterial or spiritual attributes and his or her physical form or existence." For this, it uses quotes such as: "Supposing myself to consist of soul and body, 'tis fairly presumable that 'tis my soul that thinks" (J. Norris *Ess. Ideal World* II. i. 5), and "A difference between body and soul, between the physical and the spiritual" (A. W. M. Beierle *First Person Plural* iii. 20).

The soul can also be "The seat of a person's emotions, feelings, or thoughts; the moral or emotional part of a person's nature; the central or inmost part of a person's being." To support this idea, the *OED* uses phrases like 'He looked at her, truly looked at her, deep, deep into her soul" (S.-E. Welfonder *Knight in my Bed* 15). Finally, the word can mean "Strength of character; strongly developed intellectual, moral, or aesthetic qualities; spiritual or emotional power or intensity; (also) deep feeling, sensitivity." This definition is illustrated with phrases such as "Those fellowes haue some soule" (W. Shakespeare *Othello* [1622] I. i. 54), and "The Mouse that always trusts to one poor Hole, Can never be a Mouse of any Soul" (A. Pope *Chaucer's Wife of Bath* in R. Steele *Poet. Misc.* 19).

TITLE Definitions of the Soul

o The innermost self
o The animator of life
o That which distinguishes us as us; our personality
o Our cognition (intelligence, thought, and rationality)
o The seat of our emotional nature (the source of our deep feelings)
o The seat of our moral nature, and responsible for moral action
o The source of our will, resulting in action
o Our spiritual, immaterial essence that connects us to God

We will eventually be focusing on the idea of the soul as the essential *me*, as distinct from my body. One of the questions will be about the nature of the soul. How does it change through the experience of life to become *me* uniquely? How does it interact with the world through the body? What causes us to attribute properties to it, like strength of character or virtue? Some of the attributes we give to the word soul will be explored as we look through a potential perspective I am calling the theory of the soul in Chapter 2, where we look at animals and, as the OED suggests, the attributes we associate with souls. But first, we should look at how these ideas show up in our popular media and our imaginations.

THE SOUL IN THE MEDIA

We create language to reflect on and communicate our experiences. We are a storytelling species. It is how we remember what we have learned about how the world works and how we share it with others. We learn from others' stories to handle new experiences that we have not had before. Empathy lets us live in the experiences of others as we incorporate their stories into our own lives. It is because of empathy that the arts—whether pictures, plays, poetry, novels, movies, television, music, or games—are so influential in shaping our attitudes about concepts such as the soul and the afterlife, and help us deal with life and death.

As we will see, the soul and speculations about the afterlife have been part of the stories humans tell almost back to the beginning of storytelling itself. Beliefs shape the religious stories we tell, our evolving myths, and the rituals that have grown within our cultures about the soul and the afterlife. There is not enough space to survey all the references, of course. Still, we can do a fly-over and look at some examples that can stand in as representatives of a much richer collection of media across history up to our own time.

One place to start is *The Epic of Gilgamesh,* which dates back to around 1800 BCE. As an epic poem, it is one of the earliest surviving great works of literature; we will discuss it more when we look at Mesopotamian religion. In the *Epic,* among other adventures, Gilgamesh (the hero), in his grief over his friend Enkidu's death, sets out on a dangerous journey to discover the secret of eternal life. Unfortunately, he fails in his quest and concludes, "Life, which you look for, you will never find. For when the gods created man, they let death be his share, and life withheld in their own hands."

Much of ancient Greek literature focused on comedy, satyr plays, and tragedy (especially involving the political and social life of the time). Some works in the various genres touched on the soul and the afterlife. One example is Plato's *The Phaedo* (a.k.a., *On the Soul*). In it, Plato provides a portrait of the last days of Socrates leading up to his death. Plato clarifies that he was not present himself during the events, and you could argue that there is some element of historical fiction in the work. He uses his account to explore his ideas about the soul and the realm beyond this physical world. We will cover Plato's (and possibly Socrates') ideas about the soul in detail in Chapter 4 when we examine the philosophy of the soul. As a footnote, there are elements in *The Phaedo* that suggest a Greek chorus, a dramatic technique, that would appear later in Greek tragedy, and that provides some commentary on events much like I am attempting through this natural history. There were also references to Greek myths and the fables of Aesop in his exploration of the soul.

The Frogs was a comedy by one of the most famous playwrights of ancient Greece, Aristophanes (427 to 386 BCE). It tells the story of the god Dionysus who was fed up with the state of Athenian tragedians. He decides to travel to Hades, the Greek underworld for the dead, to bring back the playwright Euripides to set things right. To find a path to Hades, Dionysus seeks his half-brother Heracles (known as Hercules by the Romans and modern B movie producers). When Dionysus asks about the quickest way to get to Hades, Heracles says he can hang himself, drink poison, or jump off a tower. Dionysus decides he prefers the route that Heracles himself took across Lake Acheron, and Charon ferries him across. This point in the story is where a chorus of frogs provides an interlude by singing, hence the play's name.[6] When he arrives, the play's substance is a series of activities within Hades, including dealing with monsters, feasts with virgin dancing girls, torture, a debate between two tragic poets, and other comedic excitement within the afterlife. Most religions today do not have such an earthy view of heaven.

The Frogs appears in Gilbert and Sullivan's *The Pirates of Penzance, Finnegan's Wake,* Cole Porter's *Out of This World,* and a book by Aldous Huxley called *Jesting Pilate.* As a footnote, the Lake Forest Academy near Chicago named its sports teams the Caxys, derived from the song of the chorus of frogs.[7] Yale also uses the choral chant in its Long Cheer. Stephen Sondheim and Burt Shevelove adapted *The Frogs* for what became their Broadway production in 2004. Their first version performed at Yale included Meryl Streep, Sigourney Weaver, and Christopher Durang. The play was revived in London in 2017.

A classic with echoes in virtually every other medium is the *Divine Comedy* by Dante Alighieri (circa 1320). It is widely viewed as one of the greatest works of world literature. It crystalized many of the afterlife ideas that emerged during the medieval period in Europe.

Some argue that the *Divine Comedy* was one of the earliest examples of fully realized fiction as we know it today.

S. Dali
Divine Comedy

It begins with *The Inferno* (hell) and also includes *Purgatorio* (purgatory) and *Paradiso* (heaven). *The Inferno* is incredibly frightening and still haunts us. The ancient Roman poet Virgil guides Dante through the nine concentric circles of torment within the Earth. It is a realm of the "dead people," those who have rejected spiritual values by yielding to "bestial appetites or violence, or by perverting their human intellect to fraud or malice against their fellowmen." For example, there is a line of sinners in the Eighth Circle waiting to be butchered by a demon. Their wounds heal after the torture, and they return to the line. Punishment happens forever. As Dante continues from the recognition and rejection of sin in hell, Beatrice (representing divine revelation, faith, and grace) leads him through purgatory. Then Saint Bernard of Clairvaux (representing devotion) leads him to heaven. *The Last Judgment* (painted by Hieronymus Bosch around 1482), Botticelli's paintings, and works by the surrealist Dali and others have continued to shape our afterlife vision, especially of the idea of hell in the spirit of these medieval images.

The great themes in the arts are love, death, and war. Given that, as would be expected, Shakespeare (1564 to 1616) had a lot to say about all three.[8] Starting around the fourteenth century and lasting to roughly the seventeenth century, the Renaissance period was not just notable for its transition from the Middle Ages to the modern era. It was also a time when death was constantly present in people's lives, and death shaped the arts. It was an era with high mortality rates, mass deaths due to various diseases (it was not long after the Black Plague), and little knowledge of medicine and hygiene. Death was ever-present and was mysterious. Images of corpses and skeletons were everywhere in art and architecture, and the clash of Catholicism and Protestantism across Europe during the Reformation was brutal and savage. Elizabethan and Jacobean drama, in part, was a kind of cultural catharsis. It helped make sense of and work through an aspect of life that today we tend to keep on the periphery of our consciousness.

Shakespeare's plays have been translated into every major living language and are still performed more than any other playwrights'. Given his time and goals as a playwright, he drew on imagery and language that his audiences would understand. As in the Greek tradition, he spoke about the great themes and carefully worked in commentary on the events and politics of his day. He leveraged imagery and stories from Catholicism, which were still common at the time, and from the Church of England. He often drew on earlier myths and stories and religious beliefs as needed to tell the stories he wanted to convey.

Cyndia Clegg (Clegg, 2019), in her analysis of Shakespeare and the afterlife, observes, "Across the canon, the afterlife may appear as a place of religious judgment, as in *Othello*, *Hamlet*, *Merchant of Venice*; as a classical Elysium or Hades where the spirit or shadow removes elsewhere (*Antony and Cleopatra*, *Titus Andronicus*); as Abraham's Bosom—a place of rest between death and the Last Judgment (*Henry V*, *Richard III*, *Hamlet*); or an unidentifiable life to come (*Measure for Measure*, *Macbeth*, *King Lear*)." Given the importance of death and the afterlife, Clegg argues that it provides essential insight into the plays' action and characters when Shakespeare leverages this imagery. Shakespeare uses death and the afterlife in his plays, like our views often punctuate important milestones and provide meaning in our own lives.

A few passages from the Bard himself will give a sense of the range in which he uses these ideas, and in any case, are always a delight to read.

"I come, my queen. Stay for me:
Where souls do couch on flowers, we'll hand in hand,
And with our sprightly port make the ghosts gaze:
Dido and her Aeneas shall want troops,
And all the haunt be ours."
– Antony and Cleopatra (Act 4, scene 14, 44-45)

"Therefore should every soldier in the wars do as every sick
man in his bed, wash every mote out of his conscience; and
dying so, death is to him advantage, or not dying the time was
blessedly lost wherein such preparation was gain'd; and in
him that escapes it were not sin to think that making God so
free an offer, He let him outlive that day to see His greatness
and to teach others how they should prepare."
– Henry V (Act 4, scene 1, 178-85)

"Ah, my young princes! Ah, my tender babes!
My unblown flowers, new-appearing sweets!
If yet your gentle souls fly in the air
And be not fix'd in doom perpetual,
Hover about me with your airy wings
And hear your mother's lamentation!"
– Richard III (Act 4, scene 4, 9-14)

"Let not our babbling dreams affright our souls;
Conscience is but a word that cowards use,
Devis'd at first to keep the strong in awe:
Our strong arms be our conscience, swords our law!
March on, join bravely, let us to it pell-mell;
If not to heaven, then hand in hand to hell."
– Richard III (Act 5, scene 3, 308-13)

"Ay, but to die, and go we know not where;
To lie in cold obstruction, and to rot;
This sensible warm motion to become
A kneaded clod; and the delighted spirit
To bathe in fiery floods."
– Measure for Measure (Act 3, scene 1, 115-21)

In 1678, John Bunyan published the *Pilgrim's Progress from This World, to That Which is to Come*. Bunyan's work has been called the first novel written in English. It has never been out of print and has been translated into hundreds of languages. It is viewed as one of the most significant works of religious fiction. Part of what I like about it is the additional text on the first edition cover, which says, "Delivered under the similitude of a dream, wherein is discovered, the manner of his setting out, his dangerous journey, and safe arrival at the desired countrey."

In the allegorical story, the reader follows the main character Christian's journey, a character intended to represent all of us. He travels from the City of Destruction, representing this current world, to the Celestial City, which is heaven (atop Mt. Zion). In the second part, the reader follows Christiana (Christian's wife) and her two children as they journey to the Celestial City. Through their journeys, they encounter the extremes of human emotion (e.g., in the Slough of Despond), various tempters, guides providing wisdom, deserts and mountains, monsters, and torture. These themes still attract us to the movies we watch and the books we read. Indeed, they could have inspired many of the *Star Trek: The Next Generation* episodes.

L. Fournier's The Funeral of Shelley

Perhaps the first modern horror novel, with its exploration of the supernatural intruding on this world, was *The Castle of Otranto* by Horace Walpole (written in 1764). It became a Gothic novel prototype, with secret passages, slamming doors, and ghostly impact on the world around us. He was inspired by Shakespeare, who enabled him to pivot to new points of view about the supernatural. Robert Hamm (Hamm, 2009) says, "Hamlet's encounter with the Ghost becomes for Walpole, a template for terror." Walpole's approach was to present it as a translation of a manuscript printed in Naples in 1529 and ostensibly discovered in the library of a Catholic family in the north of England. He presented the story as being much older, perhaps from as early as the Crusades. The story, in essence, plays out a curse on the family of Manfred, lord of the castle of Otranto. According to Hamm, the poet Thomas Gray (1716 to 1771) said that the novel made "[S]ome of us cry a little, and all in general afraid to go to bed o'nights." This more explicit mining of the entertainment value in the supernatural continued the trend from Shakespeare's time when death and the afterlife began to be controlled through the arts' cultural lens, rather than just being feared and controlled through ritual.

Coming out of the Gothic period and entering the Romantic period with its focus on emotion and individual experience, two works continue to influence us today. Mary Shelley (1797 to 1851) published *Frankenstein or The Modern Prometheus* in 1818. Some argue this was the first true science fiction story. It came out of one of Mary's dreams. The idea sprang from a competition between Mary, her lover and future husband, the poet Percy B. Shelley, and Lord Byron (another poet). *Frankenstein* is a familiar story to all of us. The monster lives and is conscious, emotional, and rational. He has many of the characteristics we associate with the soul, but did he have one?

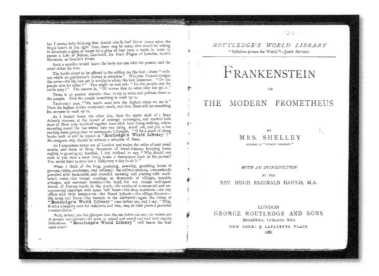

We are again discussing the ethical implications of the creatures we are creating through genetic engineering (whether manipulating human DNA for purposes like interplanetary travel, cloning, manipulating tissue to harvest body parts, or even cybernetically enhancing our bodies and minds). These discussions are intimately tied to who we are as souls, the relationship between the soul and the body, and life and death. Interestingly, Ada Byron, the daughter of Lord Byron, is considered by many to be the first computer programmer. These events were the topic of *The Haunting of Villa Diodati* (2020), an episode of *Doctor Who*.

There is a sense that just assembling all the formal elements of the soul's properties could create something sufficiently different to place the result in the category of *monster* rather than *human*. Today we call this the *uncanny valley*. The idea is that when a robot, or a voice, or an image is similar to us as humans, we may find it more familiar and comfortable.

The Brain That Wouldn't Die (1962)

When it is very different, we can categorize it as something *other* than us and interact with it on its own terms (like our pets). In between, the experience can be uncomfortable and perhaps even revolting. If you get a chance to see *Mars Attacks* (1996), you will probably experience the uncanny valley when the woman's head is attached to her pet dog's body, and her pet dog's head is attached to her body. Part of what may be affecting us is this sense that we can imagine a soul in someone else, but a human-like living thing without those soul attributes is disturbing. The robot in the classic *Metropolis* (1927) might fit into this category. For years in my field of human-computer interaction, the guidance for designers was that we should avoid anthropomorphic computer interfaces. Modern horror continues to exploit this effect in the monsters it inserts into our entertainment.

Victor Frankenstein (*Frankenstein*, 1818, selected from Chapters 3 and 4) says:

> "*I collected bones from charnel-houses and disturbed, with profane fingers, the tremendous secrets of the human frame. In a solitary chamber, or rather cell, at the top of the house, and separated from all the other apartments by a gallery and a staircase, I kept my workshop of filthy creation. The dissecting room and the slaughter-house furnished many of my materials...His limbs were in proportion, and I*

had selected his features as beautiful. Beautiful! — Great God! His yellow skin scarcely covered the work of muscles and arteries beneath; his hair was of a lustrous black, and flowing; his teeth of pearly whiteness; but these luxuriances only formed a more horrid contrast with his watery eyes, that seemed almost of the same colour as the dun-white sockets in which they were set, his shrivelled complexion and straight black lips."

In 1819, *The Vampyre* was published anonymously. Some attributed it to Lord Byron, but while the idea was part of the competition that led to Frankenstein, Byron's physician Dr. John Polidori fleshed out the story. By 1897, another seminal book, *Dracula*, was published.

Bram Stoker introduced the character of Count Dracula to the world. There had been stories and myths about vampire-like creatures before Stoker wrote his book. These included stories documented in the 1700s by Dom Augustin Calmet and others written during a short vampire craze in the 1800s. There also have been stories and myths about vampire-like creatures in other cultures around the world.[9] But the character of Dracula has been the most influential in shaping an ever-growing collection of books, movies, plays, art, and other forms of expression. Part of what is interesting is how the cultural memory of this creature is that he lives eternally, and in essence, he was able to achieve it on his own. He does suck blood, of course. Some more modern vampires suck souls or life or youth.

Dracula's motivation was presumably not unlike our own

desires for an afterlife and the efforts of those chasing immortality through life extension technologies. Stoker says of Dracula (*Dracula*, Chapter 23), originally "[H]e was in life a most wonderful man. Soldier, statesman, and alchemist. Which latter was the highest development of the scientific knowledge of his time. He had a mighty brain, a learning beyond compare, and a heart that knew no fear and no remorse…there was no branch of knowledge of his time that he did not essay." Out of his deep love for his wife, he used alchemy and black magic to live forever, and one of the unfortunate outcomes was he became a vampire. Like *Frankenstein*, these books resonate with those who see a dark side in the advance of science. The other theme, of course, is that he can share this *gift* of eternal life with others.

A zombie can be thought of as a resurrected body without its soul, a reanimated corpse without its own free will. As a body acting in the world without a soul, it is similar to a vampire. People often point to Haitian folklore as the source of the idea where the dead body is reanimated through magic. However, there are roots for the English word and the concept in African languages as well.

In contemporary media, there are many variations with slow zombies, fast zombies, zombies with personalities, good zombies, evil zombies, and even romantic zombies. An early book that shaped the Western view of the voodoo zombie was W. B. Seabrook's *The Magic Island* (1929) and the film based on the book *White Zombie* (1932). The version most of us have as our stereotype, though, is inspired by George A. Romero's film "Night of the Living Dead" (1968). There also was an earlier novel by Richard Matheson called *I Am Legend* (1954). For some, of course, the images that come to mind immediately are based on Michael Jackson's music video *Thriller* (1983).[10]

In the Haitian tradition, there are at least two different variations. One type is missing its spirit, and that is a dead person physically revived through magic by a sorcerer or a witch. The other type is a zombie astral that is missing its flesh. A sorcerer or a witch can capture the zombie astral to enhance their spiritual power by sealing it inside a special container.

One unique flavor of zombies that is particularly scary for many of us is the version where a person's body is taken over by someone else (or someone else's soul), and they are powerless as another remotely controls their bodies.[11] In this scenario, the self is imprisoned, and perhaps the soul. What would the impact be of losing control of your will?

Those of us attending Christian Sunday schools know many demon-possession stories, where demons take control of people. The Catholic Church still performs exorcisms.[12] This possession is the subject of books, movies, and games like *The Exorcist*, *The Evil Dead*, and *The Amityville Horror*. But it is also a theme in science fiction, where shows as diverse as *Fringe*, *Haven*, and *Star Trek*[13] explore the idea of one consciousness entering someone's body, overwhelming the person's consciousness, and running things.

Some argue that the examples of demon possession have a more biological explanation. Dissociative personality disorder (once known as multiple personality disorder) could present as some form of possession. I have an ancestor back in the early days of the American colonies who was killed as a witch.[14] It turns out that she had a traumatic miscarriage that impacted her emotionally, and her neighbors attributed the changes they saw in her personality to witchcraft.

As another example, I had a colleague I worked with at one point who suddenly started earnestly telling me about a conversation he had shared with his dog. The story was not the usual owner talking to a pet discussion. He believed they were having a conversation in a common language. It turns out the dosage of the drugs he was on was off due to overwork while his spouse was out of town. Other drugs induce voices and changes in behavior. Schizophrenia can cause people to hear voices, hallucinate, and have a distorted view of reality. These examples challenge thinking about the connection between mind, self, and body. A theory of the soul and its relationship to the body also needs to be able to handle these conditions.

Hypnosis might come to mind as a way of controlling another soul. Again, it captures our imagination because it represents another person or force overriding the will we often associate with our soul. It goes back to Franz Mesmer (1734 to 1815) and has been around in popular culture ever since. It is relatively mainstream in medical practice now, and research shows it can have a powerful effect on the body and our mental health. While it has been demonstrated that the widespread idea that one person can force someone to do something against their will appears to be unfounded, that fear does persist in part because it is reinforced in popular media.

A more recent development is increasingly sophisticated prosthetic technologies. Brain-controlled prosthetics are starting to appear. Brain implants can be used to control limbs, and eventually, implants may not be required. The limbs themselves could become more intelligent with built-in artificial intelligence that supports users and controls limbs and external devices on their behalf by anticipating their needs. However, the dark side was illustrated by an episode of the Netflix production, the *White Rabbit Project*. Greg Gage (co-founder of Backyard Brains) created a mind-control device where one host controlled another host's bodily movements by overriding their will. It was clear that this experience fits into the alarming category! As our bodies become more integrated with computers, this is going to be a challenge.

Is this just theory? At the end of 2020, the French armed forces' ethical committee gave the go-ahead to develop bionic soldiers who have extraordinary brainpower and are resistant to pain and stress. They assured everyone that *invasive* augmentations are not *currently* in the plans. They also noted that they are forbidding any modification that might impact their ability to manage the use of force, their free will, or affect their sense of *humanity*. Anytime someone says they will not affect your humanity, a red light should go off in your head. Their warning, of course, suggests they could potentially take more assertive control and manage that sense of humanity. They note that "[N]ot everyone has the same scruples as us and we have to prepare ourselves for such a future." They add the qualification that "It's an opinion [the policy] which isn't set in stone and will be regularly reassessed in the light of future developments."

We know that military technologies have a way of working their way into the consumer world. Virtual reality is an excellent example. Again, we have to wonder what that might imply for the souls of whoever's soldiers are impacted. Will they be held morally responsible for what their bodies do when their souls are assessed in the afterlife? What happens when they return to civilian life? Should they be able to return? Science fiction has explored the notion of the unintended consequences of super-soldiers going rogue. These characters can look and act a lot like super-zombies. We are still wrestling with the ethics and psychological implications of drone operators killing remotely, distanced from the humanity of those dying as a result of the technology.

It strikes me that another variation that is similar to a zombie is the golem in Jewish folklore. A golem is an anthropomorphic being created from something like clay or mud.[15] It is brought to life but is controlled in a way that suggests it is more like a robot than a conscious being with a soul. Marilyn Cooper (Cooper, 2017) says, "[T]he golem is a highly mutable metaphor with seemingly limitless symbolism. It can be a victim or villain, Jew or non-Jew, man or woman—or sometimes both." This image has been a stand-in for messages about war, community, isolation, and despair.

The 1930s were one of those unique cultural tipping points like the late 1800s. WWI and the 1918 flu epidemic were still fresh in memories. Entering the 1930s, the United States was still in the middle of Prohibition and all the changes that came with it. The decade began with the Depression and ended with WWII. Their climate crisis, including the drought that led to the Dustbowl, filled the middle part of the 1930s. It is also true that the *Jazz Singer* marked the end of the silent film era, and so perhaps it is not surprising that one type of cinema that exploded was the first golden age of the horror film. The dark side of variations on the soul and the afterlife resulted in movies that we are still watching, updating, and evolving today. These films include *Dracula, Frankenstein, Dr. Jekyll and Mr. Hyde, Island of Lost Souls, The Most Dangerous Game, The Mummy, Murder in the Rue Morgue, White Zombie, The Invisible Man, Werewolf of London, The Golem,* and *The Walking Dead.*

Since the 1930s, the Horror Films' genre has continued to grow, but so have comedies designed to make fun of the monsters. Mocking the things that frighten us acknowledges its power and underlying truth but is also a way of giving us control. Another genre that has developed is movies exploring and shaping our more optimistic and thoughtful views of the afterlife, and our relationship with the other side. Here are a few of my personal favorites:

- *A Christmas Carol* (22 film versions)
- *Topper* (1937)
- *Heaven Can Wait* (1943, 1978)
- *Blithe Spirit* (1945)
- *It's a Wonderful Life* (1946)
- *The Ghost and Mrs. Muir* (1947)
- *Abbot and Costello Meet Frankenstein* (1948)
- *Harvey* (1950)
- *Ghostbusters* (1984)
- *Beetlejuice* (1988)
- *Field of Dreams* (1989)
- *Flatliners* (1990)
- *Ghost* (1990)
- *The Sixth* Sense (1999)
- *Coco* (2017)
- *Soul* (2020)

Another category of movies encourages us to think and feel more empathetically about animals, aliens, and artificial intelligence. While they do not necessarily speak to their souls, the characters often have attributes that we typically associate with ourselves and our souls. That is what makes them compelling. These movies, and the books and stories that inspire them, have had a way of pointing to technologies we are exploring today. They frequently warn of the unintended consequences that we should anticipate. Typical movies include:

- *The Day the Earth Stood Still* (1951)
- *Colossus: The Forbin Project* (1970)
- *Westworld* (1973)
- *Bladerunner* (1982)
- *2001* (1968)
- *Total Recall* (1990)
- *A.I. Artificial Intelligence* (2001)
- *WALL-E* (2007)
- *Avatar* (2009)
- *Ex Machina* (2014)
- *Chappie* (2015)
- *The Planet of the Apes* Series
- *Hitchhikers Guide to the Galaxy*
- *Star Trek* Series
- *Star Wars* Series

One of the television shows my family and I have been binging during this pandemic summer has been *The Good Place*. I must admit that watching it might have helped motivate this desire to explore the soul's natural history. The twist of someone who has lived a completely selfish life ending up in the Good Place unexpectedly and then gradually discovering that it is a more sophisticated version of the Bad Place (especially in contrast to the Dante's *Inferno* alternative) was compelling. Add in the ongoing discussion of alternative theories about what an ethical life might be like and how one should be judged as worthy of the Good versus the Bad Place, and the show is well-positioned to capture theology and philosophy nerds. Furthermore, watching the plot evolve towards, in essence, creating a kind of purgatory to resolve the apparent injustice of hell led to a lot of discussion in the Lund household.

Another series well-suited to this period in our history is *Upload*. Since I have been working in artificial intelligence for awhile, I cannot help but wonder what would be required to attribute a soul to a conscious artificial intelligence. In *Upload*, of course, the physical body is removed from the equation. Just before a person dies, their consciousness and memories are uploaded into a kind of heaven, and there is a connection between the synthetic afterlife and the physical world. There is the possibility of virtual reincarnation, as well as reincarnation inside a synthetic body. The virtual person has attributes that we might associate with a soul, but an underlying question is whether the soul still exists.

We have also seen variations on these themes while binge-watching *Eureka* (from back in 2006 to 2012) and *Fringe* (2008 to 2013). My family even started to watch *iZombie*, which uses the zombie variation closest to Dracula in that the zombie has all the characteristics of a soul (personality, rationality, and emotion). As a zombie, she does not have a soul, can live eternally (except for certain fatal events), and unfortunately needs to eat brains. More shows are being turned out faster than I can watch them (e.g., *Dark Mirror*, *Tales from The Loop*, and *Altered Carbon*). The new TV series *Sweet Tooth* introduces human-animal hybrids, and you are forced to decide between the "humanity" of some of the humans versus the Sweet Tooth human-deer character. One of the attractions of these shows is they challenge the assumptions we make about who we are and how we fit within this world by asking, "What if?"

Then there are the many video games that let us step inside the characters and explore virtual worlds. I will not even try to list all of these, but I would note that often they cannot help but create empathy for *the other* that *we* get to possess. They support a sense of dualism where the self can transmigrate to other bodies and experience things in new ways. There is a story in *ScienceDaily* (Spoon, 2018) that finds evidence that kids playing video games designed in the right way can demonstrate greater connectivity in the areas of their brains associated with empathy and with being able to take on different perspectives.[16] There are also suggestions that they are better at regulating their own emotions. The article notes:

"The realization that these skills are actually trainable with video games is important because they are predictors of emotional well-being and health throughout life, and can be practiced anytime — with or without video games,' says Tammi Kral, a UW-Madison graduate student in psychology who led the research at the Center for Healthy Minds.

"Richard Davidson, director of the center and a professor of psychology and psychiatry at UW-Madison, explains that empathy is the first step in a sequence that can lead to prosocial behavior, such as helping others in need."

WHAT WE THINK ABOUT THE SOUL

Religious Affiliation

One of the influences on popular attitudes about ideas like the soul and the afterlife through history has been the rise of religious institutions within societies, as communities become more complex and hierarchical. Our beliefs are often the mix arising from sources like the arts and sciences to which we are exposed; what we read or hear in the news; our education; interpretation of our experiences; and the stories we tell each other. But all tend to be filtered through the lenses of our chosen communities, and those can include our religious communities and traditions. The filter of shared religious belief is especially relevant when considering the soul and the afterlife. So before jumping into what Americans say they believe, we should look at those religious perspectives that influence us, at least as a context within which we live. We will dive deeper into the theology of different religions in Chapter 5.

The Pew Research Center points out in their 2012 study on religion worldwide (The Global Religious Landscape, 2012) that more than eight in ten people identify with a formal religious group across two hundred and thirty countries and territories. Christianity is the largest faith on Earth, accounting for roughly thirty percent of people, with the Catholic Church being the largest Christian community. Christians in Europe are dying faster than they are born, although births greatly exceed deaths in Latin America and Sub-Saharan Africa.

Islam is followed by twenty-four percent of the world's population. Muslims are by far the fastest-growing group, especially in the Middle East and North Africa, the Asia-Pacific Region, and Sub-Saharan Africa. Hinduism accounts for about fifteen percent (with most living in India and the greatest growth in the Asia-Pacific regions). With its unique perspective on the soul and the afterlife, Buddhism is followed by seven percent of the population; about half of them live in China. Roughly six percent of the world follows various folk and traditional faiths with their roots in beliefs that pre-existed other more formal systems. Sixteen percent have no formal religious affiliation worldwide but often hold some more general spiritual faith in a God or a universal spirit.

In the United States, the stereotype is that it is a Christian nation, and you could make that case based on the numbers.[17] Most of the population (sixty-eight percent) identify with Christianity. Given the early years of immigration from Europe, this probably is not surprising. Twelve of the original colonies were Protestant, and Maryland was the only Catholic colony. That being said, there are significant divisions within the Christian communities in the United States. Furthermore, many of those identifying as Christian are not necessarily actively practicing Christians or very familiar with their church's doctrinal positions. A recent study, for example, suggests that twenty percent or more of those identifying as evangelical conservatives virtually never attend church or actively practice their faith, and identify more as a political statement than theologically. Almost as large as any individual type of Christian is the category of those who do not identify with any religious group. Roughly twenty-three percent of the population of the United States says they are Unaffiliated.

While the Christian faith held by the majority influences

many of the concepts we have about the soul and the afterlife, it is essential to be careful about painting with too broad a brush. Over America's history, various Christians have been quite vocal in their arguments about the vital importance of the differences in their beliefs. Many argued that other Christian groups would not be with them in heaven. Early Puritans would probably look askance at virtually all Christians in the United States today. As we will see, many contemporary churches might not welcome some of the views of the original Protestant Reformers. We have only recently elected the second Catholic as President, for example. This issue was a significant one back when Kennedy was running for election in the 1960s.

According to the latest Pew Research study of the religious landscape (Pew Research Center, 2021), Catholics make up about twenty-one percent of the United States population. The various groups of Protestants have declined from sixty-two percent of the United States in 1972 (when I graduated from college) to fifty-one percent in 2010, and to more like forty-seven percent today. Mainline Protestants account for about fifteen percent of the population, and the Black Protestant churches account for close to seven percent. The Black Protestant churches have long been an essential and culturally unique branch of the American church community.

Evangelicals are an interesting group. They generally have the most specific view of the soul and the afterlife. The beliefs are typically based on what they believe is a literal interpretation of the Christian Bible's scriptures, although even among themselves, the word *literal* may be defined differently. While all together, until recently, they have accounted for about twenty-five percent of the population, there are two flavors of evangelicals.[18] One group, which a Pew Research Center study (Conservatives, 2020) suggests is about thirty-six percent of evangelicals, has integrated conservative political and social views very tightly with their theology. This group emerged around the 1960s and 70s.[19] There are conservative strains within Catholicism and mainline Protestants as well, but the largest percentage and the most visible in the popular press is the politically conservative branch of evangelicalism. Given the Pew number, that would be about nine percent of Christians overall, with the remaining sixteen percent as independents or more progressive evangelicals. A recent editorial by *Christianity Today* (Dalrymple, 2020), the leading evangelical magazine (founded by Billy Graham in 1956), discusses how comprehensive this division is and how it reflects very fundamental differences in beliefs about the evangelical faith in these times. While political views can be quite distinct for these groups, specific beliefs about the soul and the afterlife are at least as diverse.

Those who actively practice Judaism account for two percent of the population. Some estimates suggest more Jews are living in the United States than are living in Israel. California and New York are home to forty-two percent of American Jews. Mormons account for a little less than two percent of the population in the United States, and about forty percent of Mormons live in Utah (the headquarters of The Church of Jesus Christ of Latter-day Saints). Buddhism, Hinduism, and Islam account for another two percent or so of the population. Finally, as with the global population, one of the largest groups and growing in the United States is the twenty-three percent of the population who identify themselves as not affiliated with any formal religious group (atheist, agnostic, and nothing in particular).

Some underlying trends in these numbers are essential to recognize, especially when rationalizing how beliefs showing up in surveys can differ from the formal doctrinal positions of various religious groups. The Pew Research survey in 2017 found that those who identify as religious and spiritual[20] in the United States have dropped over 2012 to 2017 from fifty-nine percent to less than half of Americans. At the same time, those identifying as spiritual but not religious (e.g., not regularly following a group's practices or formally engaged in a specific religious community) have grown by more than forty percent. The group identifying as neither religious nor spiritual has increased from sixteen to eighteen percent. There are some variations in these numbers, of course. The Public Religion

Research Institute (PRRI) in 2017 surveyed two thousand American adults and found eighteen percent identified as spiritual but not religious, and thirty-one percent identified as neither spiritual nor religious. We will talk more about this as we look at this trend from the perspective of how it might impact cultural beliefs about the soul and the afterlife.

There is a general trend in contemporary culture around mistrust of organizations and formal structures. Younger people are trending away from the formal practices of religion. As a result, some religious institutions are increasingly seen as out of touch with the growing cultural diversity and the implications of emerging technologies in our lives. It will be interesting to see how over time, this influences the divergence from more orthodox views of the afterlife, who or what has a soul, and individual ethical systems.

Tara Burton (Burton, 2017) captures these trends with a quote from one person who was a dog walker in New York describing the discomfort she felt being gay in her church, "I essentially shed all of my religious ties out of self-preservation. It was easier not to have the hard 'gay and Christian' conversations, so religion grew even more into this very private and personal thing for me that not a lot of other people were involved in." Another person described by Burton, who works in a yoga studio, says, "The practices I consider spiritual are the things I do to care for myself in a deep way, to calm myself when I am distressed, to create meaning out of the experiences of my life."

Harry Bruinius (Bruinius, 2017), in an article in *The Christian Science Monitor,* shared the opinion of Andrew Walker, the director of policy studies for the Ethics and Religious Liberty Commission (within the Southern Baptist Convention). Walker says, "They grew up in a nominal Christian culture, where it's no longer of a cultural or social benefit to identify as a Christian…To add to that is there's often not only no social prestige to gain, there's also social prestige to lose, if you say you are a Christian in our society."

We will spend a considerable amount of time at various points in this book looking at the beliefs about the soul and the afterlife. However, I have focused a little more time on spiritual but not religious beliefs because we will see that the common beliefs we hold in our culture are not necessarily tightly aligned with any set of formal religious doctrinal beliefs. This socially constructed view of who we are, and our destinies may in part be a result of how our traditional religious practices have been changing in recent history within our culture.

Surveying Our Beliefs

In the United States, our beliefs were initially molded by the early waves of immigrants from Western Europe that shaped the new country and displaced indigenous populations and faiths. Western European religious beliefs, however, have continued to evolve and influence us, and so may be a bell-weather for trends happening here. Looking forward, according to the Pew Research Center (Europe, 2015), the percentage of Europeans identifying as Christian is projected to decline from roughly seventy-five percent in 2010 to sixty-five percent in 2050. It should be noted that according to the Pew Research Center report in 2017 across Western Europe, the largest group of those identifying as Christians are non-practicing Christians (a median of forty-six percent of the total, versus eighteen percent identifying as church-attending Christians). Many of those leaving the religiously Christian column switch to Unaffiliated (going from nineteen to twenty-three percent during the same period).

Another Pew Research study on religion in Western Europe (Sahgal, 2018) finds that while half the people in Europe say they are neither religious nor spiritual, if they must identify with a religion, they will select Christian. In every country except Italy, non-practicing Christians outnumber regular attenders. The Pew Research Study (Attitudes Towards Spirituality and Religion, 2018) on "Being Christian in Western Europe" found that the less active and committed Christians are in their identified Christian faith, the more negative their views towards their religion. Ninety-four percent of religiously Unaffiliated have mixed or unfavorable opinions of religion.

Even with the numbers identifying as Christian, there is a clear trend towards secularization in Western Europe. In the long term, as the diversity of Europe continues to increase with this secularization and through immigration and the infusion of other faiths, one would expect the average beliefs of the religious would continue to evolve. Across history, Christianity has gradually adapted the religious beliefs and practices it has encountered and local cultural practices into its rituals and traditions (e.g., Christmas as a classic example), just as it has influenced the cultures it has encountered.

The 2017 Pew Research Center review of religion in Western Europe also asked people why they were leaving the religion they were raised in to become Unaffiliated. People could select more than one answer. Sixty-one percent selected gradually drifting away from religion as the answer. It will be interesting to see if this increases as a result of the social distancing that happened during the recent pandemic as community ties loosened. Fifty-eight percent cited disagreeing with their religion's positions on social issues, and these issues can shift quickly. In 2004, thirty-one percent of Americans supported same-sex marriage, and now sixty-one percent support it. Fifty-four percent chose no longer believing in their religion's teachings, and fifty-three percent were unhappy about scandals involving religious institutions and leaders. In the United States, this category may include the lavish lifestyles some televangelists live. Reports in the United States suggest people here are shifting in their religious beliefs for similar reasons. Across these explanations, there could be implications for how people view who will make it to heaven and who will not. Much smaller percentages cited spiritual needs not being met and religion failing them in a time of need, suggesting that local communities continue to serve their members reasonably well in these areas.

Engagement in religion and spiritual beliefs does tend to increase with age.[21] On the other hand, as we have been observing, it might not be a surprise to find the younger, better educated demographic growing up in a changing, pluralistic world is increasingly finding some of the formal institutions' extremes unattractive. They might be expected to either reject them outright or keep the parts that feel right to them and reject the identification that comes with all the baggage. Many non-practicing Christians say they do not believe in the God "described in the Bible" but do believe in some other higher power or spiritual force in the universe. In the United States, we also live in a consumer culture that lets us shop not just for things, but also for ideas that we can assemble into personalized belief systems.

Of course, summarizing Christianity in Western Europe is like summarizing beliefs in the United States (Attitudes Toward Spirituality and Religion, 2018). Communities across and within the states can have widely different beliefs, and beliefs across various Western European countries can be similarly diverse. The first place to look is those identifying as *religious* (including *religious and spiritual*, and *religious and non-spiritual*). These account for about forty percent of the sample in the Pew Western Europe study. They tend to affirm what you might expect. They believe in the God that they find in the Bible, and they think there are spiritual forces at work in the universe. They believe in a dualistic view of the soul and the body. They feel their faith helps them choose between right and wrong, and they generally think that religion does more good than harm.

The ten percent or so who described themselves as *spiritual but not religious* tend to say that they do not believe in the God they read about as described in the Bible. However, they do believe in a higher power or spiritual force in the universe. They are as likely as those who are more religious to think they have a soul but are less likely to say that religious beliefs help them make ethical choices. A little more than half (fifty-seven percent) believe that religion does more good than harm.

A third group is the roughly fifty percent of those in Western Europe who call themselves *neither religious nor spiritual*. Interestingly, as we have noted, many of these still identify as Christian. They are more likely to say they do not believe in any God or higher power. Only about a third believe there is a connection to something bigger and more transcendent or believe in spiritual forces. Almost half do believe in the soul and an afterlife (perhaps reflecting the common sense of ourselves and our hopes beyond death). They tend to reject the statement that religion helps them choose between right and wrong, and their views vary widely depending on their country as to whether religion does more good than harm. Seventy-three percent of religiously Unaffiliated nonbelievers believe that science makes religion unnecessary in their lives.

Let's shift our gaze a little closer to home. My stereotype is that Canada is one part Europe, one part the United States, and one part...Canada, eh? Joseph Brean (Brean, 2018) wrote an article entitled "Millennials are more likely to believe in an afterlife than are older generations: Do you believe in life after—well—life?" for the *National Post*. It described a survey reported by Reginald Bibby, a sociologist at the University of Lethbridge. The survey focused on Canadian Millennials' beliefs but also looked at those beliefs across different age groups.

Two-thirds of Canadians believe in the core Christian doctrines, including an afterlife and heaven. The belief in hell is much lower, at forty-two percent. Almost half of Canadians believe they can contact and communicate with the spirit world, and about the same percentage believe they have experienced God's presence. A little more than half of Canadians believe in guardian angels.

As in the European data, the belief in God or a higher power increases with age, as does the idea that God or the higher power cares about us. The traditional Christian belief about Jesus as the Son of God who resurrected from death also increases with age. The increase in the strength of more traditional concepts contrasts with the decrease with age in what might be considered more contemporary spiritual ideas about contacting the spirit world and the dead. Brean relates this strength in belief about contacting the spirit world and the dead, and believing in the afterlife, to the recent rise in spiritualism among younger generations. That rise is happening at the same time as—and perhaps in reaction to—the tremendous leaps in science and engineering that have been taking place.

This echoes what was happening when Dr. MacDougall was doing his research.

One finding that pops out in the data from Canada is that while the strength of core religious doctrinal beliefs increases with age, the belief in life after death slightly decreases with increasing age. According to Brean, Bibby explains it in terms of what is happening in popular culture. He says, "It's not that older people have given up and figure there's no life after death. It's just that, in addition to those preachers and priests and others that were drilling into people in days gone by the fact that there's life after death and you better shape up or you might go to hell, that kind of stuff, we're just saying the life-after-death theme has been given an incredible shot in the arm from culture as a whole, and from the most unlikely places, particularly the entertainment industry."

This view would be consistent with our discussion of the ideas of the soul and the afterlife in popular culture. Brean, in turn, says, "[T]he noted skeptic and professor of psychology at York University James E. Alcock puts it in his forthcoming book *Belief: What It Means to Believe and Why Our Convictions Are So Compelling*, belief can mean trust, confidence, faith, optimism, and varying degrees of certainty, among other things." He also says that distinguishing between imagination and the concrete world is getting more complicated since "Modern technological culture has increased the possibilities of human imagination, and allowed access to vastly more reality, including practically limitless numbers of other people."

From Europe and Canada, we turn to the United States. Jean Twenge, Ryne Sherman, Julie Exline, and Joshua Grubbs (Twenge, 2016) wrote an article entitled "Declines in American Adults' Religious Participation and Beliefs, 1972-2014".[22] Twengy et al. found that while earlier studies found some declines in religious affiliation, they did not see as much change in cultural-religious beliefs and practices. But in their most recent survey, they found significantly less participation in regular formal religious practices and associated official beliefs. This finding was especially true among the eighteen to twenty-nine-year-old cohort. Fewer people in the United States are praying and attending religious services, and there are fewer who say they take the Bible literally or that believe in God as described in the Bible. Concerning key age trends, they note, "Nearly a third of Millennials were secular not merely in religious affiliation but also belief in God, religiosity, and religious service attendance, many more than Boomers and Generation X'ers at the same age. Eight times more 18- to 29-year-olds never prayed in 2014 versus the early 1980s."

Twenge et al.'s analysis notes that the differences show up strongly when comparing Generation X'ers with Boomers at the same age and reflect changes broadly across society over the period they studied. They see the decline in religious commitment as most pronounced among men, Caucasians, the college-educated, and those in the Midwest, Northeast, and West. The decrease was nearly absent among Black Americans and was small in the South. As a result, Twengy et al. view the data through a filter of high social power and privilege, and how that might make people less likely to have a significant need for religion.

Jenn offers a different explanation about trends in religious practices and spiritual beliefs. She has an interesting blog called "The Search for Life after Death" (Jenn, 2016). She began it based on a significant personal event that stimulated an interest in this area. Her blog focuses on evidence for the afterlife, such as "near-death experiences, deathbed visions, past-life memories, instrumental transcommunication, out-of-body experiences, after-death communications, and mediumship." In "SDSU Study: Religion Down, Afterlife Belief Up Among Millennials; Reason? Feeling 'Entitled' to get 'Something for Nothing'" she says you have to look at how religious and spiritual beliefs now correlate with confidence in science and evidence, political party, and other potential factors. You need to look at the internet's growth in general and social media (particularly how we all now get information). It seems likely that many who are not devoted to a specific religious framework will pick and choose ideas based on their needs and lives. They may choose from the spiritual Walmart of alternative beliefs that exists amid the rapid scientific, technical, and social evolution in which we live. They will assemble the set of ideas that help them cope.

As mentioned, consistent with the notion that Europe may point to trends here, the share of the population in the United States that is religiously Unaffiliated is comparable to Western Europe. The *nones* here, however, are more religious than their European counterparts. They are more likely than their European cousins to pray and believe in God. Interestingly, even some self-identifying atheists say they believe in God. This choice suggests their selection of an atheism option could be more about rejecting formal religious institutions or indicates a belief in a universal spirit but not a classical Judeo-Christian God.

Getting Specific.

Mortier's Map to Paradise

In this next section, alas, we need to turn up the volume just a bit on the flood of surveys and statistics. This can be a little frustrating because, as we know from recent elections, the nature of surveys is that there can be considerable variability in specific numbers based on who is sampled and how the questions are asked. Nevertheless, I am going to attempt to pull out the highlights and the interesting general trends. So do not worry too much about specific numbers unless you are inclined to go back to the source documents in the Bibliography.

We generally believe in God or a universal spirit, although younger people are more skeptical. Frank Newport (Newport, 2011) wrote an article entitled "More Than 9 in 10 Americans Continue to Believe in God: Professed belief is lower among younger Americans, Easterners, and liberals". Newport reported the positive answer to "Do you believe in God?" was around ninety-two percent in 2011. But the research found belief in God or a universal spirit was lower for younger Americans, liberals, those living in the East, those with postgraduate educations, and political independents. When asked in surveys about whether they believed clearly in God or at least in a concrete god that is something other than a universal spirit, confidence dropped to around seventy-five percent. In Newport's update (Newport, 2016), he reports that in the 1940s, about ninety-six percent of people said they believed in God or a universal spirit. By 2016, this had continued to drop from the 2011 number to around ninety percent, and again was much lower for those without doubt.

Nearly three-quarters of us believe in heaven and an afterlife. Hell...not so much. In Newport's 2016 update, seventy-one percent said they believe in heaven, and sixty-four percent said they believe in hell. The Roper Center at Cornell University found similar results. They surveyed various studies relative to the afterlife from NBC, Pew Research, Gallup, and others since 1944 and summarized them in an article called "Paradise Polled: Americans and the Afterlife" (Center, 2020). Over the years, afterlife belief has been remarkably stable at about seventy-three percent of the United States.

Interestingly, eighty percent of people say they believe in heaven; and sixty-seven percent say they believe in hell (with thirty percent saying they do not). An earlier 1998 Harris poll found that eighty percent of Christians believed in hell (versus the ninety-six percent who believed in heaven and the ninety percent who believed in the afterlife), and so as with other beliefs, the trend is down. For non-Christians, only about forty percent believe in hell (about the same as those believing in the Devil). Roughly sixty percent of non-Christians, according to Harris, believe in an afterlife and heaven. A 2013 Pew poll found even lower numbers, with about twenty-seven percent of agnostics and thirteen percent of atheists believing in an afterlife. The Roper Center suggests people may be interpreting "the afterlife" as something specific that might include hell.

We tend to anticipate becoming spiritual beings, not physical ones. The Roper 2020 study also reports that an early ABC News/Washington Post poll found a high level of support for the concept of heaven (eighty-seven percent). Of those, eighty-two percent said we will exist there just spiritually and not physically. Roper also mentioned a 2005 update by ABC that found seventy-eight percent said we would live in the afterlife spiritually, eight percent believe we will exist physically,[23] and nine percent said both. Some of these differences are likely to reflect the specific beliefs about the nature of the afterlife, heaven, and possibly hell, and how respondents read various questions in the different surveys.[24] In Chapter 5, we will contrast these convictions with the beliefs of the major religions in the United States.

If we believe in heaven, we are confident we will go there. In the 1998 Harris Poll (Taylor, 1998), eighty-four percent of all adults believed in the afterlife, and seventy-six percent of those who believed in heaven were confident they would go there. Four percent thought they would go to purgatory, and two percent felt they would go to hell.[25] In the ABC News poll, eighty-nine percent believed in an afterlife, and eighty-five percent thought they would go to heaven. These high numbers have been mostly consistent across these and other studies for thirty years (Sussman, 2005). While the numbers probably reflect our fundamental beliefs about our own goodness and aspirations for the afterlife, they contrast with the more exclusionist views of some religious traditions.

For most, however, it is probably more about people feeling that basically, we are good. We know or know of some amazing, loving, selfless people. Even though we might not reach that elite status ourselves in the big scheme of things, we care for our friends and families and generally *try* to be good. Many would say the *evil* people should either go to hell or not get to live beyond death. A key question is how bad does one have to be to qualify as evil? Or how much more punishment must we go through for our guilty mistakes given the consequences we have already endured and the lessons we have learned? Our self-esteem would have to be pretty beaten down if we were going to believe in heaven and not think we would be there (although note the two percent in the study cited earlier). One of the entertaining aspects of the series *The Good Place* is who thinks they should make it to heaven, and the revelation of who does and does not make it is part of the show's premise.

We generally feel the good will be in heaven, whatever their faith and possibly even those without a faith. According to Roper's "Paradise Polled" study summarizing the research, they confirmed what most of us probably hear from our friends if the topic comes up when we get together. People who believe in the afterlife tend to think the good people we know will be in heaven. In a Harvard University poll, eighty-four percent said a good person of another faith would be able to go to heaven. An ABC News poll found sixty-nine percent believed that both Christians and non-Christians could go to heaven (just twenty-four percent believed only Christians would be allowed in). That would be a common-sense view of a loving God and reflect most people's sense of justice.

Evangelicalism often teaches the more exclusionist view where only the *saved* will make it to heaven. Individual American evangelicals themselves, however, are more diverse in their beliefs. Even twenty-two percent of evangelicals think there could be atheists in heaven, and fifty-one percent think Muslims will be there. Mainline Protestants and Catholics are even more accepting of the idea that those with different faiths (or even no faith) will be in heaven.

More believe in reincarnation than you might think, even some Christians. Roper notes that according to a PSRA/Newsweek poll in 2005, they found that while sixty-seven percent of people think the afterlife is a heaven and perhaps a hell in the traditional sense, thirteen percent believe the soul may live in some sort of spiritual realm. That study also found six percent believed there is no afterlife, and five percent believed in reincarnation. They report a 60 Minutes/Vanity Fair poll in 2010 that found sixty-five percent believed in heaven, hell, or purgatory. An additional seven percent believe in another spiritual dimension, two percent believed the dead become ghosts, and six percent believed in reincarnation. Thirteen percent did not believe in an afterlife at all.

Some of these numbers may be artifacts of the nature of forced-choice surveys. Still, Roper does note that more traditional Christians also believe in reincarnation and ghosts. In the 2011 poll, fifteen percent of Protestants and twenty-four percent of Catholics said they believed in reincarnation. Roper's review of afterlife studies suggests that the belief in reincarnation has held relatively steady since 1968 at around one in five people, varying slightly from year to year. This finding is also consistent with the Harris poll in 1998 that showed twenty-two percent of all Christians believe in reincarnation, while thirty-two percent of non-Christians believe in reincarnation. Some of these numbers may be influenced by Eastern religious beliefs, and/or the differences between those religious who align with a specific doctrine and those who just identify with a faith without much involvement and those who go to services but don't bother to internalize the formal beliefs.

We've got some interesting intuitions about what we'll find in heaven. In one study reported in the Roper "Paradise Polled" report, there was a deeper dive into detailed afterlife beliefs. In that study, people were offered a series of statements about heaven and asked whether they believed each statement, did not believe it, or were not sure. At least seventy-five percent shared beliefs that I have heard echoed widely among the people with whom I have speculated about heaven. They believe heaven will be peaceful, we will be happy, and people will love each other. God's love will be the focus of the experience (e.g., we will feel the love of God deeply), and we will be in the presence of God or Jesus Christ. We will be living forever, and those who suffer from disabilities will be healed.[26] We will see friends, relatives, and spouses.[27] We will grow spiritually through eternity. Spiritual growth as a focus of the afterlife, of course, would be one of the most common beliefs across different religions globally.[28]

The middle category of responses (between a fifty and seventy-four percent positive response rate) includes believing there will be humor.[29] We will satisfy others' spiritual needs. There will be other spiritual beings (e.g., angels or devils).[30] People tend to think we will have responsibilities. I have always felt that there should be something to *do* that is meaningful through eternity—although that might reflect one of my personality flaws—and this might be similar. Finally, there is a belief that people will grow intellectually; and I would add that Plato would approve of this view.

There is roughly the same agreement and disagreement on whether we will have a human form in heaven. As noted earlier, most do not think we will have a body per se, but slightly more people believe we will be recognizable as the same person as on Earth. On the other hand, less than a third think we

Dante Meets Beatrice
by Gustav Dore

will be the same age in heaven as when we died.[31] There will be plenty of good food—perhaps not beer, but I would have to guess certainly wine.

A third believe we will be able to minister to people's spiritual needs back on earth, and a bit fewer believe we will have some other contact with the living. This sense of connection with the other side is not too different from those who believe they have experienced ghosts. Twenty percent take material comforts a little further and believe there will be sports and other leisure activities (probably not digital ones, however). Fourteen percent anticipate there will be sexual relations with spouses. In short, for some, there seems to be the idea that whatever heaven is, it certainly would include those things which have made us happy on Earth. These ideas of heaven as a continuation of this world's best have a long history in afterlife beliefs that go back at least to the Egyptians.

Voices from the Other Side

Example 1

"Mom never got a chance to meet my son's daughter. She could no longer travel and we were trying to figure out a time that her grandkids could bring their new baby to meet great-grandma. The baby was asleep in her crib. My son and his wife were asleep in their room. The baby had the baby monitor on next to her. My daughter-in-law suddenly heard a lullaby being hummed. In a panic, she grabbed the monitor and started to get out of bed to see if someone was in the baby's room. Looking at the monitor, she saw the baby staring out at someone only [the baby] could see. The baby did not move. My daughter-in-law just watched on the monitor. When the lullaby was finished, the sound just stopped. The baby closed her little eyes and went back to sleep. When I called the kids to tell them mom had passed away in the early morning, my daughter-in-law told me she believed mom came to see the new great-granddaughter and told me what had happened."

Example 2

"I was 17 leading up to dad's trip to hunt in Canada. Dad and I butted heads a lot! I was outspoken and got under dad's skin (I was 100% a teenager). The night before dad left on his trip, I asked if I could be home to say goodbye. He knew the time would be limited, so he would not have time to pick me up at school. I solved the problem. I went to school on the bus and then, at lunch, just walked off the school's grounds. I had my backpack and homework, and I walked home. I made it home before dad's friends picked him up. Dad did not get mad. He hugged me and told me how much he loved me. I told him how much I loved him, and dad walked out of the house. He turned and looked back at me and threw me a kiss. I threw a kiss back at him. At that moment, a feeling washed over me. I was never going to see dad again.

"I tried shaking off the feeling. I tried to talk with mom about it, but she just said I was being silly. I think that is why I was not surprised when I picked up the phone, and it was dad's friend on the phone asking to speak with mom. I kept

pushing, but he would not tell me anything. He just kept ask-ing for mom's work number. I gave it to him then timed how long it would take for him to call mom at [her job]. Then I called. I could tell mom was in shock when I spoke to her. She said she was heading up to [Hope, British Columbia in Can-ada] where he was in the hospital. Dad's friend's wife was coming to pick up mom. We needed to pack a suitcase for her. By the time they made it to Hope, dad had passed away.

"That night was the first of many experiences that went on for several years. When I went to bed, I started to cry. 'Daddy, I am so sorry. I wasn't nice. I never meant to hurt you.' I had not told dad about a father-daughter dinner at school. I felt like an awful person. I felt a presence. It was so calming. I did not see a person, but I felt a touch as I laid in bed crying—a caress on my cheek. I fell asleep.

"My next experience was about a week later. I was over-whelmed. Grandma came and took me aside and told me I needed not to bother my mom. And, she said, as soon as I graduated, I needed to move out because mom could not afford me. She also said I had a responsibility to protect my mom and not tell her about our discussion. That night I was again crying. 'Daddy, I don't know what to do. How can I live without you?' That was when I saw dad. He sat on the edge of my bed. It looked exactly like him. He did not touch me at that moment, and I think at some level, I knew not to touch him. He looked sad but told me I would be ok. He was always there for me. I fell asleep. I swear I felt a brush of a kiss/caress of my hair, but he was gone. Again, I felt comforted.

"I called out to dad many times over the college years. I cried the night before I got married. I wanted dad so bad. He was always planning our weddings when we were kids. That night I just talked to dad. I cried but was able to just talk with him. Again, I felt his presence and the words that appeared in my heart/head. 'I will be there.' I felt dad that day. It felt kind of bitter-sweet.

"Life went on, and then after many miscarriages, I found out I was pregnant (with our son). Confined to my bed. I spent the time praying and talking to my daddy. Again, I felt a* *presence. 'All will be well.' After I had [our son], I was in the hospital for several days. When I finally got to hold my baby, I said out loud. 'Dad, I so wish you were here to see your first grandson.' I cried. Ok, probably hormones, but I was mourning what I lost because dad wasn't there. A peace came over me. Dad knew. No question, he knew."*

Example 3

"When [our son] was one year old [my husband] decided we were moving to Seattle. He got his transfer and moved up to Seattle with our only car. I needed to take [our son] to the doctor for his 1-year checkup before I flew up to meet [my husband]. I, of course, over-packed baby stuff: stroller, diaper bag with enough stuff to feed and change him for three days, and my purse. I had ridden a bus in CA and was very scared. I got settled but was in a panic state. I never really noticed people getting on and off the bus. I was too consumed with my fear. I looked up, and from behind, I saw a man that looked just like dad. At that moment, I thought dad isn't dead! He turned and looked at me and spoke, 'You are doing ok. You will be fine.' The bus pulled up to the next stop. Dad got off the bus. I tried getting all my stuff together but failed. Dad walked to the edge of the crowd. He turned and threw me a kiss and raised his hand goodbye. He then turned and before my eyes was gone."

Example 4

"The final experience I had was when [my husband] was in the hospital. I was so overwhelmed. After visiting [my husband], I decided to visit [the cemetery where my parents are buried]. I went and sat next to dad's grave. I started to cry and talk out loud. 'Daddy, I don't know what I am supposed to do.' I was at a very low point. My world was so shaken. I felt a presence again. Through my tears, I looked around. In the silence and tears, there was no one there. I was touched. I heard the whisper, 'I am here. You will be able to handle this.' A peace came over me. I sat in silence alone but not alone. I was there about an hour just sitting. I felt dad gradually leave me. I have not had any more experiences like these. Maybe dad and mom will be there to welcome me into heaven when the time comes."

I am a little hesitant to touch the potential third rail of ghosts and spirits. Opinions for and against can be extreme here. However, for this natural history, it is essential to acknowledge that *many* believe they have experienced something from the afterlife or a spirit world. Without necessarily identifying specific experiences with disembodied souls returning to this realm, it is essential to consider *why* these experiences occur and *how* they impact us. Chapter 6, where we examine some of the science of the soul, will look at the contexts and physical states in which the experiences tend to arise. They are important to understand, they can be profoundly meaningful for those who experience them, and there still is much left to explain.

Upfront, we should clarify the language. Most of us use the term ghost or spirit interchangeably, and I will use them as synonyms in this discussion. For parapsychologists, however, they are different things. According to Hans Holzer (Holzer, 2012), a professor of Parapsychology, "Ghosts are similar to psychotic human beings, incapable of reasoning for themselves....Spirits, on the other hand, are the surviving personalities of all of us who pass through the door of death in a relatively normal fashion." Ghosts may be tied to the location of their death, while a spirit is more like a soul without a body that presumably can return to this physical world and come back to help a loved one.

When exploring the soul and the afterlife, we can also distinguish among these spirit world experiences. One category is the sense that there is something out there that is unseen, but that is watching us. It could be friendly or hostile. Another category is the *Ghost Hunter*'s quarry, ghosts that may haunt a place and that people periodically see. When my wife and I were visiting York, England, we visited what may be the most haunted bar in England, where people have posted pictures of what they claimed were ghosts. A third category is the spirits of loved ones or friends who have passed away. This third category seems the most relevant to beliefs about souls and the afterlife since the experience is most likely to provide some direct value to the living and to communities.

In Roper's "Paradise Polled" review of various research, a Gallup study in 2005 found that thirty-two percent of people believed in ghosts, and nineteen percent were not sure. A CBS News study found in 2011 that forty percent of people believed in ghosts. In 2005, nearly half of Americans (twenty-one percent believing, and twenty-three percent not being sure) believe or at least do not disbelieve in contact with the dead. There has been a slight increase in the belief that you can hear from or contact the dead, with it floating around one in five people believing over roughly the last twenty years. Fox News (Gervis, 2018) reported a study (that admittedly might not meet academic requirements of validity) by the market research firm OnePoll that surveyed 2000 people. They found sixty percent said they had seen a ghost, and more than forty percent said they think that their pet had seen one. Those numbers seem high to me.

A 2009 Pew Research Center study reported by Michael Lipka (Lipka, 2015) found nearly one in five adults in the United States believe they have seen or been in the presence of a ghost. Twenty-nine percent say they have felt in touch with someone who has recently died. Lipka notes that Claude Fischer, a sociology professor at UC, Berkeley observed in his blog that roughly a third of people believe the spirits of the dead can come back, and that forty percent are convinced they have *felt* the presence of someone who has died. Fischer (Fischer, 2013) says:

> *"Lest you think this is all just a vestige of an older, passing, superstitious age: Belief in ghosts has soared in recent decades, from one in ten Americans to one*

in three. Moreover, young Americans are about twice as likely as old Americans to say they have consulted psychics, believe in ghosts, and believe in haunted houses. (Oh, and political liberals are more likely than conservatives to endorse these beliefs.)"

David Lester (Lester, 2005) notes that while he studied death and dying for years, he remains a skeptic on this topic of life after death. Still, in his book *Is There Life After Death? An Examination of the Empirical Evidence* while critiquing the interpretation of the research, he does document a wealth of work about the experiences people use to infer life after death. One category that he examines is deathbed visions. These visions include the spirits of family and friends that the dying seem to be seeing but who are not seen by others in the room.[32]

It also includes visions that others who are remote have of those who have just died. Lester describes a survey conducted by Osis (1961). Osis contacted six hundred and forty physicians who reported more than thirty-five thousand observations from dying patients. More than a thousand saw apparitions, mostly of deceased relatives appearing in the hospital room. In general, the apparitions' goal was to "take the person away," or as Lester describes it, to be *deathbed escorts*. At least half (more for those who were fully conscious) were calmed by the experience. Overlapping with this category are near-death experiences that we will be discussing in Chapter 6 on the science of the soul.

Another study by Osis and Haraldsson (1977) looked at four hundred and seventy-one reports of deathbed apparitions in both the United States and India. Generally, they were similar, but there were some variations in the details. For example, the experience tended to be a little shorter for Americans than for Indians. Americans may see Christ or Jesus, while Indians might see the god of death and his messengers.

A second category that Lester describes is what he calls *widow hallucinations*. It is a relatively common experience for someone whose spouse has died to sense their presence after death. Lester notes that the word hallucination carries an unfortunate implication of not being *real* that does not quite apply here. Instead, in this context, the term is best used technically in the sense of something experienced by a person that is not experienced in the same way by others who may be present. Indeed, it is important to remember that love itself is another one of those fundamental human experiences that exists within ourselves. Lester focuses on spouses, but as in the examples I provided at the start of this section, children who are close to their parents can have these experiences as well. He lists studies such as the following to give an idea of how common these experiences are, even across cultures. Widow hallucinations were experienced by:

- 73% of 22 widows in London (Parkes, 1970)
- 35% of 104 widows in London (Marris, 1958)
- 47% of spouses in a town in Wales (Rees, 1971)
- 61% of widows in nursing homes (Olson et al., 1985)
- 74% of a sample of Norwegian widows, soon after the spouse's death (Lindstrom, 1995)
- 82% of widows and widowers in a Swedish town (Grimby, 1993 and 1998)
- 90% of 20 Japanese widows studied (Yamamoto et al., 1969)

We will see in Chapters 3 (The Evolution of the Soul) and 5 (The Theology of the Soul) it is clear there has been a long history of religious beliefs and rituals around the possibility that souls might return to help or harm the living. Some take the form of ancestor worship (e.g., in China), and some take the form of encouraging the dead to stay put and rest in peace (e.g., in Egypt). It does not seem like a stretch to imagine these experiences that seem so ubiquitous and emotionally significant to those who experience them have shaped the development of religious explanations for the experiences and cultures. The experiences may have been selected for in our evolution and could have contributed to our survival as a species. They are certainly common. In addition to religious traditions, as we have observed, we see a fascination with these experiences from Shakespeare (e.g., Macbeth and Hamlet) to movies like *Coco* (and the Day of the Dead) and TV shows like *Ghost Hunters* (and the 40+ similar programs listed on Wikipedia).

While Judeo-Christian theology is not as open to ghosts as many Americans are, different groups do have a variety of views arising from Jewish and Christian scriptures. In 1 Samuel 28, Saul, in his fear of the Philistines and frustration at not getting an answer to his prayers from the Lord, consults a medium (a.k.a., the Witch of Endor) and appears to conjure up Samuel's spirit. The spirit is identified to Saul's satisfaction, and then Samuel shares God's displeasure with Saul and predicts David's ascendency. On the other hand, in Deuteronomy 18:10,11 God forbids inquiring of the dead, seances, or attempting to contact the dead as Saul did. Some Jewish scholars argue that this implies it is possible to interact with the dead, but just that it was forbidden. Others say that the medium fooled Saul into thinking he was talking with Samuel, and there was no ghost. Given Saul's earlier expulsion of mediums and spiritists, however, giving Saul such bad news would seem at best counterproductive if not terminal.

Some Jews believe that souls in the afterlife have no bodies and cannot appear to the living. The Talmud, on the other hand, does contain stories of interaction between the dead and the living, and some argue that in exceptional cases, the dead can sometimes appear in physical form. Others (e.g., Maimonides) read these references non-literally and say there are no ghosts or spirits.

In Matthew 17:1-13, the disciples see Jesus talking with the spirits of Moses and Elijah. In Luke 24:37-38, the disciples think they see a ghost, and Jesus convinces them he is not a ghost. It appears that a common assumption, at least in parts of ancient Jewish popular culture, was that indeed there were ghosts and that the existence of ghosts might explain some of what they experience. Jesus' parable about the rich man and Lazarus (Luke 16:19-31) is viewed by some who interpret it literally as suggesting that it might be possible to communicate from the afterlife to this world. In it, Lazarus in Hades asks

Abraham to tell his five brothers to repent or send someone to tell them. Abraham does not say it cannot be done. He says they already have what they need to know how to live. Catholics point to Revelation 5:8 (NIV) as indicating the saints hear our prayers for those who have died and that they present the prayers to God. It reads, "And when he had taken it, the four living creatures and the twenty-four elders fell down before the Lamb. Each one had a harp and they were holding golden bowls full of incense, which are the prayers of God's people."

For Catholics, the case for ghosts is somewhat less clear. There are accounts of souls appearing to living saints requesting prayer, penance, or masses. These would be souls in purgatory, and what they are asking for is help to get to heaven. In his *Summa Theologiae*, Thomas Aquinas says that "[A]ccording to the disposition of divine providence, separated souls sometimes come forth from their abode and appear to men." Protestants, of course, do not doctrinally believe in ghosts. Churches tend to attribute anything like ghosts to Satan deceiving people. Although as mentioned, there is a difference between traditional doctrinal beliefs and the experiences of ordinary people.

The overall experience of ghosts across history among many people diverges somewhat from more formal Judeo-Christian views of ghosts. First, the experience of ghosts seems far more common than religious traditions would seem to predict. Second, the experience of spirits tends to be about supporting either the living or helping the dying on their way to heaven; versus an appearance requesting the living to help the dead (which is more common in religious rituals).

The nature of what appears to be a disembodied spirit that is typically only experienced by one person makes it a challenge to study empirically.[33] Lester, in his survey, concludes there have not been any studies with verifiable evidence so far. Given the ubiquity of these experiences not only today but in the past, however, and their impact on culture, the question of why people have the experiences is worth asking. It seems like there must be some survival value for our species that, at the very least, is linked to how our minds work.

As mentioned, one category of experiences is of an unseen presence, and another is of ghosts associated with a specific location. These two strike me as being associated with how we are wired as human beings. We are pattern detectors. We look for threats and rewards in noisy environments and detect patterns in new environments that were meaningful in the past. We are biased to detect patterns in random data (e.g., seeing a face on the moon and figures in clouds). Some patterns we detect and add meaning to are what our minds infer are important because they suggest movement and proximity. Our brains create models of how the world works as we interact with it, and we apply the models to understand and predict what will happen in new situations. When data are missing (e.g., in memory gaps or where perceptual data are missing), our brains fill in the gaps to make sense of it, based on our experience and biology. As a result, these sensed presences can happen for isolated people in extreme or unusual stressful environments (e.g., a dark, empty house; sleeplessness; in deep meditation, while on a vision quest, sailors on the open sea, and solo mountain climbers).

According to Frank McAndrew (McAndrew, 2015) in an article on why people see ghosts in *Psychology Today*, Olaf Blanke's research has identified the parts of the brain that can be associated with a feeling of presence. The key ones are the temporal and frontoparietal brain areas related to the representation of knowledge about the world, particularly about actions (in other words, models of the world). McAndrew also says that environmental psychologist Peter Suedfeld believes that while we usually are processing the rich combination of external sensory inputs, we may start focusing on inputs originating within ourselves when entering a kind of sensorily deprived environment. McAndrew believes the "agency-detection mechanisms" proposed by evolutionary psychologists could help explain the experience. The fight or flight instincts we typically talk about are attuned to potential threats in ambiguous situations, and the entire system then gets activated. Our brains may be drawing parallels between past experiences and acquired models, and new situations. The experiences may be a by-product of properties of our brains that enable us to adapt to and survive in the rich variety of environments we experience as humans, including the new and unexpected.

Storytelling helps communicate these mental models across our culture, and our brains often prefer the content they create to make sense of experience over the real thing. Michael Shermer (Shermer, 2008) says, "I argue that our brains are belief engines: evolved pattern-recognition machines that connect the dots and create meaning out of the patterns that we think we see in nature." But as we know from the persistent existence of superstitions, he also says, "Unfortunately, we did not evolve a Baloney Detection Network in the brain to distinguish between true and false patterns. We have no error-detection governor to modulate the pattern-recognition engine." There has been survival value for humans in our ability to infer patterns and relationships, and traditionally there has been little evolutionary cost for erroneous cognition or too much caution. Add a little seasoning of stress and too little sensory stimulation, and it is easy to see how our brains might fill in an ominous presence or a sense of something that others cannot see.

While the unseen presence or the suggestion of a ghost in a dark alley can often be explained as a byproduct of how our brains work, the ubiquity of people *seeing and hearing loved ones* who have passed away in various situations is worth more exploration. These experiences are more personal. They touch us more deeply, and they occur at significant moments in our lives as opposed to those occurring in ambiguous environments. So what causes the experiences, and do they bring some value from an evolutionary perspective? Are they part of working through the five stages of grief by bringing needed personal comfort during stress? Are they a way that God or some other spiritual influence triggers a natural process in the body to answer our prayers or perhaps meet our deepest needs? Are there times when the curtain between the physical world we live in and other dimensions is thinner?

Drugs or isolation that stimulate spiritual experiences may be intentionally used for heightened religious experiences (e.g., by shamans) or to stimulate creativity. While various pathologies cause some cases, others may result from the body healing or protecting itself, a kind of immune response. For example, the cold and flu symptoms we complain about are typically the body doing what it needs to do to fight illnesses. While I am not aware of studies investigating this hypothesis per se, it strikes me that visions of and interactions with loved ones either during the process of dying or by loved ones suffering intense grief after someone has gone may be coping mechanisms that have evolved in us as social or spiritual beings. In the philosophy of the soul discussions, we will note William James's argument that one test of truth is how well it works for us as individuals and as a species. He also makes the case for not dismissing ideas just because we cannot yet test them. For many, these experiences of the spirits of loved ones feel true, and they can change lives for the better. Various faith traditions, in turn, would argue that, at least for some, the ultimate causes might be triggered from elsewhere in a larger reality that includes the spiritual realm where we may end up someday, again working through the body to heal.

Last Judgment by Fra Angelico

TITLE Summary of Popular Beliefs in the US

o Most people believe in an afterlife, and that we will live forever after death
o More believe in heaven than in hell (by around 15%)
o There is a much stronger belief that we will only have a spiritual form in heaven than those believing in a physical form
o Most believe we will be happy and peaceful there
o It will be a place where we feel God's love, and everyone there will love everyone else
o Most who believe in an afterlife believe they will go there, and if they believe they will be there, they believe they will be in heaven
o We tend to feel good people, whatever their religion and possibly even without religion, will be there
o There is a strong belief that we will see and recognize friends, relatives, and loved ones
o A surprising number believe in reincarnation
o About the same number believe in communicating with the dead (e.g., interacting with ghosts)

---

[6] None of the other examples of heaven or hell we will discuss involve frogs.

[7] When I was in seminary, one of my jobs was to serve as a chauffeur for a young heiress of the founder of the Quaker Oats company. I used to drive her in my old VW Bug to school at the Lake Forest Academy. I was her karma, the punishment her parents inflicted in this life since she had almost met her own end when she smashed up her new BMW.

[8] Just to give context, the King James Version of the Bible was assembled about this time.

[9] Ryan Boyd (2017) even has written an article called "10 Places Where Vampires May Exist" that is published on the Fodors.com travel site: www.fodors.com/news/photos/hunt-vampires-around-the-world.

[10] My daughter and I attended one of the zombie walks held by a

local community here (in Fremont, WA) that had over 4,800 zombies. Various cities around the world have attempted to set new Guinness World Records with the most zombies in their walks, and Fremont was attempting to regain its crown. Part of the experience is everyone dancing to *Thriller*.

11 For some of us, this is what locked-in syndrome must be like where someone is conscious but has virtually no ability to control their bodies.

12 This does raise interesting questions. When assuming a demon or evil spirit is a kind of soul, does that mean a body can house more than one soul (or in the case of the Mark 5:6-10 in the New Testament a legion of souls) at the same time? What does that say about the relationship between our soul and the body?

13 See the list of tropes at: tvtropes.org/pmwiki/pmwiki.php/Main/BodySnatcher.

14 As it happens, she may have been killed with one of my wife's ancestors in the crowd. I always keep this in mind during our arguments.

15 This can be read as an echo of God's creation of Adam from dust, and it is easy to think of it as a foretaste of the implications of a recent headline from DW.com (2021), "Scientists Create First Complete Human Embryo Model in Petri Dish."

16 This possibility of rewiring the brain, suggests it may be possible to intentionally shape the soul. The soul presumably changes through its existence in the body, and so intentional manipulation of experience could be, in a sense, programming the soul.

17 On the other hand, Russia has more Christians than the United States both in numbers and in percentage of the population. Greece is ninety-eight percent Christian, Mexico nine-two percent, Italy eighty-three percent, Denmark seventy-nine percent, Norway seventy-six percent and Finland seventy-one percent. Even Cuba and Sweden have roughly the same percentage of Christians as the United States. So we do need to be a little humble about claiming the United States is a uniquely Christian culture and that we will receive special rights and privileges as a result.

18 Aaron Blake in a recent article in the Washington Post (Blake, 2021), reports new data from the Public Religion Research Institute. Their survey showed that white evangelical Christians have dropped from twenty-three percent of the population to around fifteen percent since 2006, and the largest change has been during the last

administration (from 2018 to 2019). As with trends more generally, the biggest change has been in younger people no longer wanting to identify as evangelical.

[19] In the early 1900s, evangelicals and fundamentalists were largely motivated by separating themselves from a society that was viewed as unseemly and dirty. Many were not even registered to vote. Their belief was that Christ would be returning soon anyway, so they should be focused on what matters most, the afterlife.

[20] One question you might have is the difference between being religious and being spiritual. There are several ways, of course, to distinguish the two; and based on what I have learned about questionnaires these terms could differ quite a bit depending on the audience being sampled, and the nature of the questionnaire. For the Pew Research study, they have defined spirituality as "beliefs or feelings about supernatural phenomena, such as life after death, the existence of a soul apart from the human body, and the presence of spiritual energy in physical things such as mountains, trees, or crystals."

[21] A recent article in the AARP magazine, does observe that as people near senior ages the church provides a stable community of friends and routines in which they can become active. Research shows that we tend to affiliate with those who have beliefs like ours, and we tend to adapt our beliefs to match those of our friends.

[22] 1972 was when I graduated from college, and I had my eye on potentially being drafted to fight in Vietnam. My father had passed away unexpectedly the year before. These events concentrated my mind wonderfully, as Samuel Johnson would say, on my spiritual future and the afterlife.

[23] Although a physical existence without a spiritual one is a little hard to imagine. In the popular culture discussion, this described zombies and vampires.

[24] For example, it isn't clear whether people might have viewed a spiritual form as something abstract and without form, or as more of a ghostly body that can interact in a spiritual realm in the way a physical body interacts in this one.

[25] This could be related to those suffering from severe depression or related illnesses at the time of the survey. It may, however, underrepresent some groups. LGBTQ+ kids in very conservative families are often taught they are going to hell, and then may be made homeless by their families. Those that are driven to suicide in some

families may also be taught that suicide is an automatic ticket to hell, and sadly that is the only escape they may see for themselves.

[26] It is worth observing that in the disability community there is pushback on the medical model of disability where the disability is something to be *fixed*. A social model of disability is being advanced that treats disabilities as more neutral, where the issues are less about "healing" the person and more about "healing" the world that is the source of the problems experienced, the physical structures, norms of institutions and social attitudes that exclude or denigrate people. This contrasts with those who imagine a new body in heaven as being perfect in some *literal* sense.

[27] There is clearly some tension between Jesus' comments about the lack of marriage in heaven in Matthew 22:20 and verses like Luke 14:25-27 and Matthew 12:46-50 that suggest the focus in heaven will be on God and not family; and those that claim scriptures and tradition that speak to the importance of marriage and the recognition and care of others by those in heaven. In our current world, it is a little more complicated. Thirty-three percent or more have had at least one divorce in their lives. Many now have co-habited for some period of time and are no longer together. So, there is the question of how exes will interact if they all end up in the same place. Perhaps it will be a little more like the ideal of the communes in the 60s where everyone loves everyone else.

[28] I have to say this observation that so many people are looking forward to spending forever growing spiritually, when in general they typically spend hardly any time intentionally growing their spiritual muscles in the here and now, is to say the least curious.

[29] Humor is an interesting addition. Much of humor is based on something with a darker edge. I wonder whether respondents are confounding humor with happiness.

[30] I cannot help but believe this item elicited responses based on angels being there, and not so much on devils being there (except perhaps on their way to punishment).

[31] We will discuss this more in a later chapter where we address the possibly of being given a new body. Of course, almost no one wants to be old if we died when we were old, or a baby if we died when we were a baby. Everyone wants to be young, beautiful or handsome, and in the prime of life. But even Jesus still had the marks of being on the cross. What age would we be, and why?

[32] As we think about this situation, we should remember that no two people experience the world in exactly the same way. Each of our brains constructs "reality" based on the specific samples of data that our senses absorb, our unique biology, and based on our past memories and experiences. I was a witness to an auto accident a few months ago, and each of us who were on the scene remembered at least some of the details in significantly different ways.

[33] Although in the spirit of Dr. MacDougall, today we could imagine an environment where neuroscientists might try to capture a record from the brains of some having these experiences, especially during the process of actively dying. I would be willing to volunteer when the time comes!

Chapter 2

ANIMALS, AFTERLIFE, AND OUR ROOTS

"But ask the beasts, and they will teach you; the birds of the heavens, and they will tell you; or the bushes of the earth, and they will teach you; and the fish of the sea will declare to you. Who among all these does not know that the hand of the Lord has done this? In his hand is the life of every living thing and the breath of all mankind."
- Job 12:7-10 (ESV)

There are several ways to approach this topic. One is to think about whether we will see our pets or other animals in heaven. That question probably is what comes to mind first for many of us when we immediately think about animals and the afterlife. Then there is the question more broadly of whether animals have souls, and whether or not they are the same as ours. In Chapters 3 (the Evolution of the Soul) and 4 (the Philosophy of the Soul), we will see that there are threads that address this question reaching far back into history both philosophically and theologically (e.g., from the ancient Egyptians to the modern Hindus). A third approach is to think about how the characteristics we associate with our souls have evolved in the animal kingdom to give shape to who we are, and what that might imply about whether other animals might have souls and what form those souls might take.

In this discussion, I will take a point of view that is sometimes known as evolutionary creationism, knowing that it can be controversial. It recognizes the evidence for a process of evolution that has resulted in Homo sapiens. But as with other laws and processes in the universe, I will also assume in this discussion a creative hand that sets everything in motion, and that sustains and influences it. The idea of a creative God would be consistent with my specific faith and most major religions throughout history.[34] So in a modern version of the Judeo-Christian tradition, the result would be God creating human beings in the "image of God" (*imago Dei* in Latin) through an evolutionary process. However, I also recognize the continuing debate about the fullness of what that image means. In broad strokes, especially as it speaks to our human souls' nature, it is foundational to how many think about identity, ethics, stewardship of creation, and life itself. There are other ways, I am sure, to rationalize science and theology. Still, I find this one useful as I reflect on how the characteristics we associate with *our* souls have appeared in various forms and combinations *elsewhere in the creation* and eventually led to us.

The human-animal relationship in Western Europe and the United States started to significantly change culturally in the nineteenth century, with the rise of interest in transcendentalism, Theosophy, Buddhism, Hinduism, and Darwinism; and the realization that animals are rational and intelligent. One way this showed up is in the anti-vivisection movement. While the Anglican and Catholic churches, in general, maintained a strong theological distinction between humans and animals, the Christian anti-cruelty campaigners were vital to the most comprehensive animal protection laws in Europe passed in Britain (Bates, 2017). They recognized animals not just as things, but as living beings that have a connection to us.

WHAT WE WANT TO BELIEVE

"If there are no dogs in heaven, then when I die I want to go where they went."
– Will Rogers

"If man could be crossed with the cat it would improve the man, but it would deteriorate the cat."
— Mark Twain

"There are two means of refuge from the miseries of life: music and cats."
— Albert Schweitzer

"How we behave toward cats here below determines our status in heaven."
— Robert A. Heinlein

"I care not much for a man's religion whose dog and cat are not the better for it."
— Abraham Lincoln

Ron Manipulating Emotions

By some estimates (and admittedly, the numbers vary widely depending on the surveyors' biases and interests), more than thirty-six percent of United States households have dogs, and thirty percent have cats. Still, I point out to my cats that there are at least seventy-five million cats in homes plus another seventy million feral cats in the United States, versus a mere seventy million dogs. Cats being the cute predators that they are, win. Of course, many other households have pets like the fish, turtle, burro, crow, hamster, sheep, rabbit, and cockatiel I had at different points in my life. As delightful as I have found them and as fond as I have been of my pets, I have not found personally that *all* have projected that same spark of intelligence and emotional connection that we often associate with souls. While many see that spark in our cats and dogs (and perhaps my cockatiel Grendel), you do not have to watch too many episodes of *The Yorkshire Vet* or *Dr. Jeff: Rocky Mountain Vet* to know the diversity of the animals that we humans love.

Of course, we only want to believe that beloved pets will

be with us in heaven (just like many probably don't envision their exes being in heaven with them). We usually do not talk about whether some pets might end up in the Bad Place. I can personally say, however, that our family had a dog named George when I was growing up that we privately referred to as the devil dog, even though he was my dad's favorite. I would not be surprised if he might have a job herding human souls in the Bad Place. The way we imagine being with our pets in the afterlife does tend to be selective.

In a *Psychology Today* article, Hal Herzog (Herzog, 2016) reports a study by a research group led by Kenneth Royal, April Kedrowicz, and Amy Snyder from North Carolina State University, who looked at our animal afterlife beliefs. The research published in *Anthrozoos* may be the first to explore American attitudes in this area systematically. They conducted a Mechanical Turk study that sampled eight hundred people that appeared to fit the United States' demographic pattern regarding sex, age, and geographic region. It had diverse races, ethnicities, and religious affiliations, and seventy-seven percent were pet owners. Forty-eight percent of respondents felt animals definitely or probably had souls, and twenty percent were undecided. Of the roughly sixty percent of participants who believed in a human afterlife, three-quarters believed in an animal afterlife. Buddhists tended to believe in a pet afterlife, as you might expect (about eighty percent), but also about sixty percent of mainstream Protestants and roughly the same percentage of Catholics did as well. For those with no formal religious identification, twenty-three percent said they believe in a pet afterlife.

As a side note, in another study that Herzog reports, not all animals are viewed as being equally likely to be in heaven. Dogs, cats, horses, farm animals, and the like have a bit of an edge over reptiles, fish, and insects (although those expecting them in heaven are still relatively high). When we think about the afterlife and are not pressed for ratings, it is probably more comfortable for us to think about our current beloved pets as being with us there than about the cow, pig, fish, or chicken that we just had for dinner as being there. We probably really do not want to think about the icky spider, cockroach, or 17-year cicada we just squished as being there, despite their essential roles in the ecosystem.

Interestingly, while forty-five percent of pet owners thought animals went to heaven, so did thirty-eight percent of non-pet owners. That might reflect a population of people who are *between* pets. As for whether animals (incl. their pets) have souls, roughly forty-eight percent of pet owners leaned towards yes (twenty-two percent definitely, and twenty-six percent probably), while about twenty percent were unsure. Of course, making it to heaven does not necessarily require the same type of soul as we have as humans.

These results are consistent with other studies of beliefs in the United States about animals and the afterlife. For example, an ABCNews/Beliefnet poll in 2001 found that forty-seven percent of pet owners and thirty-eight percent of non-pet owners believe pets go to heaven. About the same number (forty-one percent) felt that *all* animals go to heaven. Perhaps not too surprisingly, younger people tend to think they will see their pets in heaven. Their parents may be facilitating those beliefs, of course, as we have been known to do about other things that might comfort our children.

Why does this matter? Dr. Kedrowicz (one of the North Carolina researchers Herzog mentioned) notes, "Spirituality and beliefs about animals, including the animal afterlife, undoubtedly impact what clients think, how clients feel and what decisions they make. So veterinarians should explore and acknowledge client perspectives to build trust and actively engage them in the process of animal care." It seems likely that these beliefs may also impact how many of us interact with environmental concerns, mostly when reacting to animals that are particularly popular among Americans. When these beloved family members die, the memories and grief affect us long after the events.

When my wife and I lived near Boulder, CO, the ordinances didn't refer to dog owners, only to dog guardians. Many of the vets we have taken our cats to refer to us as the cats' dad and mom. Richard Fern (Fern, 2002) observes that language changes to reflect our responsibilities to other living (and especially sentient) creatures. While changing our relationship with our animals reveals cultural differences, it does not necessarily impact law. However, according to Suzanne Monyak in the *New Republic* (Monyak, 2018), in the United States, two states (Illinois and Alaska) have recently passed laws that start to position pets a little more like children in custody battles. It forces courts not just to allocate pets to the divorcing people like property but also to consider the animals' well-being.

Monyak, in her *New Republic* article, also reports that according to Tony Eliseuson, a senior staff attorney at the Animal Legal Defense Fund, "In the last five years or so, it's gone from sort of this very fringe area of the law to very mainstream." Monyak notes that this idea that animals might have rights has emerged recently, and in the past, there were few penalties for harming animals. Monyak says, "For much of the twentieth century, the law considered pets and companion animals property—akin to a rug or a toaster." Research by Gregory Berns, a professor of neuroeconomics, was reported in the *New York Times*. He used an MRI to scan dogs' brains and concluded, "dogs are people too." Susan McDonald, in a piece in the *Guardian,* described the rationale as "If Canis lupus familiaris can be shown to have emotions, and a level of sentience comparable to that of a human child, there is a moral imperative to reassess how they are treated under law" (McDonald, 2014). In 2009, the European Union recognized animals as "sentient beings" as part of the Treaty of Lisbon. The French National Assembly did something similar in 2015, as did New Zealand and Quebec.

As we will see, life and sentience have at various points been identified with having a soul. Most of us also recognize our animals as having a personality, something that makes them unique. We will even be talking about cognition, emotion and consciousness, and other attributes as they have evolved in the animal kingdom. These capabilities have been used throughout history to define what it means to be human.

The interest pet owners have in someday being reunited with beloved pets is reflected in the wealth of books available to help us deal with our sorrow after our favorite pets have died. Stanley Coren (Coren, 2013), in his *Psychology Today* blog, says that around eighty percent of dog owners and nearly two-thirds of cat owners view their pets as "part of the family." He notes that with this commitment to our pets, the population of veterinarians in the United States grew by fifty-five percent in the previous fifteen years. When a family feels it has lost a member, they need to manage their grief. Just a few of the ever-growing list of examples from Amazon.com include:

- *All Animals Go to Heaven* by George MacDonald
- *Biblical Proof Animals Do Go To Heaven* by Steven H. Woodward
- *I Will See You in Heaven* by Jack Wintz
- *Signs From Pets In The Afterlife: Identifying Messages From Pets in Heaven* by Lyn Ragan
- *Do Pets Go to Heaven? Now There's Biblical Proof You Can Believe In* by Dennis Callen
- *Cold Noses At The Pearly Gates: A Book of Hope for Those Who Have Lost a Pet* by Gary Kurz
- *Will My Pet Be in Heaven* by Ed King
- *Do Our Pets Go to Heaven?* by Terry James
- *Pets and Heaven What the Bible Says About our Animal Friends* by Reverend Dr. Neal Otto Hively

I will set aside the books by those who claim psychic or prophetic vision and leave those to others to explore. For our purposes, it is the books focusing on the human grief of losing a pet, the need for counseling, and inferences based on theology that are more interesting. These books tend to be in the Judeo-Christian tradition and so heavily reference Jewish and Christian scriptures. This meeting of grief and pastoral counseling may be helping shape our cultural attitudes about the afterlife since the language often overlaps with that used when we lose human friends and family members. Many of the books represent efforts by ministers and counselors trying to help people deal with their grief.

The Vatican at times talks about pastoral messages, as

opposed to setting forth specific doctrinal positions. This group seems to fit into that pastoral goal to help the individual and provide hope rather than developing theology. Billy Graham was perhaps one of the most famous modern Christian evangelists. When asked about pets making it to heaven, he replied, "God will prepare everything for our perfect happiness in heaven, and if it takes my dog being there, I believe he'll be there." His perspective seems to fall into this pastoral category.

Helen T. Gray (Gray, 2008), in an article in the *Chicago Tribune* on "Will your pets be waiting for you in the afterlife?" shares several stories that capture this spirit. One interview is with Jack Vinyardi, an ordained interfaith pet chaplain. He says he is asked all the time if there is an afterlife for animals. He observes his job is about comfort, and "I believe we each can find answers to divine questions if we look deeply in our hearts and ask for guidance there. Although our answers may differ from the answers others have found, they are our own, and they will comfort us." He argues at the very least, we will carry the memories and emotional relationships we have had with our pets into our afterlife.

George MacDonald, in *All Animals Go to Heaven* (2019), also takes this pastoral view when he says, "I know of no reason why I should not look for the animals to rise again, in the same sense in which I hope myself to rise again – to reappear, clothed with another and better form of life than before. If the Father will resurrect his children, why should he not also resurrect those whom he has taught his little ones to love?"[35]

Another group of books takes the next step and tries to infer a position on animal souls in general based on relevant verses and themes in the Christian Bible. These authors do recognize that there is not much said explicitly and definitively about the topic, but see a theme across scriptures about all of creation as it could extend into the afterlife. They generally cannot imagine a heaven without animals. The key arguments include ideas such as:

- **God created both the animal Kingdom and us from the same stuff, the earth.**
  - o "G-d created the great sea-monsters, and every living creature that creepeth, wherewith the waters swarmed, after its kind, and every winged fowl after its kind; and G-d saw that it was good." – Genesis 1:21 (JPS)
  - o "G-d said: 'Let the earth bring forth the living creature after its kind, cattle, and creeping thing, and beast of the earth after its kind' And it was so.'"– Genesis 1:24 (JPS)
- **Animals and humans will eventually return to the earth.**
  - o "In the sweat of thy face shalt thou eat bread, till thou return unto the ground; for out of it wast thou taken; for dust thou art, and unto dust shalt thou return." – Genesis 3:19 (JPS)
  - o "For that which befalleth the sons of men befalleth beasts; even one thing befalleth them: as the one dieth, so dieth the other; yea, they have all one breath; so that a man hath no preeminence above a beast: for all is vanity. All go unto one place; all are of the dust, and all turn to dust again. Who knoweth the spirit of man that goeth upward, and the spirit of the beast that goeth downward to the earth?" – Ecclesiastes 3:19-21 (JPS)
- **God cares not only about us but also the creation.**
  - o "G-d spoke unto Noah, and to his sons with him, saying: 'As for Me, behold, I establish My covenant with you, and with your seed after you; and with every living creature that is with you, the fowl, the cattle, and every beast of the earth with you; of all that go out of the ark, even every beast of the earth.'" – Genesis 9:8-10 (JPS)
  - o "Six days shalt thou labour, and do all thy work; but the seventh day is a sabbath unto HaShem thy G-d, in it thou shalt not do any manner of work, thou, nor thy son, nor thy daughter, nor thy man-servant, nor thy

maid-servant, nor thy cattle, nor thy stranger that is within thy gates." – Exodus 20:9-10 (JPS)

o "Thy righteousness is like the great mountains; thy judgments are a great deep: O LORD, thou preservest man and beast." - Psalms 36:6 (JPS)

o "Are not two sparrows sold for a penny? Yet not one of them will fall to the ground outside your Father's care." – Matthew 10:20 (NIV)

- **God charges us to be good stewards of the creation.**
  o "G-d said: 'Let us make man in our image, after our likeness; and let them have dominion over the fish of the sea, and over the fowl of the air, and over the cattle, and over all the earth, and over every creeping thing that creepeth upon the earth.'" – Genesis 1:26 (JPS)

  o "He said to them, 'Go into all the world and preach the gospel to all creation.'" – Mark 16:15 (NIV)

- **Animals, like all creation, are suffering in a less than perfect state and someday will be rescued in a way similar to the new life we will have.**
  o "For the creation waits in eager expectation for the children of God to be revealed." – Romans 8:19 (NIV)

  o "In that day will I make a covenant for them with the beasts of the field and with the fowls of heaven, and with the creeping things of the ground: and I will break the bow and the sword and the battle out of the earth, and will make them to lie down safely." – Hosea 2:18 (JPS)

  o "[T]hat the creation itself will be liberated from its bondage to decay and brought into the freedom and glory of the children of God." – Romans 8:21 (NIV)

  o "We know that the whole creation has been groaning as in the pains of childbirth right up to the present time." – Romans 8:22 (NIV)

- **All creation will "cry out" in praise of God.**
  o "Beasts, and all cattle; creeping things, and flying fowl: Kings of the earth, and all people; princes, and all judges of the earth: Both young men, and maidens; old men, and children, Let them praise the name of the

LORD: for his name alone is excellent; his glory is above the earth and heaven." - Psalms 148:10-13 (JPS)

o "Let everything that hath breath praise the LORD. Praise ye the LORD." – Psalms 150:6 (JPS)

o "Then I heard every creature in heaven and on earth and under the earth and on the sea, and all that is in them, saying: 'To him who sits on the throne and to the Lamb be praise and honor and glory and power, for ever and ever!'" – Revelation 5:13 (NIV)

- **In the future, there will be a new Earth.**
    o "Then I saw 'a new heaven and a new earth'...He who was seated on the throne said, 'I am making everything new!'"– Revelation 21: 1,5 (NIV)

    o "The wolf also shall dwell with the lamb, and the leopard shall lie down with the kid; and the calf and the young lion and the fatling together; and a little child shall lead them. And the cow and the bear shall feed; their young ones shall lie down together: and the lion shall eat straw like the ox. And the sucking child shall play on the hole of the asp, and the weaned child shall put his hand on the cockatrice's den. They shall not hurt nor destroy in all my holy mountain: for the earth shall be full of the knowledge of the LORD, as the waters cover the sea." – Isaiah 11:6-9 (JPS)

A BRIEF REVIEW OF ANIMAL AFTERLIFE BELIEFS

When my wife and I were visiting Europe the summer before the COVID-19 pandemic hit, we missed our cats. As a result, we always looked for cat images in the museums and galleries that we visited. It was hard to find evidence of pets in art. That was not a problem in Ancient Egypt, however. When you watch programs about Ancient Egypt, one thing that gets many of us excited is how visible pets were in their art. The Egyptians had domestic dogs, cats, falcons, and monkeys, and their temples honored crocodiles, antelopes, hippos, and lions. They saw their pets often as having divine powers, and they mummified them to accompany themselves into the afterlife. They even believed that given the divinity associated with animals, their pets might accomplish significant things in the afterlife with their masters.

The death of a dog, as it does today, caused tremendous grief. Some were so moved they would shave their entire bodies in their distress. Cats were more common than dogs in Egypt, as they are in the United States. Partly this was due to their association with the goddess Bastet. Bastet was the goddess of fertility, childbirth, and domesticity. During one period in Ancient Egypt, cats were revered so much that you could be punished by death for killing a cat for a reason other than ritual sacrifice.

Some Native American tribes also believe that animals have souls, since all are connected to the great Universal Spirit. In some tribes, if they need to take an animal's life, they will perform a ritual of thanks and respect. In Helen Gray's (Gray, 2008) interview with Gary Langston, a Northern Cherokee, Langston says, "All living things are children of the Earth. It doesn't matter if we have feet or wings or roots." The implication is there is definitely an afterlife for animals, and we will see them again. "We all are going home, back to the Creator...The dog I had as a kid, his spirit never left me; he just moved into a different dimension."

Hinduism is one of the oldest religions on Earth, and followers not only believe that animals have souls, but the souls might also be ours. Fundamental to Hinduism is its concept of eternal life through reincarnation and rebirth, as we evolve to be one with Brahman. Often reincarnation as an animal might be punishment for living a bad life, but it can also be a part of the journey to enlightenment. Therefore, harming an animal could be injuring a soul; that, in turn, can count against your karma. The result might be walking in the paws of those we have hurt.

For Hindus, though, thinking about an animal as having a soul that lives eternally is the wrong way to think about it. In Gray's interview with Anand Bhattacharyya, a member of the Kansas City Hindu community, Anand says, "Because of the soul's inherent urge to be united with its source, souls in animals will ultimately evolve to the human plane. Once the soul is in a human body, it is capable of union with God in eternal bliss." Whatever the form, human or animal, it may take many reincarnations to liberate the soul. Gray says that according to Linda Prugh of the Vendanta Society, animals have souls, but unlike us, they do not reason and discriminate between right and wrong as humans do. They go from birth to death to birth in a cycle until they reach the human plane.

On the other hand, Anand shared a story with Gray. It is in the Hindu epic *Mahābhārata* about Yudhisthira, the eldest of five brothers. When he finally ascended to heaven, his faithful dog followed him. "Yudhisthira was allowed to go to heaven, but not his dog. But he didn't want to enter heaven without his dog. On Yudhisthira's insistence, both were allowed to enter heaven in eternal peace."

Buddhism has a somewhat different view of karma. The two are similar in that reincarnation in an animal is generally viewed as a step backward in the journey to enlightenment and self-mastery. In Buddhism, though, there is the belief that pets, in particular, have souls that need help, and many will involve their pets in their religious rituals and worship. Marnie Hammer (from Gray's interviews in 2008) summarizes her experience as "I've had three cats that I've shared my life with and have made my life richer, but I don't know if I'll see them again. That's not the question." She said the question is whether she herself is making life "more peaceful and generous for everyone, " and I'm assuming that includes her pets.

When we look at Western religions, it is worth starting at the philosophers that influenced subsequent early Christian theologians. Socrates' (470 to 399 BCE) and Plato's (roughly 428 to 347 BCE) beliefs are a little complicated since they are often expressed in stories, and animals per se were not the primary focus of their interests. The site AskPhilosophers.com contains a response by Nickolas Pappas (Pappas, 2017) to the question "Did Socrates believe that animals possessed souls?" that captures some of this complexity. Pappas starts by saying the soul may be that which is aware of ultimate reality, Plato's

Forms. It may be the source of life or perhaps of motion. It may also be the source of moral behavior.

Depending on how one thinks of the soul then, animals may or may not have souls. If the soul is about life or the cause of motion, then sure, everything alive has a soul. As Pappas observes, though, "[I]f the essential property of the soul is that it knows the Forms (beauty as such, justice as such), souls in non-human animals would seem to be impossible. Nothing in any Platonic dialogue suggests that a squirrel has a conception of true justice, or that a spider knows what largeness as such is." When thinking about the afterlife more generally, though, Socrates is well aligned with the Pythagorean philosophers. They believed in a kind of reincarnation, and so like in Hindu and Buddhist beliefs, animals may have souls that have belonged to human beings. Pappas says, "You are human now but you might come back as a dog, and then (it seems) come back from being a dog to a new human life." Although as described in Plato's *Republic*, while some might, that does not mean that all will have human souls. Some animals may possess souls that belonged to their ancestors, and you would not necessarily be able to distinguish whether two animals were different in the types of souls they possess.

Aristotle (384 to 322 BCE) not only believed animals have souls, but he also believed plants have souls.[36] Plants and animals (including us) are living things, and it is our souls that make us alive, that give us the form of a living thing, and that causally engage in the activities of life. Animal souls also have the powers of perception and locomotion. Humans, in turn, have the properties of animals and plants, but we also can reason and think. We have rational souls. For Aristotle, though, the soul is not separable from the body. We all share a human soul, but we are not, strictly speaking, souls and are not distinguishable as individuals by our souls. Presumably, that would be true for animals and their souls as well.

We will be talking more about Descartes' (1596 to 1650 CE) views about the human soul in Chapter 4, where we look at the philosophy of the soul, but his idea also has implications for animal souls. At the core of his philosophy, embodied in the "I think therefore I am" statement, he felt that thoughts and minds were core properties of the soul. He argued we have our subjective experiences because we have immaterial souls. He did not believe that animals have rational souls. They do not, he argued, have language. They do not seem to be rational beings for Descartes. As a result, he concluded that they could not have souls. They are, essentially automata, or machines, not much different from cuckoo clocks or watches, or perhaps our Roombas. He does, however, in some of his writings weaken a bit and distinguish animals from machines in that he recognizes, as Aristotle did, that animals have sensations. He even acknowledged they might have emotions like anger and happiness.

Given the long history of Catholicism, attitudes about animal souls and the afterlife are a little more complicated. On the one hand, there is a tradition within the Church dating back to Descartes of viewing animals almost as automata, essentially moving mechanisms. St. Augustine, following Aristotle, argued against animals having a rational soul, a soul that is capable of rational thought and able to make moral decisions as humans do. In his *Summa Theologica*, Thomas Aquinas says, "He that kills another's ox, sins, not through killing the ox, but through injuring another man in his property." In the nineteenth century, Pope Pius IX argued that heaven is for those with a soul and a conscience, and animals do not have either.[37][38] This is also an argument made by traditional Protestant theologians who oppose the idea of animals having a soul and a place in heaven. The Pope purportedly worked against creating the Italian chapter of the SPCA (the Society for the Prevention of Cruelty to Animals). In 2008, Pope Benedict XVI upset some when he said that only humans were "called to eternity."

To be fair, those who do not see animals in heaven often acknowledge the requirement that we as humans should not be cruel to animals, and we noted earlier the role of Christians in the antivivisection movement. We should care for the creation of which we are a part. When asked in 2002 about the exploitation of animals, Pope Benedict said, "That is a very serious question. At any rate, we can see that they are given into our care, that we cannot just do whatever we want with them. Animals, too, are God's creatures….Certainly, a sort of industrial use of creatures, so that geese are fed in such a way as to produce as large a liver as possible, or hens live so packed together that they become just caricatures of birds, this degrading of living creatures to a commodity seems to me in fact to contradict the relationship of mutuality that comes across in the Bible." Furthermore, the Catechism of the Catholic Church says, "Animals are God's creatures. He surrounds them with his providential care. By their mere existence, they bless him and give him glory. Thus, men owe them kindness."

If we were going to speculate on which voices from Catholicism might have a more sympathetic view of animal souls,

St. Francis
Sermon to the Birds

many of us would probably name St. Francis of Assisi. The Humane Society (Society, n.d.), probably not too surprisingly, says, "Francis' devotion to God was expressed through his love for all of God's creation. St. Francis cared for the poor and sick; he preached sermons to animals and praised all creatures as brothers and sisters under God."

In Helen Gray's (Gray, 2008) article about the likelihood of seeing our pets in heaven, she interviews Reverend John Schmeidler (a Capuchin Franciscan) of St. John the Evangelist Catholic Church. Reverend Schmeidler responds to some of these tensions within the Catholic Church by noting, "St. Thomas Aquinas wrote about animals having a soul, but it wasn't similar to that of humans, and St. Francis of Assisi saw animals as God's creatures to be honored and respected." While he pointed out that the Church traditionally believes that animals do not go to heaven, "[A] lot of people have a hard time with that, and I do, too, when I see a grieving pet owner. I know God wants us to be totally happy in heaven, and if our dog will help make us fully happy, and if God can resurrect us, I'm sure he could resurrect a dog too." Even Aquinas said, "[W]e must use animals in accordance with the Divine Purpose lest at the Day of Judgment they give evidence against us before the throne," which suggests our pets and other animals could be called as witnesses and will be around somewhere.

In 2014, there was a kerfuffle in the Catholic Church and Press when it was reported that Pope Francis was said to have comforted a grieving boy who was sad about his dog dying by saying, "One day, we will see our animals again in the eternity of Christ. Paradise is open to all of God's creatures." It turns out *he did not* say that, but it is one of those myths that got started because of how many people wanted it to be true. Since then, it has been attributed to Pope Paul VI. Others have since pointed out that Pope John Paul II, in a 1990 papal audience, did say, "[T]he animals possess a soul and men must love and feel solidarity with our smaller brethren" and that they are "as near to God as men are."

In his encyclical on the environment, Pope Francis also said, "Teach us to discover the worth of each thing, to be filled with awe and contemplation, to recognize that we are profoundly united with every creature as we journey towards [God's] infinite light." Pope Francis, in the encyclical, Laudato Si (#243), also wrote, "Eternal life will be a shared experience of awe, in which each creature, resplendently transfigured, will take its rightful place and have something to give those poor men and women who will have been liberated once and for all." The spirit of Pope Francis' thought is that in the future, there will be the ultimate restoration of all creatures to their intended state at the end of history.

Finally, Pope John Paul II, in his message for the celebration of the World Day of Peace in 1990, said, "I should like to address directly my brothers and sisters in the Catholic Church, to remind them of their serious obligation to care for all of creation. The commitment of believers to a healthy environment for everyone stems directly from their belief in God the Creator, from their recognition of the effects of original and personal sin, and from the certainty of having been redeemed by Christ. Respect for life and for the dignity of the human person also extends to the rest of creation, which is called to join man in praising God (cf. Ps 148:96)." On or around October 4, many churches celebrate the Feast of St. Francis with the blessing of the animals.

In mainstream Judaism, animals are not viewed as having souls and an afterlife. Indeed, we have cited Ecclesiastes 3:17-20 (JPS), where it says, "I said in mine heart concerning the estate of the sons of men, that God might manifest them, and that they might see that they themselves are beasts. For that which befalleth the sons of men befalleth beasts; even one thing befalleth them: as the one dieth, so dieth the other; yea, they have all one breath; so that a man hath no preeminence above a beast: for all is vanity. All go unto one place; all are of the dust, and all turn to dust again." But as we will see, early Judaism also didn't see human souls in quite the same way they are seen now.

There is a recognition of animals as being part of the miracle of created life and deserving respect, including at the end of their lives. God created everything, and it was "good." Life is a gift, and it is sacred because God created it, and life itself honors God. Judaism recognizes responsibility for animals and their welfare, which comes from our position over them. A recent article on Jewish views on animal rights notes laws in the Torah and the Talmud reflect sensitivity and compassion for animals (BBC, 2020). Examples include:

- "A farmer should not plough with an ox and an ass together because the ass, which is the weaker animal, would have difficulty keeping up" (Deuteronomy 22:10).
- "An ox should not be muzzled while it is treading out the grain so that it could eat some of the corn if it were hungry" (Deuteronomy 25:4).
- "Animals are given some of the same rights as humans, e.g., they should be able to rest on the seventh day, as humans rest" (Exodus 20:10).

There are, of course, various individual views among

rabbis (Rabbi Brawer, 2017) who have written about the question, but a common thread tends to be "We don't know." In Chapter 5 (the Theology of the Soul), we will discuss the evolution of the idea of the soul within Judaism and in the Hebrew Scriptures (the Tanakh) more generally. For example, the Hebrew word *nefesh* literally means soul, but is more often thought of as the life force that both animals and humans have. However, there is also an idea of a divine soul in the Tanakh that God breathes into us to make us "in the image of God."

In Helen Gray's (Gray, 2008) interviews, Rabbi Scott White of Congregation Ohev Sholom expresses a similar spirit in the context of his faith. He says that God plans a "blessed existence" for those who have lived virtuous lives. Rabbi White concludes, then, that "It's only fitting that such an existence includes the pet that inspired the greatness….For myself, paradise with my own mutt [Rescue the Wonder Dog] is a perfect inducement to pursue virtue."

One different view is also worth noting. It is part of the Kabbalah (the ancient Jewish tradition of mystical interpretation of the Bible) and is associated with the Hasidic movement's growth in Eastern Europe. Some Hasidim believed in the transmigration of souls, in other words, reincarnation. Those who were not quite ready to move on to Paradise at their deaths might be sent back to earth to exist perhaps as inanimate objects, plants, and animals before living a human life again (Segal, 2002).

While many Protestants believe in an afterlife for their pets, Protestant theology typically does not include pet souls or an animal afterlife. Protestant denominations officially take the Biblical reference to humans being made "in the image of God" to mean that humans are fundamentally different from animals, especially in having souls. However, there have been notable exceptions even from the foundation of the Protestant movement. For example, John Wesley (1703 to 1791), the founder of Methodism, considered that animals' souls could persist after death. Martin Luther believed there would be animals in heaven, based on Acts 3:21 where it refers to God "restoring all things," and Romans 8:18-22, which describes the suffering of the entire creation, its expectation for the future, and its release from bondage. The Quaker George Fox (1624 to 1691), some Anglican theologians such as Bishop Joseph Butler (1691 to 1752), and others were in this club as well. I've already shared Billy Graham's quote, which was based on thinking about the "peaceful animals" and "new Earth" texts of Isaiah 11:6–8, 65:17 and Revelation 21:1.

John Wesley delivered a sermon entitled "The General Deliverance." He wrote, "The whole brute creation will then, undoubtedly, be restored, not only to the vigour, strength, and swiftness which they had at their creation, but to a far higher degree of each than they ever enjoyed. They will be restored, not only to that measure of understanding which they had in paradise, but to a degree of it as much higher than that, as the understanding of an elephant is beyond that of a worm. And whatever affections they had in the garden of God, will be restored with vast increase; being exalted and refined in a manner which we ourselves are not now able to comprehend."[39]

Margaret DeRitter (DeRitter, 2019) shared an interesting quote from Rev. Greg Wood, senior pastor of portage First United Methodist Church, about Wesley's reflections on the Garden of Eden and its aftermath.

> *"John Wesley (the 18th-century Anglican cleric who was a co-founder of Methodism) believed in the general resurrection and that animals would be resurrected and would be sentient beings and that they would be able to reason and relate....Of course, it may have been that he loved his horse more than he loved his wife."*

A few curious notes in the Bible seem relevant to the nature of animals, and that one could use to argue for the enhanced nature of animals on a new Earth. In the Jewish Tanakh, there is the story of Balaam's donkey in Numbers 22:20-39. In the story, a prophet named Balaam is riding a donkey and is met by an angel who is blocking the way. The donkey sees it, but Balaam does not. In the encounters, Balaam is injured. He beats and berates the poor donkey. That leads to a conversation between Balaam and the donkey. Some scholars believe these verses were a later addition to the larger story of Balaam, and most would suggest the text is just a story to make a point. Taken on its own, though, it has a donkey that is aware of things going on in a spiritual state that the human cannot see. The donkey can also reflect on its relationship to its master, and when given a miraculous voice, the donkey can have a conversation with the master. Furthermore, Balaam does not seem too surprised that he suddenly has a talking donkey.

In Matthew 8:28-34, Jesus meets a demon-possessed man. This man is not possessed by just one demon, but an entire legion of them. Jesus casts out the demons and sends them into a herd of pigs. A demon might not be identical to a *soul* per se, but they presumably have some similar properties. Therefore, it is interesting to note that the pigs could *house* these spiritual beings and perhaps be controlled by them or respond to them by committing suicide. Of course, many of the tissues now being transplanted into humans come from pigs; so perhaps we are more closely related than we might expect.

Then, of course, there is Eve's lack of surprise in Genesis 3:1 (NIV), where it says, "Now the serpent was more crafty than any of the wild animals the LORD God had made. He said to the woman, 'Did God say, "You must not eat from any tree in the garden?"'" Eve did not respond, "Hey, a talking serpent!" The other animals might have been less crafty, but they must have been pretty impressive if speech was a common attribute (and this seems to be Wesley's observation as well). If heaven, in some ways, is a return to the state of the Garden of Eden, then animals will not only be there, but it seems like they may have even more characteristics that we would typically associate with souls.

Gray (Gray, 2008) provides what I suspect would be a typical quote that is easy to imagine coming from many pastors. Gray interviewed Thor Madsen, the academic dean at Midwestern Baptist Theological Seminary. Madsen acknowledged people's desire to see their pets again, but concludes "We really have no biblical grounds for an assurance that our pets will be resurrected along with us." He does realize that while some

Christians feel that heaven would be missing something without our pets, and he observes, "[T]he Scriptures imply that heaven's overwhelming treasure for us is the fellowship that we, the followers of Christ, will have with our Creator and Savior. Nothing will seem to be absent at that point." Certainly, a new Earth or heaven without the animals and other living things God has created seems like it would feel incomplete.

ANIMAL EVOLUTION AND THE THEORY OF SOUL

"No one understands animals who does not see that every one of them, even amongst the fishes, it may be with a dimness and vagueness infinitely remote, yet shadows the human."
– George MacDonald, The Princess and the Goblin (1872)

"There is no fundamental difference between man and the higher mammals in their mental faculties…If a young chimpanzee be tickled as is the case of our young children a more decided chuckling or laughing sound is uttered."
– Charles Darwin, The Descent of Man (1871)

Humans have long argued that we are different than our fellow animals. We called ourselves the species that invented and uses tools. We pointed out that we are the only species with language and use it to teach others. We are the species that produces art. There were periods where some argued we were the only species that had emotions (Bates, 2017).[40] We have argued we reason and have cognition,[41] and other animals do not. We take pride in the fact that we think abstractly and that we can imagine alternative actions. We experiment and solve problems; we are scientists. We have argued that we are the species with a theory of mind and the species that knows ourselves. We believe we are the moral species, although we recognize that we can also be immoral. Researchers have found each of these attributes in our various animal cousins (Hogenboom, 2015). Researchers have even found the kinds of personality traits we associate with our individuality in reptiles, birds, fish, and various mammals.

Juliane Bräuer, Daniel Hanus, Simone Pika, Russell Gray, and Natalie Uomini (Bräuer, 2020) identify nearly forty thousand citations and more than three thousand six hundred publications exploring these areas of similarity between animals and humans. More recently, some have argued the differences are in degree and not in kind. More accurately, researchers are recognizing that perhaps it is the specific combination and the degree of development that distinguishes us from the rest of creation. Evolution seems to be an experiment with different combinations of these attributes in various animals to enable each to prosper in its unique niche in the world.

In her BBC Earth article, Melissa Hogenboom (Hogenboom, 2015) shares a story of Kanzi the bonobo and notes that Kanzi not only likes fruit but likes to cook marshmallows over a fire using a stick.[42] She says, "He points to what he wants on a lexigram, a computerized touchscreen device on which each symbol represents a word. Kanzi can use 500 words, and when he is talked to, he can understand a few thousand...Although he cannot talk like us, Kanzi transformed our ideas about our primate relatives – and in turn, our ideas about ourselves."

As other attributes have faded as the definitive characteristics that distinguish us from the rest of the animal kingdom, the one left, at least from the perspective of some religious views, argues that we are the species with God-created souls. In the Judeo-Christian tradition, we are the species made in the image of God (and in particular, the spiritual image of God, represented by our soul). The idea is we have an element of the spiritual within our essential nature, and so we can relate to each other and God in a unique way.[43] This argument might be the most resistant to scientific inquiry unless we pivot our perspective and think about the soul's attributes as they emerge in animals and study how those attributes have grown, changed, and combined to define our humanity. As we will see, in practice, we tend to define our soul as more than just an abstract, everlasting spirit with some connection to the divine.

We have noted that for most of us in our culture, the boundary between human and animal spiritual natures is not quite as distinct as it is in some more formal religious doctrines. Even in the area of religious beliefs and their scriptures, there are different perspectives. Certainly, the absence of a description of animal souls in a literature aimed at humans does not necessarily mean there is an actual lack of some kind of soul in animals. Indeed, more than fifteen percent of the planet believes that animals have souls because the souls may be our souls in different bodies and are in the process of evolving to a more divine, spiritual state.

G. Scotin and J. Cole

One way to explore the soul is to think about the specific characteristics that we associate with our souls and explore how they show up in animals. In psychology, there is something called the *theory of mind*. It refers to our ability to attribute mental states to ourselves and others, which is critical for effective social interaction. We could imagine something like a *theory of soul*, grounded in how we see ourselves and others in this more spiritual sense. What is it about ourselves that gives us the confidence that we have or are souls, and what do we see in others that confirms our belief that they have souls? Given that, do we see any of those properties in our animal cousins? Is there a role that these attributes play in how other animals and we manage to exist, prosper, and evolve in a rapidly changing world?[44]

At the very least, if the body was designed for its ability to enable and house a soul that reflects the divine, it is an interesting exercise to look at how some of those attributes that we associate with our souls began to emerge in the evolution of various animal species. For example, the soul has been associated with the spark of life itself, of course, and its absence with physical death. Animals and humans both have that spark. When we think about the soul as being uniquely us, there is a sense of it reflecting our personality. You don't have to talk to many pet owners or zookeepers before you know animals have individual personalities as well.

When we think about ourselves, we are not just Star Trekian Mr. Spocks or Datas. Part of those stories and how we see ourselves are as emotional beings. Those Star Trek and similar stories that involve the humanization of robots and artificial intelligence often are associated with the emergence of emotion, and especially emotions like love and grief (as opposed to what are sometimes referred to as fight and flight, and more primitive emotions grounded in hunger and desire). As we will see, there is ample evidence of a rich set of emotions in various animal species.

Theologians and philosophers have associated consciousness and rationality with the soul. This conscious rationality includes the ability to reflect on our experiences and ideas and make inferences and judgments. With rationality, some of that reflection is associated with making the moral judgments for which we are responsible, and that may impact the nature of our afterlife. We feel our self, our soul, is a source of the will that moves us in the physical world and is part of why we may hold others responsible for what they do.

So let's look a little more at consciousness, for example,

most of us feel that our conscious awareness of self is tightly bound with our soul. We will see across the history of philosophy and religion the definition of who we are—our souls, in essence—has increasingly relied on our being rational conscious beings. The mind that gives rise to consciousness then interacts with the world through the mind-body connection. Ideas about the difference between life and death, and even deciding on the point of ensoulment (when the soul appears in a body), also often depend on the presence of consciousness.

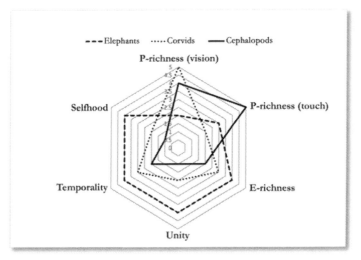

Jonathan Birch, Alexandra K. Schnell, and Nicola S. Clayton (Birch, 2020) have a nice discussion in *Trends in Cognitive Sciences* that describes some of the work in animal consciousness. They offer a hypothetical model (and they emphasize it is very speculative at this point)[45] that can serve as a framework for future comparative research across species. They note that an interdisciplinary community around animal consciousness is forming (including neuroscientists, evolutionary biologists, comparative psychologists, philosophers, and animal welfare advocates). There is even a journal called *Animal Sentience*. They argue that there is a growing consensus that the research is supporting various forms of animal consciousness. Their framework outlines some of the dimensions they identify, including perceptual richness (p-richness, including recognizing different senses like vision and touch), evaluative richness (e-richness), integration at a point in time (unity), integration across time (temporality), and self-consciousness (selfhood).

Perceptual richness is about the level of detail that is recognized consciously in the world. Evaluative richness includes the ability to experience feelings ranging from pain, fear, grief, and anxiety, to pleasure, joy, and love. Unity, in essence, is about the experience of being in the *now*, being conscious of this moment at each moment. Temporality, on the other hand, is about connecting moments into a continuous stream. As we know from our entertainment media (e.g., movies), our brains are built to give us a continuous experience instead of a series of snapshots of the world. Finally, selfhood includes the awareness of our internal experience of self versus the world outside and our body as being ours and existing within the world.

While the authors note the field is relatively young and still is debating both what consciousness is and how to measure it, there is a goal to explore animals' consciousness (their experiences and feelings) rigorously. There is also a goal to connect research on animal consciousness with the work on human consciousness. It strikes me that this approach provides a helpful way to connect animal consciousness with the Cartesian view of the human soul represented in Descartes' "I think therefore I am." It could be extended, I believe, by adding other dimensions that we associate with the soul, such as ethical judgment, culture, and empathy.

Two other examples that have been used to define how humans might differ from animals are tool-making and language. University of Oxford researchers have found that New Caledonian crows can make tools such as bending pieces of wire into shapes for scooping food out of containers. They use sharp objects in their natural environment to dig grubs out of tree trunks.

Chimpanzees, elephants, ravens, and many other species are tool users. One kind of tool is language, and it helps in transferring knowledge within cultures. While we are particularly good at language, most of what is needed for us to develop language and use it effectively is also shared with other species.

According to W. Tecumseh Fitch (Michel, 2017), a cognitive biologist from the University of Vienna, "The main difference that we have from other species is not that we have something to think about, but that we can communicate what we think about." Even that, however, is more about degree and richness rather than being an exclusive ability. Indeed, it is not a big jump to imagine that different creatures may simply have other things they are interested in reflecting about, whether or not they have rich linguistic abilities.

Fields like comparative psychology, evolutionary biology, and convergent evolution are not just interested in individual characteristics like consciousness, problem-solving, language, and tool making in different species. They are also interested in how different combinations occur together to meet specific needs. They are investigating how those combinations that occur can become the multi-purpose instruments that help with various problems a given animal has not yet encountered (e.g., like a multi-purpose *tool* such as our hand). Fitch showed that the study of more distant animal relatives could lead to valuable insights in understanding human cognition and what makes us who we think we are. Let's look at a few key species in more detail that, in some ways, seem most like us in these attributes we may associate with our souls: primates, orcas, and elephants.

Examples

Interestingly, the animals that show behaviors that are the most similar to us in some of these soul-attributes emerged in the evolutionary tree about the same time as we did. We all seem to have evolved rapidly through the extreme conditions of the latter part of the Pleistocene epoch (from about 2.5 million years ago to around 10000 BCE). Remember Darwin's survival of the fittest and the German philosopher Friedrich Nietzsche's adage that "what does not kill me makes me stronger"? The second half of this period is commonly known as the Great Ice Age.

Part of what is notable about this period is the connections and separations caused by glacial and interglacial cycles. By this time, the continents had moved to where they are now. The Isthmus of Panama connected North and South America. Asia and North America were connected by the Beringia and Laurentide ice sheet. The changing climate not only drove species to search for new places to live over these and other potential natural highways, but researchers are also studying the impact of these changes on the evolution of various species. One would expect that it would weed out some of the competition for some species while selecting some of those with the higher-level traits that we find in ourselves and that enable a species to adapt to novel situations quickly. Like us, primates, elephants, and orcas have a long evolutionary history, and under conditions like those that shaped us, they have also developed abilities and behaviors that seem familiar.

Gorillas split from the hominids around seven million years ago. The eastern and western gorillas emerged around two million years ago, with subspecies appearing about four hundred thousand years ago. Chimpanzees and our human ancestors became a different species approximately three to four million years ago (or perhaps somewhat earlier). The chimpanzees we know today appeared in the tree about one to two million years ago (the oldest fossil chimps date back to two-hundred and eighty to five hundred thousand years ago). Homo habilis, one of the earliest members of our genus, emerged around the beginning of the Pleistocene. Towards the end, Neanderthals and Homo sapiens (i.e., us) were spreading throughout the world.

Asian elephants and mastodons appeared in their family tree around six million years ago. Modern African elephants emerged in the next three million years (perhaps as recently as between one and two million years ago). Elephantoids migrated to and from Africa several times as they spread around the world. Bernice Wuethrich (Wuethrich, 1995) noted, "The world's largest collection of elephant fossils may help to show how changes in climate and landscape led other large species, including early humans, to migrate from Africa to other continents."

Homo sapiens started to expand around three hundred thousand years ago. They had spread widely across Europe, Asia, and Oceania by eighty thousand years ago. They reached the Americas about twenty thousand years ago (Early Human Migrations, n.d.). Humans and elephants often lived in similar environments, and elephants are known for their regular migrations over extended areas as conditions and seasons change. So it does not seem far-fetched to imagine that the *highways* that elephants and their ancestors created worldwide over millions of years may have served our ancestors well as we also began our global spread.

Orcas, like elephants, have had a long time to evolve; but the Pleistocene was an excellent forcing function on the various orca species as well. While they diverged from other cetaceans as early as twenty-three million years ago, that original mammal was more like a typical dolphin. Modern orcas appeared on the tree about two hundred and fifty thousand years ago. According to Rus Hoelzel, a professor in the School of Biological and Biomedical Sciences at Durham University, "Killer whales have a broad worldwide distribution, rivaling that of humans. At the same time, they have very low levels of genetic diversity." Their work suggests the extreme conditions of the last Ice Age could be responsible for reducing the diversity (Chow, 2014).

It is worth looking at these species' characteristics that in humans are often associated with having a soul. While they are not usually compared with adult humans, they are frequently compared to human children. If children have a soul, you would have to wonder about primates, orcas, and elephants. If a child's soul grows over time, perhaps for these species, their souls are evolving to a higher level of maturity. They may have a unique kind of soul, which may say something about the souls of sentient beings we may meet in the future or that might emerge from human attempts to re-engineer life itself.

Primates.

"Now we must redefine 'tool', redefine 'man', or accept chimpanzees as humans."
– Louis Leakey

Our closest evolutionary relatives, of course, are primates. We share more than ninety-seven percent of our DNA with chimpanzees, bonobos, and gorillas (some estimates for the first two are as high as ninety-nine percent). Chimpanzees build nests, form alliances with other chimps, use simple tools, and even have gestural language. They not only have facial expressions that reflect their emotions, but they can also read each other's facial expressions.

Fishing for Termites

Like human children from a young age, there is evidence that the great apes also exhibit theory of mind skills. They can figure out what others think and their intentions. They make inferences (empathize) with what others might know (Hogenboom, 2015). This evidence suggests they know their own mental state, which implies some level of chimpanzee consciousness. While philosophers and psychologists are debating and studying the nature of consciousness, most of us would probably associate our consciousness with our sense of being a soul.

Hogenboom reports that Frans de Waal of Emory University in Atlanta observed the intricate social interactions of chimps and the link to reading each other's emotions. With empathy often comes some level of what could be called moral behavior. For example, they noted that two chimps might be willing to accept equal *wages* (a cucumber) for the same task but would get upset if another were given a grape instead. On the other hand, while chimps can act selfishly over food, sharing behavior has been reported with others even when there is no apparent benefit for themselves. They have also been documented helping others (including humans) reach for hard-to-get objects. Hogenboom observes, "In the wild researchers have witnessed chimpanzees helping disabled group members, adopting unrelated orphans, and helping friends escape from poachers' snares. This sense of altruism must run deep in the animal kingdom because rats will also save a friend from being soaked with water, even if it means getting wet themselves." He cites de Waal as saying, "People say that morality comes from God, from religion, but we can see the roots of morality in many other species."[46]

Chimps and other primates are even being studied in terms of the cultural characteristics they exhibit. There may be similar behaviors across groups, but individual groups can also develop different tools and courtship behaviors. They can even pass those norms from generation to generation. In laboratory settings, they have been seen to conform and adjust their actions to fit into the group. According to Cecilia Heyes (Heyes, 2012), Whiten and Erdal argue there are "five major components of the 'human socio-cognitive niche', five dimensions on which humans excel—cooperation, egalitarianism, theory of mind, language and culture." When they survey the evidence, they find that each of these capabilities can be found in the common ancestors of both chimpanzees and humans.

Chimps in the wild have demonstrated a variety of grief responses. Mother chimps have spent the night with a dead baby or carried a child's corpse for weeks. While it is not universal, groups have been recorded exhibiting agitation after one of their own dies. James Anderson has documented various responses by chimpanzees when faced with the deaths of others (Anderson, 2018). Anderson observed, "Chimpanzees—and probably other great apes—understand that death 'is different from life and permanent.'" Bridget Alex, writing for *Discover Magazine* (Alex, 2018), says, "[U]nlike children, who can be told about death, chimps must learn from direct observations. Therefore, chimps' variable responses are likely due to their differing prior experiences as well as relationships to the deceased."

Anderson describes four concepts that our kids would have to grasp to understand death. They include the idea that the dead cannot think or feel (non-functionality). It also consists of permanence (irreversibility), inevitability (universality), and causality. He believes mature chimps could observe death's irreversibility and non-functionality. In addition, he thinks they can grasp some sources of causality (e.g., their aggression), but it is not clear whether they understand that they or others will die inevitability (universality).

They seem to know they can die and that they can kill other creatures. But concerning some kind of afterlife, Anderson concludes, "Chimpanzees have been prematurely described as engaging in 'ritual practices' in the presence of dead conspecifics, contributing to evidence of an analog to human religion. However, although death in chimpanzees appears psychologically more impactful than death in other species, compelling evidence for any notion of a spiritual life after bodily death in chimpanzees is not forthcoming." What if we could talk with chimpanzees to discover what they believe about death?

My degree is in what is now called cognitive psychology. When I was in graduate school, my wife and I would periodically be invited over to my professor, Dr. B. J. Underwood's home for dinner. Those evenings were always stimulating. Underwood was the kind of person who, in response to a story about a day we had spent at Chicago's Lincoln Park Zoo, would ask, "Why in hell would anyone want to go to a zoo?" What he was interested in was provoking conversation and reflection.

At one of those evenings, he also invited Drs. Allen and Beatrix Gardner to dinner, and we had a chance to talk about their research. They began teaching a chimp named Washoe

American Sign Language in 1967. Washoe was born in West Africa and had been captured by NASA for use in the space program. Washoe most recently lived at Central Washington University in Ellensburg, just on the other side of the Cascades from where we live now. Washoe learned three hundred and fifty signs and taught some of the signs to her son. It seemed like a promising approach since chimpanzees use gestures to communicate with each other.

Washoe expressed fear, joy, and happiness, and named things and concepts she encountered. There was even some evidence that she recognized herself in the mirror. Donovan and Anderson (Donovan, 2006) shared one story that communicated some level of empathy. They noted that Washoe often reacted like a child might when someone they care about does not show up at the expected time. Washoe might give them the cold shoulder for a while. In one case, though, a caretaker named Kat apologized to Washoe for being late and explained that her baby had died. "Washoe stared at her, then looked down. She finally peered into Kat's eyes again and carefully signed 'cry,' touching her cheek and drawing her finger down the path a tear would make on a human (Chimpanzees don't shed tears)." That interaction revealed more to them about

Dr. Patterson and Koko

what was going on inside Washoe than stacks of data on language acquisition.

Another example of primate communication is Koko (Morin, 2015). Koko was a female western lowland gorilla born at the San Francisco Zoo in 1971 and later moved to the Gorilla Foundation. The Foundation was created specifically to focus on exploring language with Koko and other gorillas. During Koko's 46 years of life, Dr. Francine Patterson taught Koko a modified version of American Sign Language (which she called Gorilla Sign Language) beginning in 1972. Koko learned more than one thousand signs and reportedly understood more than two thousand words spoken in English in addition to the signs. Koko taught some of these signs to another gorilla, Michael. The two gorillas even developed unique signs they just used with each other. While she stayed at a relatively rudimentary level of communication, around the level of a human child, she scored between seventy and ninety on an IQ scale.

Koko had several pets, and her first one was a gray male Manx kitten she named All Ball. Patterson observed that she cared for the kitten as she might have cared for a baby gorilla and was very gentle and loving with it. Unfortunately, All Ball got out one day and was hit and killed by a car. When Patterson signed to Koko that All Ball had been killed, Koko was very distressed. She signed "Bad, sad, bad" and "Frown, cry, frown, sad, trouble." It was reported that later she was making a sound like human weeping (McGraw, 1985).

According to Patterson, in an *Atlantic* interview, there was another conversation that Koko had with her caregivers about death. At one point, Patterson showed Koko a skeleton and asked whether it was alive or dead. Koko signed "Dead, draped," and draped can mean "covered up." Then Koko was asked, "Where do animals go when they die?" Koko replied, "a comfortable hole," and gave a goodbye kiss.[47] In the article, Patterson also mentioned that gorillas in zoos had been observed burying dead animals.

Many animals, like us, are mental model builders. It is easy to imagine when the models involve themselves and the social groups with whom they are connected; you have the beginnings of a concept that could eventually grow in humans to an idea of a soul. Part of what we have learned from the grief of the animals that seem to express it is the recognition of otherness coupled with attachment. This other who has died is some being that is the same as me, part of my family. It speaks of the emotional as well as cognitive, sensory connection. Washoe and Koko also could project those feelings onto their caregivers.

Finally, the Gorilla Foundation has described insights they

received from Koko and Michael (Progress and Plans, 2020). While doing their work, they recorded more about gorilla inventiveness and how Koko could use language to express more sophisticated concepts. They learned about the range of Koko's emotions, from many human-like emotions such as happiness, sadness, anger, and pain, to more subtle emotions like frustration, embarrassment, guilt, anticipation, jealousy, and boredom. They believe they demonstrated gorilla empathy for other humans and animals. They argued that Koko could express herself through art. Koko seemed to show self-awareness and eventually saw herself as being in the same category as her human caregivers.

Orcas.

If we were going to look at attributes that we associate with being human and that might have contributed to what became our souls, looking to primates is a natural step. Some of these attributes occur in other species as well. In the Seattle area, where I currently live, there was a story in the press around 2018 that many of us followed for weeks. It was about an orca named Tahlequah (the scientists, more prosaically, called her J35), in the southern resident orca population. The people of the Lummi Nation refer to the orcas as "qwe lhol mechen" or "people that live under the water" (Duin, 2018). The Kwakiutl tribes believe that ocean hunters' souls can turn into orcas when they die, just as forest hunters' souls can turn into wolves. Eventually, their souls will be reborn as human once again.

Tahlequah was pregnant, and the entire area was excited. The southern resident orcas are endangered, and every pregnancy creates news. But unfortunately, her calf was stillborn. What broke the hearts of many of us is that she carried her dead calf for more than one thousand miles over seventeen days (Grantham-Philips, 2020). Observing this behavior, a person living in the area shared that at the beginning of the journey "At sunset, a group of 5-6 females gathered at the mouth of the cove in a close, tight-knit circle, staying at the surface in a harmonious circular motion for nearly 2 hours...[After dark] they stayed directly centered in the moonbeam, even as it moved."

We do not know what was inside the mother orca's head, of course. Perhaps it was an orca version of wishful thinking, but it was interpreted as grief. *Smithsonian Magazine* (Daley, 2018) reported a study by Giovanni Bearzi of Dolphin Biology and Conversation, where he and his co-researchers did a meta-analysis of seventy-eight scientific reports of grief-like displays in cetaceans throughout 1970 to 2016. They found twenty of the eighty-eight species currently have shown signs of what they called "postmortem-attentive behavior," which could be interpreted as grief. Most (about ninety-three percent) of the behaviors were exhibited by dolphin species, and most of those (seventy-five percent) were females mourning their calves. If you are wondering, Tahlequah has recently given birth to a new calf, and the calf is doing well!

Orcas are the largest species of dolphin. According to recent research in Spain (analyzing the personality of twenty-four orcas at SeaWorld, Orlando, SeaWorld San Diego, and Loro Parque in Spain), orcas exhibit personality traits similar to those seen in chimpanzees and us (Captive Killer Whales, 2018). They ranked each animal on thirty-six personality traits and mapped those to a Five-Factor Model of personality (FFM) used to study human personality. The traits include things like playfulness, independence, stubbornness, sensitivity, and protectiveness. These attributes, in turn, map to the five factors which may seem more familiar: extraversion, agreeableness, conscientiousness, dominance, and carefulness. Next, they compared the results with previous studies of chimpanzees and people. The orcas were like humans and chimpanzees in extraversion (including playfulness, gregariousness, and sociability). But orcas were more like chimps in conscientiousness and agreeableness. The lead researcher, Yulán Úbeda, observed, "These similar personality traits may have developed because they were necessary to form complex social interactions in tightly knit groups that we see in killer whales, humans, and other primates." This similarity is a possible example of evolutionary convergence where there is value to the species in these characteristics that define us as unique, but that also enable us to cooperate.

Killer whales have life spans like ours, living into their 90s in some cases. They are social, and they live in tightly-knit pods that hunt together, share their food, and use communication skills to cooperate. As with human cultures, they can pass on specialized hunting and other behaviors across generations. They even use different dialects in communicating. Cetaceans also show similarities to chimpanzees in cognitive abilities, and their encephalization quotient (measuring brain size relative to body mass) is similar (2.6 for orcas versus 2.3 for chimpanzees). Orcas have the second-largest brain of any animal, second only to sperm whales, although their larger bodies require more brain volume to manage the body itself.

Their large brains have thick cortical areas (the areas associated with memory, attention, language, thought, and consciousness in humans), with much higher gyrification (the amount of wrinkling and folds) than humans. Gyrification is associated with the ability to process larger amounts of data and to do it faster. Orcas, relative to us, have much higher development in parts of their brains responsible for spatial memory and navigation. They also have larger areas that are associated with emotion and long-term memories. They have one of the most elaborated insulas of any animal in the world, including us. The insula is involved in consciousness and is linked to functions associated with emotions such as compassion, empathy, perception, self-awareness, and interpersonal experience (The Social Intelligence of Orcas, n.d.). You could speculate that they might even be *more* conscious than we are.

Orca, dolphin, and whale brains also have spindle cells, and only humans, great apes, and elephants also have spindle cells. Spindle cells appear to be a unique adaptation that has evolved in species with large brains, to increase the speed of information processing (possibly in response to more sophisticated social interaction). The cells may help with regulating emotional states. In us, abnormal development of these cells can result in distortions in thought and the sense of reality, and schizophrenia.

Orcas are an excellent example of a species similar to us in many ways and yet optimized for their unique environment. It is worth reflecting on the fact that the human sensory system is different and often more limited than it is for many other animals, especially orcas. Our *reality* is fundamentally different from that of orcas and elephants, and even from our cats and dogs. They experience things that we do not.

Elephants.

> *"[Elephants are] the animal that surpasses all others in wit and mind."*
> – Aristotle

> *"There is no creature among all the Beasts of the world which hath so great and ample demonstration of the power and wisdom of almighty God as the elephant."*
> – Edward Topsell (1658)

Elephants, who also have a lifespan about as long as ours, show a brain complexity similar to orcas and other dolphin brains. Their brains resemble ours in structure, complexity, and functional areas. Elephants have a large and highly complex neocortex, and the volume of their cerebral cortexes, the center of cognitive processing, is larger than any primate species other than us. Their brains are also more convoluted than human brains, and as in orcas, the convolution is used for more complex intelligence functions. The elephant hippocampus, which houses emotion and memory, is proportionally larger than humans and other intelligent species.

With those brains, they show many of the attributes we typically see in ourselves. They have complex social lives and family structures. They exhibit behaviors we would often associate with love. They protect and nurture their children, and as in human culture, they pass skills and knowledge on from generation to generation. They teach their young where to feed, how to use tools, and how to fit within their social structure. They can reason, show and recognize emotions, including joy, playfulness, grief, and mourning. They have been seen self-medicating, using tools, and showing compassion and altruistic behaviors. They have been documented coming to other species' aid, including helping humans who are in distress. Some suffer from the equivalent of post-traumatic stress disorder. They even display recognition of themselves in mirrors (Landen, n.d.).

One article in MentalFloss.com by Jessica Hullinger (Hullinger, 2017) entitled "7 Behaviors That Prove Elephants Are Incredibly Smart" discusses several interesting observations about elephants. Researchers at the University of Sussex in the UK have evidence that elephants can distinguish different languages. One Asian elephant named Koshik (an Indian elephant at Everland Amusement Park in South Korea) could apparently mimic a few words in Korean. Researchers even have evidence that elephants can understand some human gestures like pointing.

It is common knowledge, of course, that they can use tools. One seven-year-old Asian elephant figured out how to reach the fruit placed out of its reach by finding a large plastic

block and positioning it to stand and reach the fruit. But then the elephant realized that it could stack even more blocks to go higher. They show empathy, and as we are going to discuss more, they mourn their dead. Not surprisingly, given their habitats and their need to be nomadic, they have been shown to have remarkable memories that persist over long periods.

In other research, two elephants collaborated to pull each end of the same rope to obtain a reward (Aldhous, 2011). Another study showed how elephants could keep track of how many apples were dropped in two buckets, and they picked out the bucket with the most apples seventy-four percent of the time. The humans they tested were only successful sixty-seven percent of the time. A study reported in *Discovery News* demonstrated that elephant problem-solving to get food rewards uncovered shortcuts that not even their handlers had imagined.

The string-pulling task has been used to explore "insight learning" in birds since the 1950s. The bird must figure out the process of pulling a string with some food on the end, holding it with its foot, drawing some more, saving it, and so on until it gets the food. It involves understanding, at some level, cause and effect, and the relationship between string, food, and body parts. This experiment has been successfully repeated with seven Asian elephants as they figured out how to retrieve sugar cane attached to a retractable cord.

Carl Safina (Safina, 2015), writing for *PBS NOVA*, provided an excellent summary of research on "The Depths of Animal Grief." For many people, because of coverage in nature shows we have watched over the years, when we speculate about animal grief we think about elephants. Safina recounts a story of a researcher who played a recording to the herd of an elephant who had died. The family went wild, calling and searching for the missing member. The dead elephant's daughter called out for days afterward.

Safina notes that elephants almost always react to the remains of elephants who have died. Safina also shared a comment by Joyce Poole, who says, "It is their silence that is most unsettling. The only sound is the slow air blowing out of their trunks as they investigate their dead companion. It's as if even the birds have stopped singing." They touch the body or bones. They sniff. They explore. They go through behaviors they would have used when meeting and greeting other elephants, and they generally do not do this with other species. Sometimes elephants will cover dead elephants with soil and vegetation, perhaps as a kind of simple burial.

These death rituals are common among elephants and are relatively rare beyond elephants, humans, and Neanderthals. The San Diego Zoo (Researchers Study Elephants, 2020) published an article describing a research project led by Dr. Shifra Goldenberg and Dr. George Wittemyer. The study reviewed thirty-two original observations of wild elephant carcasses across Africa. Goldenberg says that while it is hard to know motivations, "The most commonly recorded behavior of elephants towards their dead included touching, approaching the dead animal and investigating the carcass....For example, some elephants made repeated visits to a carcass, and it's possible that temporal gland streaming by a young female at the site of her mother's carcass is associated with heightened emotion." Wittemyer observes, "Witnessing elephants interact with their dead sends chills up one's spine, as the behavior so clearly indicates advanced feeling. This is one of the many magnificent aspects of elephants that we have observed, but cannot fully comprehend."

Safina shared another story, this time from Cynthia Moss, director of the Amboseli Elephant Research Project in Kenya. It was about a matriarch called Big Tuskless. Big Tuskless had died, and Cynthia brought the jawbone back to the lab to study it. Sometime later, the elephants from the family passed through the camp, including moving past other jawbones that were being investigated. They went right for hers, and they spent some time with it smelling it and touching it. Finally, most of them moved on. "After the others left, one stayed a long time, stroking Big Tuskless' jaw with his trunk, fondling it, turning it. He was Butch, Big Tuskless' seven-year-old son."

Is this grief? If a young elephant dies, mothers can show behaviors that look like depression for many days, trailing far behind the family group as they travel. Sometimes mothers will carry sick or dead babies in their tusks, and Safina shared a story of one Amboseli elephant that carried a prematurely born, dying calf about fifteen hundred feet into the calm seclusion of a grove of palms. Elephants (and apes, baboons, and dolphins, for that matter) who carry dead babies for days are not seen carrying healthy youngsters in that same way.

Safina eloquently shares an observation of grief from anthropologist Barbara J. King. She says for it to be grief, survivors need to exhibit changes in their behavior. They might eat or sleep differently or appear agitated, and they might attend to the body and later to the grave. These behaviors are exhibited by non-humans and by humans. "Sadness is not a kilogram lighter than grief, and mourning isn't two meters shorter than happiness. Yet science thrives best on things that can be measured."

Sir John Tenniel Illustration in
Alice's Adventures in Wonderland

What we see in our primate cousins, orcas, and elephants may not always appear to be identical in degree or combination to what we often attribute to human souls. But these characteristics do feel like they are similar in character to attributes we associate with souls. The attributes serve a function within the various species' ecological niches, just as the attributes' unique combination and characteristics have helped us succeed as a social species. For humans, these attributes have helped us grow in goodness and creativity across generations. Looking at other species may remind us that it is not always about distinguishing others from ourselves. The Hebrew word nefesh[48] (נֶפֶשׁ) is often translated as soul, but it also carries the idea of life. It can capture aspects of sentience (e.g., a living being, life, self, person, desire, passion, appetite, emotion), and in Genesis, both humans and animals have nefesh. The issue could be more about how the attributes we associate with the soul in different combinations may provide survival value in each species' unique environment and how we evolved to be who we are. It may be a specific combination and degree of development that defines us as human souls.

TITLE Example Animal Soul-like Characteristics

o Life
o Personality
o Cognition (incl. reason, problem-solving, and abstract thinking)
o Creativity
o Emotion (incl. feelings of love and grief)
o Moral behavior and empathy
o Will, including planning ahead
o Tool invention and use
o Consciousness and theory of mind
o Complex social behavior
o Awareness of self
o Culture and the ability to pass it on

---

[34] Of course, in some cases a creative god responsible for humans and the world as we know it might be one of several gods in a pantheon.

[35] As a side note, ViaGen Pets is making a business out of cloning pets for up to fifty thousand dollars for a dog and thirty-five thousand dollars for a cat. That certainly would seem to reflect the very personal and profound emotional needs of people with sufficiently large bank accounts. It is also a living experiment that could be

relevant to thinking through the soul's implications for a future where humans may be cloned. Are the clones the same animal as the original, or physically the same but fundamentally unique?

[36] Even vegetarians and vegans need to eat mindfully.

[37] There is growing evidence that several species do exhibit behaviors that look like guilt or a sense of right and wrong, and those of us who are pet owners usually can provide stories of times when this has happened.

[38] Pope Pius IX also came up with the doctrine of the Immaculate Conception; so he was working on more of a systematic theology which in turn shaped some of his positions.

[39] This view of the new state for animals seems like it could be scaled to how different our own future state might be as well. One might speculate about whether the animals will have eternal life, along with their other enhanced abilities.

[40] Frans de Waal of Emery University in Atlanta mentioned that there used to be a taboo against attributing emotions to animals. A variety of articles note that some of this was to provide cover for animal experimentation and the unfortunate way animals have often been treated going back to the 1800s.

[41] Cognition can be defined as "adaptive information processing in the broadest sense, from gathering information through the senses to making decisions and performing functionally appropriate actions, regardless of the complexity of any internal representational processes that behavior might imply" (Shettleworth, 2000, as quoted by Brauer, et al., 2020, in www.ncbi.nlm.nih.gov/pmc/articles/PMC7555673).

[42] Perhaps we are unique in that we also create s'mores.

[43] Note however, the scriptures we have cited that suggest animals also have a spiritual awareness and can give praise to God.

[44] We will see later, this is one of the fundamental attributes of whether something is even alive.

[45] This figure was created with the permission of the authors (January 4, 2021).

[46] To be fair, Hogenboom also notes that chimps can be fairly Machiavellian. The dark side that comes along with these capabilities is something we have inherited as well, and that may be a property of the free will associated with our souls.

[47] It strikes me that this is how an early human ancestor might begin to describe an idea that could eventually become a definition of the underworld.

[48] The Hebrew word נֶ֫פֶשׁ is sometimes written nephesh and sometimes nefesh. I will be using nefesh in this natural history.

Chapter 3

THE EVOLUTION
OF THE SOUL

*"[S]ince what may be known about God is plain
to them, because God has made it plain to them.
For since the creation of the world God's invisible
qualities—his eternal power and divine nature—
have been clearly seen, being understood from what
has been made, so that men are without excuse."*
– Romans 1:19-20 (NIV)

In most religions, God created the heavens and the Earth,
and our current best guess is that process began with the
Big Bang about 13.7 billion years ago. The age of the Earth
is typically discussed in geological eras, periods, and epochs.
Human life emerged during the Pleistocene Epoch, and
modern civilization arose during the Holocene that followed
the last glacial period. There is a growing effort to recognize
the epoch we currently live in as the Anthropocene. As with
previous epochs, this human epoch is being framed in terms
of a significant event (known as the *golden spike marker*) that
shows up in the geologic record. Those arguing for the
Anthropocene are looking for evidence that demonstrates the
beginning of a major change in the human impact on the
planet. The debate among scientists is what that event is and
when the epoch began. We will look at this epoch in terms of
modern human society and culture, and our philosophical and
religious beliefs. But we should start by looking back to the
roots of these beliefs.

The Pleistocene Epoch, sometimes known as the Great Ice Age, started around 2.6 million years ago and ended about 11,700 years ago. This Epoch included the period of the most recent ice age and the period in which humans emerged and expanded across the Earth during the Old Stone Age. Around 22,000 years ago, there was a period of maximum glaciation. Then, approximately 13,000 years ago, about three-quarters of the large animals went extinct, possibly from a comet or asteroid hitting the Earth, or some combination of climate change and overkill by our ancestors. This would have forced changes in how humans organized to ensure they had enough food and would have required innovation to adapt. What was left are many of the species—including primates, orcas, and elephants—that we know today. This period's stresses played a role in filtering out many species, and as we suggested in the last chapter, those that survived and spread (including ourselves) would have been selected for particularly adaptive characteristics.

While the Earth's age is described geologically, *our* evolution is defined in terms of archeological periods. These periods are ways of organizing different stages and groupings of archeological artifacts that reflect social and cultural development. That means, of course, that the periods might be defined differently by various researchers and depend on which parts of the world are being studied. For the sake of looking at the evolution of the soul and the afterlife, associated burial practices, and the emergence of more complex religious beliefs, I will adopt the timeline approximation used by Lesley Kennedy in her History.com article (Kennedy, 2019). In the Table I have included, you will see the four main periods: the Paleolithic, the Mesolithic, the Neolithic, and the beginning of the Metal Ages (Copper, Bronze, and Iron).

Paleolithic	Mesolithic	Neolithic	Metal Ages
c. 300000 to 10000 BCE	c. 10000 BCE to 8000 BCE	c. 8000 to 3000 BCE	Starting about 3000 BCE
Caves and Simple Huts	More Complex Shelters and Communal Buildings	Mud Brick Houses and Villages	Stone Buildings, Cities, and Empires
Hunting	Hunting and Gathering Nomadic Groups	Farming and Agriculture Food Storage	Government, Law, and Warfare
Fire Simple Stone and Bone Tools Language and Storytelling	More Refined Tools, incl. Bows and Arrows Domestication of Animals	More Complex and Innovative Tools and Weapons Writing	Metal Tools and Weapons Wheel Commerce
Early Abstract and Figurative Cave Art Small Figurines (e.g., Venus figures)	Symbolic Art Pottery and Textiles Decorative Arts	Sewing and Weaving More Sophisticated Decorative Objects and Art	Potter's Wheel and New Textiles (e.g., wool) Metal Decorative Objects and Art
First Intentional Burials and Rituals Some Grave Goods Ancestor Worship Shamanism	Religious Centers More Complex Burials and Richer Grave goods	Tombs and Other Mortuary Structures	Organized Religion and Structures Mounds, Cremations, and Monumental Structures (e.g., pyramids) More Elaborate High-end burials

The Paleolithic archeological period roughly corresponds to the Pleistocene Epoch. The earliest members of the genus Homo appeared around 2.5 million years ago in Africa and were using stone tools. Evidence of one of the earliest great inventions, fire, is associated with Homo erectus around 700,000 years ago or earlier. Our modern Homo sapien ancestors appeared with anatomical changes suggesting a capacity for spoken language around 200,000 years ago.

For humans, we started chatting at least as early as 100,000 years ago. Language helps people work together. It helps us make sense of the world, enables knowledge to be passed on, and supports imagining alternative futures. Stories would be a natural use of language as it developed. Definitive evidence of our fire management dates to around 60,000 years ago, but probably goes back much further. It does not take a great leap of imagination to picture the importance of sharing stories around the fire of trips taken and making plans to find the next paradise. Around 80,000 years ago, we were clearly stretching our legs and aspirations beyond Africa and colonizing the planet.

The earliest intentional burials by humans and Neanderthals date back to around this time. About 50,000 years ago, there was a flowering of human skills. While there had been tool use earlier, the sophistication and innovation in tools began to explode. Figurative paintings started to appear as early as 40,000 years ago. They put the stories on the walls. The images probably played both a documentary role as well as a role in trying to manipulate the world. Ancestor worship emerged around this time, Venus figurines were starting to appear, and by 20,000 years ago, there was evidence of shamanism. Religion was emerging, and people were probably enriching their views of who they were and the nature of what will happen after their bodies are laid in the ground. Around 30,000 years ago, burials were becoming more complex. They included ceremonial attributes like red ochre and positioning of the bodies, along with objects used in daily life, weapons, and jewelry. Evidence of groups adopting common rituals began to appear.

The Mesolithic period (the Middle Stone Age) overlaps the end of the Paleolithic and the beginning of the Neolithic. We noted earlier that the dates of these periods are not defined as much by calendars and carbon dating as by the characteristics of how the people lived. As a result, the Mesolithic spans different periods across geographic areas. Researchers marking the beginning of the Mesolithic are looking for the signs that hunter-gatherer communities are forming. Mesolithic humans continued to improve their tools and weapons and applied their artistic and crafting skills to pottery, clothing, and decoration. By the end of the Mesolithic, farming communities were beginning to form, new agricultural tools and techniques were being developed, and there were even some walled cities. Stories and rituals binding communities together would be becoming richer as they persisted across generations. It is worth reminding ourselves that the desolation from the global changes 13,000 years ago would not have been too far in the rear-view mirror in the big scale of time. It would not be too surprising if, as the Earth recovered from the devastation and warmed from the Ice Age, creation stories would begin to form as religion continued to evolve. Flood stories, significant conflicts, disasters, and important ancestors would provide a framework for emerging societies and cultures to define themselves.

The Neolithic was the period when the next great leap in human social and cultural evolution happened. Farming communities and cities provided a fertile ground for the flowering of innovation in tools and the arts. These social changes came with more sophisticated governments, support structures (like the military), and religions. Religious beliefs were fleshed out within cultures, and with it, end-of-life practices became more elaborate. Trade and writing enabled groups to influence each other culturally, including in their beliefs about the afterlife and its implications for living a good life in the here and now.

As the Neolithic was ending, it ushered in the Metal ages. Metallurgy grew, as pottery kilns could be applied to metals. Ceramics and polished stone were in use. Many animals were domesticated as part of that farming culture, including our cats. New forms of social organization emerged. Burial practices became more elaborate, often including grandiose burial mounds and artifacts. Just think about Egypt and the pyramids, and you will have a good idea about what was happening.

The Sumerian civilization formed about 4000 BCE in Mesopotamia. The Egyptian civilization dates to roughly 3100 BCE, and the Xia Dynasty in China to 2070 BCE. Cuneiform and hieroglyphics appeared before 3000 BCE in Sumeria and Egypt, respectively. Writing may have developed in China around 2000 BCE, and characters have been found carved into bone and tortoiseshell that date back to the Shang dynasty (between the eighteenth and twelfth centuries BCE). With these civilizations came more sophisticated religious institutions, including both creation myths and visions of the afterlife. The patriarch Abraham, who Judaism, Christianity, and Islam look to, may have lived around 2000 BCE. This was about the time Hinduism was emerging further east. Civilization was on a roll. Let's explore these periods a little more deeply to look at the evolution of their ideas of the soul and the afterlife.

THE PALEOLITHIC AND MESOLITHIC PERIODS

Our understanding of how we as Homo sapiens evolved to be who we are continues to grow. The story began around two hundred thousand years ago, and it starts a bit behind the evolution of Homo neanderthalensis (commonly known as Neanderthals). They split off from our ancestral line from three hundred to eight hundred thousand years ago. Homo sapiens in Latin means "wise man," and the name carries the idea of how we like to think of ourselves. The Neanderthals largely disappeared around forty thousand years ago, and we are still here. But, of course, we now know they are still here as well, having interbred with us. Many humans carry somewhere between one to four percent Neanderthal DNA, presumably without damaging their souls. There is also some Denisovan DNA floating around in our gene pool. The Denisovans (Homo denisova) lived around this same period. Melanesians and aboriginal Australians have about three to five percent of their DNA coming from this group. Emerging research has shown that this interbreeding has led to susceptibility for some conditions that still plague us, like type 2 diabetes. Yet, it has also provided unique super-powers like the Denisovan DNA that helps Tibetans survive at high altitudes.

Neanderthal DNA has a relatively small difference from our DNA. Still, of course, minor genetic differences can functionally be quite significant, as we know from the recreations of them we see in magazines and museums. The Neanderthal average cranial capacity was about fourteen percent larger than ours. They had their own culture and built primitive homes. They used bone and stone tools. They probably had a language, developing at about the same time as it did for Homo sapiens. They buried their dead, and some researchers believe they were at least somewhat spiritual.

Some of the earliest burials were probably Neanderthals, who were known to have buried their dead in shallow graves along with stone tools and animal bones. Neanderthals and humans both lived together around one hundred thousand years ago in Es-Skhul in Israel, around Mount Carmel, and Qafzah, near Nazareth. At Qafzah, evidence of the first intentional human burial may date back to this time (Martin, 2020). Human skeletal remains covered in red ochre were found at both Qafzah and Es-Skhul, along with various grave goods such as the mandible of a wild boar in the arms of one of the skeletons (Lieberman, 1991). This would be at the time when humans were starting to migrate out of Africa, they would have been communicating, and they would have been...dating. While some might hesitate to assume that animals have souls, it would seem to be a smaller step to imagine these cousins of ours had souls. If they had souls, then there is an open question of when souls started to appear elsewhere in our genetic ancestry.

Human Burial Practices

Often the early burials were in hard-to-reach areas of caves. These locations might represent the spiritual significance of some sites. They are in the earth, and between the light and the dark. They are quite literally in what could be called an underworld. Burial items such as garments, wearable items and trinkets, and food could accompany them. Red ochre was often used for ceremonial painting of bodies and grave goods, as well as caves. It is likely that, especially for the powerful, feasts accompanied the passing. There is also evidence of areas expressly set aside for children and families to be buried together.

In ancient times, burial was both a matter of hygiene and indicated respect for the dead, just as it is today. It prevents the odor of decay and the transmission of disease. It removes the discomfort of seeing the decay of one we have known and perhaps loved personally. It also helps provide emotional closure with a marking event, a ritual. Philip Lieberman (Lieberman, 1991) suggests that burial may be one of the earliest forms of religious practice, as it can show "concern for the dead that transcends daily life." Over time, that closure process probably has helped us reflect on *what* persists, *how* it continues, and our fates.

The extent to which these rituals and practices represent afterlife beliefs is debated. For example, it has been observed that afterlife beliefs are largely absent from contemporary non-state societies such as the Hadza hunter-gatherers of Tanzania, the Nuer pastoralists of Sudan, and the Pirahã people of the Amazon basin. But the burial practices that go back, say one hundred thousand years, with elaborate ornamental grave goods do seem to suggest a belief in an afterlife (Stewart-Williams, 2018).

Paige Madison (Madison, 2018) wrote a fascinating article about early burials. Mortuary rituals are important since they often give us a window into the developing ability to think symbolically, and symbolic thought lets us unite our past, present, and future. Language, which is an embodiment of that symbolic thought, is important; but it does not fossilize. Madison notes burials are important because they are concrete and visible. They reflect the spiritual and things that are meaningful to individuals and communities. They allow researchers to trace the evolution of beliefs, values, and ideas that represent cultures. She also notes that "We imbue nonpractical things with meaning. Art and jewelry, for example, communicate concepts about beliefs, values, and social status. Mortuary rituals, too, have been put forward as a key example of symbolic thought, with the idea that deliberate treatment of the dead represents a whole web of ideas." These rituals and the stories and language that go with them are a complex cognitive process that enables us to imagine and share that which is not

British Museum Burial Goods from One Early English Grave

immediately present. Processing our feelings about our dead lets us connect our past with a future in which we also will die, and potentially beyond. This value was true then, and it is true today.

Other sites in Africa dating to around this time also show the growing use of red ochre, possibly being used because of the symbolic value that was becoming associated with it. More elaborate religious behavior is currently assumed to have emerged around thirty to forty thousand years ago and possibly earlier. Dr. Leften Stavrianos (Stavrianos, 1991) argues that religious ceremonies involving the full participation of bands of humans were becoming increasingly common. The growing use of grave goods and the appearance of anthropomorphic images in paintings around that time may also suggest the emergence of the belief in supernatural beings (Mithen, 1996).

139

In Eurasia, around ten to thirty-five thousand years ago, a study by the Univ. of Colorado, Denver found considerable variation in human burial practices. While most were plain, some were lavish; the practices varied depending on context and time (University of Colorado Denver, 2013). The study examined eighty-five burials from the late Paleolithic period. In general, men were buried more often than women, and adults significantly more often than babies. There were examples of ornate burials in Russia, Italy, and the Czech Republic from that time. The more common graves primarily included items from daily life. Often ornaments (e.g., of stone, teeth, or shells) would be found on the body's heads or torsos. In many ways, they were similar to some Neanderthal graves, where they also put bodies into pits with household items.

Burial with grave goods is probably partly about honoring the dead. Still, it is known that there is a long history of these grave goods, in some cases being more ceremonial and potentially even being part of the ritual that ushers the dead into their next life. Bodies may be dressed in their favorite clothes, their best clothes, or ceremonial clothes. They may have been buried with personally meaningful objects or with things that were part of daily life. Items that were symbols of their role in society might also be buried with them (e.g., the weapons buried with an ancient warrior).

The Emergence of Symbolic Art

Tree of Life
c. 40,000 BCE

A study in *Science* (Hoffmann, 2018) reported a new dating technique that showed Neanderthals created abstract paintings of dots, lines, and handprints some sixty-four thousand years ago in Spain's La Pasiega Cave. The conclusion is that these paintings, whatever they meant, must have been significant. Some were painted in areas deep in the cave that would have required light sources to be brought in, and of course, the pigments themselves probably took special effort to prepare. They would have been meaningful symbols in meaningful places. Dr. Alistair Pike (Standish, 2018), an archeologist from the University of Southampton, UK (who coauthored the study), said, "It wasn't simply decorating your living space. People were making journeys into the darkness."

Early humans lived in caves, huts, or tepees. They used

basic stone and bone tools, and stone axes for hunting. They cooked their prey, which consisted of birds, smaller game, deer, bison, and wooly mammoths using controlled fire.[49] They fished and harvested berries, fruit, and nuts. Cave painting used combinations of ochres, minerals, burnt bone meal, and charcoal, mixed with water, blood, fat from their prey, and tree sap.[50] They carved figurines and designs from stones, clay, bones, and antlers. Towards the end of the Mesolithic period and into the Neolithic (as the Stone Age ended), humans used small stone tools and created tools and weapons with polished points attached to antlers, bone, or wood spears and arrows. They would move as groups to be near rivers and other bodies of water to find food.

Like the Neanderthal paintings, the oldest known images

of early humans are also non-figurative, abstract paintings like handprints, and various marks on walls. There were paintings of this type dating to forty-four thousand years ago in the Franco-Cantabrian region in Western Europe and also in the caves in the district of Maros (Sulawesi, Indonesia). But the next leap in the evolution of human expression was figurative painting. There are figurative paintings that date to forty thousand years ago in Lubang Jeriji Saleh's cave on Borneo's Indonesian island, and figures illustrating pig hunting in the Maros-Pangkep karst in Sulawesi. The earliest known European figurative cave paintings are those of Chauvet Cave in France (around thirty thousand BCE).

Cavers have found figures in caves in Romania, Australia, and elsewhere around the world. Frequently the animals are highly detailed, and the humans are less so. The humans, however, are often hunting the animals. In other words, what is beginning to emerge are visual representations of the stories of their lives. Stories help create a culture, and they construct and transmit models of how the world we experience works and how we should interact with it. We show our direct experience in art, but we can also represent alternative experiences and reason about cause and effect through sketching like this. In my field, we would call these examples of storyboarding, which is used today to layout movies and other interactive media. Through these images, they may have been trying to control or at least influence how the world works. Their imaginations would be reaching beyond the here and now to larger forces that might be at work.

David Lewis-Williams (Clottes, 1998) has offered another theory based on ethnographic studies from hunter-gatherer communities. He argues that shamans made the paintings. The shaman would work their way into the dark, isolated areas of the caves, enter a trance state (perhaps with herbal help), and paint images of their visions. This effort could be tied to a sense of the power of the earth and nature itself. The emergence of the shaman would be an indicator of symbolism and storytelling beginning to depict another world that influences our reality, a world that we can influence to our benefit. Special people in the social group, shamans, or leaders, might have unique access to this other world. The stories emerging around these influential people would begin to create a model of this physical world and its relation to the next. It is easy to imagine as the stories are retold, partially to the benefit of the teller, people might imagine they might be able to enter the world, at the very least, by going through the gate that leads out of this one (Peoples, 2016).

Given the great apes' communication capabilities and the evolution of our ability to articulate richer sounds, language emerged in humans and Neanderthals as we evolved. But some believe that global events like the "nuclear winter" following the eruption of the super-volcano Mount Toba in Sumatra seventy thousand years ago and the global chaos thirteen thousand years ago may have accelerated the formation of tribes, tight family groups, and cooperation. It may have driven innovation in culture, tools, and art as well. As noted earlier, of course, many primate groups are highly social. Social, cooperative behavior is a hallmark of other animals with more sophisticated cognitive abilities as well (e.g., orcas and elephants). That cooperation among social groups was probably critical in our ability to survive and occupy a broad range of environments worldwide, especially during global environmental catastrophes (Andrei, 2015).

We find hand marks stenciled on the wall across the Neanderthal and Homo sapiens caves in Spain, France, and elsewhere. When you crawl back through the dark, narrow, slippery passages of ancient caves, you can find hand marks stenciled on the walls from thousands of years ago. They typically are outlined in red ochre, which was probably blown out of the mouths of the ancestral artists. Jonathan Jones (Jones, 2018) recounts the observation made by Jacob Bronowski as part of his TV series *The Ascent of Man* when visiting the caves in northern Spain. Bronowski observes, "The print of the hand says, 'This is my mark. This is man.'"

I would argue the mark also says this is *me. I* was *here*. I breathed this image out of myself. It may say this is mine. It reminds me of the initials on a freshly smoothed cement sidewalk, or a tag on the side of a railroad car or under the freeway on a support post. The meaning of these marks strikes me as a first step in the journey to I am *me*, a *soul*, and I can create. Imagining and portraying an image that documents a hunt or imagining what a future hunt might be like is the beginning of moving beyond my physical body's limitations and into desirable futures.

Red Ochre Rituals

It is fascinating to discover inventions, tools, ideas, and practices that seem to arise almost simultaneously in many different places. One of those is the importance of the rusty colored red ochre for Stone Age people, especially in rituals around death. Gemma Tarlach (Tarlach, 2018) wrote an article for *Discover Magazine* entitled "What the Ancient Pigment Ochre Tells Us About the Human Mind." As mentioned, some of the earliest human burials date back one hundred thousand years, and the skeletal remains were covered in red ochre and buried along with a variety of grave goods. Red ochre is the oldest known pigment used by humans in the world (Hirst, 2019). According to Ernst E. Wreschner, et al. (Wreschner, 1980), red ochre practices have persisted from the early Paleolithic (beginning with Neanderthals, possibly two hundred and fifty thousand years ago or more) to modern times and show regular patterns of use, including those around death, life, and kinship.

One of the oldest human burials is in Poland at Janislawice, dating to the Mesolithic period. Its pit walls were colored with ochre, and the corpse was sprinkled with it. The cave site of Arene Candide has a burial of a young man covered in ochre from around twenty-three thousand years ago. In a burial site in the Paviland Cave in the UK, from roughly the same time, red ochre was so liberally used the body is often referred to as the Red Lady. Tarlach mentions that Tammy Hodgskiss, an archaeologist at the University of Witwatersrand in South Africa, found sites such as the Rose Cottage Cave where ochre was used for more than sixty thousand years.[51]

Chemically ochre is known as Fe2O3, an iron-oxide, although there are many rocks in this class. Archaeologists typically define ochre as any iron-rich rock used for pigment. They usually are natural minerals and compounds composed of varying proportions of iron (Fe$_3$ or Fe$_2$), oxygen (O), and hydrogen (H). These pigments might include yellow ochre goethite (with varying amounts of manganese) and hematite.

Most often, red ochre is what today we might think of as rust color. When heated to four hundred and eighty degrees Fahrenheit, yellow ochre crystal structure changes and can be transformed into the red ochre hematite. Hodgskiss (cited by Tarlach) notes when describing the period from fifty to two hundred and eighty thousand years ago, "[T]here seems to be a preference for red – a larger percentage of the ochre used was red….It's possible some of the red ochre we find may have been yellow once."[52] If we were going to speculate, transforming yellow to red might even have been a first step in the long road to harnessing fire for ceramics and metals.

The pigment was used for a wide variety of things. Besides its ritual and possible symbolic use in burials, it was used for many of the cave paintings we have described. It was used in medicine. It has also been used for pottery, tattoos, and decorating bodies. The ground of dwellings could be decorated with ochre. It turns up on tools and weapons and is used as an adhesive. It was helpful in tanning hides, as sunscreen, and as a mosquito repellant.

Tarlach says that Brooks observes, "[S]ome languages have only two words for color: red and non-red. A language may not have a word for green or blue, but there is always a word for red." Brooks also notes, "There are lots of rocks that come in powdery form that aren't red and didn't get used. Ochre has importance because it signals to others."

According to Giulia Sorlini (Sorlini, 1985), "Neolithic burials used red ochre pigments symbolically, either to represent a return to the earth or possibly as a form of ritual rebirth, in which the colour symbolizes blood and the Great Goddess." While some of the value of ochre could have involved the practical uses described, it is clear red has had a rich symbolic significance through recorded human history, with its association with the color of blood, war, life, and love. Indeed, the effort used to mine and process ochre, and the cognitive and possibly linguistic abilities implied, suggests that its uses were symbolic and ritualized. If it signified life, return to the earth, and other animistic beliefs, it would speak to early ideas about the soul and the afterlife. Some believe that ochre may have fueled brain development and contributed to the expansion of Homo sapiens worldwide.

Storytelling and Early Religion

"In the beginning story-telling was not an affair of pen and ink. It began with the Warning Examples naturally told by a mother to her children, and with the Embroidered Exploits told by a boaster to his wife or friends. The early woman would persuade her child from the fire with a tale of how just such another as he had touched the yellow dancer, and had had his hair burned and his eyelashes singed so that he could not look in the face of the sun. Enjoying the narrative, she would give it realistic and credible touches, and so make something more of it than the dull lie of utility.

"The early man, fresh from an encounter with some beast of the woods, would not be so little of an artist as to tell the actual facts; how he heard a noise, the creaking of boughs and crackling in the undergrowth, and ran. No; he would describe the monster, sketch his panic moments, the short, fierce struggle, his stratagem, and his escape. In these two primitive tales, and their combination in varying proportions, are the germs of all the others. There is no story written today which cannot trace its pedigree to those two primitive types of narrative, generated by the vanity of man and the exigencies of his life."
– Arthur Ransome (Ransome, 1909)

We are storytellers. It is how we are built and shapes who we are as individuals and the cultures we create. The stories help us make sense of our experiences with the world around us and serves as a vehicle for communicating our experiences to others. While we cannot directly experience what another experiences, we can build empathy by virtually living through the stories we share. The stories themselves reflect the explicit and implicit models we have developed within ourselves as we interact with the world. Learning the stories of others and expressing our own stories helps us uncover those internal models and adapt them in anticipation of new contexts. Storytelling, therefore, is a robust tool for describing how we interact with the world, and it helps us predict and deal with the future.

Storytelling is likely to have been one of the developments in our evolution that led to the emergence of richer concepts about ourselves, our place in the universe, and our state beyond death. Those concepts are fundamental for the development of religion, and both early Jewish and Hindu scriptures emerged from stories passed from one generation to the next. Storytelling requires language and the ability to think abstractly.

Indian Kathakar Storyteller

It requires the ability to create conceptual models of the world and imagine alternatives and the resulting outcomes. With a concept of the self as an element in the models, stories become a way for us to manage our own experiences, react to the unexpected, explore the unknown; and share our reflections and insights with others. The emergence of storytelling is on the critical path to the formation of ideas about the soul and the afterlife.

As we have noted, language evolved around a hundred thousand years ago and possibly earlier, along with the emergence of modern Homo sapiens. Then, around fifty thousand years ago, the pace of tool use accelerated along with the tools' quality and sophistication. Interestingly, human figurative and symbolic cave paintings started to emerge around this same time.

Early humans in this later Stone Age period were beginning to communicate personal experiences socially. They would be learning about what has worked well and not so well as they hunted and dealt with the forces of nature that would surround them. They would be figuring out how the world works and the actions they might take to influence it. These models of the world would include dealing with the deaths of family and friends. They might express their understanding through language to coordinate activities. They would tell stories. The stories would communicate experience and insight, and bind groups together. The stories and lessons would help create culture. Their version of PowerPoint might even have been wall painting.

Ferris Jabr (Jabr, 2019) quotes the anthropologist Andrea Migliano as saying, "There is an adaptive advantage to storytelling. I think this work confirms that storytelling is important to communicate social norms and what is essential for hunter-gatherer survival." This observation is consistent with that of researchers such as Skylar Bayer and Annaliese Hettinger (Bayer, 2019). They argue, "Humans have been telling stories nearly since we became Homo sapiens, sharing them orally before the invention of writing. Storytelling may even be an evolutionary mechanism, embedded in our very DNA, which helped keep our ancestors alive." They support the idea that, essentially, we are storytellers. Stories "are central to human existence: our most instinctive and universal means of communicating. Stories help us build relationships with one another through exchanging perspectives between teller and listener." Storytelling by those with power (incl. those able to turn dreams and visions of a spiritual world into shared experiences) could be a tool to ensure influence in communities.

The procedural language needed for storytelling may not only have emerged at a critical point in human evolution, but a study by T. Morgan, et al. (Morgan, 2015) suggests it may also have accelerated our evolution by enhancing tool creation and use. They looked at the effectiveness of transmitting Oldowan tool-making skills through stories by simulating alternative ways of sharing skills among different chains of people. The Oldowan tools date to about one to two million years ago, and were relatively simple general-purpose tools made by knocking a few chips off a stone to give it a sharpened edge. The group in which gestures were used to pass on experience in making Oldowan flakes doubled the productivity in their production relative to the trial-and-error group, but the group using verbal methods of passing on learning more than quadrupled their effectiveness.

While some methodological issues have been raised, the potential value of language suggests how human expressiveness and evolution have evolved together. Similarly, language may have helped humans develop richer burial practices, rituals, and mythologies, including ideas about the relationship between this world and the next. This would especially be true if it helped people deal with sorrow and loss, and gave them a sense of control in an often hostile existence. It would also provide them with a tool to make sense of the experiences with people apparently being dead and later returning to life,[53] and experiences many still have of seeing the spirits of loved ones who have passed away.

As stories that carry truth—such as models of how to interact with the world and significant events like death—are passed from person to person, they evolve across time and cultures. We all have experienced a simple version of this phenomenon in the children's game Telephone, as a message transforms as it goes from person to person. Information is left out when it is forgotten or not deemed essential. It is transformed when it is misheard, interpreted, or simplified. Someone in the chain may fill in a missing piece of information to add a new insight or make the message more powerful and sticky. Across culture and time, these transformations act like living organisms evolving and occupying niches in an ecosystem. In Chapter 6, which explores the science of the soul, we will discuss some speculation about how ideas of the soul and the afterlife might represent memes evolving across generations and cultures.

Jabr (Jabr, 2019) observes that it is almost like they are living things. He says, "They compel us to share them and, once told, they begin to grow and change, often becoming longer and more elaborate. They compete with one another for our attention—for the opportunity to reach as many minds as possible." Jabr reports a study by the anthropologist Jamie Tehrani that imagines that the evolution of stories as being similar to the evolution of living things. If so, you might be able to apply an analysis you would use for mutations in DNA to the development of stories over time. The more similar the DNA of two species, the more recently they split in their family trees.

Tehrani and other researchers explored applying this approach to folktales and myths. They deconstructed stories to their most fundamental elements and then statistically identified the similarities and differences between the elements over time and geography to determine ancestral relationships. For example, Tehrani gathered fifty-eight variants of "Little Red Riding Hood" from around the world and identified archetypal stories preserved in France, Austria, and northern Italy as the source of the story familiar to many of us in North America. At the same time, another evolutionary branch about some goats came from an Aesopian tale from around 400 CE. The two merged with a local tale in Asia to become the "Tiger Grandmother." We will see how this approach can be applied to reconstruct the evolution of religious concepts and memes.

In the discussion on popular culture, we noted how game playing and, in effect, possessing another's body can make someone more empathetic. More and more research shows that people who read fiction and live through the characters also tend to be more empathetic. They tend to understand others better and to share their feelings. This empathy may be a factor in the interplay between ideas like the soul and the afterlife in the arts and culture explored in Chapter 1. In 2006, according to *Discover* magazine (Schmidt, 2020), the more names of fiction authors someone knew, the higher they scored on empathy tests. There is also evidence that reading itself drives the change, rather than more empathetic people tending to read.

I would observe that it is not just about walking in another's shoes; it is about incorporating the *other* into ourselves; much as if we had lived the experience of another ourselves. This identification would presumably be happening as we watch plays and movies, and engage as characters in games. Being able to immerse ourselves in the stories of others can make us more effective in handling novel situations we have never personally encountered. The stories that emerged during our evolution began to give us a framework for defining ourselves, and that helped us manage the anticipation of our own deaths and grief over the deaths of others. Some of the early stories probably helped shape the Stone Age religion, just as stories have come down to us and have shaped our popular culture and personal beliefs.

Stone Age Religion

As noted in the burial discussion, religious behavior probably started showing up in the Middle Paleolithic, between twenty and forty thousand years ago (Kübler-Ross, 1969). The behaviors of Homo neanderthalensis and Homo naledi may have included ancestor worship as well as burial rituals. Philip Lieberman (Lieberman, 1991) suggests intentional burial back in those early days, especially with grave goods, may indicate "concern for the dead that transcends daily life."

Vincent W. Fallio (Fallio, 2006) argues that the ancestor cults began to emerge in increasingly complex later Paleolithic societies (beginning around 40,000 years ago). The elites may have used ancestor worship and rituals to enhance their control over their societies. Convincing people that because of their position, certain people such as rulers, priests, and shamans have a unique link to the spirit world would tie their power in this world to the power coming with access to the spiritual realm. Secret societies and priest classes could use religious rituals to solidify themselves as part of the elite. Around this time,

Venus figurines and cave art became much more common. The Venus figures may have represented fertility as an Earth goddess or may have served as objects used in female and male shamanistic spiritual transformation processes.

An episode of NPR's *Hidden Brain* called "Creating God" discussed the research behind how this process of creating an active God or "high gods" as part of early religions likely impacted the formation of larger, more complex societies. Some believe that the rise of religions, with their beliefs about a God or gods, the afterlife, and the implications of reward and punishment based on how we live in this life, is a kind of cultural innovation like fire, tools, or agriculture (Creating God, 2018). Peoples et al. (Peoples, 2016) also provide support for the proposition "It can be argued that those societies under higher resource stress, encountering difficulties with resource extraction that demands cooperative effort, would benefit most from the shaman's skills." The global catastrophe around thirteen thousand years ago would be an example of this kind of stress, as would climate change cycles. These beliefs could have helped us survive as a species as they provide a structure that enables us to live with each other, cooperate with shared values, and manage the challenges that life and death bring.

Jeremiah Stanghini (Stanghini, 2013) provides an overview of shamanism's history and controversies within that history. He says that some researchers argue that European Paleolithic art from seventeen thousand years ago and South Africa (around twenty-five thousand years ago) suggests widespread shamanic practices. However, the earliest more direct archeological record of an excavation with evidence of shamanism is from Israel, dating back twelve thousand years. It is even possible to find these practices around the world today in areas as diverse as Siberia, North and South America, and Australia.

Most indigenous shamans do not see themselves as belonging to a specific religion. The researchers who started using the term shaman were trying to capture a category of beliefs that might be quite individual. Stanghini points out that words used for the role in various cultures include meanings like "one who is excited, moved, raised," "to know," and "to heal oneself or practice austerities." Stanghini offers one broad definition as "the term shaman refers to any practitioners who enter controlled ASCs [altered states of consciousness], no matter what type of altered state." He cites Harner (Harner, 1982) as defining a shaman as "a man or a woman who enters an altered state of consciousness at will to contact and utilize an ordinarily hidden reality to acquire knowledge, power, and to help other persons." This latter definition is important since it recognizes that while we are in this reality, other parallel realities could be sources of causality that can be accessed through appropriate rituals.[54]

Stanghini cites another definition of shamanism that is a little more specific from Roger Walsh (Walsh, 1989). Walsh says, "[S]hamanism might be defined as a family of traditions whose practitioners focus on voluntarily entering altered states of consciousness in which they experience themselves, or their spirit(s), traveling to other realms at will and interact with other entities to serve the community." Walsh, in turn, leans towards Harner's claim that "[S]hamanism is ultimately only a method, not a religion with a fixed set of dogmas. Therefore, people arrive at their experience-derived conclusions about what is going on in the universe, and about what term, if any, is most useful to describe ultimate reality" (Harner, 1985). Walsh observes, "Certainly there seems to be evidence of some innate human tendency to enter specific altered states. Studies of different meditative traditions suggest that an innate tendency to access altered states can be very precise." Most current major religions still have groups in their communities that are drawn to more experiential and mystical traditions that may leverage this tendency (e.g., Pentecostalism and Kabbalah).

Buddhists have been documenting the ability to enter specific states for more than two thousand years. Even Westerners studying in shamanic workshops have demonstrated that most people can experience altered states. Other research shows that these states can be stimulated by naturally occurring conditions like isolation, fatigue, hunger, rhythmic sound, and of course, hallucinogens. States like these may have been experienced by several prophets in Jewish and Christian history. The possibility of this ability being innately part of us will come up again as we discuss the experiences of those who have recently died or during the last stages of death itself in Chapter 6, where we look at the science of the soul.

These experiences are often pleasurable, personally meaningful, and a source of healing. Walsh argues that it is not surprising then that they are still being sought and are so ubiquitous. They are the kinds of experiences that provide personal value and could have evolutionary value to us as a species. Furthermore, the stories, traditions, and rituals (e.g., including the use of ochre), are often remembered and passed across generations. Walsh concludes by saying, "The end result is that this ancient tradition has spread across the earth and has survived for perhaps tens of thousands of years, a period which represents a significant proportion of this time that fully developed human beings (modern Homo sapiens) have been on the planet."

Peoples, et al. (Peoples, 2016) have taken a somewhat different approach than Stanghini. They looked at the relationship between groups over time, and how their language evolved to develop a timeline of how religious practices have evolved among early human societies. They point out that religion seems to be unique to humans and occurs in virtually all human cultures that have been studied. They argue this implies a deep evolutionary past. There are arguments that the rise of religion played a vital role in the out-of-Africa expansion of humans. According to Peoples et al., "A case can be made that transmission of religious concepts from one individual to another requires complex mental imaging, and a capacity for symbolic thought and communication that might include ritual, dancing, singing, gestures, art, and ornamentation, as well as language." This would be true of religion in general and concepts about the self, the soul, and the afterlife.

They also concluded that the earliest belief among hunter-gatherers was animism. Some of the early figurative cave art could be viewed through this lens. Animism led, they believe, to a belief in an afterlife. According to Sir Edward Burnett

Tyler (1832-1917), who is the founder of cultural anthropology, "Animism includes a 'belief in personal souls' as well as 'a sense of spiritual beings, inhabiting trees and rocks and waterfalls.' We define animism as the belief that all 'natural' things, such as plants, animals, and even such phenomena as thunder, have intentionality (or a vital force) and can influence human lives." Once you believe in some kind of personal soul, a sense of a spiritual world, and an afterlife, the next step from Peoples et al.'s analysis is shamanism and ancestor worship. The shaman might be a facilitator to connect with the other side, and those who have passed over would be some of the inhabitants of the next world.[55]

Finally, Peoples et al. speculate, "Once animistic thought is prevalent in society, interest in the whereabouts of spirits of the dead could reasonably lead to a concept of an unseen realm where the individual personality of the deceased lives on." Belief in an afterlife may come with a sense of "being watched" by the dead and motivation to follow approved social norms. The afterlife might also be seen as a reward and a continuation of a good life here on earth. This sense of being watched may be similar to the conditions that still lead to people feeling a sense of a presence from the spirit world and reports of seeing ghostly forms in stressful situations or when under sensory deprivation.

THE NEOLITHIC TRANSITION

The Neolithic led into the Bronze Age.[56] It was a period of hunters and gatherers becoming farmers and the emergence of settlements, towns, and eventually cities. It included the invention and broad adoption of metallurgy which ushered in the Metal Ages. It also led to the next stage in creating decorative pottery and carving patterns in the stone. Farming, of course, focused people on the seasons, the sun and moon, and weather. By the Neolithic, people had begun domesticating animals (including cats) and cultivated cereal grains.[57] They used polished hand axes, adzes for plowing and tilling, and were settling in the plains. Home construction advanced, as did art, pottery, sewing and weaving, and the decorative arts (e.g., jewelry).

All of this could be included as grave goods in burials. Neolithic communities carefully buried their dead. Graves might contain food, utensils, jewelry, and other objects. People were usually buried on their side in a fetal position. Herders sometimes used double graves, for husbands and wives. One of the oldest religious sites discovered from this time is Gobekli Tepe, from around 10000 to 7000 BCE. By the beginning of the Bronze Age, the cult of the Mother Goddess (e.g., recognizing the planting of *dead* seed and the resurrection of plants in ritual practices) was widespread in the area.

But once people started to farm, they began to gather in villages and towns to exchange supplies and production. They organized to protect themselves. They built communities and collaborated to achieve larger social goals. Culture grew and bound them together. As towns grew, organizational, political, and religious systems grew; and through that process, the villages and towns became cities. One form ancestor "worship" might take is continuing to pass on and evolve myths and stories about the ancestors, and building richer religious frameworks around them. Of course, we get to experience this process of the rise of civilization with *Age of Empires*, *SimCity*, and other simulation games.

Today, most of us live in cities, and the kinds of societies that gave rise to cities are also the kinds of societies that nourished the growth of more formal and complex religions and beliefs. According to Bridget Alex (Alex, 2021) the first cities began to emerge around six thousand years ago. The oldest cities still are being debated, in part based on how one defines the idea of a city. For this discussion, the details are not as important as realizing that the beginnings of cities were also associated with the emergence of more formal religious systems.

There were early cities in the Indus Valley (around

Pakistan and India) around four thousand years ago and in China about three thousand years ago. In the Americas, they appeared approximately two thousand years ago. According to Alex (2021), there was a settlement on present-day Jericho's site around ten thousand years ago with several thousand residents and large stone walls. Still, most archaeologists would classify it as a town rather than a city. Uruk, located between the Tigris and the Euphrates rivers[58] in what is now Iraq, was founded around 4500 BCE. It had a population of around forty thousand people (the size of Edmonds, WA where I live now) and was the kind of political, cultural, and religious center typical of a city. Further north in Syria, Tell Brak dated to around 2600 BCE. At the site of Tell Brak, you can find religious and secular monuments, workshops, and manufacturing. This whole area is part of what today we think of as the Fertile Crescent. Later, the larger area of Mesopotamia grew some of the earliest empires, including the Sumerians and Akkadians.

Rosetta Stone

The Neolithic was followed by the Copper Age (often called the Chalcolithic); then the Bronze Age and the Iron Age. The Copper Age was characterized by the use of copper mostly in its raw state and shaping it. The next stage in the evolution of metallurgy was bronze. The critical marker for the Bronze Age was the ability of a civilization to produce bronze or trade for bronze. The bronze ingredients (tin and copper) have a melting point in the range of Neolithic pottery kilns. The Bronze Age is also notable as when writing emerged. As we have mentioned, writing was beginning to support the more formal structures required for cities and religious practice, such as those appearing in Mesopotamia, Egypt, and China. Writing helped spread cultural practices across the Mediterranean area. Not too surprisingly, religious stories and wisdom that had been evolving through oral tradition began to get recorded around this time. Finally, iron, with its higher melting point, required another leap in technical and social innovation.

RELIGION AND THE START OF THE METAL AGES

Ancient Egypt

The Early Dynastic period in Egypt follows the unification of Lower and Upper Egypt (c. 3100 BCE) into a single kingdom. The aspects of ancient Egyptian civilization that we think of today, such as art, architecture, and the core religious ideas (incl. of the soul and the afterlife), appeared during the Early Dynastic Period. The first archeological evidence of Israel as a nation is on the Merneptah Stele from around 1208 BCE at the end of the Bronze Age. By way of context, the Babylonian Captivity of people from the ancient Kingdom of Judah was about 597 to 538 BCE, towards the end of Egypt's dominance.

Ancient Egypt is one of the civilizations whose culture was most fully and richly grounded in its theology and practices involving the soul and the afterlife. Religion was a critical social practice that bound people together in the society. We have noted in the evolution of the concept of the soul; these more developed beliefs and rituals, along with the priests to support them, typically helped in the formation of more complex cultures and social hierarchies.

We know about Egyptian practices from the Pyramid Texts, the oldest Egyptian religious records. The earliest ones date back to around 2400 BCE, and the texts were expanded over the next few hundred years. They were carved into the walls and sarcophagi in caves, tunnels, and pyramids. Given the importance of Egypt throughout the Mediterranean area during its height, these beliefs influenced afterlife beliefs in the entire region.

Of course, you cannot say the ancient Egyptians all were aligned to one orthodoxy during the ebbs and flows of their kingdoms. Beliefs evolved with the kingdoms, and as social, political, and economic conditions changed. There are some common themes, however, that can be used as a framework for thinking broadly about ancient Egyptian views of the soul and the afterlife.

For the ancient Egyptians, life in this world was just part of the journey that continued seamlessly into the afterlife. According to the ancient Egyptians, when the world was created, it and every living thing on it were filled with magic. The magic in humans took the form of the soul, an eternal force in every one of us. The soul, in turn, was made up of many parts. To house the soul, you need the physical body to be preserved. That physical form was required for the soul to have intelligence, and the state of the body after death was critical for a desirable afterlife. The word for that physical form (*Khet*) roughly translates to "sum of bodily parts." Objects, statues of slaves, and so on were buried with people to serve the deceased in the afterlife.

If all the ceremonies and rituals were performed correctly and the person was judged worthy of the afterlife, the spiritual body (*Sah*) that represents the physical body in the afterlife forms. This spiritual body could interact with the next world and potentially come back and interact with the physical world (e.g., by bringing revenge on people who wronged the person before they died). The soul, however, is also made up of other parts, which varied somewhat across the kingdoms. They believed that a person's heart (*Ib*) housed the person's emotion, will, and consciousness. The mind and the heart were synonymous for the ancient Egyptians. Importantly, it is the heart that is weighed against the feather of Ma'at by Anubis to determine whether the person can go on to the next stage of their journey in the afterlife. If the heart weighed more than the feather, it was consumed by Ammit, and the soul became restless eternally.[59] In other religions, these attributes of the heart would be considered central attributes of a soul.

While there was a rich set of characteristics that the Egyptians identified with the soul, three seem particularly relevant to this discussion, the *Ka*, the *Ba*, and the *Ren*. The Ka was the vital essence. It is what distinguishes the living and the dead. Death means that the Ka has left the body. Food and drink sustain the Ka when the person is alive, and the Ka of the offerings of food and drink sustain the Ka after death.

The Ba is that which makes us unique. It includes personality, but it also includes other aspects of the expression of identity. It can be a kind of embodiment of reputation. Even some inanimate objects (like a pyramid) may have a Ba. Some Egyptologists argue that it is not so much a part of a person as the person's essence. The Ba is sometimes discussed in the way dualists might talk about how the soul exists after the body is gone.

Then there is the Ren or the person's name. It was given to them at birth, and it contains the person's identity, experiences, and entire life's memories. It lives as long as it is being spoken. This importance of the name being remembered and spoken occurs across many religions and cultures across history and seems to be a desire for many even today. There is evidence that Egyptians attempted to erase the names and faces on monuments and statues of earlier rulers who were out of favor, which would be the ultimate insult.

A background assumption for ancient Egyptians was that the afterlife reflected and potentially enhanced the world in which they were living. For them, their country was the best country in the world and the most blessed. There were no works in Egyptian literature like the Greek Iliad or the Odyssey, where the excitement happened elsewhere. John Jack George (George, 2020) provides a detailed description that is worth a read that illustrates how Egyptians at one point viewed the process of passing into the afterlife. It begins at death when a part of the soul travels to the underworld, guided by Anubis, to find its way into the next life. Anubis weighs the person's heart in the Hall of Truth against a single feather from Ma'at (the goddess of truth, balance, justice, and harmony). If the person has lived a life worthy of the characteristics of Ma'at, their heart will be lighter than the feather; but if not, they will be devoured by Ammit—who was part lion, part hippopotamus, and part crocodile—and will essentially cease to exist (or became a kind of eternally wandering spirit). It is worth noting that there is not a concept of hell. The worst thing possible is to cease to exist, complete oblivion.

If they make it through that, they are judged by a jury of forty-two gods,[60] each looking to see if a specific sin was committed. The *Book of the Dead* helped the person manage the system by knowing each god's concerns. The final step is to cross the Lake of Flowers and enter the Reed Fields. According to George, part of what is unique to the Egyptians is how they thought about Paradise. "The ability to continue one's existence in essentially the same state as it was in the mortal realm spoke to a deep contentment within the Egyptians. They could not envision any place better than what they already had on Earth." Paradise was a continuation of the world they left, and if they achieved their goal, they would, in essence, live forever in their home with loved ones, animals, and pets.

Mesopotamia

Mesopotamia was made up of agrarian communities in the Fertile Crescent. The city of Uruk that we mentioned earlier was part of the Sumerian Civilization, dating from around 5000 to 1750 BCE. The Sumerians had one of the earliest forms of written language. Cuneiform dates from around 3400 BCE. Much of what was written was detailed clerical records. But by 3000 BCE, Sumerian scribes were recording essays, hymns, poetry, and myths. Two of the oldest literary works were the *Kesh Temple Hymn* and the *Instructions of Shuruppak*, dating to around 2500 BCE. The *Temple Hymn* was an ancient ode to the Kesh temple and the deities that inhabited it. The *Instructions* was a piece of wisdom literature (like Proverbs in the Tanakh). The *Instructions* take the form of sage advice from a Sumerian King Shuruppak to his son, Ziusudra. For example, one of the sayings warns the boy not to "pass judgment when you drink beer." This saying is always good advice. Another counsels that "a loving heart maintains a family; a hateful heart destroys a family."

Mesopotamian religions were polytheistic, with several main gods and many minor gods. The purpose of humanity was to serve the gods, although the high gods were too busy to worry about us. The lesser gods would relay the prayers of people to the high gods. One theme was nature's forces, often in the spirit of the early animistic religions mentioned earlier, with fertility deities displaying death and regeneration characteristics. There might be variations depending on whether the worshipers were marsh dwellers, orchard growers, herders, or farmers. Towns and communities would have patron gods. A second stage in the evolution of their religious beliefs was when various gods in more human form emerged, depending on the specific needs and contexts of different groups. By around 1000 BCE, there was a growing focus on the concepts of sin and forgiveness and a more hierarchical, monarchical structure in the gods being worshiped. This was associated with a greater faith and reliance on divine intervention in the here and now.

In general, the Mesopotamians believed in an underworld (or netherworld) that sometimes was referred to as the Great Below. It was known as "the land of no return" and "the house that none leaves who enters." Everyone, with a few exceptions (based on the nature of the death[61]) expected to go there irrespective of social status. Most of the time, it did not matter whether you were good or bad. Some might receive judgment from a god and end up living an afterlife of happiness. For everyone else, it wasn't much to write home about. Ending up there was neither punishment nor reward. They typically entered it from their graves (although there might be special entrances in cities). They would be stuck there unless a substitute was found or unless a god intervened to help them.

When a person died, their shade (a kind of ghost or spirit) would take on the dead person's memory or personality and descend to the underworld. The idea of physical immortality did not exist, and they did not have what we think of as a dualistic view of a body and a soul. Instead, in a sense, the life force of your body would be transformed into something new, a ghostly being with limited powers. This sounds like where Egyptian's might end up if their souls weren't light enough.

We have noted earlier that perhaps the oldest great work of literature, and one of the oldest religious texts, was the *Epic of Gilgamesh*, dating to around 3000 BCE. In the *Epic*, and it is an epic, the overarching story is about the conflict between humanity as represented by Gilgamesh, the hero, and fate. Gilgamesh is living a high life and is used to getting out of challenging situations through his mighty skills. The part of the *Epic* that is most relevant to us is when Gilgamesh goes on a quest to live forever that takes him to the underworld. He fails and so loses that ability both for himself and for the rest of the world. Recall that the moral, if you will, is "Life, which you look for, you will never find. For when the gods created man, they let death be his share, and life withheld in their own hands."

There were different descriptions of the underworld. As with the *Epic of Gilgamesh*, it could be represented as very dark and was a kind of experiential "returning to dust." At one point in the myth of Ishtar's descent to the underworld, it says, "[D]ust is their food and clay their nourishment, they see no light, where they dwell in darkness." On the other hand, other stories talk about ghosts as having houses and meeting with deceased family members and friends. Some accounts paint a picture where the actions of the living can impact the existence of the spirits in the underworld.

Once you were in the underworld, your relatives should make food and drink offerings in your honor to ease your existence. The eldest son in a family would typically be given an extra inheritance to help cover the offerings' costs. The underworld was believed to be short on good food and drink (e.g., the food was bitter and the water salty), and if the living did not provide it, then the ghosts would be forced to beg. It was believed that if offerings were not made, the spirits could come back and cause illnesses and other problems for the living. Necromancers would be consulted to learn whether various misfortunes were due to the dead or offenses against the gods. The Mesopotamians could also create magical knots, amulets, ointments and potions, and art that would work with incantations and rituals to help deal with vengeful ghosts.

Emerging Hinduism

Hinduism has its roots dating back more than four thousand years. Today it is the world's third-largest religion, with ninety-five percent of its followers living in India. It is not a single religion, but a family of religions composed of many traditions, philosophies, and customs. The sacred writings of Hinduism are the Vedas. The Vedas are made up of the Rigveda, the Samaveda, Yajurveda, and Atharvaveda. The oldest written version is from around 300 BCE, but the original codification in Sanskrit of the ancient wisdom probably goes back to as early as 1500 BCE.

Most forms of Hinduism worship a universal soul or God called *Brahman* and recognize other gods and goddesses. There is a part of Brahman in all living creatures, and it is called the *Atman*. They tend to feel there are multiple paths to reach Brahman. Hindus believe in the continuous cycle of life, death, and reincarnation. Three key gods are Brahma, Vishnu, and Shiva. Brahma's job was to create the world and its creatures. Vishnu is the preserver, and Shiva destroys so that re-creation can happen. They also believe in *karma*, the universal law of moral cause and effect. People's actions and thoughts directly determine the shape of their current life and their future lives. The goal is to achieve *moksha*, which ends the rebirth cycle as one becomes part of the absolute soul. As a result, they revere all living creatures. We will cover Hindu beliefs in more detail in Chapter 5 when we look at religion and the soul.

Early Israel

The oldest written reference to Israel is generally believed to be the Merneptah Stele. It mainly documents Pharaoh Merneptah's victories over the Libyans and their allies around 1210 BCE. It includes a separate campaign in Canaan, which was an imperial possession of Egypt. One line has been translated roughly as "Israel is laid waste, and his seed is not." The inscription is primarily formulaic and is often used to describe victory over defeated nations or peoples. The Canaanites were probably cities that had revolted. The question of who the Israelites in the stele were is still open. One interpretation is that the seed referenced stands for a group of people, and the Israelites were the nomadic group. Another interpretation is that the seed is grain, and so the Israelites were a settled farming people in the area. Other early references are the Mesha Stele, the Tel Dan Stele, and the Kurkh Monolith.

According to the scriptures of the Abrahamic religions, Abraham formed a covenant with God. It is estimated that he probably existed around 2000 to 1800 BCE (Archeology of the Hebrew Bible, 2008). Moses, in this chronology, would have lived around 1450 BCE. So far there is no definitive archeological evidence for the patriarch Abraham.[62] These events happened about the time when the first alphabet for writing began to emerge in Egypt (c. 1850 BCE). The alphabet itself was invented possibly by Canaanite workers in Egypt[63] and then began spreading through the Mediterranean. The oldest pieces of the Tanakh that we have today are the Silver Scrolls from around 650 to 587 BCE, containing a priestly blessing from the book of Numbers, and

The Merneptah Stele

The Great Isaiah Scroll from the Dead Sea Scrolls (c. 125 BCE). The reference on the Silver Scrolls does suggest there were earlier written forms of the Torah that we have not yet found.

One interpretation of the archeological record focuses on the hilltop villages from around 1300 to 1200 BCE, around the time of the Egyptian stele. Israeli archeologists have found remains of these villages in the hill country north and south of Jerusalem and in lower Galilee. The best evidence to date suggests less of a concept of wholesale conquest of the region and more of an evolution of Canaanites displaced from other areas. Those taking this position argue for more of a social and economic revolution rather than a military revolution. One could imagine nomadic groups migrating to and from Egypt, in particular, bringing their stories and experiences as well (including some religious ideas from the Egyptians). This radical change could presumably be accompanied by mythmaking in a Joseph Campbell sense over time, perhaps grounded in battles and other forms of conflict happening as Jewish communities defined themselves. We can imagine how the stories evolved by thinking about how the myths that are used to define ourselves as Americans have emerged and changed over the last couple of hundred years. The stories and other documentation appearing from this time are generally assumed to have drawn on earlier oral tradition and writing over hundreds of years or even longer, and then been organized and supplemented to form the accepted scriptures around the Babylonian exile period (600 to 530 BCE).

According to the account of William Dever, Professor Emeritus at the University of Arizona (Archeology of the Hebrew Bible, 2008), "It's interesting that in these hundreds of twelfth-century [BCE] settlements there are no temples, no palaces, no elite residences, no monumental architecture of any kind." Evidence of some cities being destroyed has been attributed to the sea peoples, such as the Philistines. Some argue that the people of the area began to develop their concept of God, and refined the origin story of humanity and themselves as a nation, in part to distinguish themselves from surrounding groups. They gradually developed new laws and customs, new markers, and a new culture with its memories. The Babylonian exile forced additional refinement of stories, beliefs, and practices. Of course, the history of archeology is that new things are discovered all the time.

Dever proposes that perhaps they were less "the chosen people" but instead more of "the choosing people" who chose to be free of their Canaanite past.[64] He recognizes some argue for the emergence of early Israel as a revolutionary social movement. He also sees them as more about agrarian social reform, throwing off corrupt overlords. They may have been abandoning an urban social structure that was in the process of collapsing. What he puzzles over, though, is "[W]hy these people were willing to take such a risk, colonizing the hill country frontier....I think there were social and economic compulsions, but I would be the first to say I think it was probably also a new religious vision."

Of course, Dever is approaching history from an archeologist's lens. From a faith lens, it could also be true that the people that emerged were chosen, but the choice could have been a process like creation through evolution. Thus, the Biblical stories from the period would be less about *facts* in the sense that we would think of history today and more about *facts* in the sense of the meanings that authors wanted to convey about their view of their origins and the relevance of those origins for their national identity. That would be consistent with what we know about that culture, say versus contemporary Western ways of thinking.

We will explore more about concepts of the soul and the afterlife in Jewish theology, starting from around the first century CE. But it is worth noting the ideas of the soul and the afterlife that reach back to the original Jewish views, presumably from Moses's time and earlier as carried in those stories that were eventually documented. While early Jewish views were intended to contrast with the cultures around them and may have adopted and adapted some of Egypt's afterlife ideas, some argue later Jewish views of the afterlife reflected concepts from Greek and Roman philosophical influences. This mix of ideas would have been the context in which later Christian doctrines emerged.

The concept of the soul as it is popularly thought of today does not appear in the earliest Jewish scriptures. The Hebrew words that are often translated as *soul* are neshama, ruach and nefesh.

- מה נ (neshama) - In the Genesis creation story, God "formed man of the dust of the ground, and breathed into his nostrils the breath of life; and man became a living soul" (Genesis 2.7, JPS). This "neshama" has as its root the sense of breath or breathing, and a related verb means "to pant." The verse's idea is about an animating element that brings the body to life, and it is not about personality or anything detachable from the body. God was not making a body from dust and then inserting a soul into it; instead, God's breath made the creature a soul, a whole thing that was a human.

- רוח (ruach or ruah) - Ruach is used as in "My spirit shall not abide in man forever, for that he also is flesh; therefore shall his days be a hundred and twenty years" (Genesis 6.3, JPS). Ruach often means "wind" but also is related to "breath." The sense is the movement of air when breathing. Israelites associated life with the physical movement of the chest and flaring of the nostrils when breathing, as in Genesis 7:22 (JPS) "[A]ll in whose nostrils was the breath of the spirit of life, whatsoever was in the dry land, died." Here refers to God's spirit, and it will disappear from the body at death. Later scriptures, however, carry a sense of this breath as not just disappearing, but as something coming from God that returns to God. "Then shall the dust return to the earth as it was: and the spirit shall return unto God who gave it" (Ecclesiastes 12:7, JPS).

- נֶפֶשׁ (nefesh) – The third word is nefesh, and it can be used to mean "person" or "living" being. Nefesh derives from the word for neck, as in Jonah 2:26, "the water reached the neck." More generally, across scriptures, it means being, life, self, or person and is used for derivative ideas like desire, appetite, emotion, and passion (Rutman, 2016). In Leviticus 17:11 (JPS), it says, "For the life of the flesh is in the blood, and I have given it to you upon the altar to make atonement for your souls; for it is the blood that maketh atonement by reason of the life." Here nefesh is translated as the "life" of the flesh, and its association with blood applies to animals and humans as a life force. In the Genesis 2.7 reference, nefesh is translated as "living soul." The rabbinic understanding as a "living soul" is synonymous with a living person. Brevard Childs, one of the most influential biblical scholars of the twentieth century, says the sense here is we do not have souls; we are souls. It is worth noting that at this point, nefesh does not carry the idea of immortality. For example, see Genesis 35:18 (JPS), where it says, "as her soul was in departing—for she died—that she called his name Ben-oni."

  Two other variations are interesting for this word. As with how we use the word soul today, nefesh can be used in the sense of "self." It can also refer to one's body and its desire, as in "The soul of the wicked desireth evil: his neighbour findeth no favour in his eyes" Proverbs 21:10 (JPS). Proverbs 23:2 (JPS) says, "[P]ut a knife to thy throat, if thou be a man given to appetite." In Genesis 2:19 (JPS), it reads, "[O]ut of the ground HaShem G-d formed every beast of the field, and every fowl of the air; and brought them unto the man to see what he would call them; and whatsoever the man would call every living creature, that

was to be the name thereof." The word for creature was nefesh (another place where the same
word is used for humans and animals).

While it is not as explicitly clear from the texts themselves,
many Jews of the period probably had some of the common
beliefs of the peoples around them (e.g., from the Mesopotamian and Egyptian influences) of a dualistic view of a soul and
a body. Richard Steiner (Steiner, 2015), a Bible and Semitics
scholar from Yeshiva University, makes this case and says,
"[T]he evidence suggests that a belief in the existence of disembodied souls was part of the common religious heritage of
the peoples of the ancient Near East." Indeed, by the rabbinic
period, the neshama included the idea of something that God
deposited in us to make us human.

Over time, these ideas evolved to those discussed in Chapter 6, where we look at religion and the soul. In general, it is
felt that a concept of an immaterial and immortal soul that is
distinct from our body was not commonly found in Judaism
before the Babylonian exile. Philo of Alexandria (c. 15 BCE to
50 CE) was a Greek-speaking Jewish philosopher and notable
representative of Hellenistic Judaism. Philo saw these early
words translated as the soul as compatible with Plato's view of
the soul as having three parts (i.e., the logos, the reason that
resides in the head; the thumos, related to anger and located in
the chest; and eros, one's desires, centered in the stomach).

While recognizing a dualist view of a separate body and
soul, other early sages of the Talmud did not see the body as a
kind of prison for the soul. Instead, they saw them in harmony.
For example, Tractate Berakhot in the Babylonian Talmud
says, "Just as the Holy One of Blessing fills the world, so does
the soul [neshama] fill the body. Just as the Holy One of Blessing sees but cannot be seen, so does the soul see but cannot be
seen...Just as the Holy One of Blessing is pure, so is the soul
pure." The idea is that the soul and the body are separate, but
they are indivisible partners in human life. The body is the vehicle or tool that God provides to do sacred work in the world.
As a result, the body is not the enemy; it is a holy instrument
that allows us to act.

Persia and Zoroastrianism

The early Persian view of the afterlife can be framed as an evolution from the Mesopotamian, perhaps influenced by Egyptian thinking. For the Persians, after someone died, their soul lingered near the body for three days before going to the underworld. Their underworld was governed by King Yima, the first great Persian mortal king who, while initially favored by the gods, eventually sinned and fell from grace. His job was to keep the dead in his kingdom and the living out.

Zoroastrian Tower of Silence

As with the Mesopotamians, the dead's welfare depended on the prayers and remembrances of the living. People would spend those three days after death in prayer and fasting. During that time, a person's soul would be confused and susceptible to a demonic attack. A dog might be brought near the corpse to drive evil spirits away because it was believed the dog could see into the spiritual world, and evil spirits would be afraid of it. The body might be placed on an outdoor scaffolding, also known as a tower of silence, for scavengers to pick at it, and the bones would eventually be buried. During this time, the soul would be wandering around. Still, ultimately, it would need to cross a dark river by boat, where the good and the bad would eventually be separated into their respective final homes. As with the Egyptians or the Book of Life in Revelation, there was an idea of scales held by Mithra weighing the good and the bad who were rewarded or punished as appropriate.

Over time, the living needed to keep the memory of the dead alive. The first year was especially important since the dead would be disoriented and feeling a bit lost and lonely.

These rites of remembrance could last thirty years or more, or until the next of kin's death. As with Mesopotamia, food, prayers, and other sacrifices were made for their well-being. The Sumerian equivalent of the Day of the Dead was their New Year's Eve, when the souls were thought to return temporarily.

Zoroastrianism emerged in this context. It may have arisen as early as four thousand years ago in Persia, and is considered by some potentially to be the world's first monotheistic religion. It is worth noting that an argument has been made that the three Wise Men or the Magi mentioned in the Christian New Testament were Zoroastrians, who looked to the stars to identify a messiah.[65] Zoroastrianism shares a lot of key concepts with Judaism and Christianity (e.g., monotheism, angels and demons, resurrection, and the messiah), and it is likely there was a lot of contact between Jews and Persian (now Iranian) Zoroastrians at the time (Jackson, 1906).

For Zoroastrians, a higher self places the soul in a body to fight on the side of good in this physical realm. Your higher self will try to help you in this fight. When you are weighed for good and bad deeds, you will travel to the bridge that connects the living and the dead, and you will be reunited with your higher self. Two dogs guarding the bridge will welcome the good and snarl at the bad. The good will easily pass over, and the bad will have to fight their way. You will then be judged and sent to one of the four levels of Paradise or one of the four levels of hell.

Unlike some religions, a loving God could not bear anyone being eternally lost at the end of time. Eventually, a messiah would come who would bring the end of time, and all would be reunited with their loved ones and live in peace with God eternally.

Ancestor Worship in China

Early Bronze Age China started around the Xia Dynasty (from 2070 to 1600 BCE). While ancestor worship is often associated with Confucianism today, the family was always at the core of Chinese society and government. Respect for one's ancestors has long been a part of their culture. Confucianism grew with this filial piety as a key tenet (Cartwright, 2017). During the Shang Dynasty (1600 to 1046 BCE), the royal family's ancestors were viewed as being in heaven as a part of the feudal hierarchy of spirits and gods. A shaman could be used to make contact with them. By the Zhou period (1046 to 256 BCE), the rulers' ancestors had their own temples (often within palace complexes).

Chinese Ancestral Shrine

The idea was that each person, even if not royal, had a spirit that required sacrifices. Each person was viewed as having two souls, one that went to heaven and the other remaining in the corpse. The one in the corpse required regular offerings of nourishment. While eventually, this latter soul would migrate to the afterlife, if it was hungry, it could trouble the living. To head that off, they would include grave goods with the burial that might be needed in the afterlife, and then they were required to make regular offerings.

Most did not view this as a burden but rather as a mutual arrangement between the dead and the living. The living support the dead, and the dead might participate in the affairs of the living by advising and conferring benefits on their descendants. They were seen as part of the family, in the same way as the political order on earth was viewed as part of the organization of the gods themselves. This support of the living for the dead did not just include food and other offerings; it included remembering them and reverently treasuring their names, including through the arts. In the Han period (206 BCE to 220 CE), poems and other texts were common. Lewis (Lewis, 2010) provides an example from the period:

> *"Prosperity and decline each has its season,*
> *I grieve that I did not make a name for myself earlier.*
> *Human life lacks the permanence of metal and stone.*
> *How could we lengthen its years?*
> *We suddenly transform, in the way of all matter,*
> *but a glorious name is a lasting treasure."*

Ancestor worship began for a son when his father was still alive. Once the father died, the son would wear humble clothes such as an unhemmed, coarse hemp garment, as long as three years after the father's death. At the gravesite, a stone was set up to commemorate the family member and honor their deeds. The idea was that one's words inscribed in this way would not decay and would last forever.

While there were extravagant shrines and offerings for the royalty and the wealthy, offerings were also made at family shrines by the heads of families. The offerings tended to be targeted to the senior males of the previous three generations. The homes of ordinary citizens had a room to set up a shrine with wooden tablets recording the ancestors' history, both male and female. The oldest tablets with each generation might be burned, buried, or moved to a temple if the family was wealthy. The remaining tablets might be brought out at wedding ceremonies to be honored and show the joining of families.

DEEPER DIVE

Digging Up Burial Practices[66]

Let's reflect on the progress of ideas so far and speculate a little. Early on, there was burial, and the burials tended to be close to where the family was living. Then rituals began to emerge, including burying using red ochre, positioning the bodies carefully, and including grave goods that belonged to the person buried. It appears animism emerged early, along with a sense of our personal soul (something we have, as do other living things). This sense of having or being a soul that might persist is still commonly held today. Next to emerge was a belief in another world beyond this one grew, along with a recognition of those who could interact with it and influence the forces within it (e.g., shamans). As we will see later, this belief could have been reinforced by near-death and altered state experiences among members of communities, and the sense of spirits from the other side that are common among those who are grieving for the loss of loved ones.

Around this time, an idea grew that those who have died are there, influencing this world. It would be natural to look especially to shamans who died to be there since they already have communicated between worlds and were known to hold power over both worlds' forces, and powerful people might claim a special place in the afterlife in part to reinforce their role in this one. We would, of course, want our loved ones, elders, and ancestors to be there, and families could easily feel an urge to reach out to them for their personalized help. Ancestor worship began to emerge. Add to this the evolving beliefs in a God or gods ruling out of that other realm, and the outline of more formal religions starts to take shape.

Where is this spiritual world? It could be in the heavens, in some kind of parallel existence, or in the earth where people are placed (perhaps in some sense planted) when they die. The land would be the source of life for hunter-gatherers, and the death-birth-life-death cycle would be associated with the earth. The forces of power for good or ill (the sun and moon, forces of nature, and so on), typically associated with what might be recognized as gods, might be more likely to come from above.

As civilizations began to emerge, the structure they brought to life in the here and now might be mirrored at some level in the next life, since what we know influences how we think about what we do not know. As religions became more formalized, they would need origin stories and stories about the afterlife to provide a rationale for behavioral norms in this world. Rituals either owned by or guided by shamans might be expected to evolve into priesthoods guiding cultural practices, blessed and supported by those in power who could leverage them.

Following the emergence of animism, shamanism, and ancestor worship, Anthony Martin (Martin, 2020) notes that the Sumerians and the Babylonians believed in an underworld where the dead went, and so burial provided easy access. The graves were often near where people lived, so it was easier to bring offerings such as food and beverages. These offerings might provide a better afterlife for the dead, and while they were at it might appease the gods. With their more elaborate theology and rituals, the Egyptians buried their dead with a wide variety of things they might need in the afterlife (including pets). Because Egypt was so hot and arid, mummification emerged as part of the ritual practices, and, of course, we all know about the pyramids and the special care that was taken for the most powerful. Regular people sometimes wanted to be mummified and buried near the powerful or important religious centers to get a little of the spiritual halo effect.

During their most prosperous period, the Celts (750 BCE to 12 BCE) occupied the British Isles, France, and some parts of Germany. During their earliest period, they tended to bury people in urns. As their culture evolved, they buried their dead with various personal items, some very valuable and that we can use now to track trade among communities at the time. At one period, they laid out the dead in carts and would have a large feast. There would be songs and poems in their honor. Stone cairns might often be erected at the site. While clearly they believed in life after death, not a lot is known about the details of their religious beliefs.

The Druids, as a special subset of Celts, did believe in the transmigration of souls and the power of the gods. The Irish, as they do, painted a rather lovely picture of the afterlife. Their otherworld was sometimes underground, and sometimes it consisted of islands in the sea. It was called things like "the Land of the Living," "Delightful Plain," and "Land of the Young." It was believed to be a place without sickness, old age, or death, where happiness lasts forever. A hundred years is like a day. It was similar to the idea of the Greek Elysium (the paradise of where those blessed by the gods are sent), and it may have its roots in earlier Indo-European traditions. In other words, their afterlife is much like the more common view of heaven today.

The Greeks (and similarly, the Romans) were focused on getting the body to the underworld as quickly as possible, so the pneuma (or breath) could reach its next state. The body was anointed in oil, wrapped, and buried with a coin placed under the tongue as the fee for Charon, the River Styx's ferryman. The ferry would be carrying the soul to the underworld. A procession of mourners might carry the prepared body after a day or two to a final resting place or a pyre. The Greeks, like the Egyptians, also believed that preserving the memory of people through art contributed to their immortality.

During the middle of the Roman Republic, there was a shift from burying bodies to cremation. After cremation, the ashes would be placed in urns or altars. People would put food and wine on the altars to celebrate the spirits of their dead. The proper offerings and rites would help keep the dead well disposed towards the living. The Romans might even build virtual cities outside of their actual cities, and they would be filled with sepulchers, shrines, and individual tombs. Several generations might be buried together, and the poorer might be buried up against the wealthy's more elaborate tombs.[67] According to Plutarch (a Roman historian and philosopher), a practice known as *os resectum* or "cut-off bone" emerged in the first century CE. People would cut off a single finger before cremation. Then the finger would be buried to complete the household purifaction and a connection with the Earth itself.

Towards the end of the Roman period (around the reign of Hadrian), there was a shift back to burials. Some point to the Jewish community and the rise of Christianity as the source of the return to inhumation. Others argue for the emergence of mystery religions, changes in the practices of the wealthier class due to the cost of cremation, and other reasons for the difference. Bodies were buried whole and often were preserved in stone coffins or full-size sarcophagi. According to Roman law, bodies could not be buried within two miles of the city walls. As a result, people started to dig burial networks (catacombs) in the soft bedrock under the area around Rome. The catacombs were originally tunnels dug by the Etruscans, and then adapted by the Jewish community and Christians for burials. Their use for burials gradually expanded. The miles of tunnels were lined with spaces for bodies, and included larger areas for funeral feasts and ceremonies to honor the dead and help them be comfortable in the afterlife. Later, as Christianity spread through the Empire, it was common to see people buried with their feet pointing East. The idea is that it would make it easier for them to rise at the last judgment meeting Christ face-to-face.

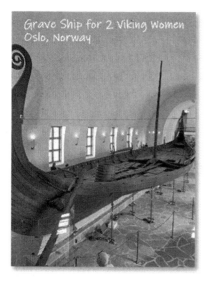

Grave Ship for 2 Viking Women
Oslo, Norway

The Vikings coming along in the early part of the Viking Age (and as the Roman Empire was ending) were inclined to cremate their dead. The ashes would then be deposited in areas that would have been meaningful, such as in the land or at sea. The belief was that the smoke would carry the spirit of the person to the right place. But as the Vikings were becoming Christian, the idea that the body would eventually resurrect meant that they started believing there should be a body to resurrect. They began to bury their dead.

In Norse mythology, their hell (Helheim) was a place for those who died a dishonorable death due to being too lazy.

Heaven (Valhalla) was for fallen warriors. When they were buried, they would be buried with the things that represented them in life. Indeed, a warrior would want to be buried with their weapons and a craftsperson with their tools. Burning ship burials, which we see in the movies, were relatively less common and probably mainly were used for ships' captains and others receiving special honor.

Elsewhere in the world, around the time of the Sumerians and Babylonians, Hinduism was emerging in India. We will dig deeper into Hindu beliefs later, and Hinduism covers a wide variety of beliefs. In general, though, the body is seen as just a vessel for the soul. When a Hindu dies, the body will be anointed by a priest with oils, incense, and water from the sacred Ganges River. Mantras will be chanted. The body will be bathed, wrapped in cloth, and cremated. Offerings will be made during the process. At some points in history, wives and servants might also be killed and be part of the cremation. After cremation, the ashes ideally will be thrown into the Ganges (the most sacred river). A less common alternative might be to leave the body out in the open on a structure erected on a hill to be eaten by carrion predators. Now we might even think of that as an early version of a green burial.

Buddhism emerged about the time of the Babylonian exile. We will talk about Buddhism more, but a core idea is that meditation and self-knowledge can help manage the suffering we experience in our day-to-day lives. Many cultures try to help ease those who are dying into a peaceful death by whispering Buddhist scriptures into their ears. Bodies would then be bathed, and along with flowers and burial items would be cremated. Early Cambodians and Indonesians believed in reincarnation, and bodies would be placed on ceremonial funeral pyres.

Also, around the time of the Sumerians and the Babylonians, and the growth of Hinduism, civilization was emerging in China. Martin notes that ancient Eastern Asian beliefs tended to be focused on ancestors, whose spirits could still influence this world. They needed to be appeased or might become mischievous.[68] Across much of Chinese history, burial practices included burial in a tomb or grave with personal property, and then there would be ritual funeral ceremonies. Representations of earthly belongings could be buried with people, as well as burial offerings that would accompany the rituals. As with the Egyptians, the idea is that people would need the things they used in life in the next life, along with their valuable belongings.

Perhaps the most famous Chinese burial for many of us would

be the terra-cotta soldiers and other grave goods buried with Qin Shi Huangdi, the first emperor of China. He lived a couple of hundred years before the Roman Empire was founded. The eight thousand soldiers and the burial complex were designed to symbolize his realm.

Another example is Xin Zhui, or Lady Dai. She lived around 168 BCE, and her well-preserved mummy was found in 1968. It was clear from the mummy and her grave goods she lived a pretty extravagant lifestyle. Her burial was notable for all the different kinds of exotic foods buried with her and everything needed to prepare them. She died with coronary thrombosis and arteriosclerosis, and other diseases associated with her, um, weight. The one hundred and thirty-eight melon seeds found in her stomach were part of the final meal that introduced her to the afterlife.

Terra Cotta Warrior

Going back to the time of the Babylonians and through the Middle Ages in Europe, civilization was prospering in the Americas as well. Martin suggests the Mayan and the Aztec beliefs were similar in some ways to those of the Egyptians. The Aztecs would bury their dead in tombs underground at the bottom of vertical shafts along with livestock, slaves, and other belongings. The Mayan elite might have elaborate tombs with masks, gems, food, and slaves buried with them, while the more common people might be buried under their houses. The various rites of the Aztecs and the Mayans depended on status and afterlife expectations. People could be buried with a green stone placed in their mouth because it represented the heart, where the soul was thought to reside. The Incas, living in the mountains, mummified their bodies. The bodies of important people might be brought out for special occasions. Eternal life for a loved one depended on making sure they were not forgotten or caused to be irrelevant, and so their bodies might be treated as advisors and confidantes.

In some cultures, the body is on display as part of the burial process. During the Victorian period in Europe, postmortem photography emerged as a way to preserve a presence of those who had died among the living (and it continues around the world today). Some dress up the bodies in their best clothes as a reflection of their lives. Others may clothe the body in shrouds that speak to their new state. They may be dressed in ceremonial garb, perhaps with sacred or symbolic objects, to aid in reaching the afterlife. They are sometimes buried with the things they will need in the afterlife. In other cultures, burial with belongings is more about just being the right thing to do. After all, since they were the person's belongings, it would not be suitable for the belongings to go to others. It is a way to honor the owners.

Post-mortem Photography

Today, we are exploring new forms of burial (e.g., green burials) that may even have desirable symbolic meaning along with practical benefits for the environment. Someday, we may leave virtual versions of ourselves. Artificial intelligence might be capable of sharing stories from our lives and providing comforting dialogue with the living. It might even do a reasonable job of representing the kind of advice we might want to give to the living. In essence, we may use technology to take ancient Chinese and Incan practices of engaging ancestors as advisors to the next level.[69] Indeed, as represented in our internet and social media footprints, our digital lives are likely to live on long after us. Deep fakes of ourselves are undoubtedly going to get better. Laws are adapting to deal with the management of those digital rights after we are gone. For religions where eternal life is partly the presence of our memories, we have to wonder whether we have to be remembered by other people who, in turn, will pass away or whether being *remembered* in the digital cloud counts.

Then there is the story of my mother. She died of Alzheimer's. During her life, she loved chocolate. It was her favorite thing to eat, and as she moved to the long-term care facility, her favorite gift was getting a box of chocolates. So as her children, when there was little else we could get her for birthdays and holidays, we always knew the chocolates would be a hit. Unfortunately, towards the end of her Alzheimer's, her memory loss meant that she sometimes forgot she had eaten her chocolate or where she had left it. She would call us in distress, convinced that one of the other patients or one of the staff had stolen her chocolates. When we buried her, my sisters and I included a box of Ghirardelli chocolate that no one will ever steal. We smile every time we remember that moment and as we think about her.

TITLE Burial Practice Observations

o Ritual burials date to Neanderthals and early humans
o Evolved with symbolic thought and art
o Cultural and personal rituals honor the dead
o Rituals provide emotional closure and relief
o Rituals preserve "relationships" beyond death
o It is important to remember those who have passed, and the memories may be sources of insight for the living
o Some grave goods rituals are for providing a better afterlife; others are about expressing honor
o Animism and shamanism helped provide some influence over forces beyond ourselves
o Religions became more complex with the growth of civilization
o Religions turned afterlife theology into culture

---

[49] Research suggests this practice also served to release far more calories for their nourishment, which in turn allowed intelligence to develop faster.

[50] As a chemist, therefore, I could argue my field goes way back.

[51] Early on, before the color red became associated with ritual behaviors, it may have come to our attention for its survival value. The ability to see red, especially against a green background, would have been a valuable adaptation for early primates. It would help primates to identify which fruits were ripe and ready to eat. As humans evolved, it could be a short step to imagine the red of the pigments as something that might carry a meaning associated with the blood of life or the change of seasons, in a world that continually reflects birth, maturing, death and rebirth.

[52] Some hearths were stacked on top of one another.

[53] We will be discussing this phenomenon more in a later chapter, when we explore the implications of the fuzzy boundary between life and death.

[54] I have been binge watching the TV series *Fringe*, and this brings a lot of resonance at the moment.

[55] In early Chinese civilization, various tribes held animistic, shamanistic, and totemic beliefs. Shamans could reach out to the spiritual world using prayers, sacrifices and offerings. By the Shang dynasty (1600 to 1046 BCE) they were worshiping ancestors and god-kings. The world was not seen as being created by a god, per se, but ancestors and kings might exist as divine forces after death that could influence this world.

[56] As a point of reference, the Neolithic lasted until around 1700 BCE in Northern Europe, and ended much earlier around 5000 BCE in the Near East. As a reminder, the patriarch Abraham, from which traditionally Christianity, Judaism and Islam sprang would have been born around 2000 BCE, during the Bronze Age in the Near East.

[57] For us cat lovers, domestication of cats (or of humans by cats) happened around 7500 BCE. Cats began being worshiped in Egypt around 3100 BCE, and of course the cats believe it continues to this day.

[58] These are two of the rivers in the Hebrew Bible associated with the Garden of Eden.

[59] This, of course, is the opposite goal from the one Dr. MacDougall had. He was interested in a soul that had some weight!

[60] For those who are fans of Douglas Adam's *Hitchhiker's Guide to the Galaxy*, we note that forty-two is the answer to the ultimate question of life, the universe, and everything. This somehow seems appropriate.

[61] Death by fire or death in a desert might not result in any ghost at all.

[62] Although there has been work on excavating Ur itself, where Abraham is said to have started his journey.

[63] There is speculation that the alphabet was derived from hieroglyphics being used at the time, in order to help with communication among the workers who may not have been able to read the hieroglyphics themselves.

[64] Not unlike the Puritans coming to America.

[65] Some believe they were Semites, and with Jews and Arabs could fit into the Torah's listing of the descendants of Noah's son Shem.

[66] In this section we will be reviewing what are known as primary burials, the initial burial. There are also secondary burials. This term refers to the situation where all or some of the remains from the

primary burial are exhumed and then reburied. Secondary burials have happened since the Paleolithic period, and continued through the Mesolithic and Neolithic through the Metal Ages up until today. They are often motivated by the reuse of burial space and construction. It might happen because of natural disasters (e.g., the flooding that used to impact the graves in New Orleans). There are examples of bones from crowded cemeteries being collected to be used in architecture (e.g., in ossuaries). Ancient Egypt, of course, is famous for subsequent grave robbing, and grave robbing has spiked at various points of history in Europe and other countries around the world. Today, it may be the result of archeological work and the need to reinter bodies in order to respect tribal traditions. I would add the way the bones of indigenous people have been treated has often not only been disrespectful, it directly impacts how the tribes view the welfare of their ancestors in the afterlife. Secondary burials may also be part of the full ritual for managing bodies or to help improve the spiritual condition of the deceased in the afterlife, and it might involve special secondary funeral ceremonies. For example, in the area of modern Syria (Levant) during the Neolithic period there was a practice of separating the skull from the body, plastering it, and giving it a secondary burial.

[67] This happened in Egypt as well.

[68] It is probably a sign of the age we live in that the idea of my becoming someone's ancestor and coming back to my great-grandchildren as a mischievous spirit makes me smile.

[69] William Shatner, for example, has announced he is creating an AI of himself that friends and family can continue to interact with even after he is gone. See www.cnet.com/news/william-shatner-turns-90-ai-version-of-him-will-live-on-indefinitely/.

Chapter 4

THE PHILOSOPHY
OF THE SOUL

"This is patently absurd; but whoever wishes to become a philosopher must learn not to be frightened by absurdities."
— Bertrand Russell

Next, we are going dip into a critical but also challenging area, philosophy. William James (who we will cover in this chapter) once observed, "There is only one thing a philosopher can be relied upon to do, and that is to contradict other philosophers." He also said, "Philosophy is at once the most sublime and the most trivial of human pursuits." My goal here is to highlight some of the ideas that have influenced discussions that continue to shape our culture today. But each idea fits within a more extensive system of thought that we will not be able to cover fully. I will attempt to give a taste of each philosopher and provide a way to think about some of the ideas relevant to our understanding of the soul. Be warned, in some areas it will take a little chewing to digest them.

I recommend three of my sourcebooks if you are interested in this area. Two which take slightly different views are Stewart Goetz and Charles Taliaferro (Goetz, 2011) and their book *A Brief History of the Soul*, and Raymond Martin and John Barresi (Martin, 2006) and their book *The Rise and Fall of Soul and Self: An Intellectual History of Personal Identity*. Goetz and Taliaferro trace the history of the soul and debate alternative views in Western philosophy from its birth to more contemporary ideas about the *mind*. Martin and Barresi approach the topic through the lens of how we define personal identity, as that idea has changed from early ideas about the soul to the more recent challenges to the concept of a unified self. A third is *Neuroscience and the Soul: The Human Person in Philosophy, Science, and Theology* by Thomas M. Crisp, Steven L. Porter, and Gregg A. Ted Elshoe (Eds.). This volume collects essays by a group of philosophers, theologians, and scientists who gathered at Biola University for a conference to explore and debate the idea that we are composed of a soul and a body (substantive dualism) versus the belief that everything about us can be explained through natural laws (physicalism).

Let's begin by going back to the roots of the philosophy of the soul. Two of the most significant ancient Greek poems were the *Iliad* and the *Odyssey*, typically attributed to Homer.[70] They were probably written down during the seventh or eighth century BCE. According to the *Stanford Encyclopedia of Philosophy* (Ancient Theories of the Soul, 2009) the soul is risked in battle and lost at death in Homeric poems. When it departs at death, it travels to the underworld (called Hades by the Greeks), where it lives a pitiful existence as a shade or image of the person who has died. The absence of the soul from the body is what defines death.

There is nothing in these early poems that suggests the soul is responsible for life's activities. The soul primarily comes to mind when it is at risk. For example, in the *Iliad,* Achilles says he continually risks his soul, and Agenor reflects on Achilles having just one soul. The soul is not a generic life force in these poems. Only human beings are said to lose their souls, and there is never a mention of the shades of non-human creatures in Hades.

By the fifth and sixth centuries BCE in Greece, however, the concept of the soul began to develop further. In the popular culture of the day, having a soul meant being alive. There was an adjective *ensouled* (empsuchos) that meant *alive*. Moving beyond the Homeric poems, it applied to everything alive, and living things move. Thales of Miletus (mathematician, astronomer, and credited by Aristotle as the first Greek philosopher) was even said to attribute soul to magnets, reasoning that magnets were capable of causing iron to move (Aristotle, *De Anima*).

The concept of the *soul* also begins to take on the kinds of properties we often use in popular language today. People were said to satisfy their souls with rich food, and both the souls of gods and humans were said to be subject to sexual desire. In moments of intense emotion, feelings of love, hate, joy, grief, anger, and shame were associated with the soul. For example, Oedipus says his soul laments the misery of his city (*Oedipus Tyrannus*). The soul becomes connected with boldness and courage, and the soul is recognized as the source and carrier of moral qualities such as temperance and justice.

According to the *Stanford Encyclopedia of Philosophy* (Lorenz, 2009), "To educated fifth century [BCE] speakers of Greek, it would have been natural to think of qualities of soul as accounting for, and being manifested in, a person's morally significant behavior. Pericles acts courageously, and Hippolytus temperately (or chastely) because of the qualities of their souls from which such actions have a strong tendency to flow, and their actions express and make evident the courage, temperance, and the like that characterize their souls." If the soul is responsible for moral action, then the next step in the evolution of the concept would be to give it the ability to think and plan. Antiphon, in a speech to a jury, says "take away from the accused the soul that planned the crime." Since the criminal's soul is responsible for the crime, it would be appropriate to remove it from the body.

With the soul as the animator of matter, the idea could be applied not just to animals but also to plants. Empedocles (the philosopher who came up with the division of earth, air, fire, and water) and Pythagoras (philosopher and mathematician that most of us know from high school math class and the Pythagorean theorem) believed plants have souls. Human souls could even have been plants at some point. Pythagoras, a little like the actress Shirley MacLaine who brought reincarnation to our popular consciousness, is said to have remembered many of his previous incarnations. Empedocles was especially interested in medicine and was viewed at the time as a miracle worker, including having brought the dead back to life. He was said to have cured illness by the power of music. As a believer in reincarnation, Empedocles claimed to have been a shrub at one point, and a bird and a fish in other lives.[71]

Pythagoreanism further explored these ideas and the implications for the continued existence of the person after death. To make a continued existence meaningful, the soul has to be more than just a generic life force or shade; it should have states, activities, and operations, representing the person's identity (incl. the personality). There is a story about Pythagoras reported by Xenophanes, an ancient Greek poet, that goes "Once, they say, he was passing by when a puppy was being whipped, and he took pity and said: 'Stop, do not beat it; it is the soul of a friend that I recognized when I heard its [i.e., the soul's] voice.'" What he was saying is that he recognized his friend's soul as doing the yelping!

By the time of Socrates' death, the human soul distinguished us as living things, experienced emotions, and had characteristics like courage and justice. Through Plato and Aristotle's time, the concept of the soul broadened to include attributes of the mind like thought, perception and desire, and moral qualities. It accounted for most of the organism's vital functions and defined what it meant to be human. As Plato and Aristotle came on the scene, the soul was not just a source of life, emotion, and virtue; it began to think. It housed our minds with properties like consciousness, thought, and desire.[72] These ideas were the context upon which Plato and Aristotle built, and their ideas (often filtered through Roman thinkers) impacted later Jewish and Christian theologians.

PLATO (428 TO 347 BCE)

"The only thing I know is that I know nothing."
- Socrates

Socrates and Plato lived at a critical time in Greek culture when scientific advances challenged traditional religious beliefs (Martin, 2006). This period is similar to the thirteenth century when Aristotle's ideas and Islamic science transformed European thinkers. It was also similar to the seventeenth century when physical science began to displace Aristotelianism, and the period around the 1900s when Dr. MacDougall was practicing. And as we have noted, we are in another time of revolutions in science, engineering, and medicine now.

Jacques-Louis David
The Death of Socrates

Goetz and Taliaferro (Goetz, 2011) provide an excellent overview of Plato's beliefs. For Plato, the *soul gives life to the body*, which means it cannot perish. The soul *is* the person, in contrast to the body or the *combination* of a soul and body. This distinction between the soul and the body is *dualism*.[73] The idea that we do not have a soul but are a soul continues to resonate with many people's experiences today (versus we are a body and therefore our existence is finite). The soul is indestructible, while the body will decay and disappear. In the *Phaedo*, in response to a question from a friend about how he would like to be buried, Plato says Socrates[74] replied, "Any way you like…that is, if you can catch me and I don't slip through your fingers….I shall remain with you [Crito and other friends] no longer, but depart to a state of heavenly happiness….You [the other friends] must give an assurance to Crito for me…that when I am dead I shall not stay, but depart and be gone." In essence, Socrates is his soul, and as such, exists without a specific body.

As context for his thinking, it should be noted that Plato did not believe the physical world was the *real* world. The real world is the *spiritual realm* that lies behind this world. This world is continually changing and is imperfect. The spiritual reality is made up of *Forms* which are the abstract, perfect, unchanging concepts or ideals that transcend time and space. This world is but a shadow of the ultimate reality of this realm of Forms.[75] The soul then is fundamentally of the realm of Forms. It is simple and essential, like a Form. Because it is simple, it is without substance. Furthermore, because it is without substance and does not depend on substance, we are essentially immortal. During Socrates' and Plato's time, many Greeks saw one's last breath as us (in the form of our souls) leaving the body. This is what my sisters felt they saw at my grandmother's end. Plato's view, in contrast, is that breath is a substance, and as substance, the breath would be divisible. If the last breath is divisible (despite what Dr. MacDougall was looking for), the breath cannot be the soul.

The Forms might be abstract objects like concepts of justice, humanness, rationality, and triangle, or the abstract, perfect versions of tree, house, mountain, man, woman, cloud, horse, cat, table, and chair. The soul is most fulfilled when it experiences and reasons about the Forms directly. The soul loves and seeks truth. The soul is less about memory than about reason and intellect. A computer analogy might be that the soul is more like the operation of an artificial intelligence *program* than what is stored on the disk *memory*. Plato says the cardinal virtues that we should aspire to are wisdom, temperance, courage, and justice; and these virtues express the true nature of our souls.

Plato also reasons that since one thing always comes from another thing, the soul must come from the realm of the *dead,* and after life is over, it will return to it. Furthermore, that coming and going for most is an ongoing cycle of reincarnation. A Greek belief in reincarnation is unexpected for many of us in

Western cultures since we usually associate it with Hinduism and Buddhism. It is, however, grounded in a rich human history of similar beliefs, and other thinkers held it at the time. Ancient humans would have noticed the rhythm of life across the seasons—its birth, life, death, and rebirth—and imagined humans as part of that cycle. According to some, you might eventually achieve the highest level when reincarnated if you have lived virtuous lives. For Plato, of course, the highest level is seeking wisdom and truth (e.g., being a philosopher). On the other hand, if you led a life of just satisfying physical desire, you might end up as a donkey. The model is similar to Hindu and Buddhist beliefs.

The idea of reincarnation, and the fundamental awareness of Forms that our souls have, has an interesting implication for Plato. In the *Meno,* Plato says, "Thus the soul, since it is immortal and has been born many times, and has seen all things both here and in the other world, has learned everything that is. So we need not be surprised if it can recall the knowledge of virtue or anything else which…it once possessed…for seeking and learning are nothing but recollection" (*Meno*). This is illustrated with a story about how a slave boy, when asked the right questions, could "rediscover" the proof for the Pythagorean theorem.

Plato shares one insightful story that brings several of these ideas together in unexpected ways (Burton, 2012). It has been seen as an inspiration for later Christian beliefs about heaven, hell, and even purgatory. At the end of Plato's *Republic,* Socrates is explaining that the soul is immortal. To illustrate it, he tells the story of Er. Er was slain in battle, but on his funeral pyre, returned to life to share his own near-death experience. During the twelve days he was dead, he went to a meadow with four doorways, two to the heavens and two to the earth below (in essence, hells). Judges were sending the good to the heavens and the bad to the hells. Some souls returned from one of the openings to a heaven, and some were returning from one of the hells. Each had been going through a thousand-year journey. Really evil people had been condemned to eternity in the underworld and could not return, and the genuinely virtuous did not return from heaven either. Everyone else on returning had learned lessons from their experiences.

Those returning got to choose their next reincarnated life from a selection of human and animal lives. But the results could be unexpected. One person returning from a pleasant existence in heaven chose the life of a dictator. It turned out that instead of getting what they wanted, among other things, they were now fated to eat their own children as a kind of punishment for not learning the lessons from their previous life. Some who had returned from the pains of the underworld chose a life that might be humble, but more virtuous. Their memories would then be wiped, and they would live through their next life and hopefully continue to improve.

If the soul does not *need* the body, what is its relationship to the body for Plato? The body is not only a kind of prison for the soul, serving as a barrier to accessing the whole experience of truth and expressing the cardinal virtues; it is a tempter to evil. The body's pleasures can be a lure for the embodied soul (e.g., through the desire for food, drink, and lovemaking). These distract the body from what it should be doing. This challenge resonates with some more fundamentalist religious views in the United States of how the body can corrupt the soul even today. Goetz and Taliaferro quote Socrates in Plato's *Phaedo* as saying:

> *"I suppose the soul reasons most beautifully [without the need for recollection] when none of these things gives her pain—neither hearing nor sight, nor grief nor any pleasure—when instead, bidding farewell to the body, she comes to be herself all by herself as much as possible and when, doing everything she can to avoid communing with or even being in touch with the body, she strives for what is."*

One more complex view that will come up with other philosophers is whether the soul is one thing or has parts. In some places, Plato does argue that the soul is simple and singular; and cannot be divided. He says that it is not changeable like a body and is more like the invisible Forms. However, in the

Republic, he proposes dividing the soul into rational, spirited, and appetitive parts (Martin, 2006). He may have reached this idea to make the argument for how a simple, unified soul can explain the behavior of our bodies. No one up to that point had laid out a theory of how the elements of human personality and cognition work together to cause action. He believed only the rational part is immortal, and the other aspects perish with the body. The rational part rules, and it exists above the neck.

The spirited and appetitive mortal parts are located below the neck. The appetites are all our myriad desires for various pleasures, comforts, physical satisfactions, and bodily ease. The spirited part is not about being spiritual. Instead, it is about the energy (e.g., the anger) that motivates us when we might see an injustice that needs to be addressed, or like the grit that helps us overcome adversity, achieve victory, take on challenges, and seek honor. In contrast to the rational part of the soul, these lower functions that are more physical and beastlike may be the source of ideas that eventually became the idea of the unconscious discussed by thinkers from Augustine to Freud and Jung (Martin, 2006). Aristotle challenges Plato's description of a unified soul with parts, arguing that if it has parts, it is not unified. Indeed, he argues that if it has parts, there should actually be more than three parts; if there is some higher level of the soul that unifies everything, then that is what philosophers should seek as the soul.

A final topic we will cover for Plato is how he thinks of the soul as collecting and reflecting on information arriving through our senses. These ideas about how a soul uses a body to understand the physical world are relevant in more contemporary animal consciousness discussions. It will also apply to thinking about artificial entities sensing information about the world and how they reason about it. According to Goetz and Taliaferro, Plato reports a discussion between Socrates and Theaetetus where Socrates asks, "Is it more correct to say that we see and hear with our eyes and ears or through them?" Theaetetus says, "I should say we always perceive through them, rather than with them." But Socrates comes back with:

"Yes, it would surely be strange that there should be a number of senses ensconced inside us, like the warriors in the Trojan horse, and all these things should not converge and meet in some single nature—a mind, or whatever it is to be called—with which we perceive all the objects of perception through the senses as instruments." (Theaetetus)

Plato recognizes that we experience through all of our senses at once. We see the lightning, hear the thunder, smell the rain and feel the breeze simultaneously. The senses must, in effect, be instruments of the soul that converge in the single point that is the soul itself, which is the source of awareness. John Searle (1997), in *The Mystery of Consciousness* (cited in Goetz and Taliaferro), discusses the *binding problem*. He recognizes that our sensory system and brain areas are specially tuned to detect attributes such as color, shape, movement, and angles. Indeed, this detection works on the myriad of signals coming from the sensors in the perceptual system. But the way we experience things in the world around us is as a unified whole. So, he asks, "How does the brain bind all of these different stimuli into a single, unified experience of an object?...All of my experiences at present are part of one big unified conscious experience." This unity of consciousness is still a subject of neuroscience research.

ARISTOTLE (384 TO 322 BCE)

"Happiness lies in virtuous activity, and perfect happiness lies in the best activity, which is contemplative."
- Aristotle

I went to the University of Chicago for my degree in chemistry. Chicago had a liberal arts culture rooted in the spirit of the *Great Books of the Western World*, the collection of writing that was curated to contain the best ideas over the last couple of millennia that an intellectually well-rounded person should know.[76] My memory, which admittedly has probably been distorted over the years, is that virtually every class I took, whatever the topic, seemed to begin with discussing what Aristotle thought about the subject. Indeed, he seemed to have opinions about everything I needed to study as an undergraduate.[77]

Aristotle and Plato Debating in Raphael's School of Athens

While Aristotle studied under Plato, his views about the soul (the *psyche*) and the afterlife were different. Aristotle was not particularly concerned about an eternal soul that survives the body. He was more interested in the soul's relationship to the body. Aristotle, who clearly liked to organize ideas, structured living things into a hierarchy. Plants, which exhibit growth, nutrition, and reproduction, have a vegetative soul. Animals with their sensitive souls have these same properties of growth, nutrition, and reproduction, but they also have the powers of perception and locomotion. They can sense and feel. They have desires. Human souls have the attributes that animal souls have, but we also have the powers of reason and thought.[78] We have rational souls.

Aristotle referred to this rational part of our soul as the *nous*. For Aristotle, the nous is that which engages in scientific thought. The emphasis here is on the "that which" as opposed to the "engages in." It is more like the idea of our *mind* or our *understanding*, rather than the process of thinking itself. Aristotle distinguished it from concepts like perception, imagination, and reason. It is a kind of basic understanding, and it enables us to be rational.

For Aristotle, everything organic has a psyche or soul, which is why it is alive. In general, the soul is inseparable from the physical body. This relationship of the body and the soul is one of the ways Aristotle differs from Plato. Plato conceived of us as souls inhabiting and, in some sense, moving bodies around; Aristotle thinks of the soul and the body as being bound together. In the past, the analogy sometimes used was that they are no more distinct than the impression of a seal can be separated from the wax on which it is impressed. Today we might say that our experience in using a computer program cannot be separated from the software and the hardware that is running it. The characteristics of the human soul (e.g., life and growth, sensing and moving, and understanding) can be thought of as faculties distinguished by how they function and the objects on which they operate. This description is Aristotle the taxonomist again.

In essence, the soul and its attributes come into being when they become associated with a body. According to Aristotle's *De anima*, the soul and the body together constitute a single living being. Aristotle has some dualist ideas, but also here is framing our nature more like a *monist* or a *physicalist* would. The one possible exception is that some believe that Aristotle felt the rational part, the nous, might be separable. Indeed, if he did hold a view of the nous's persistence after death, the nous probably did not retain the unique characteristics that define us as individuals. There is not personal immortality, in that sense, for Aristotle. Aristotle does say:

> "*Therefore, it is necessary that in [the soul] there be an intellect capable of becoming all things, and an intellect capable of making itself understand all things. And the intellect which is capable of understanding all things is...separated, not mixed or passible [i.e., perishable], and, in its substance, is action....And in its separated state, it is just what it is, and this alone is always immortal. And there is no memory, because [this agent intellect] is not*

*passible, and the passible intellect is corruptible, and
without it [i.e., the agent intellect] nothing is understood."*

What may persist would be the common property of the
nous that could have come from some kind of shared pool of
rationality and may return to it. This idea sounds like more
Eastern models of the soul, although with the focus that involves encountering truth through rationality instead of at a
spiritual level. When you set aside this one idea of the nous,
much of Aristotle's thinking seems to resonate with what
would become more functional, materialist approaches where
our various experiences can be understood through our biology. This integration of soul and body would set the stage for
Rene Descartes' ideas and eventually for William James.

Indeed, Aristotle believed that to explain how the soul
works fully, you need to explain why a particular body and a
specific soul are paired. For Aristotle, the *form* of the body is
the soul. It is the totality of how we function in the world. He
uses an analogy of an ax. Compared to a human being, the
body would be the wood and metal that make up the ax. But
the soul would be its capacity to chop. If it could not chop, it
would not be an ax. According to Goetz and Taliaferro, in the
same way, Aristotle believes the individual person is their soul-
body composite. The soul does not think, experience emotion
or pain, or deliberate by itself; it is the person (the combination
of soul and body) that does. Aristotle, in turn, says, "Perhaps
indeed it would be better not to say that the soul pities or learns
or thinks but that the man does in virtue of the soul" (Aristotle,
De anima, 408b).

While you can think of the objects we experience in terms
of particular senses, other objects are best considered as being
perceived by more than one sense. Think of the recent new
breed of apple, the Cosmic Crisp. You see it, feel it, smell it,
and taste it. Aristotle talks about a "central sense" faculty that
serves to unify these sensations. This integration is similar to
how Plato thought the information coming in through individual senses combined into a holistic experience. It also aligns
well with how we now think of the brain and the senses, with

the additional recognition we have that one sense's activity may impact what we perceive and how we experience it through another sense.[79] When COVID-19 eliminated people's sense of smell, it could also affect their sense of taste. As we have noted, the various ways of unifying sense-data enable different animal species to be uniquely adapted to their environments. There is no one definitive experience of what is "real."

Goetz and Taliaferro do raise an issue with Aristotle's views. They note that most of us can imagine inhabiting a different body. Indeed, for some today, they feel they are occupying a body of a different gender. The feature of many video games and avatars in various social media is about allowing us to show up in or virtually inhabit different characters. We may be able to experience at some level different physical bodies with varying combinations of characteristics, including those of other species. Our ability to imagine disconnecting ourselves from our physical bodies poses a challenge for Aristotle's model.

There is a *New York Times* article written by Benedict Carey called "Standing in Someone's Else's Shoes, Almost for Real." Carey (Carey, 2008) discusses neuroscience research that creates experiences in which people inhabit other characters and take on their characteristics. They can be fooled into adopting a wide variety of forms. You can create situations such as putting one gender into another gender's body, young into old, and one race into another. Researchers have found that people react when their virtual self is poked just as they would physically when you touch them.

Neuroscience confirms what we intuitively know about the power of stories, movies, games, and popular media. We can identify with the characters and imagine ourselves in other contexts faced by similar challenges. Actors do this all the time. As we have discussed, this empathy helps us pass on knowledge about how to interact with the world from one person to another and through our culture. Good stories are those where we can imagine inhabiting the character, and bad stories are those that we know do not ring true. Stories are a kind of modeling capability for the human and some animal minds.

Goetz and Taliaferro note that while Plato fails to provide a complete account of how soul and body can be integrated, Aristotle fails to provide a way to think about why each of us can so easily imagine stepping into the shoes of another.[80]

Aristotle views thinking as a critical power of the human soul. Aristotle's *rational thinking* included thinking about ideas and not just sensory experiences. Unlike other functions like sight to the eye or hearing to the ear, however, he did not see it as being specifically located in a particular organ of the body. To the extent that it is associated with a corporeal location, it would be the heart which he believed is the location of the five sensations of the body and sustains life. That seems a little surprising to me since I would guess he would have been familiar with the impact of brain injuries on warriors.

Furthermore, for Aristotle, except potentially for the intellect or the nous, the soul cannot continue without the body, and it ends when the body ceases to live. Aristotle in the *Physics* says, "[L]iving is the being of living things, and the soul is the cause and principle of this." A living being, by definition, lives, and the soul is the efficient and final cause of what it is to be a living thing. The life form is the thing that remains constant, even as the matter of the thing may change through age, surgery, accident, or whatever. Elsewhere Aristotle says, "If the eye was an animal, then sight would be its soul...the eye is the matter of sight...the body is that which exists in potentiality; but just as pupil and sight are the eye, so in our case, soul and body are the animal" *(De Anima)*.

According to Goetz and Taliaferro, Aristotle believed the soul moves the body "through some kind of choice and thought process" *(De anima)*. The way Aristotle thinks about it is in terms of objects of desire that may attract because they are good or seem good, kind of like a magnet attracts iron. Given Aristotle's conception of the soul, it seems likely that he would be sympathetic to extending his ideas to contemporary issues arising from emerging technologies if he lived today. Assuming an artificial intelligence technology (e.g., say an organic technology) could be created that meets a plausible definition of life, he might grant the possibility that it could have a soul.

His analysis would be based on the properties of movement exhibited (its behavior) in response to external conditions and internal states, and the nature of its rational thinking.

In summary, Aristotle has a rationale for how a soul and a body work together to make a unique living thing. In that sense, plants, animals, and humans each have a unique combination of soul and body. But with the possible exception of a generic nous, Aristotle does not have an idea of the afterlife. Plato, on the other hand, identifies us with our souls. Our soul is indestructible, it is rational, it provides unity to our conscious experiences, and it reasons. It has the properties that we would call mind and a sense of self. The body will go away when it dies, and many of us will get another body. A cycle of reincarnation will continue as the good are rewarded, and the bad are punished, and over time many of us become more virtuous. There are elements in each of these contrasting views that seem like they might fit within a model of the soul and an afterlife.

RENÉ DESCARTES (1596 TO 1650 CE)

"If you would be a real seeker after truth, it is necessary that at least once in your life you doubt, as far as possible, all things."
- René Descartes

The third key philosopher that I am going to look at is René Descartes. He represents another significant variation that influenced religious as well as philosophical thought. According to Martin and Barresi (Martin, 2006), Descartes takes a substantial leap into a new way of thinking that began during the period of Renaissance science. He took on the question of how the soul could fit into an otherwise material world driven by the mechanistic laws that science was uncovering. Two cultural shifts were going on at the time: one was the sense of the physical world losing its spirituality and active divine intervention as an engine of change, and the other was the broader recognition of the difference between our subjective experiences and the external physical world. Martin and Barresi point out that Descartes was the first prominent thinker to start using the word *mind* as an alternative to the word *soul*. This idea could be inferred from Plato and Aristotle, but Descartes made it explicit.

As a philosopher, he may probably be the best known today in our popular culture. After all, "I think therefore I am" is a pretty sticky phrase and is still a very contemporary perspective. The phrase comes from what is sometimes called a thought experiment. He imagines a hypothetical evil deceiver and tries to think through what the deceiver's existence might imply about his understanding of himself (Goetz, 2011).

"But there is some deceiver or other, very powerful and very cunning, whoever employs his ingenuity in deceiving me. Then without doubt I exist also if he deceives me, and let him deceive me as much as he will, he can never cause me to be nothing so long as I think that I am something. So that after having reflected well and carefully examined all things, we must come to the definite conclusion that this proposition: I am, I exist, is necessarily true each time that I pronounce it, or that I mentally conceive it.

"Finally, I am the same who feels, that is to say, who perceives certain things, as by the organs of sense, since in truth I see light, I hear noise, I feel heat. But it will be said that these phenomena are false and that I am dreaming. Let it be so; still it is at least quite certain that it seems to me that I see light, that I hear noise and that I feel heat. That cannot be false [...] [A]lthough the things which I perceive and imagine are perhaps nothing at all apart from me and in themselves, I am nevertheless assured that these modes of thought that I call perceptions and imaginations, inasmuch only as they are modes of thought, certainly reside (and are met with) in me."
– Descartes, <u>Meditations on First Philosophy</u>

This is an interesting argument, given what we know today about how the mind constructs the reality we experience. Both

Plato and Aristotle addressed this binding problem of bringing the sense data together in an integrated experience but starting from different places. Descartes sees this experience as reality, since it is our experience that is real to us. In more contemporary research, we know much that is *out there* is missed. He argued that each of us are more confident about the things we *think* than we are of the external objects around us. We *now* also know that gaps in what we perceive and our memories are filled in by the mind to make sense of the world and enable us to function. Furthermore, drugs and other altered states such as stress or the extreme absence of stimuli can alter those perceptions and influence our experiences. We have already observed that even animals experience *realities* that are different from ours, and in some cases, they are more accurate.

That being said, he is right that what I am experiencing is indeed in *me* because my mind has constructed it. That construction, the model of the world, is likely to impact how I interact with the world and how I show up to others (who, in turn, make inferences about who I am). Anil Seth, in the *Scientific American* issue on "Truth vs. Lies" (Seth, 2020), sets up an excellent overview of this literature with a quote from the writer Anais Nin that captures the spirit of it, "We do not see things as they are, we see them as we are."

Descartes knows he exists, and things appear to him as what is sensed. He argues he cannot be mistaken about what he thinks. As he says, "But what then am I? A thing which thinks. What is a thing which thinks? It is a thing which doubts, understands, [conceives], affirms, denies, wills, refuses, which also imagines and feels." When he reflects on his own experiences and thought processes, he feels their reality at some deep level. This sense of reality is similar to how most of us feel. We are confident it is *me* experiencing things, at times, even if they are dreams. For Descartes, a thing that thinks is a *mind*, and he sees the mind as the *soul*. In his *Meditations*, he makes it clear that he considers these two as equivalent. Augustine also had this idea. If we believe we have a soul, most of us believe it because the belief comes from our conscious reflections on how we are experiencing the world and how we fit within it.

Descartes also recognizes that his experience feels united with his body. My experience of a phantom limb feels real, even if the limb is missing. I lost a finger during a summer job at a machine shop when I was in high school, and I still have the experience that it is there. Descartes states, "Nature also teaches me by these sensations of pain, hunger, thirst, etc., that I am not only lodged in my body as a pilot in a vessel, but that I am very closely united to it, and so to speak so intermingled with it that I seem to compose with it one whole. For if that were not the case, when my body is hurt, I, who am merely a thinking thing, should not feel pain, for I should perceive this wound by the understanding only, just as the sailor perceives by sight when something is damaged in his vessel; and when my body needs drink or food, I should clearly understand the fact without being warned of it by confused feelings of hunger and thirst" (Descartes, *Meditations on First Philosophy*).[81]

This unity has some of that combination of ideas from both Plato and Aristotle that I mentioned. Aristotle also believed that souls give life to the bodies with which they exist and are integrated, and Plato thought that a core property of the soul is that it enlivens the body. But both cannot imagine a living body without a soul. Descartes *can* imagine a body as having its substance and potentially life without the soul. It is like a mechanism or machine where many movements can be explained without referencing the soul. Autonomous cars and robots, and even social media bots, can exhibit properties that seem alive and yet clearly have no souls at this point. Two passages from Descartes highlight some of these ideas:

"As a clock composed of wheels and counter-weights no less exactly observes the laws of nature when it is badly made, and does not show the time properly, than when it entirely satisfies the wishes of its maker, [...] [so also] if I consider the body of a man as being a sort of machine so built up and composed of nerves, muscles, veins, blood and skin, that though there were no mind in it at all, it would not cease to have the same motions as at present, exception being made of those movements which are due to the direction of the will, and in consequence depend upon the mind [as opposed to those which operate by the

disposition of its organs]. ”
– Descartes, <u>Meditations on First Philosophy</u>

“I should like you to consider, after this, all the functions I have attributed to this machine—such as the digestion of food, the beating of the heart and arteries, the nourishment and growth of the limbs, respiration, waking and sleeping, the reception by the external sense organs of light, sounds, smells, tastes, heat, and other such qualities, the imprinting of the ideas of these qualities in the organ of the 'common' sense and the imagination, the retention or stamping of these ideas in the memory, the internal movements of the appetites and passions, and finally the external movements of all the limbs (movements which are so appropriate not only to the actions of objects presented to the senses, but also the passions and the impressions found in the memory, that they imitate perfectly the movements of a real man). I should like you to consider that these functions follow from the mere arrangement of the machine's organs every bit as naturally as the movements of a clock or other automaton follow from the arrangement of its counter-weights and wheels. In order to explain these functions, then, it is not necessary to conceive of this machine as having any vegetative or sensitive soul or other principle of movement and life, apart from its blood and its spirits, which are agitated by the heat of the fire burning continuously in its heart—a fire which has the same nature as all the fires that occur in inanimate bodies.”
– Descartes, <u>Treatise on Man</u>

These ideas will be relevant when we think about ensoulment, and when we discuss the ambiguity about when the soul might leave the body. This model of the body as mechanism is also how he thinks of animals. Unlike Aristotle and Plato, Descartes believes that since animals do not think in the way we do, they are examples of mechanisms like the cuckoo clock or perhaps our Roombas that exhibit some of life's characteristics without rational thought or souls. According to Descartes (Martin, 2006), the soul is not required for life to exist. Life is just the result of the complex mechanisms operating in the world. We differ from other living things only in having non-material, immortal souls that are conscious. In some later letters, he did suggest that animals *may* have something like thought, but that it is not at the level or quite like rational human thought. Only beings, he would argue, that have non-material souls can have full consciousness with self-awareness. Lower-order beings would lack self-awareness.[82] Indeed, in response to a critique from the Jesuit Bourdin about the requirement to be able to think about thinking, Descartes replied:

> *"My critic says that to enable a substance to be superior to matter and wholly spiritual..., it is not sufficient for it to think: it is further required that it should think that it is thinking, by means of a reflexive act, or that it should have awareness...of its own thought. This is...deluded.... [T]he initial thought by means of which we become aware [adverto] of something does not differ from the second thought by means of which we become aware that we were aware of it...any more than this second thought differs from the third thought by means of which we become aware that we were aware that we were aware."*

Whew! John Locke later suggested that what Descartes took as consciousness might be understood merely as self-reflection.

For Descartes, the soul can reason to discover damaged parts of the body by seeing it. For example, the soul can recognize the damage by feeling the pain and seeing the injury to the foot. One might assume at that moment that the soul is literally in the foot. But Descartes says, "[T]he soul is really joined to the whole body, and that we cannot, properly speaking, say that it exists in any one of its parts to the exclusion of the others" (Descartes, *The Passions of the Soul*).

Goetz and Taliaferro note that there might be a temptation to argue that Descartes believes that the pains we feel are physically located in the brain. Modern physicalists like ancient materialists, without the need for the idea of a soul, might make this argument. But it is not an argument that Descartes would have made, at least at that time. They point out that for Descartes, the experience of pain is still located within the soul. The soul, in turn, is not found in space. The soul has a representation, however, of where the source of the pain is located. Because the soul has a sense of location, Descartes infers the connection to the body. Exactly how the soul and the body causally affect each other is not entirely clear from Descartes' writings. Princess Elisabeth of Bohemia, on June 16, 1643, writes to Descartes, "Tell me please how the soul of a human being (it being only a thinking substance) can determine the bodily spirits and so bring about voluntary actions." In his reply, he says, "for soul and body [operating] together we have no notion save that of their union."[83] That reply did not really satisfy her, as it probably would not have satisfied us.

In another letter, he says, "though we are not in a position to understand, either by reasoning or by any comparison drawn from other things, how the incorporeal mind can move the body, none the less we cannot doubt that it can, since experiences the most certain and the most evident make us at all times immediately aware of its doing so. This is one of those things which are known in and by themselves and which we obscure if we seek to explain them by way of other things." He is making a functional argument that William James might make. While we do not know *how* the soul or mind moves the body, we know that we exercise our will to move, and it happens.

Descartes believes the soul is potentially immortal and that God creates it, and could preserve it. While separable in death, the body is temporal and changes while it exists. In a sense, an infant's body is the same as the later adult's body, just changed in quantity and composition. It is when the body wholly and irreversibly breaks down that the soul leaves the body. "Accordingly this 'I'-that is, the soul by which I am what I am is [...] indeed easier to know than the body, and would not fail to be whatever it is, even if the body did not exist" (Descartes, *Discourse on the Method*).

Martin and Barresi (Martin, 2006) conclude by observing

that Descartes set the stage for the empirical science of psychology that started to emerge by the end of the eighteenth century, especially as represented by William James in the nineteenth. They argue that while he further developed the Platonic idea of the self, he also advanced the mechanistic view of nature. The mechanistic view would eventually be used by others to further back away from the concept of the soul in philosophy and even chip away at Descartes' own ideas about the self.

HIGHLIGHTS FROM THE EVOLUTION OF THE SELF

Renaissance (14th to 17th Century)

John Locke (1632 to 1704).

> *"No man's knowledge here can go beyond his experience."*
> – John Locke

Plato, Augustine, and Descartes thought of the person in terms of a rational soul that is an immaterial substance. Aristotle and later Aquinas thought of a person as a body filled with and given life by a rational soul. The continued existence of the soul in all of these cases defines a person's identity over time. John Locke, however, shifted the focus of this idea of what defines a person.

In the *Essay Concerning Human Understanding*, Locke says that God has the power, should he choose, to enable matter itself to think. According to Martin and Barresi (Martin, 2006), this outraged his critics since a statement like that seems like it could remove the explanatory value for why we

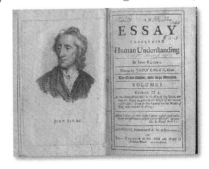

have souls. They observe that "What had always made the soul so handy for proving immortality—that it is simple, static, and inaccessible to empirical examination—is also what made it so useless for investigating human nature." Locke argued that it is not so much the soul that is important to us, but rather our consciousness. When we think of ourselves, we are thinking about our consciousness and its experiences. If that consciousness were moved to another soul, that which is us would move with it. If our consciousness moved to another body, that which is us would move with it. Consciousness is partly about considering ourselves over time; in other words, remembering ourselves in the context of our ongoing experience of the world. We now know our memories live within our brains.

The idea does not imply an unchanging body or substance since we are continually changing. We could even lose an arm but would still see ourselves as the same, and today parts of our body might be replaced with prosthetic technologies, and I would still feel I am me. When I look in the mirror through my aging body, it is my memories as a twenty-year-old that look back at me. Consciousness unifies our sense of self both over time and at each moment. Locke was not strictly a materialist, but this opened the door further to rethink how explaining the experience of self is potentially even more important than the idea of a soul for both philosophy and science.

18th Century

David Hume (1711 to 1776).

"The life of man is of no greater importance to the universe than that of an oyster."
– David Hume

Martin and Barresi argue that one of Hume's big ideas was that a philosophy of human nature (which you can think of as psychology) includes the nature of knowledge and its acquisition. The study of things and their fundamental properties, he believed, are the foundation of all sciences. This study includes abstract concepts such as being, knowing, cause and effect, identity, time, and space. It would itself be founded on experience and observation, and would explain experience and observation in the other sciences. This argument reminds me of that experience at the University of Chicago I mentioned, where it seemed like Aristotle had an opinion about just about everything I was studying. While as a psychologist, I would like to believe that my field of studying the mind is the mother of all sciences; in practice, I have acquired some humility over the course of my career. Martin and Barresi note that the field of psychology, in essence, gradually concluded that explaining the nature of reality would need to be handled by philosophers, and psychologists could more fruitfully spend their time explaining human behavior that can be observed and measured.

David Hume asked to be buried in a "simple Roman tomb" Edinburgh, Scotland

Locke focused on consciousness and how it is constructed from the memories and reflections we have about ourselves over time. Hume argues that he does not have a sense of himself at any given moment. He says he only has a sense of the ongoing sequence or bundle of perceptions. For Hume, the role memory plays is to create resemblances across perceptual experiences that cause us to infer relationships. It is this that gives rise to a sense of identity. For Hume, our identity (our sense of self) is a construct of our minds. Think of how a movie film used to be a sequence of images, and when played at the right speed, they feel like a continuous experience of movement.

In *A Treatise of Human Nature*, Hume says, "The mind is a

kind of theatre, where several perceptions successively make their appearance; pass, repass, glide away, and mingle in an infinite variety of postures and situations. There is properly no simplicity in it at one time, nor identity in different; whatever natural propension we may have to imagine that simplicity and identity." Critics argue that when Hume says he is observing these perceptions, it is, in fact, a *he* that is doing the observing.

One argument in favor of his ideas is that we tend not to be aware of that which is permanent and unchanging. As animals, our perceptual and cognitive systems have evolved to pay attention to change; that's where threat and food tend to live. If the soul exists, it would be permanent and unchanging, and we might not be aware of it. Perhaps that is why the inclination is often to talk about the soul we *have* and not talk as much as if we *are* a soul. It seems like many of us tend to separate our sense of self from this thing that carries that self into the afterlife. Goetz and Taliaferro (Goetz, 2011), though, argue that if the soul is an entity with essential powers and capacities, and these are the basis for actions, capacities, and passions, the exercise of these powers and capacities is what changes. Even if the soul is permanent and itself does not change, we can still be aware that it is responsible for change as it functions.

They cite Martin and Barresi as saying, "[A]s simple, immaterial substances, souls, are not part of the natural world. Whatever exists or obtains, but not as part of the natural world, is inherently mysterious." In essence, the idea is that while our souls are not measurable, given they are not made of something material, it is our observation and experience of our souls, our selves, as we interact with the world that we observe and experience. Those interactions give us the sense we are the same person from one moment to the next.

I do resonate with the proposition of using external evidence of otherwise hidden things to make inferences about the nature of something that cannot yet be studied directly. For example, when I was at the University of Chicago, my physics professor brought in the first "picture" of a molecule and its atoms. The picture had been made by observing the change in direction of particles that had been shot at the molecule, not by taking what we traditionally think of as a picture. This approach would be equivalent to how in psychology, we can make inferences about how the brain works by the behavior that changes when we manipulate tasks and where they are performed.

This methodology would especially be relevant in that theory of mind, and the theory of soul, that I mentioned in Chapter 2. In that approach, we make inferences about someone's behavior in response to different conditions, and we use that information to build models about the nature of their mind and potentially about their souls. Goetz and Taliaferro are correct in that I observe my experiences of the external world. I am also aware of the experience of my own internal emotions, thought processes, imagination, and decisions (including moral and ethical choices). Even Augustine and some Christian scriptures argue that we can reflect on the relationships between our souls and bodies, and we can infer souls in others by observing their behaviors. This is similar to how we would make inferences about our own minds and attribute states of mind to others. The theory of soul approach would suggest Augustine's argument could be used to make inferences about how the human soul evolved in animals along with our other characteristics.

Finally, in associating identity with memory or consciousness, Hume points out that even if the soul is composed of an immortal, immaterial substance, its continued existence after our deaths is irrelevant. He argued that memory and consciousness will end with the body. That would seem to be the issue to think about as we reflect on the afterlife. Are there mind and other properties associated with our soul that continue without a body? Are they separate from memory, consciousness, and other phenomena associated with our physical bodies? What are they? Or do we need a body, in essence, to "light up" some of our experiences that we associate with what defines us? And what if, at some point, we do receive a new heavenly body? Will our memories need to be uploaded to that body, just as we often see in science fiction movies?

Immanuel Kant (1724 to 1804).

"Metaphysics is a dark ocean without shores or lighthouse, strewn with many a philosophic wreck."
– Immanuel Kant

According to Goetz and Taliaferro (Goetz, 2011), "Immanuel Kant is without question one of the most important figures in the history of thought, and this is the case despite the fact that when one reads his work one is often not sure what he is claiming." Martin and Barresi (Martin, 2006), in turn, observe, "While it is hard to read Kant and not believe that he was up to something important, often it is equally hard to be sure what that something was." No wonder it can be hard to trace the evolution of his ideas about the soul and the afterlife!

Kant recognizes that we experience a self, an "I" that unifies the various sensory inputs and thoughts we receive. For most of us, this is how we experience our consciousness. In the *Critique of Pure Reason,* he says, "That […] the I in every act of thought is one, and cannot be resolved into a plurality of subjects, […]is something that lies already in the concept of thought, and is, therefore, an analytic proposition." But just because that is our experience, he argues, that does not prove that that is the way things are. It also doesn't guarantee that the real world is how we experience it; the experience of unified consciousness as a simple soul also does not guarantee it is.

We conclude that we are experiencing these things, but that experience is implied by having the thought itself. As I sit being annoyed by my Roomba vacuuming our condo, those experiences are unified in *my* sense of them, but that does not require that, in fact, I exist as a substantial, unified, conscious self. As Kant puts it, "In my own consciousness, therefore, identity of person is unfailingly met with….[but] the identity of the consciousness of myself at different times is therefore only a formal condition of my thoughts and their coherence, and in no way proves the numerical identity of my subject" (*Critique of Pure Reason*).

Kant distinguished two broad domains that we use in our reasoning. One is the *noumenal* world, the world of things as they are. This is the world of trees, cats, cars, and condos *out there* in Edmonds, WA. The other he called the *phenomenal* world, the realm of our actual and possible experiences; and how we reason about them. The phenomenal world includes things like truths about geometry that we derive from our experiences of the noumenal world.

He argued that thinking of the *self* as part of the noumenal world is not something we can know per se. We cannot prove its existence, let alone its immortality. However, it is essential as a *regulative* idea. It is *useful for practical purposes* and gives us the motivation to behave morally, which only makes sense if we, as souls, will live forever. Therefore, even though we cannot prove it, we cannot act as if it is not real. We need to assume it exists. While the noumenal self is never experienced, we may be able to experience a phenomenal self. Goetz and Taliaferro offer a relevant critique; however, when they point out that if we can make such vital errors in our perceptions of our own selves, one has to wonder how we avoid making errors about anything else we experience in the world. Of course, we now know from research that we make errors that show a disconnect between what is out there and what we consciously experience all the time.

19th Century

William James (1842-1910).

> *"A little philosophy inclineth man's mind to atheism; but depth in philosophy bringeth men's minds about to religion."*
> – Sir Francis Bacon

Sitting on my shelf hovering over me as I work is the *Principles of Psychology (Vols. 1 and 2)* by William James. It belonged to my PhD professor, Dr. B. J. Underwood[84], a student of a student of William James. William James taught the first psychology class in America and is often thought of as the father of experimental psychology in America (following Wilhelm Wundt's lead in Leipzig, in 1876). He was a founder of functional psychology (a.k.a., functionalism), which focuses on behavior as it suggests utility, purpose, and the inner workings of rational thought. It was a direct outgrowth of Darwin's work. He argued that psychology should be a sub-discipline within biology, and it should focus on evolutionary ideas of adaptation. A goal was to understand the biological processes of the human mind and consciousness. This is yet another step in the evolution in ideas of the self and consciousness from Descartes through Locke, Hume, and Kant.

James' father was a Swedenborgian theologian, a religious group emerging from the scientist and Swedish Lutheran theologian Emmanuel Swedenborg. It was a church based on love and charity rather than formal doctrinal statements, and it influenced various more mystical and experiential strains within the Protestant church. While James was not a follower of any religion and did not have an interest in specific institutions, he was interested in spiritual experiences. James himself studied religion (see his book *The Varieties of Religious Experience,* for example) and spiritualism.[85]

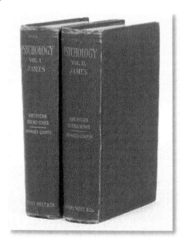

Martin and Barresi point out that one of the important things about James is that an argument can be made that he was the last philosopher-psychologist. Besides the groundbreaking *The Principles of Psychology*, he also wrote an important text in philosophy called *Essays in Radical Empiricism*. He approached many of these topics not by starting from the experiences of the soul or the self, but rather by making sense of them from how they show up in behavior. There is an interesting example from his book on emotion, where he asks if we see a bear and run away, do we run because we are afraid, or are we afraid because we run? He argued that "My theory...is that the bodily changes follow directly the perception of the exciting fact and that our feeling of the same changes as they occur IS the emotion." C. S. Lewis in *A Grief Observed* echoes this idea when he says, "No one ever told me that grief felt so like fear. I am not afraid, but the sensation is like being afraid. The same fluttering in the stomach, the same restlessness, the yawning."

Today, he would be pleased to know, there are many examples of where physiological states can be stimulated artificially (e.g., through drugs), and our brain will assign the name of an emotion to them based on other times when that combination of feelings has been associated with that label. I am a diabetic, for example, and at times when I am hypoglycemic, my brain is telling me that I am experiencing anxiety. Emotions, in turn, can bring back vivid memories of past experiences associated when the feelings occurred.

James believed in pragmatism. He tests the truth of beliefs by whether they are helpful to the believer. In *What Pragmatism Means* (1906), he says, "Truths emerge from facts, but they dip forward into facts again and add to them; which facts again create or reveal new truth (the word is indifferent) and so on indefinitely. The 'facts' themselves meanwhile are not true. They simply are. Truth is the function of the beliefs that start and terminate among them." He is recognizing something called the *observer principle*, which says the act of observing can impact the thing being observed. James acknowledges that observing the truth cannot help but impact the truth being studied empirically. As we know from research on whether witnesses can be accurate in their statements, our minds shape not only our experiences but our memories of those experiences. The physical world, the mind, and our experiences are, in essence, inseparable; they actively influence each other.

In studying consciousness, he began by reflecting on the mind within. He observes we have a natural tendency to focus on ourselves, our conscious experiences, our minds, and specific instances of "I"; and on others, as we can recognize attributes similar to ourselves. The experience of me and the experience of mine are hard to separate. "We feel and act about certain things that are ours very much as we feel and act about ourselves. Our fame, our children, the work of our hands, may be as dear to us as our bodies are, and arouse the same feelings and the same acts of reprisal if attacked. Our bodies themselves, are they simply ours, or are they us?" There is also a distinction in the self between *me* and *I*. The *me* is how I talk about myself in the context of my personal experiences. It is subject to empirical study. The *I*, however, is pure ego. It is the part of the self that persists across time and includes my reputation, self-definition, and other attributes. This *I* cannot be further divided and can be thought of as pure mind. The *me* can be divided into the material, the social, and the spiritual self. The spiritual self is one's "inner or subjective being." It includes the ability to argue and discriminate, our conscience and moral sense, and our will.

One of his main contributions to functionalism was how he thought about the subconscious. He said that in its nature, it is identical to the various states of consciousness. But it is impersonal rather than personal, and it is a simple brain state (by implication, tied to the physical brain) without a mental counterpart. There are some ideas here that Freud and Jung later spent time exploring.

All of this speaks to how he thinks of the soul. In his *Principles of Psychology*[86], he writes about how he is going to treat it (James, 1890). Up to the discussion of the soul, he has laid out explanations grounded in how our brains work to create conscious experiences. He suggests that he can account for "the unity, the identity, the individuality and the immateriality" that are typically used to argue for the soul, without requiring the soul as a concept. He says, "If I have not already succeeded in making this plausible to the reader, I am hopeless of convincing him by anything I could add now." He observes that some might call this consciousness the soul, but it is clear this experience is not itself immortal and incorruptible. He says when he pushes back further beyond the empirical explanations, if anything, he is led to a kind of *anima mundi*, a universal soul that links all living things. That universal soul does not provide for individual souls that may be rewarded and punished in the afterlife. This sounds like where Aristotle ended up with his idea of nous. James says, "as *psychologists*, we need not be metaphysical at all. The phenomena are enough, the passing thought itself is the only verifiable thinker, and its empirical connection with the brain-process is the ultimate known law."

James observes, "The Spiritualists do not deduce any of the properties of the mental life from otherwise known properties of the Soul. They simply find various characters ready-made in the mental life, and these they clap into the Soul, saying 'Lo! Behold the source from whence they flow!'....Altogether, the Soul is an outbirth of that sort of philosophizing whose great maxim, according to Dr. Hodgson, is: 'Whatever you are *totally* ignorant of, assert to be the explanation of everything else.'"

He does grant that some would argue that a concept of the soul is needed to guarantee the argument for immortality. But he says that it "guarantees no immortality of a sort we care for." Stripping away the properties of the soul associated with our bodies, "The enjoyment of the atom-like simplicity of their substance in saecula seculorum [eternity] would not to most people seem a consummation devoutly to be wished."

Another argument for the soul is it is needed for us to be rewarded or punished in the afterlife. James notes the controversy that arose when Locke suggested that our consciousness defines us as persons and not our bodies, whether we are in the same body or not. He argued that God would not hold someone responsible for something that the person did not have in their memories. He says, "It was supposed scandalous that our forgetfulness might thus deprive God of the chance of certain retributions, which otherwise would have enhanced his 'glory.'...To modern readers, however, who are less insatiate for retribution than their grandfathers, this argument will hardly be as convincing as it seems once to have been."

James concludes that the idea of the substantial soul "explains nothing and guarantees nothing. Its successive thoughts are the only intelligible and verifiable things about it, and definitely to ascertain the correlations of these with brain-processes is as much as psychology can empirically do....I therefore feel entirely free to discard the word Soul from the rest of this book. If I ever use it, it will be in the vaguest and most popular way. The reader who finds any comfort in the idea of the Soul is, however, perfectly free to continue to believe in it; for our reasonings have not established the non-existence of the Soul; they have only proved its superfluity for scientific purposes."

Despite his skepticism about the scientific value of the soul and its implication for immortality, James's lecture on the possibility of immortality is particularly interesting. The lecture illustrates how he approaches the potential tension between an empirical view of the world and ideas that, while beyond proof, provide value to us as individuals and to society. For James, four "postulates of rationality" are valuable but cannot be known in the sense other things are known. They are unprovable articles of faith. These articles of faith are God, immortality, freedom, and moral duty.

The lecture was part of a series held annually at Harvard University funded by the Ingersoll Foundation on the idea of immortality. The first one was given in 1896, and they have continued at least through 2018. Presenters have included people like Toni Morrison, Martin E. Marty, Elisabeth Kübler-Ross, Paul Tillich, and many others from a wide range of disciplines addressing the topic. James delivered the second one of these lectures, and it was entitled "Human Immortality: Two Supposed Objections to the Doctrine" (James, 1898). James argued that our wish for immortality is the source of systems of religious belief and practice (James, 1902). In his lecture, he makes a case for the viability of imagining the soul's immortality even given the biological understanding of the mind and the brain.

James does begin his fascinating lecture by admitting, "The whole subject of immortal life has its prime roots in personal feeling. I have to confess that my personal feeling about immortality has never been of the keenest order, and that, among the problems that give my mind solicitude, this one does not take the very foremost place." He does note that it is an enormous subject and that despite his personal interests, it matters to many. He cites a book by R. H. Charles entitled a *Critical History of the Doctrine of a Future Life* that has a lengthy bibliography on the topic.

He sets off the argument with, "[P]hysiological psychology is what is supposed to bar the way to the old faith. And it is now as a physiological psychologist that I ask you to look at the question with me a little more closely." He then reviews the data from physiological science about how the brain functions and concludes by saying, "During this hour I wish you also to accept it as a postulate, whether you think it controvertibly established or not; so I beg you to agree with me today in subscribing to the great psycho-physiological formula: Thought is a function of the brain." Descartes sits up in his grave at this point. James then asks whether, as it might be assumed, that these data and this doctrine logically compels us to reject the idea of immortality. He says, "Most persons imbued with what one may call the puritanism of science would feel bound to answer this question with a yes."

He then lays out his arguments, about at least the possibility that "even though our soul's life (as here below it is revealed to us) may be in literal strictness the function of a brain that perishes, yet it is not at all impossible, but on the contrary quite possible, that the life may continue when the brain itself is dead." I would note that we will be reviewing other research that attempts to account for various experiences of self, consciousness, and the transition to the afterlife. Similar to James' arguments, we will again see the idea that being able to account for the experiences based on physical explanations does not rule out additional causes that could include influences that we cannot or at least cannot *yet* measure and verify.

He says that when a physiologist says, "Thought is a function of the brain," they are thinking about the problem in the way they might say, "Steam is a function of the tea-kettle" or "Light is a function of a bulb and a circuit." He says that the physiologist is thinking of the brain in terms of its *productive function*, and so when the brain dies, the production can no longer continue. But James then lays out a series of arguments about alternative ways to model the relationship between the brain and the experience of our souls, and the justification for their potential explanatory value.

He describes what he refers to as a *releasing or permissive function*. He uses a crossbow example where there is tension as the bow is pulled back, holding the arrow in place. But when the trigger is pressed, it releases the tension, the arrow flies, and the bow springs back into shape. Similarly, with various explosives, there is a neutral state, but when some energy is applied (e.g., a hammer falling on a detonator), a chemical reaction is triggered, and energy is released. For some spiritual experiences we will be exploring, we could imagine a body primed to create an experience that is triggered by an external force.

He also suggests that thinking about a *transmissive function* is valid. Here he uses the example of a prism or a refracting lens. When light shines through it, different wavelengths bend at different angles and show up as a series of colors. The keys of a pipe organ might also be viewed as transmissive in their function. Air moves through the organ, but as the keys are pressed, the air moves through different pipes, and various sounds are created as a result. The organ does not contain "sound" per se, and the air is external to the organ, but it is a filter through which air is transmitted to different pipes that result in something new.

He then suggests at least some alternative ways to apply these ideas. I am going to take the liberty here of letting James do the work of explaining himself, since he does it so well. Keep in mind as you read his thoughts that we are now in a world of string theory, quantum physics, and dark matter where we are continuing to learn how much reality we do not yet understand.

> *"Suppose, for example, that the whole universe of material things—the furniture of earth and choir of heaven—should turn out to be a mere surface-veil of phenomena, hiding and keeping back the world of genuine realities. Such a supposition is foreign neither to common sense nor to philosophy. Common*

sense believes in realities behind the veil even too superstitiously; and idealistic philosophy declares the whole world of natural experience, as we get it, to be but a time-mask, shattering or refracting the one infinite Thought which is the sole reality into those millions of finite streams of consciousness known to us as our private selves.

"*Suppose, now, that this were really so, and suppose, moreover, that the dome, opaque enough at all times to the full super-solar blaze, could at certain times and places grow less so, and let certain beams pierce through into this sublunary world. These beams would be so many finite rays, so to speak, of consciousness, and they would vary in quantity and quality as the opacity varied in degree. Only at particular times and places would it seem that, as a matter of fact, the veil of nature can grow thin and rupturable enough for such effects to occur. But in those places gleams, however finite and unsatisfying, of the absolute life of the universe, are from time to time vouchsafed. Glows of feeling, glimpses of insight, and streams of knowledge and perception float into our finite world.*

"*Admit now that our brains are such thin and half-transparent places in the veil. What will happen? Why, as the white radiance comes through the dome, with all sorts of staining and distortion imprinted on it by the glass, or as the air now comes through my glottis determined and limited in its force and quality of its vibrations by the peculiarities of those vocal chords which form its gate of egress and shape it into my personal voice, even so the genuine matter of reality, the life of souls as it is in its fullness, will break through our several brains into this world in all sorts of restricted forms, and with all the imperfections and queernesses that characterize our finite individualities here below.*

"*You see that, on all these suppositions, our soul's life, as we here know it, would none the less in literal strictness be the function of the brain. The brain would be the independent variable, the mind would vary dependently on it. But such dependence on the brain for this natural life would in no wise make immortal life impossible—it might be quite compatible with supernatural life behind the veil hereafter.*

"As I said, then, the fatal consequence is not coercive, the con-clusion which materialism draws being due solely to its one-sided way of taking the word 'function'. And, whether we care or not for immortality in itself, we ought, as mere critics doing police duty among the vagaries of mankind, to insist on the illogicality of a denial based on the flat ignoring of a palpable alternative. How much more ought we to insist, as lovers of truth, when the denial is that of such a vital hope of man-kind!"[87]

"The theory of production is...not a jot more simple or credible in itself than any other conceivable theory. It is only a little more popular. All that one need do, therefore, if the ordinary mate-rialist should challenge one to explain how the brain can be an organ for limiting and determining to a certain form a con-sciousness elsewhere produced, is to retort with a tu quoque, asking him in turn to explain how it can be an organ for pro-ducing consciousness out of whole cloth."

DEEPER DIVES

Searching for the Soul in the Body

Across this period, philosophers, theologians, and other thinkers who assumed a soul often speculated on where it might be located. Does it exist in a realm other than our phys-ical one? Like other functions that define us, is it associated with one or more organs of our bodies? Is it non-physical but somehow co-located within the space our bodies occupy? Is it a collection of parts, similar to our consciousness, that has come to be viewed as a collection of neural activity?

It is worth pausing briefly at this point to look at the di-versity of ideas about where the soul might be located in the body. In ancient Egypt (back to 3000 BCE), we have noted that they had a view of the soul as consisting of different parts. In particular, the Ib was considered the force that brought people to life and was the center of one's being; and it was responsible for our feelings and thoughts. For the Egyptians, it was located in the heart. Because of its importance and role, it was a critical part of the heart-weighing ceremony. [88] The Egyptians left the heart in place in the mummy, even as they removed the brain and the various other organs. The Egyptians were not particularly interested in the human brain, and so during the embalming process, it was removed through the nose and discarded. The other organs would be needed in the afterlife and were stored in jars with the body.

Interestingly traditional Chinese philosophy contains the idea of the Shen. *Shen* contains ideas like mind, spirit, consciousness, vitality, expression, soul, and energy. The five types of Shen are housed in the heart (the Shen itself), lungs (the Po), liver (the Hun), spleen (the Yi), and kidneys (the Zhi).

The Stoics and Epicureans, Empedocles, and others also reasoned the soul was centered in the heart. This is because the heart would be the center of the lifeblood and so a giver of life. Epicurus believed that the soul was corporeal and consisted of tiny particles that occupy the same space as the body and are spread throughout it. Pythagoras, Plato, and Galen were more focused on the brain. Herophilus (c. 300 BCE), a famous physician from Alexandria and credited as one of the first anatomists to dissect the human body, believed it was in the brain's fourth ventricle, just above

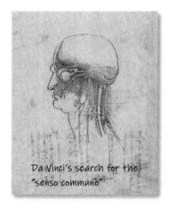

Da Vinci's search for the "senso commune"

the brain stem. Leonardo da Vinci suggested the soul was located near the brain's third ventricle, in the optic chiasm. He had observed changes in perception when that particular area of the brain was disturbed.

While primarily focused on the brain, Plato viewed the soul as consisting of three parts, the logos, the thymos, and the epithemitikon. The logos, the source of the human soul's highest and most essential characteristic, rationality, was located in the brain. The neck helped insulate the immortal part of the soul from contamination coming from the rest of the body. The thymos, the source of feelings such as bravery, hope, and rage, could be found in the chest cavity (by implication associated with the heart and perhaps lungs). The epithemitikon, which manages or controls desires and unconscious thought, was positioned near the umbilicus near the gut. One cannot help but think of Freud's superego, ego, and id as in the spirit of these reflections.

The Hippocratic Corpus, the collection of sixty or so early ancient Greek medical works associated with Hippocrates and his students, describes the evolution of thought that the soul is located within the body and is manifested in various diseases. One model of the human, for example, was that pneuma—associated with the soul or the vital spirit—or air is viewed as the warming life force. A variety of illnesses are associated with whether or not this air is moving through the body efficiently. In essence, one way to reboot the lungs was to clear the lungs of all air using a bladder and hoses. However, the air was viewed as not just being located in the lungs, but also as circulating throughout the entire body, including to and through the brain.

Later, Galen (a Roman physician, surgeon, and philosopher) explicitly used Plato's description to map the aspects of the soul to physical locations in the body. The logical part was in the brain, the spirited part was in the heart, and the appetitive part was in the liver. The heart was associated with the spirited aspects of the soul and influences actions, movements, and impulses. He saw the logical and the spirited elements of the soul as being in an ongoing conflict. The idea of the appetitive part being housed in the liver was not as developed as the others.

For Aristotle, there were different flavors of the soul, namely, the vegetative, sensitive, and rational. Aristotle explicitly states that while the soul has a corporeal form, a physical area serves as a point of contact between the soul and the human body, and that area is the heart. Aristotle states the heart is the location of the body's sensations and is responsible for respiration and life's sustenance. It has functions such as heating the body, moving the blood, and the creation of pneuma, or the life force for all animals. To Aristotle, when dead things become cold and no longer breathe, that is a sign their souls have left them. Aristotle also notes the heart is the first organ to appear during the embryo's development.

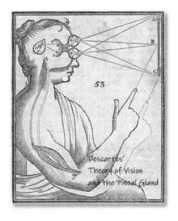

While Descartes says that the soul is joined with the entire body and is not located in space, he does note one part of the body with a special relationship with the soul, namely the pineal gland. He saw this gland as making possible the perception of passions and pains, our bodies and others, and will. However, he does not detail how it would work. Interestingly, it is possible to see a conceptual and topographical link between the modern concept of brain-stem death and Descartes' speculation.

While we might look at MacDougall's experiment to weigh the soul with some skepticism, it is worth reflecting on Sir John Carew Eccles's (1903 to 1997) work on the synapse. Eccles was an Australian neurophysiologist and philosopher who won the 1963 Nobel Prize in Physiology or Medicine. He shared the prize with Andrew Huxley and Alan Lloyd Hodgkin. Eccles was a dualist and suggested that you could look at points where the firing or inhibition of neurons might occur. He thought that these might be the direct causes and effects of things going on within the soul.

Looking across all these ideas, two general guesses of what is vital for the body's soul emerge. One is the heart and circulatory system (perhaps coupled with the lungs), and the other is the brain, associated with the nervous system. These continue to be the critical systems, while not necessarily around the soul, at least around defining life itself. In Chapter 6, where we explore life and death definitions and how they can be measured, both of these perspectives will be relevant.

Now, of course, *if* we were going to theorize about connecting the soul with one or the other of these areas, we would have to ensure the theory scales to what we are doing to modify the systems. A heart or lung can be replaced with another person's organs, tissue artificially grown or adapted from an animal, or technology. A damaged brain may receive tissue that is artificially grown. It may be connected to sensors and computers, and drugs may change its operation for various reasons (e.g., human augmentation and creativity, or medical reasons). Human brain tissue is even being grown inside animals.

When The Soul Lost Its Mind

By around 1913, religion, philosophy, and experimental psychology were heading in separate directions, with diverging methods and approaches to the questions of who we are and how our minds work. Let's go back and recap a little to see how we reached that point. By the end of the fifth century BCE, around the time of Socrates' death, the human soul distinguished us as living things, experienced emotions, and had characteristics like courage and justice. Through Plato and Aristotle's lives, the concept of the soul broadened to include characteristics of the mind like thought, perception and desire, and moral qualities. It accounted for most of the organism's vital functions and defined what it meant to be human. This idea would have reflected the popular culture in Greece at the time. Plato and Aristotle continued to develop this broad vision of the role of the soul in animating us as living things and the range of characteristics it drives and influences. They saw the soul as life-giving. They saw it as a spiritual, immaterial substance. Still, much of their focus was on the soul in its rational functions (e.g., consciousness, thinking, and feeling). Aristotle and Aquinas saw us as human beings, where our humanity is characterized by our bodies infused and given life by a rational soul.

Descartes, during the early 1600s, still believed that the soul and the mind were basically the same. Like Plato, he argued that truth is acquired by rational introspection. Descartes also argued that the soul might be the one thing of which we can be aware. Since he could imagine the mind (the rational soul) existing without the body, he concluded it must be different from the body. The soul was still immaterial. While the body and soul are different substances, it is their union that defines us. Descartes, however, did begin deconstructing the soul when he uncoupled the soul as the thing that gives life to the body. After all, animals have life but not necessarily souls in the way Descartes thought about them. What he held onto was the self thinks about itself, and that mind is what we experience as a person.

Thomas Hobbes' view from around the same time was that our mind only operates on material things, and so if we do have a soul, we cannot be aware of its presence. Hobbes says, "The soul is something of which we have no idea at all. We rationally infer that there is something within the human body which gives it the animal motion by means of which it has sensations and moves; and we call this 'something' a soul, without having any idea of it." The soul was immaterial, and to some extent, unknowable. Descartes and Hobbes's ideas opened the door to decoupling the view of the self as being identified with an enduring immaterial, eternal thing, to the self as something that emerges across time and the experiences of our physical selves. This was the time of the Renaissance when Nicolaus Copernicus and Galileo Galilei were upending the entire view of how the universe worked.

Not long after, John Locke (1632 to 1704 CE) took another step in disconnecting *us* from our souls. He says in *An Essay Concerning Human Understanding,* "Taking, as we ordinarily do [...] the Soul of a Man, for an immaterial Substance, independent from Matter, and indifferent alike to it all, there can from the Nature of things, be no Absurdity at all, to suppose, that the same Soul may, at different times be united to different Bodies, and with them make up, for that time, one Man." He argues that our thought and rationality make us people, and my sense of self results from my consciousness of being the same over time. It does not depend on an immaterial soul. We would feel like the same person, even if the soul we have is swapped out for another one. Indeed, in some sense, our bodies are already in the process of continuous change from birth to death. Our mind is bound to our bodies. In his *Essay*, he says, "When we see, hear, smell, taste, feel, meditate, or will anything, we know that we do so [consciousness is self-reflective]. Thus, it is always to our present Sensations and Perceptions." Our identity is bound up in our consciousness, and our consciousness is a property of our mind. Our mind is tied to our rational thought process. It is grounded in our physical memories, which bind together our past and present.

A couple of generations later, in the mid-1700s and shortly before the Revolutionary War, David Hume is not impressed with the arguments for the soul's immortality. He makes several points. One is that even if the soul is immortal, it must have existed before us, and if that does not define us, then its persistence after our bodies die is equally irrelevant. Furthermore, he explores a perspective that we discussed a bit in Chapter 2 as we considered the animal kingdom. Hume asks the question, "Animals undoubtedly feel, think, love, hate, will, and even reason, though in a more imperfect manner than man. Are their souls also immaterial and immortal?" He would have expected his audience to say "No!" That, he believed, forced a division between the soul and the mind.

Indeed, what evidence we have of ourselves arises from our bundle of perceptions, and it is our perceptions that make up our consciousness. He says in *A Treatise of Human Nature*, "For my part, when I enter most intimately into what I call *myself*, I always stumble on some particular perception or other, of heat or cold, light or shade, love or hatred, pain or pleasure. I never catch *myself* at any time without a perception....The mind is a kind of theater, where several perceptions successively make their appearance; pass, repass, glide away, and mingle in an infinite variety of postures and situations." And he would observe that if we have an immaterial, permanent, and unchanging soul that is different from our conscious life, can we even be aware of our souls or those of others?[89]

Emmanuel Kant did believe in a simple soul and that it

persists beyond death. He was not fond of materialism. But the soul was not subject to empirical analysis or demonstration through reason. He did believe it was required for the development of ethics and religion. In the *Critique of Pure Reason,* he calls imagination "a blind though indispensable function of the soul, without which we would have no cognition at all, but of which we are seldom even conscious." But he also identifies our rational consciousness with the body. Kant in the *Universal Natural History* says, "Man is so created as to receive the impressions and stirrings which the world must evoke in him through that body which is the visible part of his being, and the material of which serves not only to impress on the invisible soul that dwells in it the first notions of external objects, but also to recall and connect them interioriorly, in short [that body] is indispensable for thinking."

According to Martin and Barresi, by the late 1700s, more and more philosophers were dropping the idea of a soul in their theories. A conscious self, a mind, was still being used as a way of explaining human action. But Joseph Priestley (1733 to 1804)[90], a Christian and a materialist, was an early advocate of more contemporary ideas that see the difference between animals and humans as being of degree rather than kind. He argued that the idea of proposing an immaterial substance like a soul to explain human behavior was scientifically useless. Sentience and rationality are "a property of the nervous system or rather of the brain."

William James, as noted, was perhaps the last philosopher-psychologist, a philosophical pragmatist, and a functional psychologist. James points out that these early thinkers were arguing in various ways that the soul, our individuality, must somehow be *substantial.* He says they did not believe the brain could be the concrete agent responsible for our thoughts; it must be something that can think about immaterial things, as well as about material things. He says (James, 1890), "The substantialist view of the soul was essentially the view of Plato and of Aristotle. It received its completely formal elaboration in the Middle Ages. It was believed in by Hobbes, Descartes, Locke, Leibnitz, Wolf, Berkeley, and is now defended by the entire modern dualistic or spiritualistic or common-sense school. Kant held to it while denying its fruitfulness as a premise for deducing consequences verifiable here below. Kant's successors, the absolute idealists, profess to have discarded it."

In our discussion of James, we observed that he grounds his arguments about the soul in his ability to account for the properties associated with the soul (e.g., consciousness, the sense of self, rationality, and so on) in terms of how our minds work physically. In a phrase like "I know it was me who made the mistake," the "Me" part of myself is subject to study. He did see the "Me" part as consisting of material, social and spiritual parts. The "I', on the other hand, is indivisible, pure ego and is the thinking self, the mind. It provides continuity in our consciousness, and since it has no substance is not subject to empirical science. The idea of a separate soul (especially a personal one) arising from these activities we associate with a mind *may* be possible, but it has little explanatory value for psychology.

By the end of the nineteenth century, while the self as a unifying concept was still being used, philosophy and science (and especially psychology) were starting to deconstruct it into parts that could be studied more effectively. James, according to Martin and Barresi, "divided the self mercilessly," so much so, his thinking foreshadowed the demise of the self. J. B. Watson (1878 to 1958), B. F. Skinner (1904 to 1990), and others were experimental psychologists who felt they could explain us through our behavior. Sigmund Freud (1856 to 1939) framed us in terms of our id, ego, and superego. His student Carl Jung (1875 to 1961)[91] was focused on our minds as consisting of ego, personal unconscious, and the collective unconscious.

As philosophy evolved and modern science emerged, an immaterial, eternal soul as a useful theoretical assumption began to fade. While the attributes associated with the soul, such as consciousness, self, will, rationality, and morality continued, they were now associated with the mind. The mind, in turn, increasingly became disconnected from the soul, and science focused on the mind and its relationship to the body (the mind-body problem). Neuroscientists view these experiences through the lens of the patterns of brain and neural activity in our bodies. Nevertheless, religion continued to reason about the soul and its eternal destiny.

That being said, we can look across the history of how philosophers thought about the soul and look at the range of attributes that have at various points been attributed to the soul. Some probably can be eliminated since it is now clear they are the properties of the body, rather than a soul. Others may show up as properties that are highly influenced by the body, but that, in fact, are an integration of something that is physical, and something that is non-physical and more transcendent. Still others, as in James' discussion of the immortality of the soul, may be how we as souls influence and are influenced by the world through our bodies, or that connect us with a more spiritual realm that exists beyond the physical world in which we live.

We, as ordinary people, typically still feel our selfness, and most of us identify it with our souls. Moreover, as we saw in Chapter 1, we tend to believe those selves will carry what defines us into the life after this one. Our beliefs about having souls and many aspects of those souls' nature go back to the earliest Neanderthals and early humans. This persistent belief we have is different from whether the soul or the self are philosophically or scientifically helpful ideas at this point, especially in terms of the ability of the ideas to support academic theorizing about how the world works. Just like our conscious experience of reality is just a sketch of the *actual* world (and is unique to each of us), our experience of our souls may be a partial representa-tion of something larger we have yet to understand fully. Fundamentally though, as Martin and Barresi note, "Ordinary people did not have to study philosophy to know about selves and souls. They got that knowledge at their mother's knee."

TITLE Potential Properties of the Soul

o Life Force
o Sensation and Perception
o Spirit or Shade
o Source of Movement and Activity
o Center of Desires and Emotions (e.g., love, hate, and grief)
o Relationship (e.g., "true" love in the abstract)
o Embodiment of Virtues (e.g., justice, courage, and temperance)
o Moral Awareness and Judgment
o Personality
o Spiritual Awareness, Sense, and Connection Point
o Soul-body Connection
o Awareness of Fundamental Reality (e.g., truth, beauty, and forms)
o Consciousness and Awareness of Experience
o The Self (esp. the non-physical self), Essential Uniqueness
o Spiritual Self, Connection to Spiritual Realm

---

[70] Although authorship and dating are subjects of ongoing debate.

[71] I have to say, this makes me feel a little guilty over some of my past gardening efforts.

[72] As working definitions to help keep track of ideas for this discussion, think of the self, as of course, that which we would fundamentally use to distinguish ourselves from others. The mind would refer to the collection of processes like reasoning, thinking, feeling, willing, perceiving, judging, and so on. The mind would

include conscious and unconscious processes and experiences. Consciousness would be the state of being aware of ourselves, the world we inhabit and how we are interacting with it.

[73] In this book, I will be referring to dualism and physicalism (and the earlier term materialism), and naturalism. Each of these terms may be defined differently by various authors, and each has a dizzying range of variations. In general, dualism contrasts with monism and pluralism. As we use dualism, it will refer to the distinction between a body and a soul. Monism argues that everything can be explained by one common idea. Physicalism, the modern version of materialism, is a type of monism that explains everything in terms of the universe's physical laws. Naturalism here will be the shorthand for the scientific method often coupled with physicalism to uncover the laws that govern the universe. I will preserve your sanity by letting you indulge any possible curiosity by searching the internet yourself for terms like reductive physicalism (incl. behaviorism, identity theory, and functionalism), non-reductive physicalism (incl. emergentism and eliminativism), neutral monism, and reflective monism; and interactionism, occasionalism, epiphenomenalism, epistemological dualism, value dualism, and parallelism.

[74] A central character in Plato's dialogues is Socrates, and there is often a question of which beliefs are Socrates' and which are Plato's. For this discussion, it seems reasonable to treat the views expressed by Plato as his even when Socrates is a character in the story.

[75] There is a more contemporary idea in physics that is an echo of this idea called the mathematical universe hypothesis proposed by Max Tegmark. It argues that physical reality is not just describable by mathematics, but that reality is in fact a mathematical structure. We as humans are just "self-aware substructures" within the system. Michio Kaku's recent book, *The God Equation: The Quest for a Theory of Everything*, describes some of this thinking.

[76] If I had kept up with my reading of the *Great Books* from my college days, I might be nearing the end. Alas, I did not manage it.

[77] If you were looking for a way to evaluate the value of Aristotle's ideas, for better or worse, you could point to one of his students, Alexander the Great.

[78] Of course, as we discussed in a previous chapter, we now know that the rest of the animal kingdom also has varying degrees of reason and thought, in some areas superior to ours.

[79] For example, when people rate a particular video experience, their

ratings will improve as the quality of the sound improves.

[80] As we have noted, some stories could be models that carry explanations for near-death and other experiences. Our ability to empathize within stories may be part of the evolutionary benefits they offer for dealing with the stress of loss and the disruption to the community and family, and so need to be accounted for in theories of the soul.

[81] I would note that having been operated on at one point, the anesthesia that can be used has at times clearly dissociated a sense of *me* from pains in different parts of my body.

[82] Modern research, of course, suggests this is too broad of a generalization.

[83] I must say I wonder how often the royalty around now ponder these questions.

[84] B. J. Underwood is rated as one of the one hundred most eminent psychologists of the 20th century, and number twenty-three in the list of most cited psychologists.

[85] Perhaps not unlike Dr. MacDougall.

[86] The section on the soul in James' work is the only time I have seen a discussion of the soul in one of my psychology textbooks.

[87] This approach could be used to recognize that experiences of a dead loved one may have physiological roots, while also considering the possibility of a trigger or source that is not subject to empirical verification.

[88] Locating the Ib in the heart does makes one wonder about what ancient Egyptian scholars and theologians might make of artificial hearts or heart transplants today.

[89] We have mentioned earlier that Gates and Taliaferro note that Augustine makes an argument that is consistent with a theory of soul. He says we can make inferences about the relationship between what we attribute to our souls, our bodies, and behavior, and our interactions with the world. Furthermore, we can empirically observe the behavior of others and make similar inferences about their souls.

[90] Priestley discovered we breathe oxygen, and even better invented carbonated water. When I have my gin and tonic, I make a toast to Priestley.

[91] The daughter of a student of Carl Jung was as post-doctoral student in my PhD professor's experimental psychology lab. There were times when it seemed like she was looking into my soul.

Chapter 5

THE THEOLOGY
OF THE SOUL

*"The three great Western monotheistic religions,[92] with
their common origin in the Hebrew Bible, have had an
enormous influence on subsequent thinking about the self
and personal identity...most fundamentally, in each,
humans are thought not only to survive into an afterlife
where what they have done prior to their bodily deaths can
be rewarded or punished, but to resurrect, thus encouraging
philosophical reflection not only on personal identity over
time but on the identity of the body over time. Collectively,
the three religions bequeathed to the philosophy of self and
personal identity its most enduring preoccupations:
personhood, subjectivity, and identity over time."*
– Martin and Barresi

We looked at the philosophy of the soul in the last
chapter. The focus was on evolving ideas about the
soul as who we are. The ideas ranged from the soul
as a kind of life force, to the soul as our self and mind, to the
soul as virtually everything that we might use to define ourselves uniquely (e.g., including our personalities, mind, moral
judgment, and will). One recurring question that was being explored was how the soul (and later the mind) acts on the world
through the body. Another was how what we sense from the
world through the body turns into our experience of ourselves.
There was relatively less interest in the afterlife for early philosophers except in the case of ideas like reincarnation. For

religion, as we have noted, ideas about the afterlife and its implications for how we should live now are key themes in our culture and have been for societies across history.

As we turn to religion, I need to set expectations. As with the great philosophers, I am not going to try to cover the major religions comprehensively. Since I am particularly interested in ideas in American culture about our souls and the implications for the afterlife, I will focus on the major religions that shape our popular beliefs. Exploring each faith fully is simply too large of a topic and has been done elsewhere better than I can do it. Instead, I want to survey the most relevant beliefs for our natural history, and some related minor beliefs that provide a little color and context for the ideas.

For the Abrahamic religions, in particular, early Greek philosophers and their descendants influenced theologians and provided ideas that are still with us. But in general, the religious thought that impacts people's daily lives and that we saw in the surveys of popular culture is less about the mind-body or soul-body problem that interested the philosophers. Instead, in the various religions, the lens tends to be about who we are as created human beings as that gives shape to expectations about the afterlife and how we ensure we have a good one.

JUDAISM

We should begin by noting that both ancient and modern Judaism's primary concern, whether Reformed, Conservative, or Orthodox, is more about the nation, about being the Chosen People, and not as much about the person and their unique afterlife. The emphasis is on the soul of a nation versus an individual's soul. It is often about their responsibility to exercise their free will to make the world we live in better for all of us. One sermon by Rabbi Harold Schulweis (Rabbi Schulweis, n.d.) shared an interesting example that illustrates this.

> *"A...story is told of a pious Jew who boasted to his rabbi that he had saved another Jew's soul. A*

*beggar had asked him for a meal. He agreed but
insisted that first they must pray the afternoon Min-
chah prayers. Before serving him the meal, he
ordered the beggar to wash his hands and recite the
appropriate blessing and thereafter to recite the
Motzi prayer over the bread. The rabbi showed his
annoyance with his pious disciple. 'There are times,
my son, when you must act as if there were no God.'
The disciple, taken aback by this counsel, protested
'Should I act as if no God existed?' The rabbi replied, 'When someone comes to you in need, act as
if there were no God in the universe, act as if you
alone are in the world and that there is no one to
help him except you yourself.' The disciple replied,
'And have I no responsibility for his soul?' The
rabbi replied, 'Take care of your soul and his body,
not vice versa.'"*

From their earliest history, the Jewish ideas of the soul
have continued to grow richer. In Chapter 3, we reviewed the
Hebrew words in the Tanakh, and especially the Torah, often
translated in the Christian Bible as the word *soul*. These are
neshama, ruach, and nefesh. As a reminder, in Genesis 1:2
(JPS), "Now the earth was unformed and void, and darkness
was upon the face of the deep; and the spirit [wind, spirit,
breath; *ruach*] of G-d hovered over the face of the waters."
Genesis 2:7 (JPS) reads, "Then HaShem G-d formed man of
the dust of the ground, and breathed into his nostrils the breath
of life [*neshama*]; and man became a living soul [living being;
nefesh]." Job 12:7-10 (JPS), reads "In whose hand is the soul
[life; *nefesh*] of every living thing, and the breath [spirit; *ruach*] of
all mankind."

In their uses here, the words sometimes translated as soul
do not obviously carry the attributes we associate with the soul
today. Neshama is about animating the body and giving it life.
Many believe that this neshama breath is unique in making us
human and connecting us to the divine. Ruach also comes
from this sense of wind or enlivening breath, and applies to all
living things. Nefesh initially is about being a living being (incl.

239

the idea of sentience), and the word was also used for animals. It can also be associated with the blood as a sign of life.

Leningrad Codex (c. 1155)

In Genesis 2:19 (JPS), when it says, "And out of the ground Ha-Shem G-d formed every beast of the field, and every fowl of the air; and brought them unto the man to see what he would call them; and whatsoever the man would call every living creature, that was to be the name thereof," the phrase "living creature" contains the same two words used earlier for "living soul" about Adam himself. John Goldingay (2006) writes, "The life of a human being came more directly from God, and it is also evident that when someone dies, the breath (ruach, e.g., Ps 104:29) or the life (nefesh, e.g., Gen 35:18) disappears and returns to the God who is ruach."

In books of the Tanakh that were written later than the Torah, all three terms became understood to be more than just the animating spirit and grew to capture some of what it is to be what we think of as souls and the idea of souls existing separately from the body. The dualist concept of an immortal soul as separable from the body began to appear around the time of the Babylonian exile (597 to 538 BCE). It likely started to emerge in the context of Persian and Hellenistic (Greek) beliefs of the time. Around 300 BCE (roughly the time of Plato and Aristotle), the Tanakh was translated into Greek in the Septuagint. The Hebrew word *nefesh* became the Greek *psyche*, the word which we translate in English as *soul*.

Nefesh has the meaning of "person" or "living" being, but across scriptures, it could mean being, life, self, or person. It is also used for derivative ideas like desire, appetite, emotion, and passion. While psyche carries these ideas, it also grew through the Hellenistic period to have the meanings we think of today as defining the self. These meanings include concepts such as the soul, the source of will, our consciousness and uniqueness (e.g., our personality), and immortality. As the Greek words were applied to the original Hebrew, the expanded ideas were often overlaid on the original contexts by rabbis and other theologians. But some writers still recognize that the words nefesh and psyche, while often translated as soul, do not naturally in themselves imply immortality, nor the specific ideas of consciousness and rationality that were so important for the Greeks.

According to the article entitled "Body and Soul" in *My Jewish Learning* (MJL, n.d.), Hellenistic ideas had their most profound influence on Jewish and Christian thinkers around the early CE years. While individual groups took somewhat different perspectives, Philo (20 BCE to 50 CE) used these concepts of neshama, nefesh, and ruach to support Plato's view of the parts of the soul. By the Talmudic period, after the destruction of the second Temple (70 CE), the body and soul were thought of as being in harmony. "Just as the Holy One of Blessing fills the world, so does the soul [neshama] fill the body. Just as the Holy One of Blessing sees but cannot be seen, so does the soul see but cannot be seen" (Berakhot 10a).

The Midrash Leviticus Rabbah described the soul as a guest in the body, and Hillel the Elder commanded care for the body since it is created in God's image. Rabbeinu Bahya (during the medieval period) pointed out that even bodily fluids that are considered impure are only impure after they have left the human body. Sin is not presented as an unruly body asserting itself over a soul that it is pure, but rather both are a partnership with equal responsibility for actions both in this life and the next. In the Body and Soul article, it says:

> *"This concept is illustrated in the following Talmudic anecdote, from tractate Sanhedrin: The Emperor Antoninus tries to convince Rabbi Yehudah Hanasi that the body and soul can each excuse themselves from sin by claiming that the transgression is the fault of the other, since without its counterpart, it is lifeless. Rabbi Yehudah counters with a parable: Two guards—one blind and one lame—are in a garden. Together, they are able to steal some fruit from a high tree. When caught, each*

claims that he is obviously unable to commit the crime due to his disability. In the end, the orchard owner places the lame man on the back of the blind man, and they are judged as one. Similarly, God judges the actions of the body and soul in partnership after returning the soul to the body at resurrection."

One question that differentiates some philosophers and theologians is whether souls have existed forever, are created as needed, or are repurposed through reincarnation. Plato, for example, believed they have always existed. Catholics, in general, believe we are created at conception. One early church father, however, Tertullian, argued for traducianism. In this idea, only one soul was created by God, and that was Adam's. When human propagation happens, both the physical and the immaterial aspect (the soul) derive from the parents. Some early rabbis in the Midrash Tanhuma argued that all our souls were part of the Creation in Genesis and that before we take our first breath at birth, God identifies our soul and has angels show the soul how living in the new body will benefit its growth.

While there are passages in the Tanakh that suggest a model of the afterlife, it is generally believed that before around 200 BCE, there was not a well-articulated belief in an afterlife with reward and punishment. Isaiah (Isaiah. 26:19), written possibly between 740 and 436 BCE, did announce the "dead shall live, their bodies shall rise," and the "dwellers in the dust" would be called to "awake and sing."

We have mentioned the story of Saul and the ghost of Samuel before, and it is worth quoting more fully. 1 Samuel was written about 550 BCE, around the Babylonian Exile. In I Samuel 28 (JPS), Saul has banished the mediums and magicians. But he feels God is not speaking to him, so he needs some help. He goes to a medium in Endor (a.k.a., the Witch of Endor) and asks her to summon Samuel for advice. In verses 12 to 17, it says:

"And when the woman saw Samuel, she cried with a loud voice; and the woman spoke to Saul, saying:

*'Why hast thou deceived me? for thou art Saul.'
And the king said unto her: 'Be not afraid; for what
seest thou?' And the woman said unto Saul: 'I see
a godlike being coming up out of the earth.' And he
said unto her: 'What form is he of?' And she said:
'An old man cometh up; and he is covered with a
robe.' And Saul perceived that it was Samuel, and
he bowed with his face to the ground, and prostrated
himself. And Samuel said to Saul: 'Why hast thou
disquieted me, to bring me up?' And Saul an-
swered: 'I am sore distressed; for the Philistines
make war against me, and G-d is departed from
me, and answereth me no more, neither by prophets,
nor by dreams; therefore I have called thee, that thou
mayest make known unto me what I shall do.' And
Samuel said: 'Wherefore then dost thou ask of me,
seeing HaShem is departed from thee, and is become
thine adversary? And HaShem hath wrought for
Himself; as He spoke by me; and HaShem hath
rent the kingdom out of thy hand, and given it to
thy neighbour, even to David.'*

The implication is not that all the mediums and magicians
were charlatans, but rather that some could reach out to the
other side. Even so, the direction that God's people must not
use them still held (e.g., in Leviticus 19:31). John Cooper
(Cooper, 2000) says, "Dead Samuel is still Samuel....He is the
very person who was once alive....Although this is a highly
unusual occurrence, Samuel is nonetheless a typical resident of
Sheol....Although he implies that he is resting, it was still possible for him to 'wake up' and engage in a number of acts of
conscious communication."

By around 164 BCE we get a more detailed description of
resurrection in Daniel 12 (JPS), where it says, "And many of
them that sleep in the dust of the earth shall awake, some to
everlasting life, and some to shame and everlasting contempt."
Christian theologians with a more apocalyptic viewpoint see
this as an early reference to their eschatology (i.e., their ideas
about the eventual end-of-days and final judgment).

There was a sense that the dead did go to Sheol, where they exist in an ethereal shadowy world (as in Num 16:33, Ps 6:6, and Isa. 38:18). Sheol is the abode of the dead in the Hebrew scriptures. Originally this Sheol was typically thought of more as a metaphor for oblivion than where the dead might be conscious and live in any meaningful sense (see Job 3:13, Ecclesiastes 9:10, and Psalms 88:10-12). On the other hand, some texts suggest that the inhabitants are conscious and active (e.g., Isaiah 14:9-17).

Later, the idea that God would give life to the righteous dead so they can live forever grew in both Judaism and Samaritanism. Britannica (Judaism, n.d.) points to the period from the fourth century BCE to the second century CE as an important period for the development of these ideas. The concept of the resurrection of the body is found in 2 Maccabees (c. 150 BCE).[93] Towards the end of this period, the Platonic influence on Jewish thought was expressed in an apocryphal text known as the Wisdom of Solomon (c. 100 BCE) and reflected common views among cultured Jews of the Diaspora, where being righteous might let you enter an undefiled body.

So by the Second Temple literature, there was a theme among many of heavenly immortality either for all of Israel, or at least for the righteous. Philo of Alexandria, a Jewish thinker living in Alexandria during the first century BCE, believed the individual soul imprisoned in the body here on earth could return to its home in God if righteous, or if wicked would suffer eternal death.

In the *History of the Jewish War*, Josephus (in the first century CE) described the different beliefs about death and the afterlife held by various Jewish groups. The Sadducees (who represented the most conservative sect) held the older traditional doctrines we have been discussing. Josephus and the Christian New Testament say that the Sadducees did not believe in an afterlife. According to Josephus (who was a Pharisee), the Pharisees held that the soul was immortal, and they believed in the idea of resurrection. The righteous souls might "pass into other bodies." In contrast, the souls of the wicked would suffer eternal punishment.[94]

Still, before the destruction at the end of the Second Temple period (70 CE), the Talmud and Midrash had relatively less to say about the afterlife. According to the My Jewish Learning's "Body and Soul" article, the journey after death was not a focus of the ancient Jewish sages. The Talmud and the Midrash do not provide a consensus on a single set of ideas. In the Midrash Tanhuma, there were some suggestions that the body needs the soul, and the soul needs the body. However, some Talmudic Rabbis taught the soul could exist in a conscious state in an ethereal realm independent of the body.

But through the Talmudic period, scholars started pointing back to texts like Genesis 5:24, where Enoch "walked with God, and was not; for God took him," and 2 Kings 2:11, where Elijah was carried heavenward in a chariot of fire. In the following centuries, the immortality of the soul became increasingly important. Ezekiel 37 and Isaiah 24-27 were used to speak of a hope that dwellers in Sheol may be reunited with their bodies in the future. This can also be taken to imply a kind of intermediate state between death and resurrection.[95] After the Temple's destruction in CE 70 and the last resistance to the Romans (c. 135 CE), rabbinic teaching about the soul and the afterlife flowered.

Judah ha Nasi (Judah the Prince) was a patriarch of the Jewish community in Palestine from around 175 to 220 CE, and he compiled a collection of rabbinic laws called the Mishnah. By the early CE years, the dead's resurrection was recognized as a core belief of the Mishnah. In the Thirteen Articles of Faith, resurrection is the thirteenth principle. It states, "I firmly believe that there will take place a revival of the dead at a time which will please the Creator, blessed be His name." Over the next four hundred years, rabbinic teaching flourished and fleshed out codes of civil and religious practice, including beliefs about the afterlife. The ideas of immortality and resurrection became well established. In the Eighteen Benedictions recited daily in synagogues and homes, God is repeatedly addressed as "the One who resurrects the dead." Then in the tractate *Sanhedrin* 10:1, there is a warning that "anyone who said there was no resurrection" would have no share in the world to come. [96]

According to the Afterlife article in the Jewish Virtual Library (Afterlife in Judaism, n.d.), in the Talmud and the Midrash, some wrote that during the first twelve months after death, the soul could come and go until the body has disintegrated. It was argued that this is why the Witch of Endor could summon Samuel. After this interim period, the righteous would go to Paradise, and the wicked would go to a place of judgment, Gehenna or Gehinnom. It is commonly believed that Gehenna was named for a physical place where some of the kings of Judah had sacrificed their children by fire. Some references talk about this time as a kind of sleep where the righteous souls are "hidden under the Throne of Glory." Other references describe full consciousness, and the Midrash says, "The only difference between the living and the dead is the power of speech," and there was speculation about how much the dead know of the world they have moved beyond.

The Afterlife article also points out that "In the days of the messianic redemption the soul returns to the dust, which is subsequently reconstituted as this body when the individual is resurrected. It is somewhat unclear whether the resurrection is for the righteous alone, or whether the wicked too will be temporarily resurrected only to be judged and destroyed, their souls' ashes being scattered under the feet of the righteous." And an ongoing controversy (which also continues in Christian circles today) is whether there is eternal damnation for those who are evil or whether their end is annihilation. In general, according to the Talmud (although the details have been disputed over time), during the political and physical utopia of the afterlife, the righteous will sit in glory in the presence of God in a world of bliss.

Later Neoplatonist Jewish theologians saw the soul in an ascent toward the Godhead (remember Plato's vision of growing across time towards the experience of truth), and in an experience of spiritual bliss knowing God and spiritual beings, communion with them, and presumably reasoning about them. Resurrection left little room for flesh in the equation. Jewish

Aristotelians framed the intellect as the immortal part of humanity, and it would be focused on contemplating God. There was some disagreement whether all are one intellect in this state or whether there are individual intellects. According to the "Afterlife in Judaism" article, "Contemporary Orthodox Judaism, believes in the future resurrection of the dead as part of messianic redemption, and believes in the immortality of the soul after death. Reformed Judaism focuses solely on the spiritual life after death, as opposed to a literal belief in a future resurrection of the body."

Rabbi Telushkin's summarizes many contemporary beliefs about the afterlife in Judaism as:

"In Judaism the belief in afterlife is less a leap of faith than a logical outgrowth of other Jewish beliefs. If one believes in a God who is all-powerful and all-just, one cannot believe that this world, in which evil far too often triumphs, is the only arena in which human life exists. For if this existence is the final word, and God permits evil to win, then it cannot be that God is good. Thus, when someone says he or she believes in God but not in afterlife, it would seem that either they have not thought the issue through, or they don't believe in God, or the divine being in whom they believe is amoral or immoral....Because Judaism believes that God is good, it believes that God rewards good people; it does not believe that Adolf Hitler and his victims share the same fate. Beyond that, it is hard to assume much more. We are asked to leave the afterlife in God's hands."

Rabbi Harold Schulweis (Rabbi Schulweis, n.d.) reinforces this with a story that serves as an important reminder:

"A legend tells of the angels who were jealous that God was to create the human being in God's immortal image. God and his human creations would share immortality. Envious of humans, the angels plotted to hide it from them. One angel proposed that immortality be hidden from them in the mountains

above or the seas beneath far beyond the reach of man or woman. But others argued that human beings would surely climb the mountains and plumb the oceans to find it. The shrewdest angel of all suggested that immortality be hidden within and between human beings. That angel surmised that within and between would be the last place on earth people would search to discover eternal life. But we know the secret. Immortality is within and between us, and its intimations are here and now."

Many rabbis continue to point to Isaiah 64:4 (JPS), "For since the beginning of the world men have not heard, nor perceived by the ear, neither hath the eye seen, O God, beside thee, what he hath prepared for him that waiteth for him." The call is to live well and make a difference in the here and now.

CHRISTIANITY

"[Jesus Christ] suffered under Pontius Pilate, was crucified, died, and was buried; he descended to hell. The third day he rose again from the dead. He ascended to heaven and is seated at the right hand of God the Father almighty. From there he will come to judge the living and the dead. I believe in the Holy Spirit, the holy catholic church, the communion of saints, the forgiveness of sins, the resurrection of the body, and the life everlasting. Amen."
– From the Apostles' Creed

Most people in the United States, as we have noted, identify as Christian. They often define themselves as Christian whether or not they are active in any particular church or religious community. Jesus and Paul in the New Testament wanted the Christian church to be known for its unity and harmony, and its commitment to loving not just one another but also loving people who are not in the community. So what happened? Why are there so many different kinds of Christian churches? There are Eastern Orthodox, Roman Catholics, and Protestants. Among Protestants, there are Episcopalians, Lutherans, Methodists, Presbyterians, Baptists (of different flavors), and Pentecostals. While the numbers vary, there are estimates of thousands and even tens of thousands of denominations worldwide. There are even independent churches like the one I grew up in that are intentionally non-denominational (although they may form loosely organized groups whose beliefs are similar). Often, each believes they have *the correct* understanding of Christianity and God's revelation.

Churches can be filled with squabbling and be torn apart, split over what may seem to outsiders like minor issues in the grand scheme of things. There have been times where some Protestant churches believed Catholics would never make it to heaven, and vice versa. While President Biden's Catholicism was not as big of an issue as it was for John Kennedy, it did come up regularly through the campaign. My wife and I were able to spend some time traveling through Scotland and England. We regularly heard stories about the bloody wars between Catholics and Protestants as they fought for dominance, and historically there have been many wars where both sides claimed God was on their side. Religion is often a cultural identification that bonds groups as much as it is a formal set of considered beliefs that shape personal behavior.

Of course, there are similar divisions and passionate fights over politics, social issues, and other ways communities define themselves in virtually every religion. Many religions identify this as part of the characteristics and imperfections of what it means to be in physical bodies. Some Christians identify this with "original sin" and trace it to the fall of Adam and Eve in the Garden of Eden. Indeed, even Christians recognize they are not perfect. As imperfect beings—whether due to some inherited sin, or immature souls, or the tension between the soul and the nature of our bodies—we all suffer from pride, selfishness, and stubbornness. It is a little ironic that often these attributes are the consequences of the same characteristics of how our minds work that help us bond socially and form the communities that helped us survive in the past. As we have noted, some argue that formal religions with frameworks of reward and punishment in the hereafter grew to help manage this tension in society. This would make sense as tribes and villages became cities, and cities became nations.

It is also true that religious differences, as a result, are often viewed as being literally about life and death. The Catholic Church believes truth can come from the Bible, church fathers, traditions and creeds, and those in authority. Some Protestant denominations look only to the Bible and tradition. Others believe that the source of authority is their interpretation of a favorite translation of the Bible, and perhaps the guidance of their pastors. There are those who feel they or members of their communities may receive direct prophetic and other communication from God. Some churches worship with formal rituals, and others find a shared experience that is more contemporary and dynamic as meaningful. Some of us try to draw from both religious traditions and from science and other sources of human wisdom and insight. You could sort by those who are oriented towards the head and those whose foundation is the heart. While the downside might be the splits that can happen, the upside is the diversity of opportunities for each individual to find meaning in their lives.

Despite all these differences, just as with the other religions we will look at, there are many common beliefs that tend to define the core of Christianity. The two most common statements of the central tenets of Christianity are probably the Nicene Creed and the Apostles' Creed. The Nicene Creed was adopted at the First Ecumenical Council held in Nicaea, Turkey (now İznik), around 325 CE. Today's version is usually the amended form from the Second Ecumenical Council held in Constantinople in 381 CE. The Apostles' Creed emerged around the middle of the fifth century and may be traced to earlier creeds and texts. The Nicene Creed is formally accepted by the Catholic and Eastern Orthodox Churches, and much of mainline Protestantism. The Apostles' Creed is used by the Catholic Church and many Protestant churches.

In terms of the soul and the afterlife, and the rationale for more detailed beliefs about them, the Creeds are very similar. In both, God the Father is identified as the creator of everything. Jesus Christ, according to the Creeds, is God's Son. The Nicene Creed says he was crucified, buried, resurrected, and then ascended to heaven to be with the Father. In the Apostles' Creed, it adds that he descended into the place of the dead (Sheol in the Hebrew, or Hades in the Greek). This is similar to the view of the afterlife in earlier Judaism, and resonates with Jesus' story about Lazarus and the Rich Man (Luke 16:19-31). Note that at this point in the narrative, heaven and hell have not been created. Both Creeds point to a coming Day of Judgment and the forgiveness of sins (by implication for the faithful). They also each mention the resurrection of the body, which Christian scriptures ground in Jesus' resurrection. For Christians, then, as documented in the Creeds, there is an assurance of life everlasting.

The Nicene Creed also has a line that says, "We affirm one baptism for the forgiveness of sins." However, to illustrate the variations among churches, some believe baptism is specifically water baptism and is required to get into heaven. Some insist it must have happened in their denomination. Some argue any water baptism will get you there. For others, baptism is a ritual that is recommended as a demonstration of faith but not required. There are those who believe the only thing required is the baptism of the Holy Spirit, and it happens automatically when someone accepts Jesus Christ as their savior. Some believe baptism of infants gets their children into heaven. Others only see baptism after the age of accountability as meaningful. Still others believe baptism is a ritual of family commitment to how they will raise their child. Affirming that one line about baptism in the Creed covers differences that deeply matter to people.

The Soul

Over the two centuries following Jesus and the Apostles, in Christianity, the concept of the soul (psyche) increasingly began to coalesce around a more Greek (Hellenistic) meaning rather than the ancient Jewish meaning. By the third century, Origen shaped what became the views of the inherent immortality of the soul and its divine, spiritual nature, and he argued that it was infused into the body at conception.

Today the most common view across Christians is the *dualistic or dichotomous view*, in other words, that each of us consists of a body and a soul. In the early Roman Catholic Church, especially influenced by Augustine, this became the dominant

model. As we have noted, this model is less evident in the early Jewish Torah, where the emphasis is on the holistic nature of human beings. However, you can read Gen 2:7 in terms of two steps, one resulting in the physical creation and one consisting of breathing in life to create a complete human. R. Scott Clark (Clark, 2014) discusses this in an interview about Reformed and Presbyterian theology with Dr. Mike Horton from Westminster Seminary. Dr. Horton says that in the Torah and the Tanakh more broadly, you can think of the emphasis as being less about two different substances like body and soul. Instead, it is more about "lower and higher, earthly and heavenly, animal and divine."

In general, Christian New Testament scripture suggests that not only is the soul distinct from the physical body, but it can function somewhat independently of our ordinary mental processes (1 Cor 14:14 and Rom 8:16). When we die, we can act and relate to God (see Luke 23:43 and Acts 7:59). The language used at the time would likely be constrained by how the Aramaic and Greek languages were understood. The culture would shape their interpretation then, just as ours shapes us and our reading of ancient texts. Therefore, the sense of the words may be more about the independence and the continuing activity, and less about the details of what the soul can *do* in the afterlife without a body. We will be reflecting more on what this might imply later.

Philippians 1:23,24 and 2 Corinthians 5:8 point to this future state and its desirability versus the suffering and temptations of this life. However, the discussion's context is typically more focused on how we should be living on this Earth, given the relationship we should be having with God. It is not really about asking the audience to live for a particular vision of the afterlife. The spirit of many New Testament scriptures is in line with more contemporary Jewish thought that is less concerned with the afterlife than with how to live now. For the average citizen of the Roman Empire, though, an image of a paradise for believers could be pretty attractive compared to the more conventional Roman views of the afterlife and the conditions in which they were living (Figula, n.d.).[97]

While the influence of Persian and Hellenistic thought seems to have helped shape these views, the views continued to evolve in new cultural contexts. Paul Flaman (Flaman, 2008) also notes that while Plato believed the soul exists beyond death, and later theologians adopted some of his language and ideas, Plato also believed in reincarnation and that the soul existed before the body was formed. Reincarnation and the preexistence of souls are not commonly accepted among Christians. In other words:

> *"While it is true that patristic and later "traditional" Christian authors often borrowed some of the language and ideas from non-Christian authors such as Plato and Aristotle, in general they appropriated these critically. They accepted views which they considered to be true, to be compatible with Christian faith, but they did not accept views which they considered to be contrary to biblical teaching and God's revelation."*

Less common is a *trichotomous view.* In this view, we consist of three parts: the body, the soul, and the spirit. The assumption is our bodies exist in the physical world, the soul is who we are most fundamentally and is eternal, and the spirit connects us to the spiritual or non-physical world. The soul is assumed to be immaterial but also adapted to a particular body. It includes intellect, emotions, and will. The idea is everyone has a soul, and it can either serve God or turn away into sin.

The spirit most closely relates to God in this view, and in essence, it comes alive when a person becomes a Christian. Those believing in the trichotomous view would argue that it is the spirit that worships and prays to God (e.g., John 4:24 and Philippians 3:3). Part of the role of the spirit is to make the connection between the body, soul, and God. This trichotomous view was more common in the early Greek Alexandrian Church. It had some revival among some nineteenth-century Protestants, and it still is around in a few evangelical circles.

There is not a lot of scholarly support for the concept today, however. The criticism of the trichotomous model is that the words for soul and spirit are synonyms in many places. Clark (Clark, 2014) says, "The main Scriptural distinction is as follows: the word 'spirit' designates the spiritual element in man as the principle of life and action which controls the body; while the word 'soul' denominates the same element as the subject of action in man, and is therefore often used for the personal pronoun in the Old Testament, Ps. 10:1,2; 104: 1; 146: 1; Is. 42:1; cf. also Luke 12:19." The sense is represented in Genesis 2:7, where God breathes into Adam (giving him a spirit or perhaps giving him the spirit of life), and then Adam becomes a living soul. God's followers would have a spirit but are souls. Clark notes that this tends to be how we experience ourselves. We do not typically feel we have a spirit as distinct from a soul.

Often the words are used together to create emphasis. We are said to be either "body and soul" or "body and spirit." Some verses say the soul can sin (1 Peter 1:22 and Rev 18:14), and others say the spirit can sin (Deuteronomy 2:30, 2 Cor 7:1, Isaiah 29:24, 1Cor 7:34). Many of these texts read like common terms similar to how we use these words today. We talk about speaking from the heart, reaching into our soul, having a broken heart, expressing our soul, or being energized in the spirit.[98] When we hear these words, we are not speaking about a formal philosophical or theological position; we are using the words to convey the underlying poetic and expressive ideas.

A third view could be thought of as a kind of *monism*. The idea is that the soul and the body are fully integrated and are not separable. After we die, both soul and body are together until the last judgment, and have the same fate. Monism is not a broadly held view in Christian circles. Still, it can be derived from a particular perspective of the end times, and it may be held by those thinking about what it is to be human through a Christian lens applied to a more materialistic view of the world. Flaman (Flaman, 2008) says:

> *"In general Christian authors who support non-reductive physicalism argue that viewing human beings as only physical organisms ontologically is in accord with the Hebrew view of the Bible. They also consider this view to be in accord with empirical scientific data including the findings of neuroscience which demonstrate a tightening of mind-brain-behavior links. In general they argue that the traditional Christian view of the human soul, beginning with many patristic authors, was overly influenced by a Platonic 'dualism.'"*

A Note on Prayer and the Afterlife

> *"[Judas Maccabeus acted] very well and honorably, taking account of the resurrection. For if he were not expecting that those who had fallen would rise again, it would have been superfluous and foolish to pray for the dead" (2 Maccabees. 12:43–45).*

Christians tend to believe that prayers on behalf of others (Christian or non-Christian) are important. In Romans 15:30 (NIV), for example, Paul requests it. "I urge you, brothers and sisters, by our Lord Jesus Christ and by the love of the Spirit, to join me in my struggle by praying to God for me." In Job 42:8 (JPS), God says, "Therefore take unto you now seven bullocks and seven rams, and go to my servant Job, and offer up for yourselves a burnt offering; and my servant Job shall pray for you: for him will I accept."

Some believe that the dead can intercede on behalf of the living. Both those in favor of the idea and those against the idea point to Luke 16:19-31 (NIV). This is a classic story that is cited a lot (including through this book), so let's look at the text. In Luke, Jesus shares a parable (although some believe it was a historical account):

> "There was a rich man who was dressed in purple and fine linen and lived in luxury every day. At his gate was laid a beggar named Lazarus, covered with sores and longing to eat what fell from the rich man's table. Even the dogs came and licked his sores. The time came when the beggar died and the angels carried him to Abraham's side. The rich man also died and was buried. In Hades, where he was in torment, he looked up and saw Abraham far away, with Lazarus by his side. So he called to him, 'Father Abraham, have pity on me and send Lazarus to dip the tip of his finger in water and cool my tongue, because I am in agony in this fire.'
>
> "But Abraham replied, 'Son, remember that in your lifetime you received your good things, while Lazarus received bad things, but now he is comforted here and you are in agony. And besides all this, between us and you a great chasm has been set in place, so that those who want to go from here to you cannot, nor can anyone cross over from there to us.'
>
> "He answered, 'Then I beg you, father, send Lazarus to my family, for I have five brothers. Let him warn them, so that they will not also come to this place of torment.' Abraham replied, 'They have Moses and the Prophets; let them listen to them.' 'No, father Abraham,' he said, 'but if someone from the dead goes to them, they will repent.' He said to him, 'If they do not listen to Moses and the Prophets, they will not be convinced even if someone rises from the dead.'"

As we have mentioned, while Abraham does not act, there is a sense that he could have under other circumstances. There is another account in 2 Maccabees 15:14-17. Maccabees is considered canonical by Catholics but not by Jews or Protestants. It describes Onias telling a story about Jeremiah, the prophet who had been dead for more than four hundred years at that point.

> *"Then Onias answering, said: 'This is a lover of his brethren, and of the people of Israel: this is he that prayeth much for the people, and for all the holy city, Jeremias the prophet of God.' Whereupon Jeremias stretched forth his right hand, and gave to Judas a sword of gold, saying: 'Take this holy sword a gift from God, wherewith thou shalt overthrow the adversaries of my people Israel.' Thus being exhorted with the words of Judas, which were very good, and proper to stir up the courage, and strengthen the hearts of the young men, they resolved to fight, and to set upon them manfully: that valour might decide the matter, because the holy city and the temple were in danger."*

The Saints, as mentioned, have a special place in Christian eschatology (the final judgment of humanity). There was a belief that martyrs passed immediately at death to the presence of God and sit on thrones. The Eastern Orthodox, Oriental Orthodox, and Roman Catholic Churches all believe in the doctrine of the intercession of the Saints. They believe that in praying through the Saints, the Saints will present these prayers to God and intercede on behalf of those offering the prayers. This practice can be traced to the third century in various Christian writings. On the other hand, Protestant churches strongly reject prayers to the Saints. Instead, they point to 1 Tim 2:5 (NIV), "For there is one God and one mediator between God and mankind, the man Christ Jesus," and other verses that they believe make it clear that we have access to God directly.[99]

At the council of Trent, the doctrine was laid out as "[T]he saints who reign together with Christ offer up their prayers to God for men. It is good and useful suppliantly to invoke them, and to have recourse to their prayers, aid, and help for obtaining benefits from God, through His Son Jesus Christ our Lord, Who alone is our Redeemer and Savior." Gregory of Nazianzus said of his father Saint Gregory the Elder (and a father, by the way, of Saint Gorgonia one of his daughters), "I am well assured that his intercession is of more avail now than was his instruction in former days, since he is closer to God, now that he has shaken off his bodily fetters, and freed his mind from the clay which obscured it."

I worked with a colleague at one point who was a Roman Catholic and asked her why she prayed to Mary. She looked me in the eye and, speaking from a profound conviction, said something like, "Mary is a woman like me. She can understand what I am feeling, and as Jesus' mother, Jesus will be sure to listen to her." She spoke from the comfort of an empathetic connection between someone you identify with and that you feel identifies with you.

Stepping (briefly) into Hell[100]

As the COVID-19 pandemic hit in the spring of 2020, we spent some time binge-watching *The Good Place* on television. If you have watched it, you know the premise is a collection of not particularly remarkable characters who find themselves in what they believe is Paradise. They begin to realize that they might be there by mistake. If you have not seen it (spoilers), it turns out to be an experiment in an alternative hell. There is an ongoing discussion about what it means to be *good*. Eventually, it proposes a framework that recognizes various mixtures of good and bad behavior and provides a way for most of the one hundred and seven billion people who have lived so far to continue to improve until the majority end up in Paradise.

We have reviewed some of the religious systems that include various heavens and hells, and a variety of mechanisms they believe are used to distinguish the good from the bad based on our allotted three score and ten years of life that may determine our eternal destinies. As we noted in the surveys taken in the United States, most Americans who believe in heaven are confident that they will end up there whatever their religious background. Furthermore, they are remarkably tolerant in thinking that others (even atheists) will also make it. Very few believe they will probably end up in hell, and they may be dealing with other issues. A common view is that hell is a place where people who have led horrible lives and who are unrepentant will go, and natural examples are the Adolf Hitlers and Saddam Husseins of the world. It feels right to us that as the Wisdom of Solomon 6:6 (one of the apocryphal books included in the 1611 KJV, but later removed) says, "For mercy will soon pardon the meanest: but mighty men shall be mightily tormented." The average person typically does not think the minor mistakes they have made through their lives should doom them, especially since most believe we have good hearts.

It is helpful to look at its evolution across Judeo-Christian history to understand this concept. As mentioned, in ancient Jewish belief, everyone went to Sheol, a place of darkness, silence, and forgetfulness. By the time of the Second Temple period, the idea of Sheol started to have separate areas for the righteous and the wicked. During that time, of course, most non-Jews would probably be in the category of the wicked. By the first century CE, some Jews were awaiting a resurrection and judgment that would see the righteous in Paradise (the bosom of Abraham) and the unrighteous in torment. Some believe that Jesus' parable of the Rich Man and Lazarus in Luke 16:19-31 is using this common imagery among Jews at the time as it tells the story of the two areas within Hades (in the Greek), one where the poor man Lazarus enjoys bliss in the bosom of Abraham, and the other where the rich man is being tormented.

In the Christian New Testament, John the Seer (c. 100 CE) paints a picture of punishment for the wicked who had been causing havoc for a thousand years. In Revelation 20:10 (NIV), he says, "And the devil, who deceived them, was thrown into the lake of burning sulfur, where the beast and the false prophet had been thrown. They will be tormented day and night for ever and ever." Eventually, death itself and Hades will be destroyed in the lake of fire. Jesus in Matthew 25:41-43 (NIV), speaking to his disciples about the judgment, defines the pool of those who will be punished:

> *"Depart from me, you who are cursed, into the eternal fire prepared for the devil and his angels. For I was hungry and you gave me nothing to eat, I was thirsty and you gave me nothing to drink, I was a stranger and you did not invite me in, I needed clothes and you did not clothe me, I was sick and in prison and you did not look after me....[W]hatever you did not do for one of the least of these, you did not do for me."*

Images of a lake of fire connected with the impression the people of the time had of Gehenna, the burning trash area where during earlier years children were sacrificed. It would be like referencing the horrific images of the Holocaust today.

One of my professors in seminary, Clark Pinnock (an influential evangelical theologian), wrote, "Everlasting torment is intolerable from a moral point of view because it makes God into a bloodthirsty monster who maintains an everlasting Auschwitz for victims who he does not even allow to die." Another of my professors, John Stott (an Anglican clergyman and a famous evangelical leader), expressed a similar thought when he said, "I question whether 'eternal conscious torment' is compatible with the biblical revelation of divine justice." He says that "Fundamental to [divine justice] is the belief that God will judge people 'according to what they [have] done' (e.g., Revelation 20:12), which implies that the penalty inflicted will be commensurate with the evil done."

Critics of Eternal Conscious Torment also note this lack of proportional punishment. Would a loving God punish hundreds of billions of the people that He has created with an eternity of torture, each based on a single finite lifetime of failing to be perfect? According to Genesis, each has already been punished with a lifetime of pain and suffering that ends with physical death itself.

Hell as a Christian doctrine is gradually losing ground in popular culture and more mainstream denominations, but it is also being reexamined even within the evangelical community. Mark Strauss (Strauss, 2016) quotes Edward Fudge, whose book *The Fire That Consumes* is a contemporary exploration that helped stimulate the current debate. Fudge says, "What if the muting of hell is due neither due to emotional weakness nor loss of Gospel commitment? What if the biblical foundations thought to endorse unending conscious torment are less secure than has been widely supposed?"

It is one thing to read New Testament scriptures in this area as doctrinal descriptions of a literal eschatological process of final judgment. It is still another to read them through the lens of looking at Jesus and Paul as Jewish preachers trying to motivate transformation among their listeners using familiar language and images. As we look at some of the verses used to describe hell, they seem to read more like rhetorical devices designed to make larger points than attempts to define theology.

For example, Matthew 5:22 is in the context of the beatitudes, and it emphasizes the point that even being angry with your "brother" is terrible. Matthew 18:8-9 speaks to those getting in the way of innocents coming to God and is paired with saying that you should cut off your hand or foot, or remove your eye, if they might cause you to sin. Hebrews 10:27 and Jude 7 express righteous indignation at those in the church who use their faith as a license to sin or who are attacking the church, and in the case of Romans 2:7-9, it is calling out those in the church who condemn others. It seems like they are using expressions that were in everyday use to be more persuasive. Many of us have heard similar rhetorical techniques used to make a point even today, both from politicians and from the pulpit.

Strauss describes three of the current alternative views about the destinies of the "wicked." Fudge himself is a proponent of "annihilationism" or "conditional immortality." *Annihilationism* views the result of final judgment and the image of fire as implying that sinners cease to exist. A similar idea is in Matthew 3:12, where John the Baptist uses the imagery of a wheat harvest to describe the final judgment, where the chaff is burned up in a fire. He notes that this is equivalent to spiritual capital punishment and seems more merciful than an eternity of torture. Irenaeus of Lyons (a second-century bishop) in his *Against Heresies* emphasized that he believed the soul is not inherently immortal, that eternal life requires God's active intervention. "It is the Father who imparts continuance forever on those who are saved" by the resurrection of Christ. The "wicked" would fade from existence.

Preston Sprinkle (co-author of *Erasing hell*, which rose to number three on the *New York Times* bestseller list in 2011) said, "My prediction is that, even within conservative evangelical circles, the annihilation view of hell will be the dominant view in 10 or 15 years...I base that on how many well-known pastors secretly hold that view. I think that we are at a time and place when there is a growing suspicion of adopting tradition for the sake of tradition."

In the early centuries of Christianity, there was not a consensus on the nature of hell. Origen Adamantius (a third-century theologian) believed the wicked were punished after death, but the goal was to help the wicked repent and be restored to purity. This doctrine—which is still held today by many—is *universalism* and seems more aligned with the belief both of a loving God and a goal of the creation to bring all into a relationship with God. The Catholic vision of purgatory would fit into this category. Reincarnation could be thought of as another flavor of this mechanism, as it provides a way to improve by living more than one life. The larger view is that when God created us, the intent was not to just have a relationship with a select few. Instead, God would love us so much God would figure out how to ensure most *would* make it to the originally intended state of blessing.

Another view, at least as I think of it, is the absence-of-God model, and often related to that is the one-last-chance possibility. Mark Galli (the editor of *Christianity Today*) says, "I certainly wouldn't agree that hell is a place of literal fire or torment...I tend to be more favorable toward the metaphors that talk about hell as the absence of a love of God and that would be a miserable existence." There are many rich descriptions about how wonderful being in a direct, spiritual relationship with the Creator will be, and the love and joy in which we will be swimming. In contrast, if one chose to refuse that blessing, all the despair, depression, and pain representing the worst of what some have experienced in life would presumably be similarly magnified. That would be a hell.

The one-last-chance variation is that just as there is an age of accountability in this life, there probably will be a future state of accountability or a final informed point of decision. A background context, of course, might be that as some scriptures and writers have noted, there could be those who think they are welcome into heaven and who will be surprised, and some who we might not expect to be there that are welcome. C. S. Lewis wrote about his belief in this vein, where after death, he proposed everyone will face God and have the ability to decide on whether to be in communion with God in light of the reality they would then see fully.

In Acts 17:22-31, Paul visited Athens and pointed to an altar to the Unknown God. He declared he was going to tell them about that God. My father-in-law and others visiting remote, isolated tribes have found connections between what the people already believe and the messages the missionaries were bringing (different words, but common concepts). People in many different faiths have pursued—based on what they know and to the best of their ability—connecting with the Creator, spirituality, and love of others. Presumably, after we go from this limited, physical world to the next one where the barriers of awareness and understanding fall, that would be the point where we really could make the most informed decision about the afterlife. Those that even in that knowledge and experience turn from God, in essence, are in a hell of their own choosing and making.

Alternative Christian Approaches

Catholicism.

The Catholic Church believes that originally God planned for humanity to be in eternal communion with God. When Adam and Eve ate of the fruit in Eden, it meant that humanity was cursed to face suffering and death, and with that came the fear of death. Given the original sin of Adam and Eve, and our fallen state, to rescue us from death, God broke the power of the curse of death by incarnating as a human (Jesus Christ), dying on the cross, and resurrecting. That enabled anyone who

Mosaic of Christ, Roman Villa, in Dorset, England

believes in Christ and follows him to achieve salvation and have eternal life in heaven with God. Following Christ for much of history would, of course, generally be assumed to involve being a member of the Catholic Church.

The Roman Catholic Church believes that there is an immediate personal judgment when the soul separates from the mortal body at death. *Who* we are is the soul, and that is how we stand in judgment. The Catholic *Catechism* teaches, "Each man receives his eternal retribution in his immortal soul at the very moment of his death, in a particular judgment that refers his life to Christ:

either entrance into the blessedness of heaven—through a purification or immediately—or immediate and everlasting damnation." (#1022). Each person will account for the good they have done and the sins they have committed. If a person is free of sin, they will be admitted to heaven and be able to commune with God face-to-face.

It is a tall order, though, to be completely free of sin. The Catholic Church believes there is an intermediate state called purgatory. Purgatory is where the Lord will cleanse us. We will then be welcomed into heaven. However, if we have died rejecting God, have committed mortal sins, and will not repent, then we are destined for hell. Then, when the Lord comes again at the end of time, there will be a final judgment of those still living at that point and the dead.

John 5:27-29 (NIV) says, "He has given him authority to judge because he is the Son of Man. Do not be amazed at this, for a time is coming when all who are in their graves will hear his voice and come out—those who have done what is good will rise to live, and those who have done what is evil will rise to be condemned." The Catholic *Catechism* says, "In the presence of Christ, who is Truth itself, the truth of each man's relationship with God will be laid bare. The Last Judgment will reveal even to its furthest consequences the good each person has done or failed to do during his earthly life" (#1039). Those who have already been judged will remain in heaven or hell.

According to Father W. P. Saunders (Father Saunders, n.d.), "Since after the final judgment, only heaven and hell will exist, St. Augustine and others speculated that all purification of the soul—for those already in purgatory and now those faithful awaiting judgment at this final judgment—will be completed....Archbishop Fulton Sheen stated, 'For when the curtain goes down on the last day, and we respond to the certain call of judgment, we will not be asked what part we played, but how well we played the part that was assigned to us' (Moods and Truths, 75)."

The Roman Catholic Church also believes that the kingdom of God began with Christ's death and resurrection, and it is the charge of Catholics to extend the kingdom by emulating

Christ, promoting peace and justice, and seeking and following God's will. The perfection of the kingdom and Christ's ultimate triumph will not happen until the end of time and that final judgment.

While there is the official set of doctrines of the Church, there are differences within the community of Catholics. There was a time when the Catholic Church was more exclusionary. But after Vatican II, it became clear that the criterion for entering heaven is not about being Catholic per se but instead conforming to the Lord's ways. For many, more important than being a member of a specific religious group is being committed to living in a good and godly way. Currently, some believe heaven, purgatory, and hell are physical spaces; others believe heaven and hell are states where heaven is an eternal union with God and hell is a state of eternal separation from God.

Protestantism.

There are various approaches to the afterlife within Protestantism, especially when looking from more progressive churches to the politically conservative evangelical wing of the church. All typically reject the idea of a purgatory that provides a mechanism of purification. This is partly because Protestants believe that salvation is not a function of how much good one has done, but instead, it is a function of one act. Has an individual accepted the forgiveness of sins offered by God through Jesus as a Lord and Savior? All their sins before and after, at that point, are forgiven, although they are called to change their lives at that point. There are differences between believers across the range of Protestant churches about the nature of this acceptance, and there is an ongoing tension between ideas of loving forgiveness and justice. That can have implications for how many of those from the past, those around the world who have never heard the Gospel, children, and others will be treated at the final judgment.

Another source of differences is what happens immediately at death. Some believe the soul is unconscious between death and that Day of Judgment (often referred to as "soul sleep"). Others expect to go to an intermediate place such as the one described in Jesus' parable about Lazarus and the rich man, a kind of waiting room for heaven or hell. They will then resurrect at the final judgment for a second trial. There is a view that the righteous get to go immediately to be with Christ in heaven (like the thief on the cross did), and everyone else hangs out in Sheol or Hades until the final judgment. These and other ideas can be passionately held, but again, this was not a critical issue for believers at the time, and so the details of a specific timeline leave plenty of opportunity for speculation and debate. When Jesus was alive, some of his followers expected Jesus' immediate return and that they could bypass this whole question. In Matthew 24:34 (NIV), he says, "Truly I tell you, this generation will certainly not pass away until all these things have happened." Since it has been two thousand years, the time between death and the final judgment could be significant.

Reformation Broadsheet

Some of these models imply that when we are at the funeral of a loved one and the pastor says they are in heaven waiting for us, that comforting thought strictly speaking may not be accurate depending on their theological position. Quizzing them probably is not appropriate, but a more precise blessing might be that you *will* see them at some indefinite period of time in the future. I personally hope it will be like some of the medical procedures I have gone through, where they give me a shot, and while I feel like I wake up immediately, several hours will have passed.[101]

According to Protestant denominations, the end of the world's history as we know it is on Judgment Day, as it is in Catholicism. At that point, all will be resurrected from throughout human history. Most Protestant denominations believe there will be some form of a physical body that will resemble but not necessarily be identical to the bodies we possessed during our earthly existence.[102] Jesus' resurrection is the model of this, including his body's physicality and marks of his crucifixion.

Jesus' resurrection does, of course, raise some questions about exactly what our bodies will be like, especially given today's understanding of areas like human biology, transplants, cybernetics, recognition of different ages, and disabilities. Even in the accounts of Jesus' resurrection, commentators have to take some steps to explain why Jesus is not always immediately recognized in his resurrected body. However, eventually, he is recognized in his interactions with people. In 1 Cor 15:12-19, Paul argues that resurrection (by implication of a body) is fundamental to the faith.

This is not a place to go deeply into the details of alternative views of eschatology and the end times. These differences have driven a variety of significant divisions among different Christian groups. From the perspective of the soul and the ultimate afterlife, there is more continuity. The differences are in how literal to take various passages in the Bible and in the attempts to rationalize a timeline.

We can touch on these divisions to get an overview. Since the beginning of Christianity (see Matthew 16: 27,28 and Matthew 24: 25-34), there have been those that expected Christ to return at any time. This expectation is often heightened when different groups feel the turmoil and stresses of their time and place in history. Broadly speaking, there are three different models: amillennialism, postmillennialism, and premillennialism. Most Christians are either effectively amillennialists or postmillenialists, or identify with denominations that hold these views. Frankly, however, very few people I know have ever heard of these terms.

The *amillennialists* believe that Jesus is currently ruling in heaven, and the one thousand years represents an extended reign that began with his resurrection and will end when he returns. In essence, we are already in the millennium, and the thousand-year figure just stands for "a really long time." Christians are empowered by the Holy Spirit and working towards an age of peace, prosperity, and health. This age includes both elements of victory but also of ongoing suffering. Then Jesus will return, overcome Satan and evil, and judge humanity. At that point, we will enter the eternal age. We should always be living like the return will happen at any moment.

The *postmillennialists* also believe that Jesus will return after the millennium (indeed, at one point, amillennialists were called postmillennialists). Furthermore, they also think there will be a general resurrection of the righteous and the wicked and a final judgment, culminating in a new heaven and a new Earth. Postmillennialists, however, see the story as being one of a growing victory for Christianity where the majority of people on the planet will eventually be saved. They predict there will be a kind of growing utopia of peace and justice in the world. The slide in the number of people identifying as Christian in this scenario could be an issue, at least at this point in time.

Premillennialism, as you might guess, says Christ will return before the millennium. There are some differences between historic and dispensational flavors, but they generally share the same sequence of events. Christ's return will be preceded by something called the Tribulation. This is a seven-year period characterized by disasters, famine, war, pain, suffering, and persecutions of the righteous (esp. Christians). It will culminate in the return of Christ in a final battle where Satan is bound and imprisoned with Christ ruling as the king over the Earth for the millennium. When Christ returns, there will be a resurrection of believers who will rule with Christ. This idea of a rapture was depicted (and sometimes ridiculed) in some popular books and movies a few years ago. But towards the end of the thousand years, Satan is released, there is a huge global rebellion, and then after putting it down, the final judgment happens, and the new heavens and Earth begin.

Premillennialism took off around the time of the French and American revolutions, in a context of some groups seeing these revolutions as a sign of Christ's return. Over history, people have seen the signs over and over again. My mother-in-law had a tendency to see whatever terrible thing was being covered in the news as a sign of the Second Coming. Some have even attempted to do what they can to hasten it. This does remind us of the early history of humanity where we tried to exercise control over our gods.

Not too surprisingly, there are different views about what will happen around the Tribulation. For the mid-tribulationists, the church will be around during the first half when they will see the signs, but then will be raptured up to be with Christ and miss the second half, representing God's wrath. The pretribulationists believe the church will be raptured before the seven years of tribulation begins, and then with Christ will return as part of the Kingdom's subsequent millennial rule. The righteous dead will also be resurrected at this time. The posttribulationists see the church as having to go through the entire tribulation, and then it will be raptured, and the dead will resurrect to be with Christ. All the righteous will then immediately return to participate in the millennial Kingdom. Being human, while many are charting which verse defines which timeline, Jesus cautions us in Matthew 24:36 (NIV), "But about that day or hour no one knows, not even the angels in heaven, nor the Son, but only the Father."

For most Protestants, heaven is generally characterized as an eternal state of blessedness in the presence of God, as was intended from the time of the creation of the Garden of Eden. For many, in turn, hell is an eternal place of torment as a punishment for Adam and Eve's original sin, the sins committed through life, and the lack of accepting God's gift of salvation. Although here again, as we have mentioned, there are different opinions about the degree of suffering depending on the nature of one's failures or intent, whether some exist eternally in torment while others go into oblivion, or whether God will find a way to bring most into a heavenly relationship. One fundamental question for many is whether it is God that is tormenting the bulk of humanity, or do individuals end up, in essence, tormenting themselves because of the choice they have made not to accept God as Lord?

In general, the more conservative Protestant denominations believe the afterlife is in a literal heaven or hell. More progressive Protestants are less accepting of a literal hell because the image of a loving God torturing people for eternity after a relatively short physical life or as a result of what two people did back at the beginning of creation does not seem to make sense. When the discussion of hell comes up in conversations, after agreeing on those who should be there, it is common for most people to ask, "What about...?" They then start to think of a list of people that most recognize as genuinely good or those through history who were raised in cultures different from the nominal American Christian culture. Of course, in the surveys of current culture, we saw that many more people believe in heaven than in hell, and, by far, most people believe they will end up in heaven. Some Protestants even believe that salvation is living in the present and experiencing the blessedness and divine relationship in this life. Hell is living without that relationship.

Flying Up To Heaven. You might think you understand heaven and hell, but not too surprisingly, it can be a little more complicated when you get into the details. In some religions, there are multiple heavens and even multiple hells. For Protestants, the complications depend on your denomination (or even your preferred independent semi-organized group of churches). Charles Baker (1972) lays out some of the issues from a Dispensationalist perspective (the tradition of the church I was in as a kid).

Some reference the Tanakh or some of the New

Testament scriptures that say there is a place referred to as the Jewish Sheol or the Greek Hades (a place of darkness for the dead). In English, the translation might be hell, grave, or pit. Some point to Jesus' parable about Lazarus and the rich man as evidence of this place. This may be thought of as a general holding place for the dead, where souls hang out underground until the Last Judgment when they are reunited with "their" bodies (perhaps in a kind of hibernation until they awake or in a spiritual form in heaven with God). As we have described, the sense of Sheol or Hades is more of an unseen world of the dead, and typically reflects the Hellenistic and earlier beliefs. Others around the time of Christ started to distinguish a kind of pre-judgment at death where everyone gets triaged into either a good place or a nasty place. Again, Jesus's parable in Luke 16 gives this sense, and the New Testament references (and the Apostles' Creed) when it says Jesus descended into hell after his death was describing this view. When Jesus resurrected, some believe he brought the righteous who were there at the time with him. We have noted elsewhere that both many Jews and Christians just view this as an interim state that has existed in the past, but they look to a future time of bliss for the righteous and punishment or annihilation for the wicked.

The New Jerusalem

There is something in the Christian New Testament, referred to as the new Jerusalem. Some believe it describes the church itself, while others see it as a renewal and rebuilding of the existing Jerusalem. But in Revelation, it is described as a massive structure that shows up as Christ returns, coming down from heaven (presumably God's dwelling place, where it has been prepared). It would be the center of God's kingdom on a new Earth, and where he will engage with his people. As we will describe in more detail later, this new Jerusalem is quite an object (although not necessarily what most people in surveys think of as heaven). It is worth noting that given the example of the existing heavens and current Earth, the new heavens and the new Earth will take quite some time to form. For now, think of it in terms of the intent. It is the dwelling place of God (in the model of the old Temple). As a result, the new Jerusalem will not need a temple, unlike ancient Jerusalem.

Some believe the new Jerusalem is heaven; or at least the New Jerusalem is the capital city for the kingdom of God on the new Earth and that is heaven. Some believe there is a place for both Jews and Christians in the kingdom, others believe the new Jerusalem and the new Earth is the eventual home of the nation of Israel, and Christians are in another heaven.

Paul does make a reference in the New Testament to a third heaven. Some rabbis also referred to multiple heavens. Baker (1972) notes that the words distinguish our immediate sky, the stars, and then the dwelling place of God. It is this that most of us traditionally would imagine as heaven. Many view the term Paradise as referring to this as well. The relationship between Paradise and the original Garden of Eden, and this view of heaven and the new Jerusalem (and the kingdom of God on the new Earth) lends itself to various interpretations. When trying to rationalize texts that were not necessarily intended to be a consistent, integrated theological model of the afterlife, one can, as they say, lose the forest for the trees and shrubs.

ISLAM

The third of the Abrahamic religions is Islam, and Islam is the second-largest religion in the world. Moses and eventually Jesus were descendants of Abraham's son Isaac. Muhammad traces his lineage to Ishmael, Abraham's first-born son. Islam is monotheistic, and Allah is the one and only God. Moses is revered within Islam, and among the prophets described in the Qur'an (the Islamic scriptures), he is one of the five most important. Muhammad, Abraham, Noah, and Jesus are the other prophets. Just as Christians often draw parallels between Jesus and passages in the Tanakh, Muslims see parallels between Muhammad and Moses. The Torah (i.e., the Hebrew scriptures that include Genesis, Deuteronomy, Numbers, Leviticus, and Exodus) is considered to be divinely revealed to Moses. Muslims see the Torah and Moses' teaching as foretelling Muhammad. Moses is especially revered because he spoke directly with God, in contrast to the other prophets who communicated with God through intervening angels.

Islamic Gardens as a Metaphor For Heavenly Paradise
Alhambra Court of the Lions

While Muslims do not believe in a Trinity, they do believe Jesus was a prophet of God. They believe he was born to the virgin Mary. They also predict he will return to Earth before the final Day of Judgment to restore justice and defeat what Christians know as the Antichrist, the false messiah. Interestingly, Mary is mentioned in the Qur'an more than in the

Christian New Testament and is the only woman to be mentioned by name in the whole Qur'an. There is an entire chapter named after her.

In Islam, life and death are both given by God. Life is sacred, and so only God has the right to take it back. Suicide is considered a major sin. Even in conditions of extreme hardship, the prayer should be in the sense of "Oh Allah! Let me live as long as life is good for me, and let me die if death is good for me." Killing another unjustly would be considered one of the worst sins. That being said, death is inevitable. The Qur'an says, "Every soul shall taste death, and only on the Day of Judgment will you be paid your full recompense." Belief in the afterlife is one of the core beliefs of Islam, and death is viewed as a continuation of life rather than a termination. God gives life itself as a preparation and testing ground for the afterlife as we move from this physical world to the unseen, spiritual world. It is viewed as a natural process, and true believers and the righteous will welcome death when the time is right.

As with Judaism and Christianity, while some distinguish the soul, spirit, and body, the most common view is the dualistic view that we are a union of body and soul. At death, the soul is separated from the body and moves into the afterlife. There is a view that the soul has three parts. One part is like Freud's concept of the *id*, and is driven by animal urges. It is prone to evil. There is an *ego*-like part that has a moral judgment function and tries to overcome evil. The third part is a spiritual component that is focused on the relationship with Allah. According to one writer (Facts and Details, n.d.), "The spiritual component is said to be about the size of a bee and shimmers like mercury when it is removed from the body."

There are variations in some of the specifics for various groups within Islam, as with sub-groups within Judaism and Christianity. One area where you can find multiple ideas is what happens between death and the Day of Judgment. For many, people remain in their graves until the final judgment. For others, there are different kinds of testing and interrogation by angels during that time. For example, the Sunnah (a collection of traditional social and legal custom and practice) says, "When a believer is nearly dead, angels of mercy come, clothed in white silk garments, and say to the soul of the dying man, 'Come out, O thou who art satisfied with God, and with whom he is satisfied; come out to rest, which is with God, and the sustenance of God's mercy and compassion, and to the Lord, who is not angry." Martyrs, though, who died for Allah immediately enter Paradise.

There will be a final judgment when God calls us to account for our deeds throughout our lives. All who have ever lived will be raised from the dead and face judgment. As with Christian doctrine, the specific time is unknown, but the expectation is that it is sooner rather than later. Also, as in Christian beliefs, the judgment will be accompanied by earthquakes and other natural disasters, and social turmoil. As it says in the Qur'an (Don Stewart, n.d.), "When the stars darken, And when the mountains are made to pass away, And when the camels are left untended, And when the wild animals are made to go forth, And when the seas are set on fire, And when souls are united, And when the female infant buried alive is asked 'For what sin she was killed.' And when the books are spread, And when the heaven has its covering removed, And when the hell is kindled up, And when the garden is brought nigh, Every soul shall (then) know what it has prepared." There will be a cosmic battle between Satan's forces (including a false messiah) and God's forces led by the Mahdi and Jesus.

There is some debate within Islam about the fate of people of other faiths. The Qur'an does say that Jews and Christians are enemies of Islam because they do not believe Muhammad is a prophet. On the other hand, there is the belief that one's destiny depends on whether a person's good deeds outweigh their bad. Muslims do believe that Allah is forgiving, merciful, and compassionate. Allah can forgive those who have repented from their sins and who are kind to others. In Christianity, the unpardonable sin is blasphemy against the Holy Spirit. In Islam, it is worshiping anything or anyone other than Allah.

Hell is generally a place of fiery torment. The Qur'an says,

"Those who reject faith – neither their possessions nor their (numerous) progeny will avail them aught against Allah: they will be companions of the fire, dwelling therein (forever)." But on the other hand, heaven is a place of pleasure. It is referred to as a "garden of everlasting bliss" and a "home of peace," where there is no sickness, pain, or sadness. According to the Qur'an, "Other faces on that day shall be happy, Well-pleased because of their striving, in a lofty garden, wherein you shall not hear vain talk. Therein is a fountain flowing, therein are thrones raised high, and drinking-cups ready placed, and cushions set in a row, and carpets spread out."

HINDUISM

Hinduism is the world's third most common religion. It is also considered by many to be the world's oldest religion, dating back to four thousand years ago. It is not a single religion but instead describes a family of practices of various groups in India. Hindus believe in one God, Brahman. Brahman is the cause and foundation for all existence, and the gods of Hinduism that we often see celebrated represent different

Vishnu, Shiva, and Brahma

expressions of Brahman sent to help people find Brahman. The challenges some find with the Christian Trinity feel expanded here.

Hindus may have a personal god or goddess such as Shiva (the Destroyer), Krishna, or Lakshmi that they pray to regularly. In the 60s, we heard a lot about Krishna (see, for example, George Harrison's "My Sweet Lord"). Many of us in the tech industry have colleagues who celebrate Diwali, the festival of lights, that honors Lakshmi, the Goddess of Wealth. The holiday celebrates the triumph of good, light, and knowledge. Holi is another holiday that regularly makes it to the popular press. This festival of colors includes people throwing dyes and colorful powders over each other. It symbolizes the absence of class distinctions. Finally, I would note Ganesh, the elephant-headed god. One of my former employees presented an image of him to me when I was leaving to start a new job, as this is a popular deity representing new beginnings, success, and wisdom.

When thinking about the soul in Hinduism, the core idea is that there is a part of Brahman in everyone, and it is called the *Atman*. This resonates with God breathing into Adam to create humans. The Atman is the Sanskrit word that refers to the inner self or spirit, or soul. It is our true self and lies beneath our experience of the world. In its essence, it is without qualities and attributes (such as a form). This spirit in its purest state is indistinguishable, indestructible, immutable, invisible, formless, and infinite for Hindu believers. They believe they are only associated with qualities and attributes that distinguish them when they are bound to nature in physical bodies.

To attain the highest level, one must achieve self-knowledge, although there are different schools of thought about what that means relative to Brahman's ultimate reality. In the Rigveda, one ancient Indian grammarian (Yaska) interpreted the word Atman as meaning "the pervading principle, the organism in which elements are united and the ultimate sentient principle (Ātman [Hinduism], n.d.)." The Upanishads have "know your Atman" as a thematic focus. They point to the core of every person's self as this soul or self as distinct from the body, the mind, and the ego. The approach to these latter two, of course, contrasts quite distinctly with Hellenistic thought. The Atman is an eternal, ageless essence. However, everything we are is associated with it, including our free will, desires, what we do or do not do, and what is good and bad. This idea of the Atman soul as carrying the core of our being and our spiritual maturity and goodness is similar to the Christian view of the soul, although progress happens across physical lives as opposed to within a single life.

Part of the process of the soul evolving to merge with the Brahman ultimately is the mechanism of reincarnation. The idea is the soul is eternal, and souls may live in a human body, an animal body, or a plant body at any given point. A soul may live in many bodies over time. All forms of life contain a soul,[103] and souls in any form of life have a chance to experience a different form. This reincarnation process is known as *Samsara*, and is governed by *Karma*. The life you live depends on how your previous life was lived, and your past causes the Karma you experience (e.g., the misfortunes you suffer or the good). Hindus are motivated to live in a way—including responding to misfortunes and opportunities to live well—that leads to each life being better than the previous life. The ultimate goal is not a heaven (and of course, there is not a sense of hell) but rather, given Karma, lives get better or worse, and the ultimate goal is to achieve the spiritual state of becoming one with Brahman.

In Christianity, the goal ultimately is to be in a relationship with God. In Hinduism, the goal is more about becoming one with God. Through our lives, the goal is to move towards the self-realization of the truth that there is only Brahman and that nothing else exists. This spiritual goal of becoming one with Brahman is known as *Moksha*, the self-realization that nothing exists other than Brahman. One way to get there across reincarnations involves acquiring spiritual knowledge through yoga, meditation, and devotion to God (the paths of meditation, knowledge, and devotion). The other is working selflessly for the good of society (the path of good works).

One passage that conveys the relationship between the

Atman and Brahman, where Brahman is ultimately all there is, comes from Brihandaranyaka Upanishad from around the ninth century BCE.

> *"That Atman (self, soul) is indeed Brahman. It [Ātman] is also identified with the intellect, the Manas (mind), and the vital breath, with the eyes and ears, with earth, water, air, and ākāśa (sky), with fire and with what is other than fire, with desire and the absence of desire, with anger and the absence of anger, with righteousness and unrighteousness, with everything — it is identified, as is well known, with this (what is perceived) and with that (what is inferred). As it [Ātman] does and acts, so it becomes: by doing good it becomes good, and by doing evil it becomes evil. It becomes virtuous through good acts, and vicious through evil acts. Others, however, say, 'The self is identified with desire alone. What it desires, so it resolves; what it resolves, so is its deed; and what deed it does, so it reaps.'"*

BUDDHISM

Contrasting to religions where there is a God or gods, and religions like Hinduism where ultimately a believer can become one with Brahman, is Buddhism where there is not a personal creator God at all. (History.com Editors, n.d.) There is not any eternal divine being. Indeed, Buddha saw such a belief as too fatalistic and believed it would lead to some of the worst in humanity. He says, "Owing to the creation of a supreme deity men will become murderers, thieves, unchaste, liars, slanderers, abusive, babblers, covetous, malicious and perverse in view. Thus, for those who fall back on the creation of a god as the essential reason, there is neither desire nor effort nor necessity to do this deed or abstain from that deed." Along with there being no creator, the universe, of course, has no single beginning. There is an argument that Buddhism is not as much an organized religion as it is a "way of life" or a "spiritual tradition." It was founded on and inspired by the teachings of Siddhartha Gautama (called the Buddha) around the fourth or fifth century BCE in India.[104] It has more than three hundred and fifty million adherents worldwide, and its ideas have influenced a variety of Westernized spiritual practices even for those who might identify as Christian.

Much has been written about the journey of Siddhartha Gautama[105] as he followed the path to enlightenment, and grew through pain and suffering towards enlightenment and becoming the "awakened one." He had been born in a royal family protected from the suffering in the real world, and one day stepped outside and saw an old man, a sick man, and a corpse. That began a journey through the world as a Holy Man and exploring different ways of escaping the inevitability of pain, old age, and eventual death. Buddha is not a god or a chosen prophet that is speaking on behalf of God. Instead, his followers believe he is a human being just like they are, and his teachings are passing on how he achieved enlightenment so others can follow it.

Tagore's "Departure of Prince Siddhartha"

There is a cycle of birth, life, death, and rebirth for Buddhists that continues until one gains enlightenment. You achieve enlightenment by following Buddha's teachings and working with others to release an attachment to desire and the self, and to cease being selfish. It also is about avoiding being too ascetic; having too much self-discipline. Reaching that level of enlightenment is called *nirvana*, and represents perfect peace, and being free of suffering. It is the leaving of all that is imperfect. It is the extinction of all craving.

The *dharma* is a set of Buddha's teachings about virtues like wisdom, kindness, patience, generosity, and compassion.

The five moral precepts prohibit killing living things, taking what is not given, sexual misconduct, lying, and using drugs or alcohol. The Four Nobel Truths help overcome suffering, and they include the truth of suffering, the truth of its cause, the truth of its end, and the truth of the path to free us from suffering. That leads to the Eightfold Path, the ideas for ethical conduct, mental discipline, and wisdom. The Path touches on topics like understanding and thought, speech and action, and mindfulness.

This growth to a spiritual state, of course, has some similarity to other views of the ideal of a heavenly afterlife, but without being centered on a concept of God. It is important to note that Buddhism does not have a soul per se in its belief system. An individual consists of a bundle of habits, memories, and desires. Together, they provide an illusion of a stable, lasting self. This false self can even reincarnate and move from body to body. The idea, therefore, is to move beyond the false sense of self so that the collection of things that define the self disintegrates, leaving nothing to reincarnate and nothing to experience pain. What is carried on from life to life is the life force (Karma), and that Karma can be good or bad depending on how life is lived.

According to Tibetan Buddhism, after death, the departed spirit goes through three stages (the *bardos*). At the conclusion, one either enters nirvana or reincarnates. The first stage (the *Chikai Bardo*) is the initial period where the departed realize they have left their old body. This departure can be the ecstatic experience of the "white light" at the moment of death that has been reported in other near-death experiences. The more spiritual see it longer and can move beyond it to a higher level of reality. In the second stage (the *Chonyid Bardo* or the bardo of Luminous Mind), the person experiences hallucinations resulting from their life's karma. If you are not sufficiently spiritual, you may experience this as still being inside your body. The third stage (the *Sidpa Bardo*) is the process of reincarnation for those not moving directly to nirvana. Buddhism is much richer than this, and there are different variations of Buddhism depending on the country, customs, and culture.

TOUCHING ON EXAMPLES OF OTHER FAITHS

The Church of Jesus Christ of Latter-day Saints (a.k.a. Mormonism)

The Church of Jesus Christ of Latter-day Saints (often referred to informally as the Mormon Church) has close to seven million members in the United States. Its founder is Joseph Smith, who organized the church in 1830. While some refer to it as a denomination of the Christian Church, there are significant differences from historical Christianity.

Joseph Smith said he experienced a series of visions, including those from God the Father and Jesus Christ, and from an angel who led him to buried golden-plates. He said the plates connect Judeo-Christian history with an ancient American civilization. It was argued that some native Americans are descendants of Lehi, a member of the ancient Israeli tribe of Manasseh. While the Christian Bible is part of their canon of scriptures, the canon also includes other material like the Book of Mormon, the Doctrine and Covenants, and the Pearl of Great Price. Much of it was said to have been revealed by God to Joseph 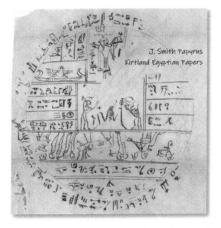 Smith personally. They see whoever the current church president is as a prophet and seer, and Jesus Christ is believed to reveal his will directly to the president.[106] While the church does believe in salvation through the substitutionary atonement of Jesus Christ, it does not believe in the trinitarian view of God the Father, Jesus Christ, and the Holy Spirit that is central to the Christian Creeds.

In the Church of Jesus Christ of Latter-day Saints doctrine, at the Final Judgment, a small number of people who have committed the unpardonable sin, the sin against the Holy Spirit, will be banished to the "outer darkness" along with Satan. This outer darkness would be a concept of hell, where there is weeping and gnashing of teeth. Everyone else will be assigned to one of three degrees of glory: the telestial, the terrestrial, and the celestial.

Those headed for the *telestial kingdom* according to the book of Doctrine and Covenants will include those "who received not the gospel of Christ, nor the testimony of Jesus," "liars, and sorcerers, and adulterers, and whoremongers, and whosoever loves and makes a lie," and "murderers, and idolaters." During the millennial reign of Christ (the one thousand years), they will be in spirit prison, and they will then receive an immortal body and be placed in the telestial kingdom. While they would not be able to be with God, the Holy Spirit will minister to them. According to Latter-day Saints beliefs, it is not a place of suffering but instead, "the glory of the telestial...surpasses all understanding."

For those who were good people but "were blinded by the craftiness of men" and rejected the gospel of Christ when it was presented to them, those who rejected it when they were physically alive but accepted it in the spirit world (where they are before judgment), and those who received the gospel but "are not valiant in the testimony of Jesus" inhabit the *terrestrial kingdom*. Ultimately sorting into the terrestrial kingdom is based on God's knowledge of whether they "would have received it with all their hearts" as manifested by their works and the "desire of their hearts." In the terrestrial kingdom, they "receive of the presence of the Son, but not the fullness of the Father."

Each believer's goal is to receive "exaltation" through the salvation (the atonement) of Jesus. When they receive exaltation, they become like God (Becoming Like God, n.d.) and inherit the attributes of God the Father (incl. godhood). They will have "all power, glory, dominion, and knowledge" and will live with their Earthly families, have spirit children, and their posterity will grow forever. This goal is reached for those attaining the highest degree of the *celestial kingdom* as they achieve spiritual perfection.

One of my hobbies is uncovering the genealogy of my ancestors, and for many years a key source has been the records of Mormon genealogists. Part of the reason why they are so interested in genealogy is because they believe if they can trace their ancestral trees, they can identify those who have not heard the "restored Mormon Gospel" and therefore did not have a chance to accept it. Because those in the afterlife exist as conscious spirits, vicarious baptisms give them an opportunity to join the fold even after they have passed. The sacrament enables multiple generations to be sealed together in the afterlife.

Indigenous People of the Americas[107]

There is not one religion across all indigenous peoples, let alone Native American tribes. After all, more than five hundred and sixty tribes are recognized in the United States today, and there were many more in the past. Rather than laying out

Sioux Funeral Scaffold

a systematic theology for this group, I will just provide a sample of the diversity of ideas across some of the tribes and a few of the common themes. A fundamental principle is that Native American beliefs are rooted in tribal cultures and histories and informed by their lived experiences. But there is also generally a sense that everything is connected, which is often described as being "one with nature." The spiritual is woven through all tangible reality.

There is no fixed set of Native rituals, rules, or specific teachings across generations like formal religions. Instead, it is more like spiritual systems (customs, beliefs, and history passed down orally through stories, songs, and dances) that permeate people's lives and evolve across generations. The beliefs change through the interaction of tribes as they share cultural practices and intermarry, and as external events and historical trauma impact the tribes (e.g., genocide, forced assimilation, wars, and disease).

Native Americans are typically not focused on reward and punishment in the afterlife. Instead, they are more focused on harmony with the creation. Traditional Navajo, for example, have little concern about an afterlife. They will find out what it is like when they die, and until then, most will not waste time thinking about it. Their orientation is towards making this life happier, more harmonious, and more beautiful.

A common idea is that life after death is a natural continuation of life before death. Most Native American tribes do not separate the natural world and the spiritual world in dramatic ways. According to an article on Native American religion and spirituality in powwows.com (Native American Religion, 2019), "The spiritual or supernatural world is the same thing as the real world. Every supposed division is completely permeable and people can access everything spiritual just as easily as they can wade in a river or feel the sun on their skin." This perspective echoes the ancient Egyptian beliefs.

Furthermore, "The concept of journeying on to another world makes sense when you consider the idea that many tribes spent a lot of time traveling in the early days. They would see a journey as a normal progression of life." For example, among the Pueblo Indians of North America, the deceased's journey to a village to live with the people they knew who have died before would be expected. Anthropologist Elsie Clews Parsons writing about Pueblo beliefs, says, "The Pueblo idea of life after death as merely a continuation of this life is incompatible with dogmas of hell and heaven. In this life, the Spirits do not reward or punish; why should they after death?"

For the Northwestern Coastal Native Americans, according to Silas Smith (Smith, 1901):

> *"These people believe in the immortality of the soul;*
> *they believe in a spirit life and in a spirit land; they*

believe that the spirit of other animals go to the spirit land as well as that of men. Their conception of the spirit land is quite beautiful and pleasing. There it is always spring or summer; the fields are perpetually green, flowers blooming, fruit ripening, and running waters diversify the scenery of the beautiful landscapes, with always an abundant supply of game, and of course the inhabitants are in a continuous state of felicity."

Many native people do not use the language of death as a termination but instead refer to "walking on." This walking on emphasizes the continuation of a journey rather than being about an endpoint. In some tribes, the souls of the dead go to a spirit world and may communicate with the living through dreams, or they may communicate through medicine people and shamans. The spirits can travel to and from the afterlife to communicate with the living. In other tribes, there is a land of the dead that may be presided over by a god or other supernatural caretaker.

Some tribes in Massachusetts and around Rhode Island believed in an afterlife to the southwest where you could find a village of ancestors that would welcome your spirit. For others, the dead may become stars or a part of the earth; but may be disturbed and turned into ghosts. The Cheyenne of the Northern Plains believed the souls of the dead travel along the Milky Way (known as "The Road of the Departed") to a place of the dead. Again, there was no concept of hell or punishment after life on earth, but rather as George Bird Grinnell wrote in *The Cheyenne Indians: Their History and Lifeways*, "the spirit of the dead man found the trail where the footprints all pointed the same way, followed that to the Milky Way, and finally arrived at the camp in the stars, where he met his friends and relatives and lived in the camp of the dead" (Some American Indian Beliefs About an Afterlife, 2015).

Howard Russell (in Indian New England Before the Mayflower, 2014) says, "The soul of the departed was believed to journey to the southwest, there to share the delights of the wigwam and fields of the great god Kanta (or Tanto or

Kautautowit), where abundance reigns and ancestors offer welcome and feasting."[108] The Narragansett Indians of the Northeast around Rhode Island also saw death as a transition and a journey by the soul to be with relatives and friends in the world of the dead. The world of the dead also was to the southwest. Passing through gates guarded by a ferocious dog, the souls would find a paradise without worry or pain, and it was full of storehouses filled with corn, beans, and squash. Strawberries were always in season, and succulent clams were abundant. Religion professor Henry Bowden wrote (Some American Indian Beliefs About an Afterlife, 2015), "the Massachusetts [Indians] expected to triumph over death by finding new opportunities in another realm, beyond the grave, where individual accomplishments could flourish again with undiminished vigor."

In the Northwest Coast culture, people believed they were surrounded at all times by supernatural beings that can interact with the physical world. Spirits were connected to all living things, and shamans or medicine men could interact with them. Other tribes believed in reincarnation, so the dead spirits might come back as new infants within the tribe. Elders would examine newborns to try to identify who they were in a past life. Sioux physician Charles Eastman wrote, "Many of the Indians believed that one may be born more than once, and there were some who claimed to have full knowledge of a former incarnation" (The Soul, 2011).

One Christian missionary (John Heckewelder), writing about a Lenni Lenape man in 1817, wrote, "He asserted very strange things, of his own supernatural knowledge, which he had obtained not only at the time of his initiation, but at other times, even before he was born. He said he knew that he had lived through two generations; that he had died twice and was born a third time, to live out the then-present race, after which he was to die and never more to come to this country again." A member of the Gitxsan (Shirley Muldon) writes, "We believe in reincarnation of people and animals. We believe that the dead can visit this world and that the living can enter the past. We believe that memory survives from generation to generation. Our elders remember the past because they have lived it."

In some tribal groups, people are seen as having multiple souls. According to the Sheepeater Shoshone, for example, there are three kinds of souls: the *suap* or "ego-soul" which is embodied in breath, the *navushieip* or "free-soul" that can leave the body in dreams, trances, and comas, and the *mugua* or "body-soul" (which we might think of as the will in other concepts of the soul) that activates the body when awake. If a person is sick because the soul has fled, a medicine person might go into a trance to search for the soul and restore it to the body and restore the person's health. In Chapter 3, when we talked about the evolution of religion, ideas like this probably would have emerged very early in human history.

The Narragansett believed one soul is active when the body is asleep, and a different soul animates the body when we are awake and leaves the body after death. This latter soul is *Michachunck*, and is located near the heart. It gives life to the person (perhaps like the Greek pneuma). The dream soul is called *Cowwewonck*, and it can roam during sleep and seek out guardian spirits. The Huron also believed in two souls, one that animates the body and one that extends beyond the physical world and activities. According to one writer (The Soul, n.d.), "In sleep, one soul communicates with spirits and with other human souls. When this soul returns to the body, dreams are how the soul's experiences are communicated. From a Huron perspective, it was essential to reenact these dream adventures to unify the two souls and make each person whole again. The failure to do this would result in serious illness which could impact the entire village."

Again, from Smith (Smith, 1901, there is a story that sounds a little like what we know today as near-death experiences:

> *They believe that when a person becomes very sick the spirit leaves the body and seeks the shores of the spirit land, and unless it is recaptured and returned to its original tenement, the person will of course surely die. In such cases the services of a skillful*

> *tamanawas doctor are engaged, and an assistant is*
> *furnished him to accompany him on his journey of*
> *discovery to the land of the dead....Should the pa-*
> *tient recover, it is proof of the great powers of the*
> *doctor, but if, on the contrary, the patient pass away,*
> *it is evidence that the spirit ran away the second*
> *time."*

As with the Egyptians and other earlier religions, many death rituals across tribes were designed to help provide a spirit with what it needs to arrive at its destination in the afterlife. These might include offerings of food, jewelry, tools, and weapons, and even in some cases, slaves, and horses for those deserving special honor. Other rituals were designed to help guide the spirit. They might even leave a gap in a burial chamber to allow the spirit to escape.

DEEPER DIVES

Made in the Image of God

We should step back from the foundations of some of these religious ideas and look a bit at "the Beginning." Who are we, really? What makes us different from the other living creatures on our planet? The creation stories are diverse. One ancient Egyptian account (Mysteries of Egypt: The Creation Myth, n.d.) describes how the sun god Re (the most powerful god and the one who created himself out of chaos) ruled over the earth. Re's eye somehow left and failed to return. When two of the other deities, Shu and Tefnut, went to fetch it, the eye resisted. It shed tears, and out of the tears, we humans were born. One way to read the story is we are made of god stuff.

An early Mesopotamian creation myth, the Enuma Elish (Mark, 2011), included a pair of male and female principles (Apsu and Tiamat). They were brother and sister, and mates. A summary is that there was a lot of palace intrigue. The two of them produced the first generation of gods. Apsu, the male and representing freshwater, decided to kill their godly descendants who were causing too much of a ruckus during the creation process. Instead, the children killed Apsu. Not too surprisingly, this irked Tiamat, the primordial goddess of the sea, and so she decided to kill the children. Tiamat created monsters and dragons to help in the fight. Alas, the storm god Marduk killed her and her champion, Qingu. Then out of the remains of Qingu, Marduk created humans to serve as helpers of the gods. There could be an exciting movie plot in this story.

In another early Sumerian poem ("The Song of the Hoe"), Enlil is the god who separates the heavens and the earth. Enlil creates humans to serve as helpers for the gods. In this story, humans were naked, and the Earth was mostly barren. So the gods created sheep and grain to give sustenance to the humans, then provided the Tigris and Euphrates, and caused civilization's rise. In a different story ("Enki and Ninmah"), the lesser gods were complaining to the ancient mother (Namma) about how much work there was. As a result, Namma fashioned some clay, put it in her womb, and gave birth to the first humans to help out.

One of the very earliest Greek myths was that humans sprang from the earth. The ancient Greeks saw nature push its way from the ground in the spring after the dead of winter, the cycle of life and death in nature, and concluded it happened with humanity as well. Initially, like other wild things, we needed to be tamed and civilized. The gods and heroes helped us learn what we needed. Later, among the alternative stories (e.g., see the *Theogony*), Prometheus created the first human out of the Earth's mud, and the goddess Athena breathed life into the creation. This account is another instance where a breath, the spirit, gives life to the body. In this story, humanity was the last to be created, and all the valuable skills went to the animals.[109] So we were made upright like the gods and were given fire as a consolation prize.

In many of these stories, the gods look and act suspiciously like humans with superpowers, but also with supersized egos, emotions and exhibiting even more drama. Frequently humans are made from the earth, and it does make me think of a possible connection with red ochre. Often, the gods seem to create humans either with some small essence of the divine in them or breathed life into the material of creation to make something that is a little like themselves. Their goal was often to create helpers who would serve them. Perhaps *our* goal was to invent gods that would let us explain the things in life that are out of our control, but in a way that might also give *us* some control over our fates. We may have wanted to invent them, in essence, to serve us.

These stories contrast with the creation stories of the indigenous people of the Americas. While there are many unique stories, a common theme is the relationship with the symbolism, patterns, and meaning found in the seasons, weather, plants, animals, earth, air, and heavenly bodies. Typically, there is a universal, omniscient Great Spirit among the indigenous peoples and a connection between all of nature (including us). There is an emphasis on the relationship between humans and animals, often with animal spirits involved in our creation. In some groups, animism is a theme; in other words, all objects, places, and creatures have souls. This idea is in contrast to pantheism, where everything shares the same soul. There may be shapeshifting between animal and human forms, marriage between people and various species, and even animals fostering children. As with other religions, there are tricksters in some of the stories, often to make the stories more compelling or to convey morals. This kind of storytelling feels like it probably goes way back in our human development.

In Hinduism, there is not a single creation story. Instead, the stories have grown and evolved across time and groups. In contrast to the beliefs we have mentioned so far and the Abrahamic religions (Judaism, Christianity, and Islam), there is not a creation of the universe per se. The cycle of creation and destruction in nature is taken to its limit, with the world being seen as eternal in itself.

Compared with many of these other origin stories, the Jewish and Christian creation narratives offer an important contrast in how to think about who we are as a species and why we are here. In the Jewish Tanakh, Genesis 1:26-28 (JPS), it says, "And G-d said: 'Let us make man *in our image, after our likeness*; and let them have dominion over the fish of the sea, and over the fowl of the air, and over the cattle, and over all the earth, and over every creeping thing that creepeth upon the earth.' And G-d created man *in His own image, in the image of G-d* created He him; male and female created He them. And G-d blessed them; and G-d said unto them: 'Be fruitful, and multiply, and replenish the earth, and subdue it; and have dominion over the fish of the sea, and over the fowl of the air, and over every living thing that creepeth upon the earth.'" The key here is the explicit phrase of "make man [humanity] *in our own image*." Again, Genesis 5:1,2 (JPS) says, "This is the book of the generations of Adam. In the day that G-d created man, in the *likeness of G-d* made He him; male and female created He them, and blessed them, and called their name Adam, in the day when they were created."

Michelangelo's "Creation of Adam"

In Latin, this is the phrase *imago Dei*, and the idea seems like it is a clue to something really important about us, either that or it represents our fundamental hubris as a species. It certainly is a puzzle. What does it really mean? God in these verses doesn't have a body. While other scriptures describe God with human-like characteristics, we now know that for us, many of those characteristics require a body. Plus, many of those characteristics we have demonstrated are shared by the animal kingdom. The imago Dei, the image and likeness of God, seems to be specifically about us as humans in relation to God.[110] However, we should be especially wary about anthropomorphizing God, and not define God in our own likeness.

On a first read, these accounts might seem similar to some of the other creation stories. However, they are not about a god creating servants per se or humanity resulting from a divine prankster's cruel joke. Instead, the idea carries more the sense of humanity being in a relationship with God and participating in God's ongoing creative plan. As an example, Adam was engaged in the "naming" of the creatures that were created, and we are charged as stewards of the care and use of the creation of which we are a part. The stories also imply free will (for better or worse), and at least the acquisition of a moral sense. God is still "the boss," but the tone of the stories seems to be different than most other creation narratives.

Paul Ricoeur (a twentieth Century French Philosopher) argued that the original author(s) probably did not have an explicit definition in mind or a complete understanding of what it could mean. It is over time that the idea of the image of God has been explored more fully.[111] He says, "In the very essence of the individual, in terms of its quality as a subject; the image of God, we believe, is the very personal and solitary power to think and to choose; it is interiority." Emil Brunner (1889 to 1996) wrote that "the formal aspect of human nature, as beings 'made in the image of God', denotes being as Subject, or freedom; it is this which differentiates humanity from lower creation." He also felt that the idea of *relationship* between God and us reflects that image. This latter idea is echoed in Pope Benedict XVI's *Imago Dei*, "Its nature as an image has to do with the fact that it goes beyond itself and manifests...the dynamic that sets the human being in motion towards the totally Other. Hence it means the capacity for relationship; it is the human capacity for God." The *Catechism of the Catholic Church* suggests that Christ in relation to the Father is a model of what this means for us. "It is in Christ, 'the image of the invisible God,' that man has been created 'in the image and likeness of the Creator.'"

One way to read these early verses about being in the image of God is from a *function or role-based* perspective. J. Richard Middleton suggests thinking in terms of the royal-functional understanding that would have been a common description of relationships between human hierarchies and their gods back in the day. He says, "[T]he imago Dei designates the royal office or calling of human beings as God's representatives or agents in the world." This approach is also held by many modern Hebrew Bible scholars, and is in the Jewish tradition recognizing that the phrase is about bestowing special honor onto humankind. They point out that the structure of the language is similar to that used in many Mesopotamian and Near Eastern cultures. In these cultures, kings were often labeled as being in various gods' images, and with that, they received divine rights and responsibilities. This structure would broaden the hierarchy from God to humankind to all of creation, and of course, the Hebrew scriptures would be read through the lens of being the Chosen People.[112]

Another example of using language in this way is that many of the promises and laws through the Torah are in the form of a suzerain vassal treaty or covenant, typically between two powers (esp. between a greater and lesser power). In the Torah, God would be the greater power, and the treaty would be codifying the relationship with Israel. This use of well-known social and political conventions and cultural language would have brought a lot of tacit (well understood) meaning to people at the time that sometimes is not apparent to us now. In this view, the creation of the first humans is just a step in the origin story of the Chosen People and their role in the world.

One aspect of this functional idea is reflected in the Jewish text Sirach, from around 200 BCE, where it positions us as sharing in God's dominion. We are, in essence, stewards of nature. In Sirach 17:1-4, it says, "The Lord created man of the earth, and turned him into it again. He gave them few days, and a short time, and power also over the things therein. He endued them with strength by themselves and made them according to his image. And put the fear of man upon all flesh, and gave him dominion over beasts and fowls."

There is also something that is sometimes called the *substantive view*, although I have to say being a psychologist, this is what I would have thought of as more about functionality or capabilities. The idea is that there are similarities between God and humanity in shared substances, such as how our rational, willful, and spiritual soul mirrors the divine.[113] It is similar to how a realistic sculpture can be said to reflect the form of the sculptor. God is spirit, and our souls are spirit. We have spiritual self-awareness. God defines right and wrong, and we have a moral sense. God is eternal, and we are created to live forever. God creates and has made us to create. While God does not need a body to have these characteristics, we may have the characteristics in part by virtue of the bodies he has evolved for us.

In Chapter 4, we discussed Aristotle's idea that the *form* of the body is the soul. There was an example of an ax, which is made of wood and metal, but its form comes from its being shaped to chop. The book of Enoch is part of the pseudepigraphic literature and was written perhaps as early as the 1st century BCE (but possibly quite a bit later). 2 Enoch 65:2 says, "He constituted man in His own form, in accordance with a similarity. And He gave him eyes to see, ears to hear, and a heart to think, and reason to argue." This would be understood in terms of being created to see, hear, think, and reason; and being enabled to do that through the eyes, ears, heart, and brain that our bodies provide. Similarly, in the Apocrypha, the Wisdom of Solomon 2:23 says, "For God created man to be immortal, and made him to be an image of his own eternity."[114] This is about our potential for immortality that was part of that initial creation.

The challenge of this approach is to separate out the forms and the substance we share with God, from the properties that we now know are inherent in the physical nature of our bodies. As with the ax, the fact that we can deconstruct some of these characteristics that we appear to share with God into components of our brains and biology does not mean we don't share those higher-level forms they enable. Indeed, as we discussed in Chapter 2, part of our evolution might have been bringing us to the point where we can be called designed in the image of God.

A third view is sometimes called the *relational* view. Karl

Barth and Emil Brunner advocated this perspective, although I tend to think of it as another aspect of the substantive or forms view. In this view, we can create and maintain complex, perhaps even *spiritual,* relationships that make us like God. It is the social and interpersonal connections that reflect the spiritual and relational connections between God and ourselves.[115] This would be reflected in us being the "religion making species" (as far as we know), and in the goodness that ensures a desirable afterlife. This aspect of being good is closely bound to our spiritual relationships and our active care of our neighbors.

Contemporary research does suggest the underlying capabilities needed for these various attributes are present in other animals, as we have discussed, and are fundamental to how we are wired as a species. Indeed, as we will suggest, many of our experiences around death may be grounded in how our relational and spiritual DNA works.

The interpretation of what the "image of God" means, of course, has evolved as the idea of the soul has evolved. It continues to be shaped by theologians reasoning from various doctrinal frameworks and our changing cultural, historical contexts. While it has been used to argue for separation and exclusion at times, it also has been used to push for the fundamental value and equality of all people regardless of class, race, gender expression, ability, or culture. Today we are continuing to uncover new implications of this idea for ecology, ableism, feminism, transhumanism, and other important issues.

Ensoulment

So when does the soul enter the body? Ideas range from at conception, to birth, to when a child can say, "Amen!" One approach to this question is to examine how our bodies develop and see if we can infer when the characteristics we attribute to the soul begin to emerge. For much of human history, the two most obvious life attributes for both humans and animals have been the heart and blood, and breathing (i.e., the cardiopulmonary system). For example, in the Tanakh:

- For the *life of the flesh is in the blood*; and I have given it to you upon the altar to make atonement for your souls; for it is the blood that maketh atonement by reason of the life." – Leviticus 17:11 (JPS)
- "Only flesh with the *life thereof, which is the blood thereof,* shall ye not eat." – Genesis 9:4 (JPS)
- "Only be stedfast in not eating the blood; for the *blood is the life*; and thou shalt not eat the life with the flesh." – Deuteronomy 12:23 (JPS)
- "Then HaShem G-d formed man of the dust of the ground, and breathed into his nostrils the *breath of life*; and man became a living soul." – Genesis 2:7 (JPS)
- "Thus saith God the LORD, he that created the heavens, and stretched them out; he that spread forth the earth, and that which cometh out of it; he that *giveth breath unto the people upon it*, and *spirit to them* that walk therein." – Isaiah 42:5 (JPS)
- "All the while *my breath is in me*, and the *spirit of God is in my nostrils*." – Job 27:3 (JPS)

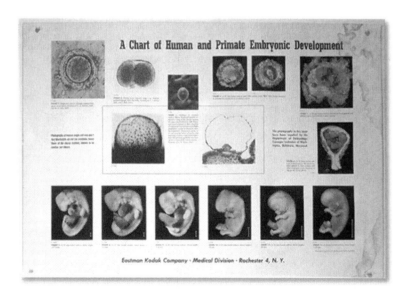

A Chart of Human and Primate Embryonic Development

Eastman Kodak Company · Medical Division · Rochester 4, N. Y.

The implication from these passages, therefore, is that the fetus is *not* alive in this fundamental sense until it has blood. It could also be read to suggest that a key milestone to being human (and by implication having a soul) is breathing; in other words, having successfully been born. Earlier, we reviewed the Hebrew words for the soul that have this fundamental sense of breath or breathing.

Another way to think about life today is to identify when a fetus is viable and can live outside the uterus (and, of course, breathe). Initially, this might be a premature birth or a Caesarean where the baby would be breathing on its own. Now, we bring technology into the process, in essence, to breathe for the baby. One could wonder whether ensoulment might require being able to be removed from the artificial devices or not.

According to the Mayo Clinic, today, at least ten to twenty percent of pregnancies end in miscarriages (and probably more, since many are not recognized as such) before the twentieth week. As might be expected, with the evolution of current medical technology, that point has changed. Forty years ago, viability was around twenty-eight weeks. Since then, it has dropped to about twenty-two weeks, but the rate it is dropping has been slowing. One of the earliest births so far recorded was at twenty-one weeks and five days.

Part of what has been advancing this is technologies to create artificial wombs and better infection and intensive neonatal care. So, in a way, babies are not as much being born that early as switching environments until they are ready to be *virtually born*. That, of course, does not mean they will survive, and it does not necessarily guarantee a healthy life. On the contrary, the earlier babies are born, the more likely there will be problems if they are delivered at all. Premature births may result in breathing problems, heart problems, brain problems, temperature control problems, gastrointestinal problems, and blood problems. Long term, there may be cerebral palsy, learning disabilities, vision and hearing issues, and behavioral and psychological difficulties. Some of these issues will return as we consider the nature of souls and bodies in the afterlife.

Within the scientific and medical communities, many would say they do not know a specific point of viability, and instead, they would rather point to meaningful milestones in fetal development. According to Arthur Caplan, the founding head of the Division of Medical Ethics at New York University Langone Medical Center, "The first is conception, the second is the development of the spine, the third the development of the brain, consciousness and so on." But the evidence for being alive, since it applies to other animals in the creation, is separate from the question of when we are ensouled (i.e., given a soul, become a soul, or when our soul is given a body). When does the soul become housed in a body, and we become *us*?

According to *Nature Neuroscience* (In Search of Self, 2002), most people tend to believe that the soul appears at conception, "[D]espite the obvious counter-arguments about twinning, nuclear transplantation and so forth. This discrepancy between what most biologists believe and what many laypeople believe has led (particularly in the United States) to bitter public controversy, culminating in regulations for human stem cell research that most biologists regard as inappropriately restrictive."

The reference here is to issues such as identical twins coming from a single fertilized egg, for example. Do they share a soul? Is the soul cloned? Does one twin get the original soul, but then a new one is added? Does fertilizing an egg in a petri dish give it a soul? When it is then frozen, what is the state of the soul? And would God create a system that so inefficiently produces souls only to condemn them to an eternity in some unknown state (or even worse, if you believe in original sin)?

Those that believe in reincarnation have a little less of an issue here. Pythagoras believed in reincarnation, and his followers felt the soul appeared at conception. Some Hindus also believe that personhood begins at conception when reincarnation happens. You could imagine that if souls are moving from body to body, if a body does not succeed in being born for whatever reason jumping to another equivalent body would not be an issue. Still, some references within the Hindu Ayurveda state the soul does not become attached to the body until the seventh month. The idea is "the occupant doesn't move into the house until the house is finished." The body has to be physiologically capable of housing human consciousness.[116]

Aristotle had the idea that the developing fetus first has a soul equivalent to a plant. Eventually, it had a soul equivalent to an animal, with both the vegetative nature of a plant's soul and the animal soul's perceptual properties. However, it was only later that it received a human soul, at around forty to ninety days. This process is called epigenesis, and it is the idea that a human is brought into existence over time. The Stoics believed that a soul only was received at birth, when the baby started to breathe, and only became a rational soul at age fourteen.[117]

Islamic tradition, according to the Hadith, is that the ensoulment process occurs about one hundred and twenty days after conception. In a passage from Sahih al-Bukhari, "Each one of you is constituted in the womb of the mother for forty days, and then he becomes a clot or thick blood for a similar period, and then a piece of flesh for a similar period. Then God sends an angel who is ordered to write four things. He is ordered to write down his deeds, livelihood, date of death, and whether he will be blessed or wretched. Then the soul is breathed into him." In this perspective, one of the ways human souls differ from animal souls is that God has a pretty clear picture of our entire lives from the very beginning.

While the verses we began this section with suggest that being alive by virtue of blood and breathing are key points in development, there are alternative views about ensoulment within Judaism. Some rabbis argue for conception, and others propose it happens at the end of the first trimester. The Babylonian Talmud Yevamot says that the fetus is likened to water during the first forty days of pregnancy. Then, it isn't truly human until it is born. By the latter half of the second Temple period, the idea of the soul joining the body at birth (when the body is ready to be fully human) and leaving it at death was the more common reading of the Talmud. Some rabbinical writings did not see it as happening until the thirteenth postnatal day for full-term infants. One view even was that it occurred when the child first answers "Amen." (Feldman, 1994).

In line with the reading of the texts about the evidence of life and being human, though, is the law in Exodus 21:22-23. If two men are fighting and injure a pregnant woman and cause her to miscarry, the punishment is just paying compensatory damages if no other harm is done. It is treated as a civil case and not a criminal case. This law can be viewed in the context of the long list of crimes that result in death. The literature that looks at how the Jewish law should be applied in various situations says that a charge of murder can only be applied to the death of "a man, but not a fetus."

If you predicted who might have the most robust case for ensoulment at conception, you might look to Catholicism. But for Catholics, the point of ensoulment can be less important than the dignity of the fetus. According to Daniel Sulmasy (a Catholic bioethicist and director of the Program on Medicine and Religion at the University of Chicago), "You might be surprised to know that the Catholic Church has never dogmatically defined when life begins. Instead, there is a recognition that there is unfolding developmental potential in the embryo, from unification between the sperm and egg to birth." He points out that the Church does not have a specific moment it identifies as when ensoulment takes place. There is a sense that "the *potential* of human life" starts at conception. The Church leans towards humans not interfering with the process. According to Sulmasy, that includes letting natural miscarriages happen, and if an infant is too sick to live, it should be allowed to die.

Pope Benedict XVI, for example, stated the sense of the Church as "'[F]rom the moment of its conception life must be guarded with the greatest care.'...With regard to the embryo in the mother's womb, science itself highlights its autonomy, its capacity for interaction with the mother, the coordination of biological processes, the continuity of development, the growing complexity of the organism. It is not an accumulation of biological material but rather of a new living being, dynamic and marvelously ordered, a new individual of the human species. This is what Jesus was in Mary's womb, and this is what we all were in our mother's womb."

Pope Pius IX did issue a document in 1869 declaring excommunication for abortions at any stage of pregnancy. The Pope, however, was in the process of reasoning about the nature of Mary's immaculate conception, and how someone having original sin could give birth to Jesus. Before then, ensoulment was assumed by the Church to occur at "quickening" when the mother first felt the child move in her womb. It was assumed quickening indicated a separate consciousness had emerged and that there was now a soul present. This was assumed to be about twenty-four weeks into the pregnancy. Before then, if there was an abortion, it was not a homicide. Of course, the best current neuroscience suggests that even then, the fetus is not conscious in the way we would define human consciousness after birth.

Consistent with the approach of the Catholic Church and valuing the individual, messaging from the Church does include caring about the emerging individual beyond birth (the point where some churches apparently relinquish shared responsibility for the health and safety of the child). The Catholic Church has also developed a rationale for the fate in the afterlife of those infants that die before the age of accountability.[118]

One final consideration, of course, is whether the new soul is good or bad. Thomas Hobbes assumed humans are inherently "nasty" and "brutish," and we need society to civilize us. Jean-Jacques Rousseau argued that we start out gentle and pure until society corrupts us through greed and inequality. Most people probably believe that their lovely babies are pure and unspoiled. I know my wife and I saw our daughters that way even as they started to move inside their mom.

But even though parents may feel that way, the parents' religions may have a different opinion. Religions that believe in reincarnation would see the soul as bringing along its karma with it, good or bad. Many religions would see the soul as a blank slate. Others would argue for inherent goodness. For example, the Jewish Talmud says, "*All* Israel have a portion in the World to Come." The idea is that being in the image of God means all begin with a bit of divinity, and are destined for reward until they do something to lose it.

However, Christians who believe in original sin at least doctrinally see infants as being born in a sinful state and, at some level, inherently wicked and deserving death. Therefore, from the start, their destiny is punishment unless they are saved. This leads to an interesting situation where groups that believe in the inherent sinfulness of infants may also oppose abortion because it is the killing of "innocents."

Contemporary research with infants supports those of us who are optimists. Babies show empathy and compassion soon after birth. Almost as soon as they can coordinate their movements, they will try to soothe others who are suffering. Even three-month-olds will respond differently to a character that helps another versus one that hurts someone. It has been demonstrated that these inclinations are at least partially inherited. It appears clear that the default at birth is having a sense of right and wrong and a tendency to lean into doing the right thing. Thomas Jefferson[119] said a moral sense is "as much a part of man as his leg or arm."

Modeling the Afterlife

Since we have considered some of the views about how we are made and what makes us unique, let's turn to how it might end. As we have seen, the models of the afterlife tend to fall into several broad categories. In different religious traditions, the specific descriptions may combine elements of each.

Annihilation and the Persistence of Memory. Materialist and physicalist views, of course, assume that this life is it. There is nothing beyond our deaths, except to the extent that we have made a difference in the world and are remembered by those who we have touched with our lives. Carl Sagan, in this spirit, once said, "We are like butterflies who flutter for a day and think it is forever." On the other hand, some religions view annihilation as the ultimate end for those who are evil. For example, if you did not make the cut to reach your reward in Ancient Egypt, you could be devoured by Ammit.

The Netherworld, the Underworld, Sheol, and Hades. In many early religions and mythologies, this is the place where our souls go after we die. It usually is a place of shade or darkness, and is indeed under the earth's surface. Often souls are, in essence, asleep there. In other traditions, the spirits of the dead are aimlessly roaming around. Generally, it is a neutral place (except, of course, you are dead). In the Christian New Testament, some passages speak about Christ descending into this realm at his death and bringing the righteous to heaven as he resurrects. In Matthew 27:52-53 (NIV), there is that rather mysterious note that rarely is preached about that says, "…the tombs broke open. The bodies of many holy people who had died were raised to life. They came out of the tombs after Jesus' resurrection and went into the holy city and appeared to many people." I can't help but think about zombie walks. By the Jewish Second Temple period (around 500 BCE to 70 CE), the Jewish and Christian understanding was that there was a fore-taste of the future in this waiting room for the dead with a place for the wicked and a place for the righteous (see, for example, Jesus' parable of Lazarus and the rich man in Luke 16:19–31).

Heaven, Hell (and Purgatory). While heaven, hell, and to some extent, purgatory are identified with Christianity, elements of these ideas can be found in other religions as well, from the ancient Greeks to the Norse and even to the Incas. Heaven especially may go by names like the heavens, pure lands, Tian (China), Jannah (Islam), Valhalla, the Summerland (e.g., Swedenborgians, Theosophists, and Wiccans), Svarga Loka (Hinduism), and Paradise. It is where "the good"[120] go and where beings such as gods, angels, jinn, saints, and revered ancestors might live. The core idea is that the good end up in a paradise as a reward, and the wicked end up being punished in a place specifically designed for them. Often, there is some kind of divine judgment where people are sorted into their ultimate destinies. The rules for who is considered good and for those who are deemed bad can vary considerably. As we know, many today struggle with the idea of eternal punishment either suffered because of some ancient event (e.g., the fall of Adam and Eve), an accident of where or when someone was born, or actions during a relatively finite physical life. As a result, some religions provide a framework for continuing purification and perfection so that a larger proportion of humanity will end up in a paradise. Rituals to speed this process may include activities of the living on behalf of the dead.

Life Here, Only Better. Some indigenous tribes, the ancient Egyptians, and others saw death more like a continuation of this life, a passage to a life much like this one only better. In principle, the sense is we are meant to live in our world, and the afterlife is a continuation of the good things we have already been given. A variation on this might be that part of our charge in this world, our purpose for being here at all, is to envision a future paradise and make it real within this world. For example, Tod Lindberg (Lindberg, 2007) argues that part of what made Jesus' Sermon on the Mount so radical was he was painting that kind of vision of how his followers should transform the world in which we live.

Reincarnation and Perfection. For most Reincarnation models from Plato to Hinduism, the point is to improve and achieve perfection. In a way, this world itself is a kind of purgatory, and reincarnation is the process. Reincarnation is a central tenet of major Indian religions, including Buddhism, Hinduism, Jainism, and Sikhism. It recognizes that one life probably is not enough to achieve all of our potential. It was also held by ancient Greeks such as Pythagoras, Socrates, and Plato. It occurs in Spiritism and Theosophy, and tribal societies in Australia, East Asia, Siberia, and South America. It even is held by some subgroups within Judaism and Christianity. If your life is well-lived, the next one is another step forward, and if your life had issues, you would take a step back so you can learn your lessons and improve. Ultimate perfection may be completely moving beyond the physical and merging with the divine. A variation on this theme might be a new heaven and new Earth idea where you also receive a new body. While the new body may be presented as a resurrected version of the old body, it is typically so transformed it seems to fall more into the category of being about undergoing transmigration to a new, perfect *host* body. It is easy to imagine that there could be more bodies and places to use them in an infinite future.

Hoping to Die

Given the ubiquity of these ideas across history, it is worth speculating a little about how we have reached this point. In our culture, we might imagine that for the average person across human history, a future paradise would be a source of hope, a time when they would be freed from the toil, diseases, and wars that characterize life for most people. We could imagine this for much of the world still today. Of course, the ideas of a paradise, as opposed to an underworld, emerged relatively late in our history.

Given how we feel about the loss of a family member or a child, their presence in an afterlife paradise would be expected to give people comfort, with the additional hope that we will get to be reunited with them again. Of course, while there is something very human about this hope, we also know cultural attitudes (including religious beliefs) have varied across time and place based on social structures, attitudes about marriage and gender roles, life expectancy for children and adults, climate, and other factors. There have been times when life was so fragile, one could not afford to invest too much in any individual life emotionally.

We have also seen the possible early evolution of ideas focusing on the powerful and holy people going to a paradise, and how that might have expanded over time to include more of the rest of us. As mentioned, there is evidence that religions, with their belief systems and rituals, grew more rapidly and with richer theologies as civilization emerged. There is speculation that reward and punishment systems in the next life served a function of helping keep social order in place in this life. But what do we know historically?

In our twenty-first-century Western industrialized culture, most people take a more personal interest in their afterlife and that of their loved ones. We want to survive in some form of paradise, and we may be anxious about whether or not we will end up in a good place or a bad place. The roots of our beliefs, however, go back to the emergence of humanity. Many anthropologists believe that Neanderthal burial stones were placed to ensure those who had died would live beyond their physical deaths. We described in Chapter 3 research that these kinds of ideas among Neanderthals and early humans could have come about through visions and dreams. They could have come from altered states caused by herbs, stress, illness, and other conditions as well. They may have experienced visits in these states from human-like spirits and imagined them either as ghostly versions of themselves or others. Ideas of astral travel and reincarnation could come from these same sources.

Martin and Barresi (Martin, 2006) do note that while early humans and Neanderthals may have developed beliefs like this, there is not much evidence even from traditional cultures today that people felt a *yearning* to survive bodily death. They point out, "[B]ecoming an ancestor is not something that traditional people long for, just one of the things that they believe happens—a fact of life, if you will, or of death."

Up until the Greek philosophers, people developed more and more elaborate systems of beliefs about the afterlife's nature, and they had faith they would exist in it in some form. But even Socrates (according to Plato), who felt that he would survive bodily death and might find aspects of the afterlife engaging, did not express a longing to survive. He expected it to be a generally positive experience where he would be freed from some of this life's distractions so he could contemplate truth. Still, he was neither anxious about some kind of punishment nor did he long to get to a paradise that could not be experienced in any other way.

Martin and Barresi suggest the focus on one's fate in the afterlife began in earnest across Europe with the emergence of Christianity. They cite Paul (1 Corinthians 15:32, NIV), "If the dead are not raised, 'Let us eat and drink, for tomorrow we die.'" They believe that Paul is saying that we should be all in on hedonism if there is no price to pay. They argue that it appears for early Christians there was less of a focus on living a good life (either for one's own sake or for others) in this life, but the focus became investing in the best possible afterlife. Martin and Barresi point to Matthew 6:19-21 (NIV), "Do not store up for yourselves treasures on earth, where moths and vermin destroy, and where thieves break in and steal. But store up for yourselves treasures in heaven, where moths and vermin do not destroy, and where thieves do not break in and steal. For where your treasure is, there your heart will be also."[121] While Greek and Roman philosophers focused on living well in this life, Christians were relatively more focused on living well eternally.

In some cases, this could be contrasted with the Humanism of the growing set of modern Unaffiliated, and with the religious traditions of Judaism and more contemporary Catholicism and mainline Protestantism. The clear trend culturally in the United States is to own the sense that we can apply our creative gifts to sail towards a better future for humanity on Earth. We can make the world of tomorrow better than the one we have today, and ultimately that may be what it really means to "store up… treasures in heaven" given our stewardship role and whatever it means to be in the image of God.

How Long is Eternity

Christianity often talks about eternal life (and sometimes about eternal punishment). As Tommy Redmon (Redmon, 2020) observes, the Greek word typically translated as eternity is complex because it was used in various ways during the Hellenistic period. "It would be like explaining what the word 'soul' means in the early twenty-first century to somebody from the forty-first century….However, if one were to dig into people's perception of that loaded word, they would find many shades of meaning: material/spiritual, immortal/mortal, and the list could continue endlessly."

The idea of eternity as we think about it today did not exist for the early Israelites. The word often translated as eternity in Hebrew is olam (עוֹלָם). The word means "beyond the horizon." Space and time are using the same word here. For space, it is looking off in the far distance, and when we look out at that distance, the details fade, and beyond the horizon, we cannot see what is there even though something is there. While we might think of eternity as a time that never ends, the ancient Jews thought of it as a "very distant time," a point beyond the horizon. There is a common phrase that can be translated "to the distant horizon and again" which means something like "a very distant time and even further" (Benner, n.d.). According to Redmon, the idea of olam is related to life, time, and projects into the future and the past. Its limit, as with a horizon, is not always known. It can be hidden and unmeasurable to humans. Presumably, instead of being a static projection from now, it may contain surprises.

Aion (αἰών)[122], the Greek word often translated as eternal or eternity, has elements of both the Jewish way of thinking and Greek thought; and to make it more challenging, the meaning has changed considerably over time. It differs based on context and the point of view of those interpreting it. For Christians, this becomes particularly important in the difference between the *Traditionalist* view of eternal punishment and the *Universalist* view. The Traditionalist view is that there is a hell, and it punishes forever. For Universalists, there are differences in whether they think hell exists or not, and if it does, its purpose may be to help people grow out of it, and it does not last forever (just a long time, and it may change in character over that time). Each can find verses that can be interpreted to support their views.

Redmon reviews some of the ambiguous roots of the word aion or age. They are not easy to summarize. Eventually, though, they start to coalesce around a set of core meanings. He says that John of Damascus (675 to 749 CE) explains the meanings of the word from an eighth-century CE Christian perspective, starting with the earliest view (probably reaching back to around the time of Christ) and then as interpreted around his time. He says, "The life of each man is called an age. Again, a period of a thousand years is called an age. Again, the whole course of the present life is called an age: the future life, the immortal life after the resurrection, is also spoken of as an age. Again, the word age is used to denote, not time nor yet a part of time as measured by the movement and course of the sun, that is to say, composed of days and nights, but the sort of temporal motion and interval that is co-extensive with eternity." He says the word began as a description of a person's actual life and then grew over time to the life or age of different things, including the largest, the universe.

Early Church Fathers like Origen and Gregory of Nyssa used aion in a more cyclical sense of an age that could be taken as implying punishment was not eternal. Only God and heaven itself were eternal. Some early Greek poets used the word in the more limited sense for humans, but as unending for gods. The Septuagint uses the phrase "from aions" that can be read as either "from an infinite" or as an alternative an "undefined/boundless" number of ages back. Redmon sees one view of the evolution of the term from small (life) to big (lifetime/age) to bigger (eternity), but notes another idea is that in aion there is life, and more broadly time, and even more broadly entirety. An *entirety* implies a limit, however large. Redmon believes that while the word could mean eternity by the New Testament period, it is not obvious what it meant to the New Testament authors who were using it.

Redmon cites Thorleif Boman on the differences. He suggests for the ancient Jews, time could be thought of in a more rhythmic, dynamic sense. An example might be the universe model with a big bang, then a big crunch, and then another big bang. He says to the Jews time was more subjective and experiential. For the Greeks, it was more abstract and static. The Greek model of the universe might be like a big bang, and then everything continues to expand forever. The Jews experienced reality through activity, and as can be seen through Plato and Aristotle, the Greeks experienced reality more through reflection, knowledge, and theory. Redmon embraces the variety of points of view about eternity as they each provide insight. The caution, I suspect, would be picking one and applying it indiscriminately across all situations and ignoring the understanding of those using a given word in a specific context.

TITLE Notes on Afterlife Religious Themes

o The Afterlife Extends Beyond the Limits of This One
o We, as Unique Souls, Continue
o This Life Influences the Experiences in the Next
o One Goal is to Connect with the Ultimate Divine (i.e., God)
o Another Goal is to Care for Others (esp. those in need) and the World Itself
o Evil Will be Punished
o Grace and the Redemptive Process are Divine Attributes
o Growth and Divine Relationship Continues Beyond this Life
o Growth Is a Journey to Ultimate Truth, Wisdom, and Completion (incl. Spiritual)
o A Theme is Participating in the Ongoing Creative Activity
o Eternal Activity and Growth Involves Embodiment
o The Beauty and Life in this World will Be Taken to the Next Level in the Afterlife

---

[92] The religions referenced, of course, are the three Abrahamic religions, Judaism, Christianity, and Islam.

[93] It also appears in the extra-canonical books of Enoch and the Apocalypse of Baruch.

[94] Paul, in the Christian New Testament, was a Pharisee and this belief may provide some context for his view that what is "sown as a natural body is raised a spiritual body."

[95] "According to another midrash, sleep, like death, temporarily separates body and soul (Genesis Rabbah 14:9). Several rituals surrounding going to sleep and waking up evolved from this belief. Like birth and death, even temporary severings of the connection between body and soul require holy acts (for example, the washing of hands or recitation of particular prayers). Jews express gratitude

to God every morning for renewal of both body and soul: 'I offer thanks to You, living and everlasting King, for having returned to me my soul with compassion and great faithfulness' (the Modeh Ani prayer)" (MJL, n.d.). This is a particularly interesting view that I was not aware of, but that echoes early Egyptian ideas as well as some indigenous tribal beliefs. This idea could be relevant as we discuss comas (both from accidents and artificially induced), as well as certain forms of anaesthesia.

[96] In 2 Maccabees 12:38-45 (c. 1st century BCE), there is evidence that some believed that one could help the deceased in the intermediate state through prayer. This idea of the power of love connecting us to the other side through prayer is an important part of contemporary Christian belief as well.

[97] "Traditional Pagan culture offered all kinds of views of death and the afterlife: ranging from a terrifying series of punishment for those who had sinned in this life, through a more or less pleasant state of being that followed but was secondary to this life, to uncertainty or denial that any form of afterlife was possible (or knowable) ... the official state cult did not particularly emphasize the fate of the individual after death, or urge a particular view of the after-life (Beard et al, Religions of Rome)."

[98] See our Oxford English Dictionary discussion.

[99] Similar ideas of the intercessory value of beseeching the righteous while supported by some (e.g., Chasidic Jews), is generally opposed by Modern Orthodox Judaism.

[100] *National Geographic* has produced an interesting video summarizing these views entitled a *Map of hell* (available on DVD through Amazon).

[101] In speculating about what the experience between death and the "final" resurrection is, it is worth thinking about what parts of consciousness and mind are tied to having a physical body, and what the soul might experience without sensory input.

[102] Recall the earlier survey data that shows more than eighty percent of those who believe in heaven believe we will exist there spiritually and not physically.

[103] Aristotle also held this belief.

[104] As context, this was after the Babylonians fell to the Persians, and around the time in the history of Israel that Ezra and Nehemiah returned to Jerusalem. Persia was forcing local communities to firm up their laws, and that may have impacted the refining of the Tanakh.

The Temple was rebuilt around 515 BCE, and around the mid-fifth century BCE the area had virtually become a theocracy.

[105] A book that was widely read by many of us back in the 1960s and 70s was *Siddhartha* by Herman Hesse.

[106] To an outsider, this does sound a little like the Papal infallibility in the Catholic church, with a unique prophetic role as well.

[107] There are a variety of religions that are very different from each other, but that are centered in ideas like communication with a spirit world, reincarnation, animism, and/or pantheism. For the purposes of this natural history, I am going to use this exploration of Native American beliefs as a way to capture some of the unique ideas about death and the afterlife that have not already been touched on by other religions we have discussed.

[108] Interestingly, for many of the eastern tribes, their ancestors would have originally come from the southwest, as they migrated over the Bering Straight and along the coast as the glaciers slowly receded at the end of the last ice age, and then the would have moved up towards the northeast. It is easy to imagine the original migration was in search of a paradise, and some of those stories may have carried on as memories of paradise and ancestors left behind.

[109] Perhaps this explains the elephants, orcas, and other primates, as well as corvids like ravens.

[110] It is conceivable, however, that animals might also have some of the characteristics, but humans wrote about the things that were of interest to us. As we have noted, there are hints in the Tanakh and the Christian New Testament about more going on in the creation than we might otherwise assume.

[111] Dr. Jeffrey Tigay in his article on "Genesis as Allegory" in *My Jewish Learning* points out that Steven Katz says, "In Jewish religious thought Genesis is not regarded as meant for a literal reading, and Jewish tradition has not usually read it so." The Tanakh itself has a variety of ways it talks about the order and the details of creation. Genesis 1, while not typical of more common ancient Hebrew poetry, contains more poetic elements than those typical of text intended as history. It seems to speak to the grand questions around "The Beginning" of the Children of Israel, in a way that probably reflects the oral tradition that preceded the documentation of the stories.

[112] From this perspective, at least some animals could theoretically have souls and share attributes of God and ourselves as well, but we would have been given a special role in the hierarchy.

[113] In Chapter 2, of course, we noted that there may be differences in the degree of the rational and willful characteristics between humans and the rest of creation, but perhaps not in substance. The major difference, presumably, would be in the spiritual (although again, not necessarily the moral) substance of being human. At this point, humans do seem to be the "religion" making species. Of course, there is the caveat of the various scriptures that do point to a spiritual sense across all of creation.

[114] On the other hand, in Genesis 3:22 (JPS) it suggests what God was concerned about was that humans would be able to make moral judgments and would live forever like God, and that was at least part of why we were kicked out of the Garden.

[115] Again, in Chapter 2 we noted the significant social bonding among some animal species, and even across species. So here the difference would need to be in particular aspects of the relationships, perhaps at the level of a deeper, more spiritual level.

[116] An interesting open question is how popular attitudes about when ensoulment takes place might change based on broader social trends in miscarriage and infant mortality rates.

[117] In the 1860s, Ernst Haeckel (a German naturalist and philosopher) suggested that "ontogeny recapitulates phylogeny." The idea is that as an animal (including human) embryo develops, it shows a chronological replay of the species' past forms through the process of evolution.

[118] As a little context, not even counting miscarriages and deaths during childbirth, in 1800 forty-six percent of children that were born died before they reached age five. The fate of those between conception and these young ages across history does need to be considered in a comprehensive view of the soul and the afterlife.

[119] Thomas Jefferson, like some of the other founders of the United States, was a deist. He believed in divine providence, and reward and punishment after death. But he did not believe in the idea of God's revelation and the core doctrines of Christianity.

[120] Across religious history there are a wide variety of ways to define "the good." Sometimes it is about holiness or perfection, sometimes sainthood or martyrdom, and sometimes it is about doing more good than bad across a lifetime.

[121] Some are not inclined to worry about the wicked problems we have today (e.g., with global warming, working towards global peace, or dealing with the health and welfare of the poor) on behalf of future generations because they are focused on their own mansions and crowns in heaven and trying to stimulate Christ's imminent return.

[122] For this discussion, the noun form (aion) and the adjectival form, aionios, will be treated as equivalent.

Chapter 6

THE SCIENCE
OF THE SOUL

*"Since the creation of the world God's invisible qualities—his
eternal power and divine nature—have been clearly seen,
being understood from what has been made, so that men are
without excuse."*
– Romans 1:20 (NIV)

*"We must behold things as they are. And having thus got rid
of the foolishness of the body, we shall be pure and hold
converse with the pure, and shall in our own selves have
complete knowledge of the Incorruptible which is, I take it, no
other than the very truth."*
– Socrates (quoted by Plato)

*"The most beautiful and most profound experience is the
sensation of the mystical. It is the sower of all true science. He
to whom this emotion is a stranger, who can no longer wonder
and stand rapt in awe, is as good as dead. To know that
what is impenetrable to us really exists, manifesting itself as
the highest wisdom and the most radiant beauty which our
dull faculties can comprehend only in their primitive forms—
this knowledge, this feeling is at the center of true
religiousness."*
– Albert Einstein

So far, we have explored the experience of the self and our
souls that most of us carry, and alternative ideas about
life after death. We have looked at how these beliefs are
represented in our culture, and how they inform the stories that
shape us. We have also reviewed the evolution of the concepts

within philosophy, and the emergence of psychology and its more empirical and naturalistic approach. Religion is one area where the soul and the afterlife are still a central focus of thought, and these beliefs in different faiths provide frameworks for how we should live our lives. As a result, we have also compared the different soul and afterlife models across prominent religious voices within our culture. Still, empirical science is dancing around the edges of some of the experiences associated with our approach to death and our feelings about our souls and those of loved ones in the afterlife.

According to Martin and Barresi (Martin, 2006), after Descartes started pivoting the focus to our own minds as the proof of existence, theologians continued to value the idea of the soul and its application to ethical theory. William James hoped to retain its value in the nineteenth century, but as a functionalist and a psychologist, he deconstructed the self so completely there was not much of the soul left. Martin and Barresi observed that even the concept of a unified self that might be identified with the soul died "if not of a thousand qualifications, then of a thousand hyphenations," despite the way most of us experience it. At the same time, they recognize that our ideas about the self and our identities are grounded in very personal concerns about who we are and our fates after death. It seems clear that well before the flowering of contemporary philosophical and scientific analyses of the self and identity, people had and still have a sense of who we are. It feels direct, experiential, and unified. This chapter will review some of the empirical work exploring the value we find in these experiences and how our bodies have evolved to provide them.

As we approach this chapter, it is worth reminding ourselves of William James' arguments about the afterlife. Just because something can be explained, does not mean the explanation is the complete answer. Science is a continuous process of growing our understanding by testing, refining, and even replacing what we thought we already knew. There is a physicalist argument that could be made, for example, that dismisses our beliefs and experiences under the assumption that they will eventually be entirely accounted for by our biology and evolutionary forces. Voltaire once argued, "If God did not exist, it would be necessary to invent him." We might respond to the physicalists by suggesting that since we have had these beliefs and experiences across human history, "If the soul and the afterlife do not exist, apparently we *needed* to invent them." If they do not exist, there still is the question of the evolutionary benefits of these beliefs, and the sensory and experiential inputs that sustain them.

Dean Hamer, for example, has a book called *The God Gene*. He argues that a specific gene called VMAT2 (the vesicular monoamine transporter 2) inclines us as humans to have spiritual and mystical experiences. Harner proposes the gene works by affecting neurotransmitter levels and that evolution has preserved this gene since religious people tend to survive longer. The comfort and optimism that comes with religion (and presumably its accompanying beliefs about the soul and the afterlife) for many have been associated with various physical and psychological benefits.

Cody Delistraty (Delistraty, 2014), in "Why Do We Believe in heaven?" takes a different approach, but that could reflect this genetic inclination. Delistraty builds on the research that shows humans are particularly effective pattern detectors. We have also shown that, as a result, we are also fundamentally story creators and tellers. Delistraty says, "Humans tend to see patterns in their lives at large. We imagine we are on Earth for a reason—that there is a Master Plan. And if the soul dies with the body, what would be the point of our entire existence? Illogical as it may be, our most rational recourse is that our emotions, our desires, our soul will last forever. Heaven is just the most sensible place to go."

Taking the point of view of theistic evolution and evolutionary creationism, we could suggest we have been designed to have these experiences in order to mature as a species. In the last chapter, I suggested that being in the image of God was a process. We may have acquired the urge for relationship, curiosity and creativity, reflection and learning, and spiritual sensitivity as properties of our souls and bodies through God's creative use of evolution.

There are many questions about how this might work, but just because we cannot *yet* study something empirically does not mean it can be ruled out. Much in science was once inconceivable. We do now know that the way we experience reality is just a tiny sample of the richness of the universe, and is not even the only way to experience and make inferences about the world in which we live. Much inherently will likely continue to be outside direct empirical verification, and will need to be inferred from the patterns that we can measure. We are already demonstrating quantum linkages that Einstein called "spooky action at a distance." Given the ideas of string theory, some of us would not be surprised if forces outside our immediate three or four-dimensional existence might impact us. That being said, let's take a look at some of the interesting research and speculation about the physical laws that shape our experiences. Some of the research may reveal the outline of things we cannot study directly. Some may suggest how we should think about how our ideas of the soul and the afterlife might need to evolve in the future.

EVOLUTION AND THE SOUL

"Animals learn death first at the moment of death…man approaches death with the knowledge it is closer every hour, and this creates a feeling of uncertainty over his life, even for him who forgets in the business of life that annihilation is awaiting him. It is for this reason chiefly that we have philosophy and religion."
— Arthur Schopenhauer

Steve Stewart-Williams (Stewart-Williams, 2018), in his paper on "Afterlife Beliefs: An Evolutionary Perspective," outlined and evaluated three major approaches to how afterlife beliefs began to appear among humans. One is that it is a beneficial adaptation of natural selection. A second is that it is a kind of evolutionary byproduct of other adaptations. I noted earlier, for example, the evolutionary characteristics that may be associated with the appearance of storytelling. Storytelling is important in the formation of culture and probably contributed to our evolution.[123] *The God Gene* hypothesis also falls into this category. A third approach is to apply evolutionary principles to the process of how culture forms. There is evidence that stories can be thought of in terms of an evolutionary process. Stories that embody ideas about the soul and the afterlife might have survived because they were useful for individuals holding them, good for groups, or valuable as they were exchanged across groups.

One of the voices arguing for its value in natural selection is that of the evolutionary psychologist Jesse Bering (Bering, 2002). He proposes that we are wired with a cognitive system that is partially optimized to produce a range of religious convictions, such as believing that the mind is immortal and can exist independently from the body. In other words, we cannot help but feel what most of us believe about our conscious experience. As the theory of mind is partially about projecting our mind's introspections onto others, this idea lends itself to imagining invisible agents (e.g., ancestors or gods) being present and observing us. Bering argues that a payoff of being able to imagine these agents is that it can motivate us to behave in a more socially responsible manner. He claims, "the general idea of an afterlife is not so much implanted in people's heads by way of 'exposure' to counterintuitive tales, as it is already present."

Bering and his collaborators demonstrated this with a variety of studies. In one, children were primed to believe there was an invisible girl called Princess Alice in the room with them. This was compared to a condition where the children were alone. When they thought Alice was with them, they were less likely to cheat on a task. In another study, children saw a puppet show of an alligator gobbling up a mouse. Children seemed to understand that the mouse's body was not working in any sense, but they still believed the mouse would be experiencing emotions and would want to be with its mother.

We have discussed how religious beliefs, stories, and rituals such as those around the soul and the afterlife serve to bond communities. Community membership offers an advantage both to the individual and the group. William Irons (2001), an evolutionary anthropologist, makes the adaptation argument. He argues that it is essential for groups to ensure all their members are committed and weed out the *free riders*. The free riders might not give as much as they take and could abandon the group when their calculation of value changes. Religious practices and rituals do that, and religious beliefs (especially with more specific detail than the more *intuitive* beliefs) might do that. Alcorta and Sosa (Alcorta, 2005) point out that "By incorporating counterintuitive concepts within belief systems, religion creates reliable costly signals that are difficult to 'fake.'"

Perhaps the approach with the most support today is the idea that these beliefs are a byproduct of other adaptations. For example, one theory is that we have developed the ability to anticipate and imagine our death, which comes with a natural dread of death and extinction. Belief in the persistence of self and an afterlife may be an effective response to managing anxiety (Jonas, 2006). A variety of studies have shown that a belief in the afterlife is associated with reduced death anxiety; as that belief is stronger, the fear is lower.

Another example is the theory of mind that we have mentioned earlier. Again, this is the idea that we can recognize others' thoughts, beliefs, perceptions, feelings, and desires; in part by projecting our reflections and experiences onto them. This ability lets us empathize with others and is a characteristic that enables stories to serve as tools for sharing models of how the world works. According to Steve Stewart-Williams (Stewart-Williams, 2018), this theory of mind ability lets us represent the world in terms of physical objects and interactions in a three-dimensional space. It gives us a way to think about our agency and mental states as well as those in others. This modeling, in turn, allows us to imagine that our minds can be potentially separable entities. It could be what gives us the dualist intuitions so many of us have, which would make it easy to imagine the persistence of mind beyond death.

The third view of cultural adaptation argues that selection shapes culture by acting on cultural formation itself. Part of what I have been looking at through this natural history is what the process might look like over human history. Stewart-Williams suggests the main ideas here are:

- Cultural elements are selected to the extent they increase the individual's survivability
- Cultural elements are selected if they are good for the group
- Cultural elements are selected to the extent they enable themselves to persist

There is a variety of research that shows the benefits of emulating successful high-status people in a culture. Part of why there is popular culture is a result of this tendency. Other research regularly indicates the value of looking like the people with whom you are trying to connect.[124] We have mentioned that in looking at the history of various religions back to prehistoric times, there was a suggestion that religions emerged as societies became more complex and benefited from structures that would keep people bonded and in line. The emergence of formal religious institutions is the kind of tendency that would come from these prestige and conformist biases. Stewart-Williams calls this an acquired adaptation.

A group-oriented variation on this begins with the assumption that different groups vary in their beliefs, norms, practices, tools, and technical development. As some survive and others disappear, the cultural elements associated with the winners persist. When they benefit group survival, these cultural elements can continue to evolve. They bring benefits to the group, live on, and become enriched. Ancient Egypt is probably a good example. The Children of Israel, as depicted through the Tanakh, would seem to be another one. While not discussed in Stewart-Williams' article, groups that want to prosper might, in essence, absorb cultural elements of more powerful groups just as individuals within a group adopt the characteristics, beliefs, and behaviors of more powerful people. In *Darwin's Cathedral: Evolution, Religion, and the Nature of Society,*

David Sloan Wilson (2002) suggests that beliefs that enhance groups' solidity would increase their ability to compete with other groups. Atkinson and Bourrat (Atkinson, 2011) point out that cross-national surveys suggest that sharing common afterlife beliefs predicts more cooperation.

The idea that there can be a characteristic in cultural elements that makes some "stickier" than others was explored by a seminal book called *The Selfish Gene* by Richard Dawkins (1976). Dawkins introduced the idea called memetics, and he brought us the concept of memes (which now has firmly entered the vocabulary of our popular culture). Memes can be viewed as analogous to genes. The memes that are the fittest and survive are not necessarily good either for the individual or the group, but they have properties that enable them to persist in people's minds.

The argument is that religious beliefs about death and the afterlife can have these properties. As they may carry stories with characteristics that allow them to enhance the value they bring to individuals and groups, they can mutate without being tied to either the individual or the group. The most useful properties will allow them to persist. The research that treats stories as having something like evolving DNA and tracking folk tales' evolution and persistence seems like it is tapping into this tendency. The evolution of ideas like the underworld and netherworld to concepts like heaven and hell, nirvana, and so on could be illustrations of this memetic mechanism.

CHILDREN AND THE AFTERLIFE

While we cannot necessarily put ourselves into the heads of ancient humans to test how some of these ideas that we find in the archeology evolved, we can look at the process as it occurs in children. David Menendez, Iseli Hernandez, and Karl Rosengren (Menendez, 2020) provide a nice high-level summary in "Children's Emerging Understanding of Death."

While early researchers such as Piaget thought death was not understood until children were nine or ten, a deeper understanding of how death is experienced has suggested a finer-grained development of the idea. They cite a study by Speece and Brent (1992), who identify four concepts that make up the overall experience of death. One is *universality*, the idea that all living things die. One is *finality*, and that refers to death as final and irreversible. *Nonfunctionality* is the third one, and that implies biological and psychological processes end. An understanding that different things can be responsible for death, *causality*, is the fourth. Recall that we explored how this model has been applied to animals, and there is evidence that various animals have demonstrated behaviors that suggest some of these concepts. Very young children (under five) seem to demonstrate universality, and that is followed by finality. Around five, they begin to understand there is a cessation of bodily processes, and by six they know death can happen due to a variety of causes.

As children acquiring cultural ideas have been studied, a fifth concept has been added. This stage could be called *noncorporeal continuity*, the idea that something exists either beyond death or in parallel to the body. Both children and adults can simultaneously hold these biological and religious (or more generally metaphysical) concepts. Kristina Olson (Olson, 2013) cites work by Jesse Bering and David Bjorkland that finds many young children start out as dualists and believe that even when the body ends, the mind continues to exist.

One study she describes asked children about a mouse that had died. While the children knew the mouse's body was dead (and so the body would not need water or have a working brain), they believed the mouse would still love its mother and would want to return home. The children came from both religious and secular families. They saw a natural predisposition towards dualism in the earliest stages, perhaps grounded in something like the growing theory of a mind that is somewhat disconnected from the body. However, the family context seems to predict how these feelings develop as the children continue to mature, whether along an increasingly dualist line or moving beyond afterlife beliefs in secular families.

The potential dissonance that a child might feel as they try to make sense of the distinctions can be reduced through the ongoing interaction they have with their parents and authority figures about the religious and cultural context in which they are developing. It has been observed that while children initially start asking questions about biological issues, some parents often respond using religious language. From what we have seen across the development of religious ideas around the soul and the afterlife, it would not be surprising if parents are not just responding for purely educational reasons but also are using the language and the ideas that they themselves use to find comfort during end-of-life stresses.

Cody Delistraty (Delistraty, 2014) reported a study from Boston University researchers. This research team looked at two groups of children in Ecuador. One group was raised Roman Catholic, and the other had no cultural pre-life beliefs. They showed the children a series of drawings with a baby, a young woman, and the same woman while pregnant. They explored what the children thought this child in the pictures would think before conception, as a baby, and in the womb. Both groups were confident the baby's emotions and wishes existed even before they were born. They felt the baby would be sad that they were apart from their family and would be looking forward to meeting their mommy once they were born. According to Delistraty, the head researcher reported, "They didn't even realize they were contradicting themselves. Even kids who had biological knowledge about reproduction still seemed to think that they had existed in some sort of eternal form, and that form seemed to be about emotions and desires."

MEASURING LIFE AND DEATH

We are exploring the doorway to the afterlife, death. It might be helpful first to look at what it means to be alive.

Indeed, what it means to be alive and what it means to be human comes up in the abortion debate that is still underway. As we mentioned earlier, Aristotle said that plants have a nutritive soul because they take in nutrition, grow from this nutrition, and eventually decay over time. You could say these properties exhibit the evidence of life. He also observed that non-human animals have these properties plus a sensitive soul, including the perception of the world in which they live. It includes their ability to remember things that happened to them, pain and pleasure, and appetites and desires. We humans have all of these plus rationality, according to Aristotle, as part of our rational soul.

In the Judeo-Christian tradition, Genesis 1 begins with giving humans and other creatures the breath of life. The idea that life is associated with breathing is a theme through Jewish and Christian scriptures. But in texts like Leviticus 17:11 (JPS), life is also explicitly associated with the blood, as in "For the life of the flesh is in the blood, and I have given it to you upon the altar to make atonement for your souls; for it is the blood that maketh atonement by reason of the life." The association was part of the rationale for sacrifices, including for Christians the importance of the crucifixion and the symbolism of the sacrament of Holy Communion.

Across most of human history, breathing and circulating blood would be signs of life. For many before the nineteenth century, the presence of a soul (especially in a human) gave us the *vital spark* that signified life; and when the soul was gone, our bodies no longer lived. The evidence of the vital spark was a heart that was pumping and lungs that were breathing. In our discussion of ensoulment, one set of milestones that probably determine when a growing set of cells with human potential are ready for a soul are these critical milestones.

As we will be discussing, we now recognize that the failure of these physical systems can be reversed under certain circumstances. The phenomena associated with the living experiencing those who return from death have a long history. While Christians would probably point first to Jesus as one who resurrected from the dead, he would be a special case since he is divine for Christians. The Jewish Tanakh and the Christian New Testament have mentioned several others who came back from the dead. In the Tanakh, these include the widow of Zarephath's son (I Kings 17: 17-24), the Shunammite woman's son (2 Kings 4:18-37), and the man raised from Elisha's grave (2 Kings 13: 20-21). In the Christian New Testament, besides Jesus, there is the widow of Nain's son (Luke 7:11-17) who was the first of the resurrections Jesus performed, Lazarus of Bethany of course (John 11), Tabitha (Acts 9:36-43), Eutychus (Acts 20: 7-12), and the mass resurrection that occurred at the resurrection of Christ. In all these cases, the sense of the texts is that the bodies were resurrected with the souls. They apparently came back as something close to who they were before they died. There have been miracles and healers in many other cultures as well (e.g., remember Empedocles, who brought people back to life and even healed through the power of music).

The tradition of what happened to Lazarus after he was resurrected is interesting. There are different accounts, of course. According to the Eastern Orthodox Church tradition, after Lazarus was resurrected, he asked Jesus if he would ever die again. Jesus told him that he would. In this story, as a result, Lazarus never smiled again in his remaining thirty years, except for once. At one point, he saw someone stealing a pot, and he grinned and said, "the clay steals the clay."

To know death, we need to know life. What is it? Biological definitions capture much of what we associate with living things that we see in our world. These definitions are heavily influenced by cell theory which dates back to the early 1800s. Some of the common properties include:

- Movement – Living things move, especially in response to stimuli.
- Sensitivity and Response to Stimuli – Living things respond to changes in their environment.
- Growth – Living cells grow.
- Reproduction – Living things reproduce and pass genetic information to offspring.

- Metabolism – Living things can convert chemicals (food, air, etc.) into the energy their cells need and excrete the waste they do not need.
- Organization and Homeostasis – Living things are composed of one or more cells (the basic units of life) and can regulate their internal environment.
- Adaptation – Living things have evolutionary potential. They can adapt to the environment over time.

Definitions of life have been based on chemical systems and biophysics, living systems theory, theology, and philosophy. There are well over one hundred documented definitions of what life is and how to measure it. There does seem to generally be a carbon-based chemistry bias, as we have built out our understanding of the world as we know it. Looking backwards to how "life" came to be in evolution, however, the roots are in things that may not meet all the characteristics of the living things that immediately come to mind. In addition, the diversity of the edges of the taxonomy of living or living-like things includes archaea, bacteria, eukaryotes, and viruses. Bacteria are recognized as being alive. But most would rule out viruses as being alive, although some include them depending on their specific definition. This is despite the "intentions" the press sometimes seem to attribute to the COVID virus as it mutates.

Further, we are in the process of synthetically creating new categories of things with various combinations of these properties. Then we have to consider what we will find as we reach out to the stars. NASA has moved from defining life per se to taking more of a systems approach. It talks about "a self-sustaining chemical system capable of Darwinian evolution." But, as we will see, others looking at artificial intelligence are skeptical about the "chemical" requirement.

Interestingly, while they began from a similar place, the conversation about how we know something is dead has taken a different path than the conversation about life. In some ways, the definition of death is perhaps less about theory and more about the pragmatics of how we must deal with it as individuals and societies. In practice, the issue is also less what death "is" (e.g., the complete cessation of all bodily systems) but instead when it occurs and how to establish it (Whetstine, 1996). In her *Lancet* article, Leslie Whetstine notes, "The nature of death…does not lend itself to one discipline; it cannot be defined without considering metaphysics, sociology, theology, and medicine. Death evades an immutable objective definition and instead is understood in subjective terms that are culturally and historically regulated." This is not unlike the definition of what it means to be alive, of course. She says that Karen Gervais says there is a "decision of significance" that "must be established before criteria to test for the definition of death can be imposed. Such a decision identifies specific features that are necessary to differentiate a living person from a dead person and the conceptual reasons why such features are significant."

It is worth reminding ourselves that the question of when someone is dead is not an easy one to answer. With all the equipment we have today, we can now measure brain activity, respiration, and heart activity in a hospital room. But it was not until the 1960s that we regularly began to harvest organs from one person to replace another person's organs[125] and so needed to certify the donor was dead. We did not always have the tools

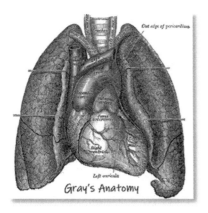

Gray's Anatomy

and metrics we use now, and the ambiguity in the past may have influenced ideas about how the soul relates to the body (e.g., in popular culture) and ideas about the afterlife.

Early on, people identified death with the "permanent" cessation of heart activity and breathing (the cardiovascular system) since their absence soon resulted in what was recognized as the entire system's failure. In the Judeo-Christian tradition, these symptoms of death were certainly the counterpart of those associated with life.

More broadly, it was obvious to the average person dealing with a family member's death or the fatalities on a battlefield that there were several signs that meant the person was "gone." As Whetstine notes, a "consensus emerged that cardiac and respiratory activities were significant for distinguishing the living from the dead. The moment of death was firmly established [in theory], but the task of creating criteria to test for the permanent quiescence of these functions provided more challenging and often had devastating results." What became clear is that there is no universal *moment* of death, but there is a *process* of death that can vary by individual and circumstance.

Until the eighteenth century, while the idea of death as being associated with the cessation of activity of the heart and lungs became quite prevalent, there were no reliable ways for doctors to certify it. For those without anything like what we would think of as a doctor, the diagnosis of death would be even less reliable. Empirical criteria to test at this time often depended on folklore, "old wives" tales, shamans, superstition, religious leaders, and so on. On the other hand, many still experience a moment at their loved one's bedside when they are confident the soul has left the body, even if some signs of physical life continue. This was the experience of my sisters at our grandmother's passing. As we know today, *apparent* death can happen from lack of oxygen, apoplexy, hysteria, overdose, concussion, and the often rampant plagues at the time. In the case of disease, there was an additional motivation to bury those quickly who had died of the plague before they infected others.[126]

Taphophobia is the fear of being buried alive due to being pronounced dead when you are not. During the 1700s and early 1800s, there were many studies and news accounts documenting cases of misdiagnosed death and premature interment. The popular press in the nineteenth and twentieth centuries loved to cover reports of unintentional live burials, and there were stories such as Edgar Allan Poe's works: "The

Fall of the House of Usher," "The Cask of Amontillado," and "The Premature Burial."

The American funeral director T. M. Montgomery in 1896 suggested that nearly two out of every hundred of those exhumed probably had been alive when they were buried. In 1905, William Tebb collected accounts of English premature burials. He found two hundred and nineteen near-live burials, one hundred and forty-nine actual live burials, ten cases of live dissection, and two cases of awakening during the process of embalming.

Fear of being alive after being pronounced dead peaked during the cholera epidemics of the nineteenth century. Safety coffins (e.g., including a bell to notify the living you were not dead) go back to 1791. Frédéric Chopin, George Washington, Hans Christian Anderson, and Alfred Nobel all wanted additional steps taken to make sure they were dead before they were buried.

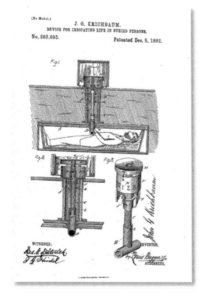

Many of the technologies used to avoid being buried alive were based on signs of movement. Some approaches were efforts to ensure death, such as an apparatus that would slowly create a vacuum while monitoring for any activity. As with the Greeks and the Romans, arrangements were sometimes made to ensure corpses began to decay before they were buried. Techniques like applying electricity, a nipple pincher device, surgical investigation to see if the heart is beating, and thrusting a needle under a toenail were used to see if they could stimulate a response that would indicate suspended animation versus death. Some widely used techniques such as inserting needles deep into the body to see if they rusted, inserting them into the heart directly, or injecting ammonia into the body to see if there was an inflammatory response persisted, despite the fact that if the person was alive the test might kill them. Across history, there have also been accounts of people *coming back* from the dead. The soldier that thrust a spear into Jesus on the cross (John 19:34) was probably confirming Jesus' death at a time when this was an issue.[127] Typically, the Thracians, Romans, and Greeks all waited at least three days for putrefaction to begin before burying their dead. The Romans might even cut off a finger to see if the stump bled (indicating there was still circulation).

As the mechanistic model of the body grew after the Enlightenment and the Scientific Revolution began, experiments began to demonstrate the ambiguity inherent in the model of death up to that point. Giovanni Aldini (a physics professor in Bologna) pioneered the electrical cardiac resuscitation that became an inspiration for Mary Shelly's *Frankenstein*. The first recorded instance of artificial respiration dates back to 1627 and became well documented in the 1700s. In the nineteenth century, the open-chest cardiac massage technique demonstrated that a "dead" heart could be brought back to life.

By the nineteenth century, while electro-resuscitation and artificial respiration brought medical benefits, it also made it clear more broadly that what had seemed to be an objective boundary between life and the afterlife was not so distinct after all. In 1861, Horace Welby, in his book *Mysteries of Life, Death and Futurity,* even provided evidence that suspended animation does not always lead to the suspension of consciousness. Suspended animation in animals was being studied with pond trout, snails, and other creatures, and they could be brought back to life after months of apparent death. One instance was recorded in 1889 with an Indian Sanskrit scholar who was known for his self-induced trances. He went into a trance as a physician monitored the reduction in his heartbeat and pulse until it could no longer be detected. He was then wrapped in a shroud and entombed for thirty-three days. When brought out, it appeared he was in rigor mortis and, against all tests, showed the signs of death. Three days later, he fully recovered.

We continue to see cases of people being frozen to death or dying of hypothermia in frigid waters without respiration, heart rate, or brain activity being brought back to life. Indeed, part of the idea behind cryogenic preservation of bodies (or at least heads) from the moments before death is based on this idea. It is likely that this happened naturally in the past and would enter folklore. Then there are the rare cases of those who have locked-in syndrome, where there is complete paralysis of voluntary muscles except those that control the eyes but who are fully conscious. This syndrome is different from either brain death, where the body is alive in some sense but the brain is not, and comas, where there may be brain activity without consciousness.

Historically, stories from families and friends dealing with loved ones in these conditions—especially where they may have returned to some perhaps restricted level of functioning—could serve as the source of ideas that evolved into what we now think of as zombies. It also could reinforce the sense of the separation of the body and a soul that can come and go (and perhaps return). A grounded theory of the soul should make sense of what happens in these various situations.

A significant change happened in the 1880s and 1890s when embalming was introduced. It became widely used during the Civil War when they had to preserve the bodies of soldiers who had died in order to transport them for several days to bring them home. It received even more recognition when Lincoln was embalmed and viewed at a series of train stops over nineteen days. A side "benefit" was that removing the blood and replacing it with chemicals ensured that the body would not come back to life. Still, as Whetstine notes, even as late as 1926, the *Medical Diagnosis for the Student and Practitioner* listed these checks on whether a person was dead or alive:

- "A deep red or purple color in the fingertips will become evident gradually if a firm ligature be applied to the digit.
- Several hours after a supposed death blood will flow persistently from a cut artery.

- If a needle thrust into the tissues and left for a time becomes oxidized, life is present.

- If any cloud repeatedly appears upon an ice-cold mirror held close to the mouth, there is respiration, but its absence does not alone suffice to prove death.

- If a powerful vesicant produces redness or blisters, there is life.

- If a body fails to take approximately the temperature of its environment forty-eight hours after apparent death, there is life.

- Pupillary response to light shows life, its absence does not prove death. Several hours after death it is affected neither by atropine nor eserine.

- Persistence of the red in and visibility of the arteries of the optic disc are signs of life, as is also persistent clearness of the media, six to eight hours after death.

- A sensitive cornea is a sign of life; absence of the corneal reflex is not a sign of death.

- Presence of electric excitability in all muscles twenty-four hours after apparent death indicates life."

Whetstone points out that heading into the 1900s, "At this juncture we see a fundamental change from being unable to determine death due to medical inadequacy to being unable to determine death because of scientific advancement." By the 1920s, kidney transplantation was being explored, and over time transplantation was more and more successful in humans. In 1967, Christiaan Bernard performed the first human to human heart transplant. The heart of Denise Darvall, an accident victim, was transplanted into Louis Washkansky. Washkansky regained full consciousness and was able to converse with his wife. While he died eighteen days later, it was from pneumonia resulting from his suppressed immune system. The introduction of cardiopulmonary resuscitation (CPR) and the use of electric shock to reverse ventricular fibrillation are now so ubiquitous that it is clear that death, as it had been defined, is not always irreversible. One cultural byproduct is many of us now try to be *very explicit* about under what conditions we may or may not want to be brought back in the journey to the afterlife.

Around 2007 I had a young employee who needed a heart transplant, and there were one hundred thousand people on the waiting list. The idea that an organ could be moved from one body to another was long in the realm of science fiction. Now the idea that an organ that has for much of human history been associated with life itself and often with the soul can be transplanted requires some adjustment of many people's views of what it means to be who we are. Even pigs' heart valves have been successfully transplanted into humans, and experiments are going on to transplant chimpanzee kidneys into patients. Pigskin grafts for burn victims and corneal transplants are common. Medicine has made the idea of what is considered *my body* much more fluid, and it begs the question about the nature of the body that might resurrect in the future.

The medical science of organ transplantation's success pushed the focus from the heart and lungs to the brain. Neurologists began to get on board with what philosophers have been arguing since Descartes, that the brain is the primary seat of integrative functioning. Physicians could use electroencephalogram (EEG) tools to measure the brain directly. By 1968, the Ad Hoc Committee of the Harvard Medical School's Report proposed that death is, in essence, *irreversible* coma (i.e., a permanent loss of brain function). This definition became law with the Uniform Determination of Death Act in 1981. It was reaffirmed by a presidential commission in 2008. Christof Koch (Koch, 2019), in his article entitled "Is Death Reversible?" notes how in recent years, the locus of death shifted from the heart and lungs to the brain, and has tended to move from a more public sphere historically to the privacy of the hospital room. He observes:

> *"This rapid and widespread acceptance of brain death, reaffirmed by a presidential commission in 2008, is remarkable when compared with the*

ongoing controversy around abortion and the beginning of life. It may perhaps be reflective of another little noticed asymmetry—people agonize about what happens in the hereafter but rarely about where they were before being born!"

Even here, however, the expectation is that as science continues to advance, the boundary between life and death, at least as we can measure it, will continue to be ambiguous, and the ambiguity may even increase. Koch reminds us that a brain-dead body can be kept *alive* for days, as we have seen in various news stories of families who are struggling with letting a loved one go.[128] Families visiting a family member that the doctors have diagnosed as brain dead may see a chest moving in and out, they feel a pulse, and the skin looks normal. Koch reports a recent study at the Yale School of Medicine under Nenad Sestan, who worked with the Department of Agriculture, where they had hundreds of pigs that they had been putting to death for various reasons (as they sometimes have to do). In experiments published in *Nature*, the researchers removed the brains and connected the arteries and veins to a device that mimics a beating heart and circulates a kind of artificial blood. The researchers compared these brains with those of control pigs whose brains were not aided in this way. Koch says these brains showed signs of being almost normal. Arteries, capillaries, and veins responded to the treatment, and tissue integrity was preserved without the extreme signs typically associated with death. Neural cells (synapses, neurons, and axons) appeared normal.

The researchers demonstrated that the cortical neurons retained their capacity to generate electrical and synaptic activity. Cells removed and studied could be excited with an electrical current and responded with stereotypical electrical pulses. Koch (a neuroscientist) asks the question of whether in the future it might be possible to apply a version of this technique to a human brain in some fashion. He provides an answer and a question. "...the technical answer is yes; in principle, this could be done. But should it be done?"

So it is clear that what might appear to be death to

observers over human history has not always been irreversible. Furthermore, it still is not. There may even be a considerable time between the outward signs of death and when it is no longer possible to recover. If ensoulment is when a soul appears as part of a body, when exactly does the soul leave the body and why? Where is the soul when the unassisted heartbeat and breathing have stopped? What about when it is being artificially maintained, but there is no consciousness? When the brain activity has stopped, but eventually it will be revived, where is the soul then? What happens when it seems like the person themselves (their soul) has "left the building," but the body is otherwise still alive? In all these situations where it is possible to bring people back from the dead, one wonders where the soul is hanging out, what it is doing until death is final, and what it may be sensing. It may be worth rereading and reflecting on the issues explored in *Frankenstein*.

WALKING THROUGH THE DOOR TO THE AFTERLIFE

Near-death Experiences

Some of the experiences where death has been ambiguous have been reversed and resulted in what are known as near-death experiences. These experiences are perhaps the closest thing we have to reports from those who appear to have walked up to the door of death and returned, other than religious figures. A near-death experience (NDE) is a profound experience reported after someone recovers from apparent physical death or a near-death event. An NDE is one of the few spiritual experiences that we have a chance to explore scientifically. Indeed, it tends to happen in a context in which the person nearing death is surrounded by an ever-growing set of devices and software tracking and analyzing everything about the body that can be measured.

Various studies suggest that anywhere from nine to

eighteen percent of cardiac patients who revive have an experience in this category, and twenty percent of critically ill people may have them. Among the general population, there are estimates that five percent of the United States population have experienced NDEs (or about ten million Americans). In Germany, there are estimates that over three million have had NDEs. NDEs have been reported in many cross-cultural studies, as well. Gideon Lichfield (Lichfield, 2015) describes some of these, including *The Handbook of Near-Death Experiences: Thirty Years of Investigation*, an anthology that includes studies of nearly three thousand five hundred people who have had NDEs. Most reported experiences tend to be positive, mystical, and life-changing, although some have been found that are quite distressing (around twenty percent or more across a dozen different studies).

NDEs may occur for people who have been subject to events like blunt trauma, heart attacks, asphyxia, and shock. Some of these would be common during times of war across human history. We all have heard about people seeing their life pass in front of their eyes as they near possibly fatal events. In other words, many of us probably know someone or know someone who knows someone who has had one of these experiences, even if they don't talk about it. The question at this point is clearly not if they happen, but rather what causes them and what do they tell us? A related question, of course, is what has their existence meant to an evolving view of death across human history?

As we have discussed, medical technology is continually improving and can bring more and more people back to life from the brink of death. Some have recovered after spending hours without a breath or a pulse when cooled in snow or cold water. Doctors sometimes artificially create this condition to slow the process of death for patients. According to Lichfield, a brain does not die just because of a lack of oxygen. If it is kept cold, it can be brought back after many hours. As a result, the boundary between whether the brain is alive or dead has gotten even fuzzier as our technologies continue to advance.

Near-death experiences go back to ancient times and have

probably shaped some of the stories and ideas that have worked their way into our various religions and popular culture. There is evidence of NDEs in early Greek and Roman literature, and there may be references in Jewish and Christian scriptures and literature that reflect these experiences. They can be found in Buddhism's history and the folklore of aboriginal groups in Australia, South America, and Oceania.

The oldest medical description is from around 1740. Dr. Phillippe Charlier found a manuscript written by Pierre-Jean du Monchaux, a military physician. In the *Anecdotes de Médecine,* he speculates that too much blood flowing to the brain might explain people's reports after coming back to consciousness. One patient, for example, reported seeing a light so pure and bright that he felt it must be heaven.

In 1892, Albert Heim reported a series of experiences such as workers falling from scaffolds, soldiers suffering injuries in war, climbers, and near-drownings. This report was perhaps the earliest recognition of these experiences as a clinical syndrome. In 1968, Celia Green analyzed four hundred accounts of out-of-body experiences and attempted to provide a taxonomy of the incidents. In Elizabeth Kübler-Ross's *On Death and Dying* and other subsequent works, she also reported near-death experiences.

However, the work that brought near-death experiences into popular culture is *Life After Life* by Raymond A. Moody Jr. (Moody, 1975). Moody was an academic philosopher who retrained as a medical practitioner. Since then, there have been many books ranging from behavioral and clinical studies to those applying lenses of religious studies, sociology, psychiatry, parapsychology, and more to the phenomena. Moody in *Life After Life* identified a series of common elements in the stories he heard from the fifty cases of people (filtered down from about one hundred and fifty) who were unconscious and near death, and who then resuscitated. The elements included the following:

Ineffability. People generally struggle with fully describing their experiences. Our brains are excellent at trying to bring sense and meaning out of complex sets of experiences. Still, they do it partly by trying to relate it to what we have experienced and how we have understood it in the past (see, for example, dreams, visions, and constructed memories).

Hearing the News. Some report hearing their doctors or people in the room pronounce them dead. As we have mentioned earlier, hearing is one of the last things to go, and there is EEG evidence that sound is getting in even when the brain is otherwise shut down. This ability to hear is one piece of evidence that those signals may be getting interpreted by the mind in an otherwise quiescent state.

Feelings of Quiet. Many report extremely pleasant feelings and experiences. Words like peace, comfort, and quietness are common.

The Noise. Some hear sounds ranging from buzzing noises[129] to bells or even music. Again, if we are getting samples of external sound, it seems possible that the brain might be constructing something more recognizable out of it as a kind of audio illusion.

The Dark Tunnel. The experience often cited as part of an NDE is some kind of tunnel. Moody says he has heard it described as "a cave, a well, a trough, an enclosure, a tunnel, a funnel, a vacuum, a void, a sewer, a valley, and a cylinder." He feels all of these are attempts to describe the same kind of experience.

Out of the Body. Perhaps the most controversial and puzzling aspect of some near-death experiences is the out-of-body experiences. As we reviewed various religious and philosophical models of the soul, some are more spiritual, disembodied views of the soul. Others view the soul as pure rationality. Dualistic views can frame the soul as a conscious, sensing, reasoning, and possibly willful thing that can exist without the body. The out-of-body stories seem to align with this last view of the soul.

Lichfield described one experience about a migrant worker named Maria, who had an NDE here in Seattle in 1977. She found herself floating outside the hospital during her cardiac arrest and saw a tennis shoe on a third-floor window ledge. The social worker went to the window, found the shoe, and believed that Maria could not have seen it from her room based on its position.

In another story, Lichfield described Pam Reynolds's case, a singer-songwriter who suffered a ruptured aneurysm in her brain. The surgeon chilled her body to sixty degrees, stopped her heart, and drained the blood from her head. To ensure the brain was completely inactive, the medical team played rapid clicks at one hundred decibels (equivalent to a jackhammer's sound) in her ears. If her brain were working, they would see evidence in the electroencephalogram, and they didn't. Despite all this, she reported an NDE when she was revived, including an out-of-body experience. She accurately recalled various things going on in the operating room, including snatches of conversation, the shape of tools, and the staff listening to the song "Hotel California."[130]

Meeting Others. Some meet spiritual beings who are there to help them along in their journey, or in a trope that has become common in movies, beings who tell them that their time has not yet come. Sometimes the being is someone that the person knows.

The Being of Light. In addition to the tunnel, the other classic element is people have the experience of encountering a very bright light. This encounter often causes the most profound effect upon the individual. The light might begin as dim and get brighter and brighter until it reaches an "unearthly brilliance." People often experience it not as an abstract light, but instead experience it as a being of light. It has a personality and emanates love and warmth, and the person feels surrounded and embraced by it. This is an experience that may be identified differently depending on the religious background of the person who is dying. Christians might recognize it as Christ, while someone who is Jewish might identify it as an "angel." An agnostic might experience it as a "being of light." This being may communicate to the person, but not in a language. Communication is more like exchanging thoughts.

The Review. There has long been a story that people have reported during crisis moments where they review their past life experiences. Here too, the being of light may present a panoramic view of the person's life to them so they can reflect on it. Some see it in order, but some experience it in essence simultaneously. It feels vivid and real. Some report just experiencing it, some report reflecting on things that could be different, and some feel they are guided through it to reflect and learn.

The Border or Limit. For some, there is some kind of gateway. It might be a body of water, a gray mist, a door, a fence in a field, a line, or something else that is the point of no return. Moody speculates that there may be a standard, ultimate experience of the physical end here that is being interpreted or experienced in different ways that are somehow meaningful to each individual.

Coming Back. Often, when people go deeper into this experience, they are reluctant to return. Presumably, if they don't return, we wouldn't have an NDE.

This experience is typically very profound. People feel it as intensely real and extremely important. Moody argues that people do not describe what happened in the way they describe dreams on waking, but rather as memories of real things that have happened to them. Many know that society will look at them skeptically, and so they are not inclined to talk about the experiences with others. That being said, people feel it gave them new insights into themselves. They typically become more reflective. They ask more questions about how they should live. Most stress the importance of cultivating a love of others, and many have a new commitment to seek knowledge.

Moody notes that while there are common elements among all the accounts, no two of them are exactly alike. Reporting all of the experiences was rare, but "very many" shared most of them. The order in which people experience the stages can vary from person to person. People who were further into the death process seem to report "more florid, complete experiences than those who only came close to death; and those who were 'dead' for a longer period go deeper than those who were 'dead' for a shorter time." Finally, the experiences are not universal, in the sense that there are people who have been brought back from near-death and did not experience anything that they remember and can recount.

These NDEs can have culturally specific elements and can be interpreted and enriched through cultural lenses as they are shared. Still, they do not fall neatly into any specific religious framework. Whether they represent an ultimate truth or an illusion created by our bodies at the end, by and large, they do give some comfort for most about what that last part of the journey from this life will be like. They seem potentially among the most interesting phenomena at the end of life that we can study. At the very least, given their ubiquity, understanding the phenomena might be expected to help yield therapeutic support for those of us heading towards the door of whatever is next and seeking to reach acceptance in the grief process.

Litchfield concludes his *Atlantic* article by quoting Susan Blackmore, a British psychologist who had her own out-of-body experience as a young woman but who is now a scientific skeptic for more spiritualist explanations of NDEs. She rejects the stark distinction between "the false and unhelpful black and white comparison between NDEs as 'true, wonderful, spiritual, etc.' [versus] NDEs as 'JUST a hallucination of no importance.' The truth, it seems to me, is that NDEs can be wonderful, life-changing experiences that shed light on the human condition and on questions of life and death."

There are various hypotheses about the brain's state at the end of life, especially around what may be experienced by the person. Some begin by arguing that despite clinical evidence of death, people are not dead. They could point, for example, back to the challenge of accurately and specifically identifying when death happens. Some suggest that the lack of oxygen (hypoxia) during the process of death might cause neurons associated with a vision to fire abnormally and generate the illusion of bright light. Hypoxia can also lead to disorientation, confusion, and hallucinations. Some suggest a problem with the temporoparietal junction, where various areas of the brain meet. This is the part of the brain associated with integrating the data from all our senses and organs into an overall perception of the body. Others counter that some had the experience before their oxygen levels changed, and many others who had abnormal oxygen levels did not have the experience. Some argue that the oxygen levels cause an acute confusional state, but critics point out that the accounts are not confused; they are lucid and profound. There are those that suggest there is too much carbon dioxide (hypercardia), which can give people a feeling of separation from their body or being in a tunnel (although the evidence for this is thin).

One study suggests "NDEs are really an instance of a sleep disorder, rapid eye movement (REM) intrusion. In that disorder, a person's mind can wake up before his body, and both hallucinations and the sensation of being physically detached from the body can occur. Cardiac arrest could trigger a REM intrusion in the brain stem—the region that controls the most basic functions of the body and which can operate independently from the (now dead) higher brain. The resulting NDE would actually be a dream" (Bethune, 2013).

There has been relatively little research on the brain chemistry and activity of humans at this point. Speculation ranges from hallucinations like those mentioned due to lack of oxygen, undetected brain activity (which could be chemical and not electrical), the release of endorphins, to stress reactions. Alexander Wutzler's team at the Charité University of Medicine in Berlin, Germany, found that when rats were given an overdose of an anesthetic, they did have serotonin levels three times the normal levels. They speculate that something similar might happen in humans. A team in the Psychedelic Research Group at Imperial College London argues that there are similarities between hallucinogenics (in their case, dimethyltryptamine or DMT) and NDEs. They found "Results revealed significant increases in phenomenological features associated with the NDE, following DMT administration compared to placebo."[131]

Robert Martone (Martone, 2019) notes that many cultures over human history have employed drugs as part of religious rituals to create transcendent feelings, possibly similar to NDEs. One recent study compared the stories of six hundred and twenty-five people reporting NDEs with the stories of fifteen thousand individuals who had taken one hundred and sixty-five psychoactive drugs.[132] They then analyzed the language used across the groups and found similarities, especially with ketamine.

The challenge—similar to explaining consciousness by studying its parts—is that NDEs do not seem to have the characteristics the explanations predict. NDEs are serene. They are structured, well-integrated experiences. They are vivid and intense. People report becoming even more alert than usual. They often claim a clear, intense form of experience.

Steven Taylor (Taylor, 2018) says that the DMT study from the Center for Psychedelic Research at Imperial College London used a near-death experience scale to assess the experience and found many similarities. There was a sense of being in an unearthly environment. People felt inner peace, altered time, feelings of joy, and heightened senses. There often was a bright light and a sense of unity or harmony in everything. On the other hand, they did not find people on DMT feeling like they were reaching some kind of door to another world, encountering loved ones who had passed away, or even having a sense of reviewing their past life experiences.

The Five Stages of Grief

Part of what we have learned about death is it is less than an event than a process, and the process can tell us something about how we might think about it and ourselves. The seminal book on how we experience approaching death was written by Elisabeth Kübler-Ross in 1969 and is called *On Death and Dying: What the Dying Have to Teach Doctors, Nurses, Clergy & Their Own Families* (Kübler-Ross, 1969). Based on seismic shifts in how we think about the diagnosis of life and death and cultural changes that were happening at the time,[133] Kübler-Ross' book entered the popular consciousness at the right moment. Kübler-Ross was a Swiss-American psychiatrist, was inducted in 2007 into the National Women's Hall of Fame, and was named by *Time Magazine* as one of the one hundred most important thinkers of the twentieth century.

When she was a junior faculty member at the University of Colorado School of Medicine in the early 1960s, she gave her first interview of a young terminally ill woman in front of a group of medical students. The focus was not on pathology but on how the patient handled the experience itself. Kübler-Ross told her students, "Now you are reacting like human beings instead of scientists. Maybe now you'll not only know how a dying patient feels but you will also be able to treat them with compassion – the same compassion that you would want for yourself."

She completed her psychiatric training in 1963 and moved to Chicago in 1965, where she began her practice and became an instructor at the University of Chicago's Pritzker School of Medicine. That is when she started the series of weekly educational seminars that consisted of live interviews with terminally ill patients that led to her model of the five stages of grief. She based her model on over two hundred interviews, but it is worth noting that this was more of a qualitative study designed to understand patterns in how the dying were experiencing and dealing with their deaths. The work was not intended to be quantitative, empirical research. It was conducted in the context of American culture, and cross-cultural validation of the ideas is still relatively rare.

The five stages of grief model is still widely taught and studied. The model has been so compelling that it has been pushed beyond the focus on the experience of the dying to family members dealing with grief, and to other trauma that can be expressed as grief. Critics argue about the number, nature, and order of the stages. Despite that, the model still is a robust short-hand that captures much of the universal

Rosemary, a beloved pet, at the end

grief people have in the face of terminal or severe illness, the loss of a close relationship, disruption in routine, or the death of a loved one.[134]

While the model is presented as five stages, which implies a serial, ordered process, the stages do not occur in any specific order, and one may move back and forth between stages. There also is no particular amount of time that one spends in a given stage. For some, they may even fixate within a stage. For others, the progress of their illness may not allow them to reach the final stage. Furthermore, those of us who have lived long enough can see that it is one thing to have a model that describes the typical stages that many people experience; and it is quite another to predict how an individual will experience grief.

The first stage is *denial and isolation.* "This isn't happening! This cannot be happening!" Recently, we have heard this a lot from people who are suffering the worst of the pandemic.

Those of us who have either experienced cancer or know of people who have, know this is an expected reaction. For most, our natural state is not to think about disaster falling on us. Part of what makes it a disaster is that while we might believe it could always happen to someone else, we tend to place these thoughts in a little protected box inside ourselves. Living with the constant feeling that something terrible might happen to us at any moment probably would border on pathology. It would be hard to live that way.

The second stage is *anger*. Anger is a way to redirect and perhaps to gain some kind of control in our life. It probably is tied to fight or flight instincts. It may be aimed at objects, strangers, or loved ones. Feeling guilt over our anger at those who do not deserve it can create more anger. I am struck by this stage's similarity to research that suggests emotions may be in part our mind's interpretation of sets of behaviors and physical responses. The emotion our mind says we are experiencing can then drive new self-reinforcing actions and responses.

The third stage is *bargaining*. Often it looks like "If only we had" or "If only I had." Growing up, I often heard stories of soldiers facing death on the battlefield praying, "If you let me live through this God, I will change my life." Or, "If only I can live through this, I'll stop smoking and will start exercising." It was a stage of searching for an opportunity to get some control over the situation. Prayer to a higher being is a common technique at this stage.

When the end seems inevitable despite everything tried, the result can be the fourth stage, *depression*. Sadness and regret are common experiences. Unfortunately, the other stages may have resulted in pushing the very people away who might have been able to help work through the feelings. Depression is a set of feelings that occur to most of us at various points when we feel most at the mercy of either forces outside of our control or are experiencing the consequences of actions we regret.

If we are fortunate, the final stage is *acceptance*. Acceptance is not a state of happiness, and for those who are dying, it may be associated with some sense of withdrawal. It is perhaps more about coming to terms with the inevitable and being at peace with it. The withdrawal may be more about centering and preparing for moving beyond this world, where the most important things are coming but are not yet here.[135]

A few additional observations are worth noting from Seamus Coyle (Coyle, 2020), an honorary clinical research fellow at the University of Liverpool. He works in the area of palliative care. He highlights a TED talk by Jill Bolte-Taylor (a neuroanatomist), who talked about experiencing euphoria and a sense of nirvana when her left-brain hemisphere shut down following a stroke. The left hemisphere is the center of logic and rational thought. She also noted that an injury to the right side of the brain can increase feelings of being close to a higher power.

Coyle reminds us that the process of death is sacred to Buddhists. The transition from living to dying when you carry Karma from this life to the next provides great potential for the mind. But Coyle notes that in his research, he does see a variety of experiences. People who have suffered physically up to that point may continue to suffer to the end. They might not benefit from a rush of endorphins or serotonin, or natural psychedelic chemicals. He has seen people with young families who struggled emotionally to the end. That would fit the situation of not reaching that last stage of acceptance in Kübler-Ross' model. He does note that those who appear to have reached that final stage seem to be more likely to have an ecstatic experience toward the end, and early palliative care and effective hospice can lead to a happier end. His final observation is, "It is possible that we experience our most profound moment in the murky hinterland between life and death. But that does not mean we should stop 'raging against the dying of the light.'[136] As the Swedish diplomat, Dag Hammarskjöld put it: 'Do not seek death. Death will find you. But seek the road which makes death a fulfillment.'"

While we do not have specific historical data about how grief in the past was experienced, it would probably be a surprise if it was significantly different. The feelings seem to be tied closely to fundamental emotional experiences and how the human mind manages stress. Given this process of dealing with grief, it is also easy to imagine how various religious beliefs and practices about death and the afterlife could evolve to help rationalize the process and give us tools to deal with it and move forward. Whether or not the spiritual sense in our DNA or cultural rituals and interpretations are the mechanisms, the needs through this process would be expected to benefit from community (relational) belief systems and practices. Critique of Kübler-Ross is often from the perspective of the culturally specific ways of dealing with the five stages or perhaps their relative importance. Still, the description of the qualitative types of experience tends to be an effective way of thinking.

The *very* last step, of course, is the final process of death itself. According to Michigan Medicine (Physical and Emotional Changes as Death Approaches, n.d.), patients may feel less interested in the outside world and daily life details as they near the end. The person who is dying may only want a few select people around. They may be focused on introspection, letting things go, and in essence, saying goodbye to everything they have known. Eventually, they enter a period called by some in the field as "actively dying." Unfortunately, my family has witnessed this process several times in the last few years.

That period may move very quickly or take a few days. As the end nears, to some, they may seem confused as they talk about going somewhere or going home; and they may experience hallucinations of dead family members and loved ones. [137]Consciousness may come and go more frequently. The appetite will typically decrease as the person weakens and their metabolism slows down.

Hearing is one of the last senses to go when someone is dying. A paper recently published in *Scientific Reports* from the University of British Columbia provides additional light on this stage (University of British Columbia, 2020). This work is the first study to look at hearing for those who are near death. Using electroencephalography (EEG), the researchers analyzed electrical activity in the brain from hospice patients when they were conscious, some when they were unconscious and unresponsive, and a control group of healthy participants. What they found was "[A] dying brain can respond to sound, even in an unconscious state, up to the last hours of life." One aspect of this that is particularly encouraging for us who are fortunate to be with a loved one at the end, according to Dr. Romayne Gallagher (a palliative care physician at St. John Hospice), is "This research gives credence to the fact that hospice nurses and physicians noticed that the sounds of loved ones helped comfort people when they were dying....and to me, it adds significant meaning to the last days and hours of life and shows that being present, in person or by phone, is meaningful. It is a comfort to be able to say goodbye and express love."

Outwardly, there may be a period of rapid breathing and periods of no breathing (perhaps even over a minute). Breathing may become moist and congested, often called the "death rattle." The part of the brain responsible for regulating body temperature begins to fail, and the person may run a high temperature at one point and then feel very cold at another. The body can appear pale and blotchy. Periods of wakefulness will tend to be shorter, and the person will be less responsive.

There can be an experience that is often referred to as the last breath. It may be several outward pants as the heart and lungs stop. Other people may give a long out-breath, sometimes followed a little later with a short intake of breath. This pattern might occur a few times before the last breath. The skin tone of the face may loosen. The person may look at peace or even happy. Some observers have a sense that no one is *home* in the body any longer. Caregivers and relatives may see something like a vapor leaving the body or hovering near the body (Being With Someone When They Die, n.d.). This observation of vapor was my sisters' experience with my grandmother when she died, which I shared in the Introduction. Dr. MacDougall may have heard stories about others making these observations, and that could have provided some of the motivation for his work. Others have described a change in room temperature, a sense of heaviness in the air, or animals behaving strangely.[138]

THE NEUROSCIENCE OF SELF AND CONSCIOUSNESS

"Consciousness is a relatively late and highly developed manifestation of the principle which the Greeks call 'soul.' That principle shows itself not merely in consciousness but in the whole process of nutrition and growth and the adaptation of motor response to an external stimulation. Thus consciousness is a more secondary feature of the 'soul' in Greek philosophy than in most modern thought, which has never ceased to be affected by Descartes' selection of 'thought' as the special characteristic of psychical life. In common language the word psyche is constantly used where we should say 'life' rather than 'soul,' and in Greek philosophy a work 'on the Psyche' means what we should call one on 'the principle of life.'"
– Alfred Edward Taylor (Taylor, 1955)[139]

The Greek term translated as soul is psyche, and it comes from the verb meaning "to breathe." That made it natural to map back to the words used in the Hebrew scriptures that appeared as soul in various translations. For philosophers, psyche came to stand, not for breath, but for that which generates and constitutes a being's essential life, and later as including consciousness or awareness. So let's explore what

R. Fudd (1600s)
Location Consciousness

we know about our consciousness and other attributes that we associate with our soul, and what neuroscience tells us about how they appear in our brains (whether arising out of our physical nature, or perhaps in an ongoing dance with it).

For most of us, our sense of our souls is heavily influenced by our experience of being conscious, and in particular, of being conscious of ourselves in the world. Reflections on our own consciousness may be at the root of the dualistic perspectives in early childhood. We experience selfness and its continuity over time, and it is easy to imagine and desire that our conscious selves will continue after death and that the consciousness of friends and family will continue as well. Near-death experiences, experiences of the dying, and the experiences of families whose loved ones have died may get viewed through the filter of how we experience our own selves as souls and our inferences about the souls of others (e.g., in what I suggested might be a theory of soul).

In a recent, fascinating article in *Nature* called "Decoding Consciousness" (Sohn, 2019), Emily Sohn notes how important understanding consciousness is. As our understanding grows, researchers are working on treatments for brain injuries, phobias, PTSD, and other mental health conditions plaguing many of us. Neuroscientists discovering signs of consciousness in people in comas was transformative. Research has shown those at the edge of struggling to respond to external stimuli might understand what is going on around them, what is being said, and might even be able to communicate in some fashion. Even Francis Crick, the Nobel laureate involved in deciphering the structure of DNA, originally wanted to explore consciousness.[140]

Still, Sohn notes that Anil Seth, a cognitive and computational neuroscientist, said, "It's still just fundamentally mysterious how consciousness happens." As recently as the 1970s and 80s, as cognitive science was emerging, consciousness was being questioned as a topic appropriate for scientific investigation. Sohn writes:

> *"'Consciousness is often described as the mind's subjective experience. Whereas a basic robot can unconsciously detect conditions such as colour, temperature or sound, consciousness describes the qualitative feeling that is associated with these perceptions, together with the deeper processes of reflection, communication and thoughts', says Matthias Michel, a philosopher of science and a PhD student at Sorbonne University in Paris."*

An interesting study in 2005 focused on a twenty-three-year-old woman who had been in a car accident and suffered a severe brain injury. She was in a state of wakeful awareness but was otherwise non-responsive. Adrian Own (a neuroscientist at the University of Cambridge, UK) and colleagues used an fMRI to observe her brain activity while giving her a series of verbal commands. When they asked her to imagine playing tennis, they could see activity in her brain's supplementary motor area. Next, they asked her to imagine walking around her home, and they could see activity in movement and memory areas. This activity was similar to what they observed in healthy controls as well. Since then, consciousness has been found in as many as ten to twenty percent of non-responsive coma patients. Work continues on tools that will better measure the conscious brain and characterize the complex activity across the cerebral cortex's surface.

The cerebral cortex has long been identified with consciousness. While we do not have the largest cerebral cortex by volume of animals (e.g., elephants have far more cerebral cortex), it is the largest relative to the overall brain volume. Chimpanzees, short-finned whales, corvids like ravens and crows, and even horses are not far behind, however. The posterior-cortical area of the human cortex is a *hot zone* responsible for our sensory data experience. People whose brains are monitored with EEGs while they are dreaming just before waking up, show more high-frequency activity in this area. Some researchers believe it may eventually be possible to identify our dreams' contents from the signals generated. Konolky et al. (2021)[141] recently reported successful work demonstrating two-way communication with people in a dream state.[142] That being said, as we continue to understand consciousness and the brain activity associated with it, it is clear that it is not just confined to one area of the brain.

One of the areas of interest for consciousness researchers is psychiatric disorders. These disorders include conditions such as schizophrenia, obsessive-compulsive disorder, and depression. The idea is that they may result from problems at the unconscious level or conflicts between conscious and unconscious brain activity. One set of researchers is studying hallucinations. They apply machine learning to identify brain activity patterns and then use a virtual reality environment to simulate hallucinations in healthy brains. This line of work may eventually help us understand visions only experienced by one person and not others present during the final stages of the process of dying, near-death experiences, and possibly among loved ones after someone dies.

While cognitive neuroscience is in its infancy, it is evolving rapidly to understand the relationship between the brain's structures and our experiences. An editorial in *Nature Neuroscience* (In Search of Self, 2002) did recognize there still is much to learn. "As philosopher Daniel Dennett memorably put it, a brain transplant is the only operation for which it's better to be the donor." The editorial points out that while our intuitions about how our brains work raise many questions, it is undeniable that it will pose challenges to our sense of who we are as understanding grows. According to the editorial, while there is no single brain structure that can be identified as the location of an experience of the *self,* there are related areas worth exploring. Key areas include the neural basis of perception, the sense of free will and decision making, autobiographical memory and reasoning, the source and activity of ethical decision making, and the experience of self-awareness. The background question I have, given my interest, is to wonder how that brain-soul connection might work, and how edge cases in some of these areas might impact the nature of a soul and its afterlife.

The editorial concludes with observations such as "It is understandable that people are drawn to a simple account in which the appearance of a new individual corresponds to the sharply defined event of fertilization. The alternative is to accept that the self is not an indivisible all-or-nothing entity, but that it instead emerges gradually, and that its origin must be explained in terms of the complexities of developmental neuroscience and psychology."

But let us dive in a little and explore the full range of attributes that have been associated at one point or another with the soul. Dr. Joel Yuhudah Rutman, a pediatric neurologist, has written an interesting article called "In Search of the Soul: Between Torah and Science" that digs into the evolving Jewish concepts of the soul in light of contemporary neuroscience. As we have discussed, Rutman says that the earliest Hebrew words in the Tanakh (nefesh, neshama, and ruach) are often translated as soul, and they are all words that at their roots relate to the process of breathing. One implication is that a characteristic of the soul might be that it provides a kind of spark of life for humans and animals, and that at the end of the death process the spark leaves. This spark of life cannot stand alone, however. It has to work through the body. We know that the mechanism of breath is typically a function of the medulla-oblongata sensing acid-base changes in the blood and causing the diaphragm to move, or its function needs to be duplicated in some artificial fashion.

Aristotle also conceived of the soul as including something like this spark, this "activating principle" of life. For him, this activating principle is possessed by plants, animals, and us. The activating principle makes living things different from the dust from which they were formed. Today, life is more likely to be defined in terms of biological system properties than in terms of some kind of vital force. Both living and non-living things can be formed from the same chemicals, although certainly on Earth, many of the more complex organic molecules (e.g., DNA) are unique to living things. In contemporary neuroscience, the idea of a vital force (perhaps enlivened by a divine breath) is not necessary to explain life in general or human life in particular. According to Rutman (Rutman, 2016), the assumptions that seem to be working well for neuroscientists are based on biochemical processes and a mechanistic model of the body. As creators ourselves, we are using this same approach to re-engineer living things, and we are opening the door to new forms of life.

Some words translated as soul in other contexts contain aspects of what we may think of as mind, such as desire and emotion, and its receptive, retentive, and creative properties. But in the Tanakh, and for much of human history, it is the heart that is assumed to be the location of the mind. Rutman does observe that a phrase like "with all your heart and with all your soul" implies a distinction between the heart and soul. But our ancestors did not have the same understanding of how the systems in the body work that we now have.[143] Even today, we use *heart* language that, while poetically useful, biologically is not technically accurate. Rutman illustrates how ideas have changed by quoting Henry Moore, a sixteenth-century English philosopher, as saying, "this laxe pithe (sic) or marrow in man's head shows no more capacity for thought than a Cake of Suet or a Bowl of Curds." He could have pointed to the ancient Egyptians throwing away the brains of people who had died. We now know the mind's functions like rational thought, feeling, planning, calculating, desiring, and so on occur in and are unified by the brain.

Some of today's thinking began with the English physician Thomas Willis (1621 to 1675), the founder of neurology. He compared his patients' behaviors and symptoms during life with the damaged areas he found in their brains after they died.

Santiago Ramón y Cajal in Madrid perfected the technique of staining cells and was able to show the network of what later was called neurons that make up the brain. Neurons generate and transmit the electrochemical signals 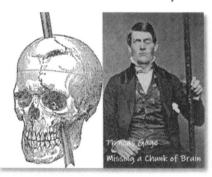 that support our cognition. Combinations of these form areas in our brains that support functions like vision, language, and memory. Together these shape mind, and out of mind arises consciousness. We have also learned from surgical interventions and accidents like the one suffered by Phineas Gage, more about how they interact. Gage, for example, lost much of the left frontal lobe of his brain and lived. But some saw his personality so changed, they wondered if he was the same man.

Of course, part of consciousness is being conscious of

ourselves, and the experience of our minds. Rutman says the mind itself, often identified with the soul, is being demystified by neuroscience. Mind is what the brain does as it functions, and so it is less helpful in explaining the soul, just as the concept of the soul is currently doing little to enlighten our scientific understanding of the mind. We have traced how philosophers and psychologists over the last two hundred years have come to these conclusions elsewhere.

Psalms 103:1 (JPS) reads, "Bless the LORD, O my soul: and all that is within me, bless his holy name." Rudman explains that the first and second parts of this are parallel, so LORD is parallel with His holy name, and "my soul" is parallel with "all that is within me." So "my soul" and "all that is within me" are trying to communicate the notion of "myself" or "my being." Often this sense of "self" was in the past explained by the concept of the soul, and for most people, we would probably say it is the sense of "self" that we would hope to persist after death, and so it must in some way be part of the soul.

It is true that neuroscience now points to the medial prefrontal cortex (MPFC), which lies along the midline of the frontal lobes, as a critical brain structure responsible for processing the data that gives us our sense of self. Evolutionarily, it is assumed that the relatively larger frontal cortex has enabled us to think in the abstract and in symbolic ways about ourselves (see, for example, the discussion of the emergence of art, stories, and rituals among early hominids). The MPFC enables us to connect past experiences into a continuum of self-relevance, our own ongoing stories, if you will. Rutman says this collected information is our self-concept and is stored in long-term memory. That is where the sense of *me* or possibly *I* resides in the brain for neuroscientists. So perhaps *the self that I experience* (which may be more dependent on the functioning of my mind) relative to *my actual self* (that which persists into an afterlife), is analogous to how *my experience of the world* is only *a constructed representation of the real world* that is "out there." What we experience are shadows or models of that which is real.

In ancient Egyptian and some Jewish thought, there is the idea that the soul leaves the body during sleep. There is a

Jewish blessing for the morning after awakening that includes the phrase "who restores souls to lifeless bodies." But, of course, we know that the autonomic nervous system keeps our heart, blood pressure, respiration, digestion, and other processes going while we are asleep. What changes during sleep are our consciousness, the awareness of our surroundings, and some of the interaction between what is going on in our brains and the connection to our bodies.

As we think about ourselves, there are different lenses that we may use. Within cognitive science, one set of studies focuses on *me*, where the *me* is an *object* of my internal and external experiences. Another lens is the dimension of me as a stand-alone self versus me *in relation* to my community and the world in which I live. Then there is the *I* who is doing the reflecting, and this might be an experience that arises out of everything else going on as it is integrated in consciousness. It might be how my body represents a reality that includes my soul.

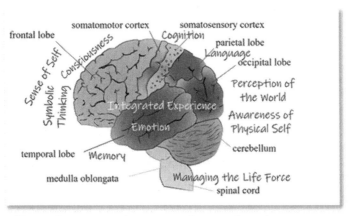

Part of our consciousness of our selves is our sense of embodiment, how we *fit* within our bodies. This touches on the long debate in philosophy about the mind-body connection, and possibly the soul-body connection. The study of embodiment is about examining how the sensory input our body receives (which, of course, differs between individuals and definitely across species) is interpreted and experienced. It includes how our bodies are positioned within and interact with the world, by constructing models of the world.

Just to toss out a little brain anatomy that you can use in Scrabble or parties (esp. if you want to end a conversation), the temporoparietal junction within the cortex is one of the brain regions that helps us integrate sensory information into a holistic experience. The extrastriate body area in the lateral occipitotemporal cortex is involved in thoughts about and exposure to our body parts as we perceive them. The left dorsolateral prefrontal cortex and the posterior cingulate cortex are involved in how we remember autobiographical (or what in my graduate thesis we called episodic) information. Episodic information includes when it happened, where it happened, and connections to how and why it happened. This information is part of what is integrated into our sense and perception of ourselves.

One attribute typically associated with the soul is the sense of morality and how it results in action in the world. Paul in Romans (the Christian New Testament) recognizes that some principles are baked into how the world is structured (see Romans 1:19,20). Many believe this sense comes to humans as part of that "being in the image of God." However, in both the Tanakh and in the Christian New Testament (as well as a wealth of research on how children develop a sense of morality), we also see how ethical principles are passed to us socially through culture. So we would expect there are areas of our brain devoted to our sense of right and wrong, and indeed there are. The anterior and medial prefrontal cortex and the superior temporal sulcus are activated by feelings of guilt, compassion, or embarrassment. The mesolimbic pathway is activated by guilt and passion, and the amygdala shows the effects of indignation and disgust.

Our ideas of ourselves can change with age. When adults perform tasks associated with retrieving self-knowledge information, their prefrontal cortex and the medial posterior parietal cortex tend to be activated. Adults tend to activate the medial prefrontal cortex's posterior precuneus in these tasks, while children tend to activate the anterior precuneus and the posterior cingulate. Children's brains are spending less time introspecting about themselves than adults. They have a decreased specificity in skills and show more activation during spatial tasks. They tend to be more concerned about their surroundings and the environment, as, of course, those who have had children frequently observe. Pfeifer, J. H., Lieberman, M. D., and Dapretto, M. (2007) wrote an article that describes this work. It has the wonderful title "'I know you are but what am I?!': Neural bases of self and social knowledge retrieval in children and adults."

This plasticity of our brains and how that would impact the way we experience the world and our sense of selves, does reinforce the idea that if the soul is influenced by the brain, the soul presumably may change and develop over time as well. Just as with physical development, intentional management of experiences might, in essence, be able to guide the development and maturity of the soul. Furthermore, the soul's maturity could impact how we experience whatever comes next after this life. This potential relationship shows up in religions such as Buddhism, and more monastic and ascetic practices in other religions.[144]

Much of what some of us think of as a mind that is identical with our souls is, in fact, at least largely associated with the functioning of our brains and sensory organs. Rutman is led as a neuroscientist to something that might be called a "soul of the gaps." The attributes that the average person might identify with our selves or our souls over human history turn out can mostly be reduced to capabilities associated with our bodies.

He then suggests that another way to look at the question is along a continuum that ranges from physiological to mental, but then it extends to the spiritual. The solely reductionist neuroscience argument works as science, and at this point, we can admittedly see areas of the brain associated with experiences like self and consciousness, will, and moral judgment. But it is not yet clear that the phenomena of how we experience ourselves are fully explained in the aggregate. Further, we could imagine that having a soul *lights up* some of these experiences in a distinctly human way that distinguishes us from other animals, and perhaps this is also part of being in the image of God. William James would argue that we need to allow for these possibilities until they can be eliminated.

Genesis (e.g., 1:27, 5:1, and 9:6) is read by Rutman as not just God's breath giving life to a lump of clay, but giving it properties of his image and giving it *something* that defines it as human and unique in the Creation. He sees this idea as positioning us in the universe as being exceptional in reflecting

God's image. This perspective of being in God's image is our dignity and gives our lives meaning. He quotes a morning prayer that includes, "My God, the soul You placed within me is pure." Rutman believes this soul that lives on beyond our bodies "will never be replaced by neuroscience." It seems to me that what this does suggest is that while one vision of the afterlife could be more of a spir-

itual communion with God (similar to Platonic, Hindu, or Buddhist ideas), the afterlife that many of us envision requires some form of a body to house us as souls if we are going to act and continue to mature in the afterlife. Jewish tradition, especially, seems to position this right with the idea of a unity of soul and a body, a combination that is tightly bound together, as being important in fulfilling our purpose.

Rutman acknowledges that some argue against this idea of a spiritual soul by saying it is just an illusion generated by our brains. He says perhaps, in the end, they might be correct. He also recognizes the evolutionary argument that this *feeling* of being in the image of God, this element of divinity, may have helped us survive. But Rutman argues that neither of these, even if true, negates the possible underlying truth of our fundamental nature. He says, "We can dismiss the idea of an ethereal or divine soul as resulting from an evolved way of thinking in human beings that has no basis in the way things really are. Or, we can integrate a concept that feels meaningful to us into the fabric of our lives, to give us hope and dignity, despite the fact that we will never know whether or not such a soul exists. I choose the latter."

TITLE Miscellaneous Notes from the Science

o Attributes of Our Souls Have Evolved Over Time
o Components of Our Unique Souls are Grounded in Our Bodies
o Our Sense of Our Souls as Our Selves Seem to Transcend Its Components (so far)
o The Experienced Soul/Self May be to the Actual Soul what Experienced Reality is to the Real World
o Our Stories and Sense of the Afterlife Help Manage Individual and Social Grief, and Provide a Path Forward
o Concepts of the Soul and the Afterlife Appear to Support Cultural Evolution
o However Experiences of Spirits are Triggered, They May Emerge from Within and Provide Personal and Social Value

---

[123] Some recent research suggests that music is another one of these things that is a combination of evolving capabilities in the human, but also of invention and our ability to associate it with meaning and emotional experience.

[124] There is a downside with a lack of diversity as it reduces innovation within a society and a culture. The mix of beliefs about the soul and the afterlife within our society would be expected to evolve and better serve our needs over time as the diversity becomes richer.

[125] Transplantation presumably does not transfer "pieces" of soul, although there continue to be stories of some connection between living donors and those receiving organs.

[126] I cannot help but be reminded of the "Bring out your dead!" scene from *Monty Python and the Holy Grail.*

[127] The typical crucifixion could take thirty-six hours if not hastened, and so Jesus' death on the cross as noted in the New Testament was faster than expected. It may in fact have been an example of exhibiting all the characteristics of death, but then was finalized by the thrust of the spear allowing the water and blood from a state of hypovolemic shock from the torture he went through to leak out.

[128] For example, the story of Jahi McMath was reported in the *New Yorker* (1968). While the law and her doctors considered her dead,

her family maintained her on a ventilator in a home care setting in New Jersey for five years until her body suffered liver failure.

[129] This reminds me of the rather annoying and mysterious tinnitus many of us experience, perhaps after too many rock concerts when we were young (I blame Edgar Winter).

[130] Since spending four years in the San Francisco Bay area, I am not sure the sound of "Hotel California" will ever be out of my head.

[131] Meinch (2021) described a variety of studies that are starting to use psychedelics therapeutically, and the experiences reported do sound strikingly similar to NDEs.

[132] I must say, this must have been quite a party.

[133] She was at the University of Chicago at roughly the same time I was there, and that was in the midst of the social turmoil and protests of the 60s.

[134] The loved one might even be a pet.

[135] While completing this book, my older cousin became unexpectedly ill and passed away. He went through all of these stages, in part with the hands-on support of my remaining brother-in-law (the other one died a few months ago). His reaching the acceptance stage gave us great peace.

[136] From Dylan Thomas' poem:
"And you, my father, there on the sad height,
Curse, bless, me now with your fierce tears, I pray.
Do not go gentle into that good night.
Rage, rage against the dying of the light."

[137] The word "hallucination" here is again being used to refer to that which one person sees but others do not. It could, theoretically, be something present that others do not see or detect. It could be something that the person's brain constructs based on physical need or condition, or it could be the result of some external (perhaps spiritual) trigger that is specific to the individual.

[138] I have to admit, however, that my three black cats often behave like they are seeing mysterious, unseen forces. Research definitely shows they can see things that I cannot.

[139] Cited in Goetz and Taliaferro (2011).

[140] Clearly this might have been a good thing from a historical perspective, given his contributions to our understanding of genetics.

[141] Konkoly, K. R., Appel, K., Chabani, E., Mangiaruga, A., Gott, J., Mallett, R., Caughran, B., Witkowski, S., Whitmore, N. W., Mazurek, C. Y., Berent, J. B., Weber, F. D., Turker, B., Leu-Semenescu, S.,

Maranci, J., Pipa, G., Arnulf, I., Oudiette, D., Martin Dresler, M., and Paller, K. A. (2021). "Real-time dialogue between experimenters and dreamers during REM sleep," *Current Biology*, 31, 1–11. Retrieved from: doi.org/10.1016/j.cub.2021.01.026.

[142] Remember that there have been those that have argued the soul (or a soul) is in a unique state during dreams. Some believe it may be communicating most directly with a spiritual realm. Freud and Jung, of course, also recognized the importance of dreams as it reveals what was going on within us. Contemporary sleep research is also uncovering new insights about the importance of dreaming for our mental health.

[143] As we have observed, the ancient Egyptians thought so little of the brain they removed it before embalming. It was the heart, kidneys, liver, and other organs that contained what mattered about emotions, mental, and spiritual functions, and that were preserved in canopic jars.

[144] This idea of the influence of the conscious experience of the brain on the maturity and shape of our souls suggests we could manage that process intentionally. A brain trainer using virtual reality and perhaps appropriate (legal) chemicals could at least in theory simulate the experiences of monks, ascetics, shamans, and others to intentionally grow us as souls more efficiently. Research reported in Meinch (2021) does provide some case studies of where an appropriate psychoactive drug treatment along with a managed physical experience can meaningfully change personality, along with emotional, and behavioral traits for years afterwards. One wonders whether or how the soul might be changing.

Chapter 7

FINAL THOUGHTS AND QUESTIONS

"For much of the early part of the 20th century mind and consciousness got somehow pushed out of science. For how could science explain learning? How could it explain the reconstructions and revisions of memory we make throughout our lives? How could it explain the processes of adaptation? Of improvisation and creativity? How could it explain consciousness? Its richness, its wholeness, its everchanging stream and its many disorders? How could it explain individuality or self?"
– Oliver Sacks

I have been fortunate to stagger through a few marathons and half-marathons in my life, and there is a point of euphoria and a little burst of energy when I am on the home stretch and see the finish line. That is where you are now. In this final chapter, my goal is to do three things. First, I want to wrap up a few of the arguments that help pull together the various threads we have been considering. Second, I want to share some of my learning based on this research, including several more significant questions still open for me. I suspect I will not have answers to these until I see what is on the other side myself. Third, I will reflect on a few of the emerging areas resulting from research in areas like healthcare and technology that I see as tests for whatever ideas of the soul and the afterlife that we hold. I do want to provide a fair warning that since this is where I will be sharing more of *my* conclusions, remaining questions, and speculations, there will be a little more explicit reflection given *my own* more progressive and certainly evolving Christian perspective. Furthermore, it will be through the lens of my interest in the future of science and technology, and its impact on society. I am assuming your lens will be equally as unique.

A CRITIQUE OF CRITIQUES

Throughout this exploration of the natural history of the soul, the contrast to the dualistic view of the soul and the body has generally been the physicalism arising from earlier materialism. In other words, it has been a debate between whether we assume a soul and a body, or whether the physical laws of the universe can explain everything. Goetz and Taliaferro (Goetz, 2011) critiqued a series of the materialistic arguments against the idea of the soul. They endorse the position that we are, as souls, more than the sum of all the bodily processes and states that can be associated with our bodies. Deconstructing us into our measurable parts, they argue, does not capture the holistic experience most of us have as we reflect on what defines us. I identify with this position.

Rembrandt's The Philosopher in Meditation

One argument against the idea of the soul is the "Ghost in the Machine Objection." Gilbert Ryle argued that the Cartesian view of a soul-body relationship is like having a ghost inside the body's machine. Ryle summarizes the division of the mind and the body by contrasting them. The body is located in space, is subject to mechanical laws, and is public. The mind is not in space, is not witnessable by other observers, and it is private. He argues that according to Descartes' Cartesianism, "The mind is its own place and in his inner life each of us lives the life of a ghostly

Robinson Crusoe. People can see, hear and jolt one another's bodies, but they are irremediably blind and deaf to the workings of one another's minds and inoperative upon them." Ryle argues that based on *his* reflections, each of us *is* a unified whole. We *do* see, hear, and touch each other.

He gives an example of what he believes the problem is, which is treating something as independent when it is not. In his example, he talks about someone visiting a university in Cambridge and seeing colleges, libraries, fields, and museums, and then complaining that he has not yet seen the University. Ryle argues that, of course, it is the sum of things that is the university. He argues the self is the sum of all the physical aspects of our bodies.

Goetz and Taliaferro respond that while there is a sense the example is true, it is also not true. As a professor, I know that my University is indeed more than the sum of all the buildings, grounds, and people that compose it. It exists as a unique entity in law, tradition, and the experiences and imaginations of faculty, students, and alumni. That entity can persist as its component buildings and organizational structure change. That entity, in turn, can influence the collective forces that impact that physical structure over time. Similarly, as we have reviewed in the research, our experience of ourselves, while tied to the nature of our bodies, also feels like it is more than just our bodies. When a part of my body is replaced or as I age, I do not feel I am a different person. On the other hand, there can be conditions when I feel I am a different person and yet have the same body.

While Ryle says we do not kiss a loved one's soul, Goetz and Taliaferro propose that the experience most of us have is that we do indeed kiss that person's soul in its embodiment. When that soul, in some sense, is *elsewhere* preoccupied, we can certainly sense it when one of us is being romantic, and the other is thinking about Facebook posts. We have discussed earlier a kind of theory of the soul that proposes, like the theory of mind, that there are reflections that we attribute to the operation of our souls in the world and that we use to infer the souls in others. This mutual recognition may be part of the evolutionary value ideas of the soul and the afterlife have for our species as we form cultural communities.

Another objection they describe is Ludwig Wittgenstein's "Private Language Argument." This one is not quite as intuitive or easy to understand. After all, it is Wittgenstein. As we have discussed, Descartes argued that we have direct and immediate access to our minds, our own mental, subjective states. Based on this, we can be confident in our existence and about our experiences. This is what most of us feel in ourselves. Wittgenstein argued that any language, to be a language, must be subject to correction to ensure it is not in error. Wittgenstein, ever the philosopher, argues that if we have privileged access to our internal states, we should, in principle, be able to create a private language, a language that only we know and perhaps that only we can know is accurate. He then argues that this is impossible. He argues that if the soul exists and has privileged access to its status, there may be mistakes in meaning (e.g., if I point to something that I experience as blue, but someone else experiences it as yellow). There would be no way of knowing the difference and correcting which one of us is in error.

Goetz and Taliaferro point out that as with much of Wittgenstein's work, while some hold the argument up as a critical thrust at the heart of a dualist view, it is not clear that the implications of Descartes' ideas are being correctly understood. They take issue with Wittgenstein's assumption that certainty in language *must* be possible. I would argue that complete certainty in language given our different experiences may at best be rare. In one management course I took, an example was given about a conversation between someone from the East Coast and someone from the West Coast. They talked about fishing for dogfish for hours, but they were talking about two different species of fish. They eventually did discover the difference, but that does not mean the continuing conversation did not carry any ambiguity. I've already shared stories about how culture influenced understanding during my wife's formative years in Brazil. We could also point to the unique perspectives of people with various sensory disabilities (e.g., color blindness) and their impact on communication.

Research that we have mentioned through this natural history has also repeatedly highlighted the constructive nature of experience. While the input we receive from others helps us align our internal model of the world to the external, there is always a difference in the full set of meanings behind what one person says, and the other set that helps the listener interpret what they hear. Furthermore, it strikes me that the proposition that someone might create a language that only they can know around an internal experience of their own mind is a straw argument. I do not know of evidence that anyone has attempted to try it as Wittgenstein describes it.[145] Perhaps it is possible, but the set of associations any one of us has in our brains around an experience on which we are reflecting is inherently unique to us no matter what our language.

Goetz and Taliaferro do share a quote from Wittgenstein that suggests even he acknowledges that some aspects of our mental life may not be reducible to the physical:

> *"No supposition seems to me more natural than that there is no process in the brain correlated with associating or with thinking; so that it would be impossible to read off thought-processes from brain processes. I mean this: if I talk or write there is, I assume, a system of impulses going out from my brain and correlated with my spoken or written thoughts. But why should the system continue further in the direction of the centre? Why should this order not proceed, so to speak, out of chaos? It is perfectly possible that certain psychological phenomena cannot be identified physiologically, because physiologically nothing corresponds to them. Why should there not be a psychological regularity to which no physiological regularity corresponds? If this upsets our concepts of causality, then it is high time they were upset. (Wittgenstein, quoted in Kenny 1998, 344)"*

There is a principle in science called *Ockham's razor*, the idea that you should not make things more complex than they need to be. A third objection to the soul then is the "Ockham's Razor and Identity" objection. This argument is based on the idea that the physicalist position grounded in the material world is sufficient and is simple. If the scientific method does not require the idea of the soul to explain what it means to be human, why adopt an idea of the soul? The history of science, the argument goes, is that we continue to make progress in identifying the properties of the body and our minds, and how they work. We should have faith in the project of understanding the nature of higher-order things like how consciousness and the experience of self arises from physical systems.

Goetz and Taliaferro begin by looking at what it means to be a person and whether the nature of our mental life can be reduced to an understanding of brain states like we reviewed when talking about neuroscience research. On the one hand, they cite Paul Churchland as a warning about the limits of relying on inner reflection as a data source. Churchland correctly observes (as we have elsewhere) that our perception is a constructed experience. When we look at an apple and it appears red, or feel the surface of the chair I am sitting on, we are not seeing the reflection of the photons of light or feeling the matrix of molecules that compose them. The argument is that our ability to introspect stops at the constructed reality and does not penetrate to the hidden details. This even might suggest our reflections on our experience of our selves, our souls, might be, in essence, a kind of shadow of our real souls existing in a more spiritual realm.

On the other hand, and serving to demonstrate the importance of that inner experience, one example they give is from my field. During the 60s and 70s, B. F. Skinner was actively advancing behaviorism. Skinner argued that you could completely define every aspect of our mental lives in terms of our bodily behavior. He was a master of reframing almost anything in terms of conditioning paradigms. Being in pain, for example, could be explained in terms of the behaviors of wincing and cursing, and the conditions causing them.

But Goetz and Taliaferro share a thought experiment from A. C. Ewing, which shows the practical limit of this kind of argument. Ewing advises you to heat a piece of iron red hot and then grab it with your hand.[146] Whatever you measure about behavior or the physical burning effects or activity in the brain, the actual internal experience will be more than any constituent things you can measure. Love also continues to be an experience that is more than just the hormones and other processes we have measured to date.

Goetz and Taliaferro recognize that Ockham's razor says not to make things more complicated than they need to be. They argue, however, that it is a mistake to confuse simplicity for adequacy. I know I am frequently reminded of Albert Einstein's qualification that "Everything should be made as simple as possible, but no simpler." They believe, and I agree with them, that if we have experiences of pleasure and pain, and if we have a sense of self and perhaps even the persistence of self, the experiences need to be adequately explained. They argue that there is a long history of arguments from Plato and Aristotle to Augustine and Descartes that have demonstrated the explanatory value of the soul if not for scientific theory, at least for understanding our social, moral, and spiritual natures. That helps us act in a way that provides survival value for our species. A long history of practical, human self-awareness has supported its value.

SPECULATIVE QUESTIONS AND THOUGHT EXERCISES

"Hic sunt dracones" (Here be dragons)

What does it mean to be human?

> *"The word 'human' refers to something more than the bodily form or even the rational mind. It refers also to that community of blood and experience which unites all men and women on the Earth."*
> – C. S. Lewis

"The nitrogen in our DNA, the calcium in our teeth, the iron in our blood, the carbon in our apple pies were made in the interiors of collapsing stars. We are made of starstuff."

— Carl Sagan

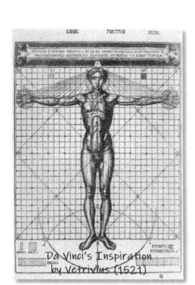

Da Vinci's Inspiration by Vetrivius (1521)

Our interest here, of course, is in the human soul and our afterlife. Still, we all may feel, being human, we know at least something about our souls and what makes us who we are. But what does it mean to be human itself? When pressed, we might start by pointing to our genetics. We have twenty-three pairs of chromosomes. But of course, so does a Chinese barking deer. Both chimpanzees and potatoes (naturally) have twenty-four pairs of chromosomes. It is also a fact that while that is the norm, roughly one in two hundred babies are born with a chromosomal abnormality (e.g., Down syndrome), and it is estimated that these abnormalities account for half of the many miscarriages that occur. About two percent of the population does not have the expected XX or XY combinations of chromosomes typically associated with being female and male. The incidence of XXX, XXY, X, and others is about the same as the incidence of red hair.

Our DNA serves as the set of instructions that determine the genetic influence on how our bodies grow. Our DNA provides the code for our cell's activities, while our RNA converts the code into the proteins that carry out cellular functions. But our DNA is actually on a continuum with other animals. For example, we share as much as ninety-nine percent of our DNA with chimps and bonobos and about eighty percent with cows.

Interestingly we share eighty-four percent of our DNA with dogs, and for us cat people, we share ninety percent of our DNA with cats. People with European ancestry may have as much as two percent of their DNA from Neanderthals, and people from Melanesia may have as much as six percent of their DNA from Denisovans.

This influence might, for example, prompt an interesting question. If we have souls, did the Neanderthals and the Denisovans? They indeed exhibit early behavior such as art and burial rituals similar to early humans. If they had the same soul as Homo sapiens, when did souls appear in our family tree? Did they appear selectively among various species, or did the human soul evolve as our bodies did? If you have a lot of Neanderthal and Denisovan DNA, is your soul any different from someone who does not?

Of course, it is also true that the body that feels so *us*, is not the same body from one moment to the next. Our cells are regularly being replaced with new cells. Some estimates are that our body replaces virtually all its cells every seven to ten years, with some parts being replaced more rapidly than others. Current research suggests we are not fully adult, especially from the perspective of brain maturity until we are twenty-five. Even in law, those under eighteen are treated as not being fully responsible for what they do. It is almost as if they are more potential humans than fully human, and I suspect my parents thought that about me when I was a teenager. On the other hand, the number of neurons in our brains is at its highest in our twenties and then starts to decline, so there is that.

Our optimal childbearing years are in our twenties and thirties, and as we near our forties, more systems are starting to feel the lives we have led. Our life experiences continually cause an accumulation of damage to the DNA. The telomeres are the regions of repetitive nucleotide sequences at the ends of our chromosomes. They get shorter each time our DNA divides, and as a result, they are a kind of internal clock that partially drives how long our actual three score and ten years of life turns out to be.[147] At each moment, as several of the philosophers we have discussed have observed, what I am experiencing as my body is mostly my memories knitted together to provide continuity. The fact is that we require bodies to exhibit the characteristics of mind and a sense of self often associated with souls. Still, our bodies continually change, and that says something about the relationship between our souls and our bodies. Heraclitus once said, "No man ever steps in the same river twice, for it's not the same river and he's not the same man." That would also be true about the idea of resurrection. Our souls probably cannot leave and then step back into the *same* body, because our souls presumably grow and our bodies continually change.

To make this even more interesting, only about forty-three percent or even more of our body's cells are human. The rest includes things like the microbiome. As we are learning, the microbiome not only influences our health and how we experience the world, but there is also evidence that the microbiome can influence what we do by producing neurotransmitters that affect our brain. Earlier, we talked about a particularly scary zombie controlled by someone else and stories of demon possession. In a sense, external factors are continually possessing us, at least in some small but often important ways.

As with diversity in the creation itself, human diversity is why we have been successful as a species. That diversity comes in many forms. In addition to the variations we have mentioned already, some of us are born with disabilities, and others of us are acquiring disabilities as we age. Some of us have genetic predispositions for specific diseases and conditions. Still, we are also finding that some potential genetic problems may have entered the human gene pool to help defend against other diseases and conditions ravaging various groups. And a "deficit" in one area may lead to growth in other areas. Fixing a "problem" may have unintended consequences over time. There is no *perfect* human body even in the afterlife that would still be human, at least as we would define it in this world.

We have also been increasingly able to replace various parts of our bodies with prosthetics such as artificial hearts, and human-to-human transplantation has been used since the

1950s. Xenotransplantation (animal to human transplantation) has become more successful since the 1960s. There have been claims that human embryos have been cloned, but at best, the attempts have not yet been particularly successful. Still, the necessary technologies are increasing rapidly. Edinburgh's Centre for Regenerative Medicine (where the sheep Dolly was cloned) has created brain tissue from patients suffering from various brain diseases. Other researchers have been using CRISPR to do experimental edits of the DNA of embryos. It is easy to imagine that eventually, this will be more common, not just for curing congenital disabilities, but also for optimizing humans for new goals. These goals might include preparing for eventual long-term colonies on Mars and, judging from history, creating designer babies for those privileged with the necessary resources.[148]

Assuming humans have souls, as many of us do, will this increasingly diverse human community be changed beyond being defined as human and in the imago Dei, the image of God? What are the implications for the souls of these future humans that are presumably so different from Cain, Abel, and Seth? What would determine the limits? How might we change the definition of what it is to be human, or perhaps our understanding of what it would mean to be suitable for housing a soul?

Currently, the debate is about the boundaries that should be placed on science. Still, it is in the nature of science and the *creative* essence of being who we are as humans, especially in a world like ours, that if it can be done, it probably will be done at some point somewhere. If it is useful, the practice often has a way of becoming accepted in popular culture. Perhaps the human body is better imagined as the sensory, cognitive container (a kind of plugin) for a soul that enables it to grow in the image of and relationship to God under different conditions.

What is the soul, after all?

I described an article by Dr. Joel Yehudah Rutman (Rutman, 2016), a pediatric neurologist, who looked back at ideas of the soul in the Torah through the lens of neuroscience. One by one, he argued, most of the attributes that have been associated with the soul are either attributes of the body itself or are our experiences emerging from physical phenomena related to our bodies (especially our brains). He concludes that in the Jewish tradition—and I would suggest in this area also in the Christian tradition—what persists after death are the things that are more than just the physical components that contribute to our experience. But the thought exercise is to think about the possible time between death and the final judgment; if there is a soul in heaven or elsewhere without a body, what is it really like? In this exercise, you would need to edit out all the characteristics we associate with being a living human that are related to our bodies. Perhaps what we are left with is something like the state of being of the same essence, in some sense, as God (e.g., Brahman in Hinduism).

The soul without the body, for example, may be the God-stuff—that which distinguishes humans from the rest of creation—and our unique self and personhood that allows us to be in relationship with God and with others. It may be the part of us that connects us with a larger spiritual reality. Furthermore, while there are learned ethical rules from our culture, we may share with God the more fundamental sense of right and wrong touched on in Genesis and rooted in something universal. This might be the source of behaviors that can appear to violate social norms, such as sacrificing one's self for another.

The self and personhood could be what distinguishes us from one another and makes being an individual meaningful. It would not necessarily involve something like a personality. What we often think of personality is typically associated with patterns in our behavior as perceived by others and ourselves in different situations in the physical world. Personality, perhaps as opposed to something the Greeks might think of as character, is intimately tied to the characteristics of our body, the combination of nature and nurture. While our life experiences in our body presumably have molded the clay of our souls in unique ways, our souls might be the image in the wax of our experiences.

I would also assume the soul needs to be engaged in the will since that presumably is what makes us ultimately responsible for what we do both as it influences intention and plays out through how we interact with the world through our bodies. This is the soul-body question I have mentioned earlier, the question of how the soul connects to what the body does. That engagement suggests some kind of source intent and will that can be one of the triggers of activity in the body.

The soul's essence may be these characteristics as they exist or extend beyond the four-dimensional constraints of the physical world.[149] William James might say that while this idea is not subject to empirical verification, as with the concept of eternal life, it cannot easily be dismissed either. A more transcendent soul might be what lets us connect with a God who is more all-encompassing than the constraints of our physical world. This latter idea seems a little like what Plato had in mind with his spiritual realm of ultimate reality (incl. his idea of Forms). It also appears to resonate with the Hindu view of how the Atman after multiple reincarnations matures until it is absorbed into the Brahman (the supreme divine force present in all things), and the Buddhist idea of nirvana. However, in the Judeo-Christian origin story, it would involve the Creator who breathed the essence of humanness into us, and our ability to have a personal, spiritual connection with that Creator.

If we have a body in the afterlife, what will it be like?

For Eastern religions like Hinduism and Buddhism, the physical body is a barrier to reaching the ultimate spiritual state. In the process of reincarnation, one moves from body to body, either moving forward or in reverse, depending on karma. In contrast, in Judeo-Christian theology, while there is a distinction between the soul and the body, they are intimately linked. Based on the discussion so far, I believe we do have some kind of transcendent soul that defines us as in the image of God. I agree with the philosophers and theologians who point out we do not have souls; we are souls. And as we have observed, research makes it clear our bodies are continually changing and, coupled with our experiences, shape what we feel makes us unique. Much of philosophy and theology over the last couple of millennia have been trying to understand the relationship between the soul and body, and how they interact.

While the Talmud's early sages recognized a dualist view, the body was not seen as a prison for the soul. Being human is, in essence, the soul and body acting in harmony. Tractate Berakhot in the Babylonian Talmud says, "Just as the Holy One of Blessing fills the world, so does the soul [neshama] fill the body. Just as the Holy One of Blessing sees but cannot be seen, so does the soul see but cannot be seen." The body is not an enemy but is a holy instrument that allows us to fulfill God's mission in this world. The body is how we as souls interact with the world, and that fulfillment of the seed of the soul planted in a unique body is what allows us to flower in the life where we find ourselves. It is easy to imagine that what happens in this world, as Native American traditions, ancient Egyptians, and others believe, is both preparation and a precursor for what life might be like in the next.

From the beginning, God had work for us to do in this world. In Genesis 1:22-39 (JPS), it says:

> *"G-d blessed them, saying: 'Be fruitful, and multiply, and fill the waters in the seas, and let fowl multiply in the earth' And there was evening and there was morning, a fifth day. And G-d said: 'Let the earth bring forth the living creature after its kind, cattle, and creeping thing, and beast of the earth after its kind' And it was so. And G-d made the beast of the earth after its kind, and the cattle after their kind, and every thing that creepeth upon the ground after its kind; and G-d saw that it was good. And G-d said: 'Let us make man in our image, after our likeness; and let them have dominion[150] over the fish of the sea, and over the fowl of the air, and over the cattle, and over all the earth, and over every creeping thing that creepeth upon the earth'.*
>
> *"And G-d created man in His own image, in the image of G-d created He him; male and female created He them. And*

G-d blessed them; and G-d said unto them: 'Be fruitful, and multiply, and replenish the earth, and subdue it; and have dominion over the fish of the sea, and over the fowl of the air, and over every living thing that creepeth upon the earth.' And G-d said: 'Behold, I have given you every herb yielding seed, which is upon the face of all the earth, and every tree, in which is the fruit of a tree yielding seed—to you it shall be for food; and to every beast of the earth, and to every fowl of the air, and to every thing that creepeth upon the earth, wherein there is a living soul, I have given every green herb for food' And it was so."

Much of the Tanakh and the Christian New Testament is about fleshing out the details of that mission. Jesus summarizes the top priorities in Mark 12:30,31 (NIV) as "'Love the Lord your God with all your heart and with all your soul and with all your mind and with all your strength.' The second is this: 'Love your neighbor as yourself.' There is no commandment greater than these." To carry out that function as individuals and as groups, we need our bodies to let us, as souls, interact with the world and the people around us. As a species, we needed our bodies to grow in our effectiveness in the roles that were designed into us as creative, relational, and rational beings over the long span of human history. I cannot help but believe that our physical maturation and growing body of experiences grows us as souls and our ability to be closer to that image of God. In that sense, the goals of reincarnation, ideas expressed by philosophers like Plato, and the spiritual focus in scriptural texts that led to prophets, monks, sages, and shamans seem to reflect this urge.

When this body dies, in most religious traditions, the soul continues. In Christianity and some Jewish traditions, there is a resurrection of the body. In popular culture in the United States, people are split on whether they will have a physical body in the afterlife versus a more spiritual body or even existing just as a spirit. The Egyptians had a kind of hybrid view, and many early religions (e.g., the Chinese) believed they could equip souls with at least symbolic food and other objects from this life that would enable them to "live" and act in the next one. Those who believe in a spiritual body often lean towards a body that is somehow recognizable by their loved ones. Often the activities in heaven are described by religious traditions that place value on the physical in terms that imply having a body, just as John the Seer describes the activities of God, the saints, and the angels in the throne room of God's kingdom. But it is not a surprise that as humans think about the afterlife, they think in terms of a self in a body like the one they experience every day (e.g., including in their typical clothing and other cultural trappings).

The classical Greek word used in many of the New Testament resurrection verses is ἀνάστασις or anastasis. It means making to stand or rise (a more literal usage) and raising the dead (perhaps a more conceptual usage). While it is not always explicit in its use, for Christians, the understanding given the model of Jesus' resurrection would be that a body is being resurrected and reassociated with its owner. For example, in Romans 8:11 (NIV), "[H]e who raised Christ from the dead will also give life to your mortal bodies because of his Spirit who lives in you." 1 Corinthians 6:14 (NIV) says, "By his power God raised the Lord from the dead, and he will raise us also." A body dies and is resurrected in some form, and the soul is eternal.[151]

Christians point to verses that say we will be resurrected just as Christ was. As we have noted, while often not initially recognized by his friends, Christ made it a point to demonstrate the wounds he continued to have after resurrection. While there may be "no more death or mourning or crying or pain" (Revelation 21:4, NIV); we apparently could have imperfections. Christ was able to walk through walls and then ascended to heaven. Finally, in Matthew 17:2 (NIV), his transformation continued as "There he was transfigured before them. His face shone like the sun, and his clothes became as white as the light." So it is not *exactly* the same body, and there is the issue of very culture-specific clothing being "resurrected" as well. Other appearances of the "ghosts" of the dead such as Moses and Elijah, were apparently recognizable even though the disciples had never met them. Presumably if they died when they were old, they stayed old. Visions of what is going on in heaven in Revelation reflect throne rooms, clothing, and rituals that seem frozen in Israel during the Roman empire.[152]

The nature of all these physical and spiritual bodies is not clear. In the Westminster Confession of Faith (dating back to around 1645), there is a section on the resurrection of the dead which says, "all the dead shall be raised up, with the selfsame bodies, and none other (although with different qualities)." The parenthetical qualification seems to be trying to balance the idea that Jesus resurrected in his body (as he demonstrated with his wounds and its physicality), with the idea that he could pass through walls and perform other miracles. The sense of the Confession is that we similarly will be raised in our bodies, but our bodies will also have new characteristics. This does give one a slight pause, since if there are different qualities, it is not the selfsame body, just a similar one.

During much of the latter part of her life, my mother-in-law looked forward to the entire family being caught up when the Rapture happened. She hoped that we would all be there in heaven and pretty much be recognizably the same family that we are on Earth. My grandmother did not want to be cremated because she was convinced she and her daughter needed to have bodies if they were going to be raised from the grave to meet Christ on his return, and she wanted those bodies at some fundamental level to be the ones they had when they died. Like in the Westminster Confession, the idea seems to be that our existing bodies are somehow us in whatever stage of life they are in at death. But on the other hand, the hope is that anything we do not like about ourselves will be *fixed*.

As we have pointed out from what we know about biology and the universe's physical laws, having the "same" body as the one we died in is not literally possible. Cells change in real-time, some of our cells will have already been recycled, and as we noted, many of the cells that define us are not us. We have also identified some of the unanswered questions, like how old will babies be? How old will the elderly be? What, if anything, would be "cured," and if it were, is the person the same person? And as we know from modern drugs and anesthetics, a soul could theoretically be without crying or pain without requiring wholesale changes to the body.

When ghosts or spirits appear in the form people who knew them recognize, that does not necessarily mean they are like that in the spiritual world. It only says that whatever their underlying state, they can appear in a form that is meaningful to those who observe them.[153] This is a theme widely explored in science fiction stories, and is the common experience across human history of those visited by the spirits of their loved ones. The appearance of those being encountered may come as much from within as without

While resonating with the idea that there will be a body for us, I am not concerned about the details of the specifics of a physical body. I hold onto a possible spiritual "connection" that allows one person to recognize another without a body. I know the love my wife and I share persists and has grown even as our bodies have changed considerably since we first fell in love. I am also left with the idea of a body fitted to help us grow and fulfill our duties, our purpose, in the afterlife. Indeed, across an eternity (especially given the early Jewish definition of olan), I am inclined to believe there may be additional bodies that we might have in the future as needed. As some philosophers have pointed out, God could provide them if required. That is what we as a species are working towards here on Earth even now, as we manipulate and reengineer our bodies.

This leads me to the verses that promise something new. Philippians 3:21 (NIV) says, "[Christ], by the power that enables him to bring everything under his control, will transform our lowly bodies so that they will be like his glorious body." You could say this is the same body, but it seems only the same in having the same soul and perhaps some version or imprint of the memories that define the character of the same mind. Otherwise, it seems to me to be quite different. Paul expands his thoughts in 2 Corinthians 5:1-10 (NIV), where he says:

"For we know that if the earthly tent we live in is destroyed, we have a building from God, an eternal house in heaven, not built by human hands. Meanwhile we groan, longing to be clothed instead with our heavenly dwelling, because when we are clothed, we will not be found naked. For while we are in this tent, we

groan and are burdened, because we do not wish to be unclothed but to be clothed instead with our heavenly dwelling, so that what is mortal may be swallowed up by life. Now the one who has fashioned us for this very purpose is God, who has given us the Spirit as a deposit, guaranteeing what is to come.

"Therefore we are always confident and know that as long as we are at home in the body we are away from the Lord. For we live by faith, not by sight. We are confident, I say, and would prefer to be away from the body and at home with the Lord. So we make it our goal to please him, whether we are at home in the body or away from it. For we must all appear before the judgment seat of Christ, so that each of us may receive what is due us for the things done while in the body, whether good or bad."

I Corinthians 15:35-54 (NIV) provides the most detailed description of this future state:

"But someone will ask, 'How are the dead raised? With what kind of body will they come?' How foolish! What you sow does not come to life unless it dies. When you sow, you do not plant the body that will be, but just a seed, perhaps of wheat or of something else. But God gives it a body as he has determined, and to each kind of seed he gives its own body.

"Not all flesh is the same: People have one kind of flesh, animals have another, birds another and fish another. There are also heavenly bodies and there are earthly bodies; but the splendor of the heavenly bodies is one kind, and the splendor of the earthly bodies is another. The sun has one kind of splendor, the moon another and the stars another; and star differs from star in splendor. So will it be with the resurrection of the dead.

"The body that is sown is perishable, it is raised imperishable; it is sown in dishonor, it is raised in glory; it is sown in weakness, it is raised in power; it is sown a natural body, it is raised a spiritual body. If there is a natural body, there is also a spiritual body. So it is written: 'The first man Adam became a living being'; the last Adam, a life-giving spirit. The spiritual did not come first, but the natural, and after that the spiritual.

The first man was of the dust of the earth; the second man is of heaven. As was the earthly man, so are those who are of the earth; and as is the heavenly man, so also are those who are of heaven. And just as we have borne the image of the earthly man, so shall we bear the image of the heavenly man.

"I declare to you, brothers and sisters, that flesh and blood cannot inherit the kingdom of God, nor does the perishable inherit the imperishable. Listen, I tell you a mystery: We will not all sleep, but we will all be changed—in a flash, in the twinkling of an eye, at the last trumpet. For the trumpet will sound, the dead will be raised imperishable, and we will be changed. For the perishable must clothe itself with the imperishable, and the mortal with immortality. When the perishable has been clothed with the imperishable, and the mortal with immortality, then the saying that is written will come true: 'Death has been swallowed up in victory.'"

Billy Graham takes the approach of imagining a general principle of "it will be great," whatever it is (Graham, 2011). He says, "What will we look like in heaven? The Bible does not say, exactly—but you can be sure that all our weaknesses and imperfections will be gone, and our bodies will be perfect and ageless. The baby who died from a crippling disease won't be a baby any longer; the old person who was feeble and frail will have perfect health." I personally think Reverend Graham is over-promising here. While there are promises of a new body with some sketches of it being special, we are reminded that we have no idea of how this will be implemented. 1 John 3:2 (NIV) says, "Dear friends, now we are children of God, and what we will be has not yet been made known. But we know that when Christ appears, we shall be like him, for we shall see him as he is."

Will our soul have a gender?

I believe the answer is no... sort of. This clearly is my opinion, but let me describe how I think about it. I have checked with several people whose expertise I value, and no one knows of any place in Judeo-Christian scriptures where this is addressed directly. While God is often described in male terms, given the patriarchal nature of the cultures at the time and the desire to communicate about God as the ultimate in the most powerful roles that would be familiar to their audiences, that would not be a surprise. Many have noted that God also is portrayed in feminine roles in the scriptures, and except for speaking about Jesus, most would not seriously portray God as physically a man. The exception would be a few who argue that some ancient Israelites worshiped both a male God, Yahweh, and God's wife, Asherah (e.g., Raphael Patai and Francesca Stavrakopoulou).

Similarly, when God created Adam in God's image in the origin story, many religious scholars argue that Adam is portrayed without gender. Some rabbis even proposed that Adam had both genders. The image sometimes used in this last idea is Adam with two faces, and a body almost like conjoined twins. The formation of Adam and Eve, in this story, was a very literal split as the genders came into existence.

The word for Adam may come from Adamah, ground or soil, and also references Adom, which can mean "red." That might suggest Adam came from red soil or clay, and given the etymology, Adam could best be referred to as an Earthling. In breathing into Adam, God brought the clay alive and made it human. Interestingly, this could reflect the historical use and symbolism of red ochre for early humans. Once Adam was human, God formed genders. Genesis 1:26 (JPS) says, "G-d created man in His own image, in the image of G-d created He him; male and female created He them." The sense is that Adam's soul was not gendered, and then two gendered physical bodies were created, each with souls.

Some might point out that the spirits of those who died and were seen again retained their gender identities from their physical lives. But as we have mentioned from the research, that may be about how "perception" or at least experience of the otherwise unseen works for those seeing the spirits. From a more metaphysical perspective, it may be similar to how angels are said to manifest themselves in this physical world.

People often see what they hope to see, or they may be shown what they need to see; irrespective of the nature of the souls in the afterlife when they are separated from bodies.

Matthew 22:30 also says, "At the resurrection people will neither marry nor be given in marriage; they will be like the angels in heaven." Except for the Church of Jesus Christ of Latter-day Saints, there is not much argument that there will be procreation in heaven.[154] Gender would largely be irrelevant at that point. Our future bodies will likely be considerably different than they are now anyway. So recognizing each other in the afterlife seems like it would be less about preserving a snapshot of a body in period clothing than recognition between souls at a more spiritual level.

None of the major philosophers have argued that souls were gendered. Some have pointed out that our consciousness and self-hood could even be dropped arbitrarily into any body, and we would still be us. That is, of course, a popular trope in films. We also mentioned research that suggests we are wired quite effectively for imagining ourselves in other forms. Dissociative identity disorders that demonstrate gender identity independent of the physical body are well documented. Furthermore, as has been established, often experienced gender identity does not match assigned identity (e.g., from the high incidence of non-standard chromosomal combinations, the way hormonal systems have developed, and other factors).

So, given our discussion of what a soul is, removing characteristics that are clearly associated with our bodies' biology suggests that there is nothing inherently gendered about the soul itself. On the other hand, I support the importance of the intimate relationship between our souls and our bodies. I do believe, like several philosophical and theological traditions, souls do not begin fully formed. They grow and develop their uniqueness through their existence in a body interacting with God, others, and the world. Like a photograph developed through a filter, the specific image will be shaped by gendered identity and experiences. That is part of the diversity that makes us interesting and uniquely able to adapt and survive as a species.

Given that view, I can find it relatively easy to imagine my soul being the same even as my body goes through considerable physical change as I age. I would be the same even if I went through dramatic surgical, hormonal, and other interventions. Changes in the body would influence the development of my soul, just as existing in a virtual or augmented world like we create with games could, in essence, "program" not only my body but also shape my soul. If I can imagine that, it is a small step to imagine that beyond the foreseeable edge of forever God might move my soul into yet another body (perhaps with an alternative gender or even a genetic map suitable for another world) if that fit a divine plan.

What is heaven like?

"Would you know my name if I saw you in heaven?"
– Eric Clapton ("Tears in Heaven")

"There are more things in heaven and earth, Horatio, than are dreamt of in your philosophy." – Shakespeare

Most modern religions do not attempt to flesh out a lot of detail about heaven or the equivalent. Christians (especially evangelicals), Mormons, and Muslims[155] tend to think and talk the most about it. In Judaism, for example, there is little about heaven within the Tanakh. This is partly because, as we have mentioned, the focus of Judaism tends to be on life in this world. God wants people to enjoy this world to the fullest and make it better, and the Torah promises worldly rewards and punishments for the faithful and the faithless here on earth. In general, it does not dwell on heaven for the righteous or threaten hell for the sinful (Heaven, Hell, and the Afterlife in Jewish Thought, n.d.). It has even been noted that if a person abstains from permitted pleasures in this world, they may be taken to task for it in the next.

However, Rabbi Tully Bryks paints a nice picture of the Jewish afterlife with a series of rabbinical and Talmudic sources (Bryks, 2017). People will experience external pleasure in the next world, where a moment will be as intense as an entire life here on earth. Bryks points to sources that suggest the level and intensity of the pleasure correspond to our good deeds and the observed commandments when alive. There will be complete clarity in understanding God and our purpose.[156] Some of a person's acts in this world can continue to have ripple effects and benefit them in the next (e.g., charity, kindness, teaching, and saving someone's life). In the Jewish concept of the afterlife, departed souls may watch over loved ones who are still alive and share in the joy of the living. Importantly, Judaism believes that all of God's children, Jews and non-Jews alike, can enjoy the world to come.

In the Catechism of the Catholic Church (Catechism of the Catholic Church, n.d.), it says, "This mystery of blessed communion with God and all who are in Christ is beyond all understanding and description. Scripture speaks of it in images: life, light, peace, wedding feast, wine of the kingdom, the Father's house, the heavenly Jerusalem, paradise: 'no eye has seen, nor ear heard, nor the heart of man conceived, what God has prepared for those who love him.'" The Catechism also says, "We shall know the ultimate meaning of the whole work of creation and the entire economy of salvation and understand the marvelous ways by which [God's] Providence led everything toward its final end." Pope Benedict XII, in his Apostolic Constitution, Benedictus Deus, of Jan. 29, 1336, says:

"By virtue of our apostolic authority, we define the following: According to the general disposition of God, the souls of all the saints...and other faithful who died after receiving Christ's holy Baptism (provided they were not in need of purification when they died...or, if they then did need or will need some purification, when they have been purified after death...) already before they take up their bodies again and before the general judgment — and this since the Ascension of our Lord and Savior Jesus Christ into heaven — have been, are and will be in heaven, in the heavenly Kingdom and celestial paradise with Christ, joined to the company of the holy angels. Since the Passion and death of our Lord Jesus Christ, these souls have seen and do see the divine essence with an intuitive vision, and even face to face, without the mediation of any creature."[157]

Even though many point to the I Corinthians 2:9 verse that suggests we have no idea of what heaven will be like and, in fact, cannot have an idea, that does not stop many of us from speculating. As we saw in Chapter 1, if you asked the average person in the United States to imagine heaven, you might get attributes like:

- Everyone will be worshipping and singing praises to God.[158]
- It will be peaceful.
- There will be angels.
- We will be able to be with those we love (at least those who are in heaven).
- Everyone will love everyone else.
- We will be healed from anything that is wrong with us (e.g., disabilities).[159]
- We will continue to grow spiritually.
- Everyone will be happy.
- There will be humor.
- It will be beautiful.

- There will be no diseases.
- No one will be hungry.
- No one will be sad.[160]
- Everything we want will be there.[161]
- We will all feel present with Jesus Christ.
- We will have crowns and mansions.

Billy Graham, again, expands on this "Whatever it is, it will be wonderful!" vision that many Protestant pastors sketch for heaven. He said, "heaven will be a place of perfect happiness for us—and if we need animals around us to make our happiness complete, then you can be sure God will have them there. Heaven will be glorious—far beyond anything we can fully imagine. It will be glorious first of all because it will be perfect. All the sufferings, conflicts, and disappointments of this life will be over, and death will no longer exist. Sin will be banished, and Satan will never again have any influence over our lives."

Scripturally, while many pastors have made plausible projections from various definitions of perfection and personal wishes, literally, the specific promises are a little narrower. The essential promises are immortality and the ongoing relationship with God. There is a theme of reward in heaven for a life well lived and storing up "treasures" in heaven. Still, those things that might be seen as rewarding within a secular world are unlikely to be what is meant by a reward or treasures in heaven, where the reward is more likely to be an expression of God's approval. The treasure is most likely about the relationship between the individual and God, and one might assume whatever one's starting point, that relationship would continue to grow across eternity. It is hard to imagine it will be static and frozen forever. The lesson from here on Earth is that growth (including spiritual growth) generally comes from doing things, having new experiences, and overcoming challenges.

As we have noted, there is a promise of new heavens and a new Earth, and some kind of resurrected but considerably changed body.[162] In John 14.2, Jesus teaches the disciples that there is plenty of room in heaven for the billions (estimated) of his followers,[163] as you might expect. Jesus mostly talks about the kingdom of God, and his listeners would relate his messages to the kingdom of Israel, especially as contrasting with the Roman world in which they were living. But on the cross, he tells the thief on the cross next to him (Luke 23:43) that he will see him in Paradise. The word used for Paradise was originally Iranian, and the Greeks modified it into a word meaning something like an "enclosed park." In the Septuagint, this was the word used to refer to the Garden of Eden. In Hebrews (11:16 and 13:14), the author speaking to what was probably a largely Jewish-Christian audience spoke of a vision of a city to come that was probably in the spirit of a new Jerusalem.

The verses that are often drawn on the most are from the vision of John the Seer in Revelation. A favorite is from Revelation 21:4 (see also 7:17) "He will wipe away every tear from their eyes, and death shall be no more, neither shall there be mourning, nor crying, nor pain anymore, for the former things have passed away." Often this is claimed more in the specifics of the absence of mourning (since death is gone), and the absence of crying and pain. The "former things have passed away" is interpreted as all of the things in people's lives that they consider painful and disappointing, and those things that may be associated with sin (especially violations of the Ten Commandments). But, of course, it could be more explicitly contrasting the new state of being with God for eternity with the distance that was characteristic of the past (especially between existing in a physical world and connecting with a spiritual one).

It might not be a universal proclamation that there will never again be crying. Not all crying is unfortunate, some is from happiness and some is from love.[164] It is hard to imagine there would not be crying over the pain of any loved ones not in heaven. Certainly, it would not preclude the satisfying effort—and strain that might come with it—that it might take to fulfill a mission in the future world that we know at least in this world would help our souls and our bodies grow, and that would contribute to God's creative goals.

Another source for some descriptions of heaven is the Beatitudes, from Jesus' Sermon on the Mount (Matthew 5:3-12). Tod Lindberg (Lindberg, 2007) points out that this is, in essence, Jesus' inaugural speech. It is the executive summary of his teaching and paints a picture of the world Jesus is in the process of creating. As Lindberg says, "The Beatitudes provide a dizzying commentary designed to turn upside down the political and social world of the Roman Empire of Caesar Augustus and of the Jewish religious elite of Judea and Jerusalem. This is the opening move of a more drastic and fundamental reassessment of political and social affairs, applying not only to its own time but to all future times, down to our day." It is a blessing, and it is a call to remake the current world. Indeed, it seems reasonable to project this vision to a future kingdom of heaven.

But there are just three verses that explicitly mention the coming kingdom of heaven. One is "Blessed are the poor in spirit, for theirs is the kingdom of heaven," one is "Blessed are those who are persecuted because of righteousness, for theirs is the kingdom of heaven," and one is the extension of this last one which reads "Blessed are you when people insult you, persecute you and falsely say all kinds of evil against you because of me. Rejoice and be glad, because great is your reward in heaven, for in the same way they persecuted the prophets who were before you." The tone of these verses is that some of our billionaires might not get the special treatment they have received in life.

Revelation itself has to be viewed in the context of a vision that speaks to larger themes about God's victory at the end of this world and not necessarily as what some might think of as literal history. After all, while the new Jerusalem is described in a way that would be meaningful to the audience of the day (especially during the Roman empire), it does not quite strike many of us in the same way now. The building is presented as a cube one thousand three hundred and twelve miles on each side. As context, it would cover most of the United States, and since space starts at roughly sixty-two miles up, this would extend way beyond that. Its volume would be about half the size of the moon. Logically, today, a literal structure made of the metals and the gems described would not be particularly special for those in it. Most of us would not even consider it particularly beautiful, even if its impact on a global environment made sense. I would expect God, who invented the fractals that define the wonders of nature that bring us such awe, would design something more aesthetically pleasing.[165] As a result, I am inclined to look more at this vision of a new Jerusalem in terms of what it says about how God will be more directly connected to us and a general "it will be better than anything you have ever seen," whatever that turns out to be.[166]

One puzzle is in the references to people sitting on thrones ruling.[167] Who is being ruled? What are those being ruled doing? What is the nature of the ruling? Why would it even be required? Bottom line, the best approach is probably to embrace I Corinthians 2:9 and realize, "No eye has seen, no ear has heard, no mind has conceived what God has prepared for those who love him."[168]

What happens to the innocents who die?

From "Sistine Madonna" by Raphael

For women who know they are pregnant, roughly fifteen percent of pregnancies end in miscarriages. The March of Dimes suggests that as many as fifty percent of pregnancies can end in miscarriages. In most of human history, another twenty-five percent of babies often died during their first year of life, and fifty percent of children died before puberty. So what is the fate of those who are lost while still in their innocence?

Eastern religions that believe in reincarnation, of course, have a way to handle these losses. In contrast, for Christianity, these are challenging edge cases in discussions about the soul and the afterlife. Augustine of Hippo (354 to 430 CE) originated the term and fleshed out the doctrine of *original sin*, based in part on a mistranslation of Romans 5:12 "Therefore, just as sin entered the world through one man, and death through sin, and in this way death came to all people, because all sinned." His position argued that when Adam and Eve disobeyed God, all of subsequent humanity by definition have a tainted nature and inclination to disobey God. The argument brings the idea that all deserve death and punishment as a result, and it is only by deciding to accept salvation through Christ that one can avoid that fate. Augustine's idea influenced subsequent Catholic thought and also became quite popular with the Protestant reformers.[169]

Origen, who introduced the interpretation that led to the concept of original sin, had a belief that all souls are created before conception. Therefore, it made sense to him that all were treated as having sinned because Adam and Eve sinned. However, the more accurate translation is that we follow those original ancestors' footsteps when each of us does something bad. We are responsible and will be judged for *our own actions*.

You can imagine Origen's position could pose some difficulties as we think about those who have not reached the age at which they can make a rational decision to accept salvation. One hope people seize on is 2 Samuel 12:23, where David responds to the loss of his infant son who died when he stops mourning and declares, "[H]e can't come to me, but I will go to him." Technically, that does not necessarily speak as much about the afterlife theology and children as perhaps it does about resolving his own cognitive dissonance and stress over the penalty he is paying for *his* sin, especially given early Jewish views of the afterlife. Other than that, the Bible does not say much about what happens to babies and children when they die.

During the Medieval period, Catholic theologians proposed the idea of Limbo. It recognized that if you have not been saved (or baptized), you cannot enter heaven. On the other hand, babies cannot accept salvation; and while they have inherited original sin, they have not committed a personal sin. While Augustine imagined a quasi-hell for this situation, these Medieval theologians imagined a kind of quasi-heaven. This Limbo would be a place where they could enjoy a natural stage of happiness but would not enjoy the full, direct beatific vision of God in heaven. This doctrine, however, has never become an official doctrine of the Church.

Among Protestants, you can find a wide variety of opinions online. Some say we just do not know because the Bible does not speak about it. Some argue that God does not provide a soul until the first breath (or perhaps even after, since God would know what might happen), and so at least for the preborn, it is not an issue. Others, especially those who do not accept the theology of original sin, would point to the various verses that say we will be judged by what we have done, whether good or bad (e.g., Matthew 16:27, 2 Corinthians 5:10, Revelation 20:12, and James 2:14). Some also point to verses like Matthew 19:13-14 (NIV), "Then people brought little children to Jesus for him to place his hands on them and pray for them. But the disciples rebuked them. Jesus said, 'Let the little children come to me, and do not hinder them, for the kingdom of heaven belongs to such as these.'" [170]

It is one thing to believe there are consequences for making bad decisions in life. It is another to believe that those who have not been born (especially if they do not yet have souls) and infants have a price to pay. It does not fit with how most of us think of a loving God. Certainly, God would cut them some slack at the final judgment.

Then there is being married to the right person. I Corinthians 7:14 (NIV) is another verse that some claim, which reads, "For the unbelieving husband has been sanctified through his wife, and the unbelieving wife has been sanctified through her believing husband. Otherwise, your children would be unclean, but as it is, they are holy." While the church I grew up in did not believe in adult water baptism as a requirement for salvation, let alone infant baptism, those who believe in infant baptism sometimes argue that in baptizing, the parents are standing in "surety" for them until they reach the age of accountability.

Some take the hard line that they are all, alas, condemned. But I have to admit, for me, "That does not compute." For those arguing for the hard-core position that babies and children are lost, presumably, there is an *extra* obligation to ensure society cares and provides for those children until they reach the age of accountability. Otherwise, those believing this position would potentially seem to fall under Jesus' curse in Matthew 18:6 (NIV), "If anyone causes one of these little ones—those who believe in me—to stumble, it would be better for them to have a large millstone hung around their neck and to be drowned in the depths of the sea."

Even More Speculative

Will aliens have souls?[171]

Imagining Life on the Moon
John Wilkins (1638)

Honestly, we do not know based on what we have got. But let's think about it. It is clear that the medieval view of the Earth as the center of the universe is wrong, and it seems unlikely that human beings are the center of the universe in any sense. That would just feel like a waste of a universe. Based on string theory in physics and alternative views besides the Big Bang, even the universe may not be the center of all creation. Assuming a supreme Creator that spans the multidimensional all-that-there-is, there is no reason why God could not create creatures with souls on other worlds. Indeed, we have speculated that Neanderthals may have had souls, and some of our genetic engineering and cybernetic technologies may modify ourselves significantly.

Indeed, God filled this planet with various creatures that may have souls in some form or at least attributes of souls, and we have evolved in this dynamic system that was created. It seems like God would utilize the diversity of creation across this and possibly other universes to create other beings that God could interact with as directly as with us. In essence, we might be part of a larger, divine experiment. Perhaps some succeeded where we as a species partially failed. Maybe some accepted whatever form God used to manifest within their world. If God did not have a literal moment before which there were no humans with a soul and after which we all had souls, but instead evolved souls along with the creatures that grew to become us, we could expect God would do something similar elsewhere. Some of those worlds are likely to be far older and more mature than ours. So, chances are, if we encountered another sentient being, we could potentially find them worshipping the same God that we do, but with concepts, rituals, and stories that are theirs.[172]

Would my clone have a soul?

This question is interesting. I think that one of the precedents to look at would be identical twins. Across the traditions of human history and current medical knowledge, it is difficult to believe that a soul is implanted when an egg is fertilized. If it is, does a soul divide when the first cell divides to start the process of twining?[173] At some point, each developing person reaches a stage where they receive the soul that will be them—perhaps at their first natural breath or some time after. Given the nature of divergent experiences, each soul would further differentiate into a unique soul. This would include being responsible for its own moral choices.

Similarly, I have to believe that whatever the conditions are for a soul to appear inside the body of a twin would apply to cloning. These would be the conditions required to make it human and express the image of God. They would apply even

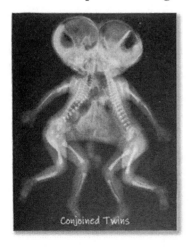

Conjoined Twins

if my clone (my virtual twin) was nurtured to a mature physical state inside a surrogate mother or a lab. It could also apply to the situation where I might be cloned as an adult. The point where those conditions were equivalent to either of the infant twins when a soul appears should also be valid for the clone. However, it will be more of an issue when the cloning is to grow replacement parts for my body. At the very least, the process *should* stop short of ensoulment. That suggests we need to work towards more clarity on what the conditions for ensoulment are (e.g., consciousness) in order to guide future policies.

Is there an artificial intelligence with a soul in our future?

This one is trickier. I have just argued that life could have been created elsewhere, and if so, there is nothing that constrains God from creating in that life whatever the soul is, an imago Dei. Science also recognizes that what we call life could be biochemically quite different from what defines life here on Earth. Over human history, our DNA has never been *pure* in any sense, and we are continuing to edit it. In time, as we have observed, we will likely customize our DNA for unique environments and needs. Furthermore, the definition of life continues to evolve, and where there is life, there eventually is likely to be a rational mind and consciousness. From a theory of the soul perspective, if the attributes of the soul have appeared in other creatures on Earth and possibly elsewhere, it is not a huge leap to imagine "artificially" creating many of these attributes.

While there is the idea of artificial intelligence as we think about it today receiving a consciousness, it is also true that we are already starting to create computers from living tissues. We are exploring merging ourselves and various intelligent technologies. We are implementing models of artificial intelligence that are inspired by ourselves as well as other living creatures.

An Early Cyborg

As a thought experiment, if I replaced pieces of myself one piece at a time, is there a point where my soul would leave, and what is it? Even at the level of the brain, it is not too far-fetched to imagine portions of the brain being replaced by cloned tissue and external storage, bit by bit, until there is an entirely "new" brain. It seems like there would not be a point that is identifiable as death.

Given that, with a kind of dualist model where the body is merely a vehicle with the suitable properties to *receive* and be complementary to a soul, there is no reason I can imagine that God could not provide an appropriate *artificial being* with a soul. Those properties would be those we speculated on earlier as variations of the characteristics that map to our souls, including consciousness as the meeting place of a soul and its ability to interact with the world and to be in relationships with others. So is there an expectation that artificial intelligence might become conscious?

In 1997 the Association for Computing Machinery held a conference to celebrate the first fifty years of computing and to imagine the next fifty years. In the book written to accompany the event, *Beyond Calculation*, Gordon Bell and James Gray wrote a chapter entitled "The Revolution Yet to Happen" (Bell, 1997). In it, they argued that by 2047 virtually all information about people, things, knowledge, and art will be in cyberspace. It feels like we are already there, but certainly, we are easily on track given how fast things have moved since 1997. Back then they projected that computers would begin to outpace the processing power of the human brain around 2047. They estimated the brain's processing power as around one petaflops. To provide a little context, to match what a one petaflops computer can do in one second, you would have to perform one calculation every second for 31,688,765 years. They also projected that there would be a massive supply of essentially zero-cost, specialized computers on a chip embedded in everything around us. Today we are living an early incarnation of this idea in the Internet of Things.

The vision of a computer with the power of the brain, though, is worth a second look. IBM's Roadrunner supercomputer achieved the one petaflops target in 2008, well before the target date of 2047. Of course, the bar has moved, and now there are estimates of the brain's processing power as being around one exaflop (or one billion calculations per second, equivalent to 1,000 petaflops). Some believe that this goal from a raw processing power perspective could be reached in 2022 or shortly thereafter, and a distributed computing system reached this goal last year. There is something called the Human Brain Project (HBP), which is a ten-year research project that will be built on exascale supercomputers.

However, the human brain is a combination of, in essence, its hardware and its software. Having the processing power and being connected to a virtually unlimited memory is not quite enough. It needs to learn and process like a human brain. While that is likely to be far out, progress over the last twenty-five years is getting faster and faster. The University of Manchester in the UK has created a neuromorphic supercomputer that can simulate a mouse's brain. The National Institute of Standards and Technology for the United States has created a synthetic synapse that is more than two hundred times faster than our own. That is certainly a start. Whether the goal of a human brain equivalent is thirty years in our future or not, it is pretty clear it will be in our future. That could cause a paradigm shift (sometimes known as "the singularity") in technology, society, and our culture.

The idea of computers becoming conscious has been a topic not just of science fiction but also among cyberneticians and neural network analysts since the early days of artificial intelligence work. In 2001 (at the Cold Spring Harbour Laboratories, a center for biomedical research), a seminal meeting brought together neuroscientists, philosophers, computer scientists, and roboticists to discuss "Could Machines be Conscious?"

Some say no, at least in the relatively near term. In 2003, as one of The Long Now Foundation's "Long Bets: the Arena for Accountable Predictions," Nova Spivack offered the bet, "By 2050 no synthetic computer nor machine intelligence will have become truly self-aware (i.e., will become conscious)." He lays out a very articulate rationale for his position. But consider how much the world has changed since Dr. MacDougall's research, and with each generation, it is changing faster as one technology helps breed the next wave of innovation. While waiting thirty years for 2050 seems like a long time, thirty years ago, the internet was just getting started, mobile phones were rare and huge, and personal computers were mainly in the garages of nerds. We now carry the equivalent of massive IBM mainframe computers in our pockets, and throw them away every couple of years when something cooler appears.

Antonio Regalado explores another view in his article on "What It Will Take for Computers to Be Conscious" in the MIT Technology Review (Regalado, 2014). He interviews Christof Koch, who left Caltech in 2011 to join the Allen Institute (here in Seattle). He is working on an "integrated information theory" that suggests consciousness emerges from how our brains are structured for storage and in their interconnections. He believes that if he can develop such a theory, it could help diagnose degrees of consciousness within people whose brains are damaged, across different species, and even among machines. Furthermore, Koch believes that while consciousness is a fundamental property of the universe, there is a difference between simulating consciousness and being conscious.

He does, however, recognize the significant group of people (e.g., Daniel Dennett and Ray Kurzweil) who are even further along the functionalist dimension of "if you can simulate everything about consciousness, it is conscious." This is a little like the character Data on *Star Trek: Next Generation*, who is always searching for his own emotions and neglects the obvious that he often is expressing them. Across this growing field of artificial intelligence, as it moves at an accelerating pace, this debate is growing ever more intense. It is likely to continue as the technology enables more and more sophisticated capabilities. Stephen Hawking (1998) provides an appropriate caution when he says, "Some people say that computers can never show true intelligence whatever that may be. But it seems that if complicated chemical molecules can operate in humans to make them intelligent, then equally complicated electronic circuits can also make computers act intelligently. If they are intelligent, they can presumably design computers that have even greater complexity and intelligence."[174]

CONCLUDING REFLECTIONS

I began by sharing some of my own biases as a Christian exploring and refining my beliefs in the context of our contemporary understanding of our world and ourselves. But I have also shared the questions that began my journey through this natural history of the soul and new questions that have emerged.

In Chapter 1, it became clear that the soul and the afterlife pervade our American culture. Our everyday, common-sense beliefs are a melting pot of all the different ideas that we have absorbed through history. The forces that have shaped us include biology, evolving cultures and creative expression, various religious traditions, and that which provides emotional value to us as individuals and social value as it helps us live together in communities.

We want to be in heaven, and just as the Egyptians did, we often want our beloved pets there with us as well. Chapter 2 surveyed our beliefs about pet souls and the afterlife. This desire probably is a bit of wishful thinking, but what does seem like a more robust idea is that if the Judeo-Christian afterlife is a new world, that world would have animals in it. Furthermore, there are suggestions within Jewish and Christian scriptures that the creation has a connection to the Creator, is suffering now, and will rise up in praise as the master plan unfolds. One of the charges to humanity is our stewardship of the creation of which we are a part. In addition, of course, there is a long tradition of the idea of reincarnation, and in that tradition, we not only will be with our animals, but we might also be our animals for a few lives.

We also looked at some of the attributes in animals that we commonly associate with our souls. I speculated that just as the animal kingdom evolved to become us, perhaps some of the attributes we use as evidence of a soul also evolved in the process until they coalesced within us. This, in turn, suggests another way of thinking about the experiences we have around death and how we make sense of them in terms of their evolutionary value. This approach also encourages us to think about our continuing evolution as a species, the technologies we are creating, and what we might find out in the universe.

Chapter 3 traced the early emergence of a sense of an afterlife and rituals around death (incl. art and burial practices). These early end-of-life beliefs and activities, and probably the beginning-of-life fertility rituals, eventually evolved into rich religious frameworks. As our storytelling skills emerged and our ability to think more abstractly grew, we started giving voice to our experiences of death and grief, and finding ways to manage them. Some of our experiences are probably associated with the properties of our bodies that we saw evolving in Chapter 2, and shaped and were shaped by the emergence of our communities and cultures. The experiences that we commonly have today in these areas have a long history. They and the characteristics that enable them apparently have provided survival value to us as a species.

Religions fleshed out and gave structure to our stories and rituals around the soul and the afterlife (incl. how we came to be). As writing and culture developed, an engine emerged for developing and testing ideas based on the value they bring. A common theme is if we believe in God, we should show it by exhibiting love and compassion for our neighbors (esp. those in need). Loving our neighbors makes the here and now better, as well as the afterlife. We see a great arc across human history and individual lives pushing towards a deeper understanding and appreciation of a spiritual dimension that can influence our activity and development in the physical world. This could be a kind of virtuous cycle of cultural evolution. We also began seeing documentation of the ongoing influence of how we as humans have managed our grief (individually and collectively), our experiences of what feels like contact with a spiritual world, and the stories emerging from the ambiguity at the boundary between life and death.

As cultures became more sophisticated, philosophers began to step back and start thinking in detail about how the world works. They speculated and reasoned about the sets of principles that could explain the world as we see it and our place within it. Chapter 4 covered several philosophers whose ideas are still with us today, including those that certainly have influenced Judeo-Christian theology's evolution over the last couple of millennia. Philosophy, especially, explored the nature of who we are (incl. as souls), how our minds and bodies work in concert, and how we understand ourselves within the world.

Chapter 5, in turn, went deeper into some of the religious traditions with the most followers, especially in the United States. The major division in models of the soul and the afterlife are the Judeo-Christian family of beliefs and the Eastern religions. There are some concepts in each, however, that are similar. That overlap is probably why we see influences of both in contemporary culture. Religion has largely been ceded ownership of the idea of the soul at this point, but its special interest is generally in answering questions about what happens after this life and the implications of that afterlife for how we should behave in this one.

In philosophy, a more empirical analysis initially of the soul, and then eventually the self and consciousness (and the mind-body problem) led to the growth of a more scientific approach. Materialism and physicalism became the standard perspective for a working scientific, naturalistic method. Psychology split off from philosophy, and it, in turn, evolved into functionalism, neuroscience, and other common approaches today. Chapter 6 examined some of the various ideas relevant to our understanding of the soul (or self) and the afterlife. This began with an approach that takes the spiritual experiences we have—including around life, death, and the afterlife—and treats them as data that reflects evolutionary biological forces. The argument is related to the one made in Chapter 2. We then explored the fuzzy, ever-moving boundary between life and death. We looked at the experiences of those who have approached death and returned, and then what we go through during the active dying process. We examined attributes that have been associated with our experience of the soul and their biological bases. Some of these functional areas have also been associated with phenomena that we see at the end of life, and they may be the mechanism for providing some of that evolutionary value.

A key observation is that increasingly with modern technology's reductionist approach, we can tie many of the attributes we experience and see in others (and in higher animals) to specific biological functions. The challenge still is adequately explaining the meta-phenomena that we experience, things like mind, consciousness, and self, and our spiritual natures. This is the same challenge that contemporary philosophy has as well. As with quantum physics and astrophysics, when you cannot measure something, it is challenging to get your arms around it. Still, at the same time, modern physics and mathematics are uncovering alternative perspectives on reality that push the edges of our imaginations. String theorists are thinking about dimensions beyond those in which we live, including multiverses and parallel universes. In psychology, we already recognize that the reality we experience is just one version constructed by our minds. Practically, finding meaning is often about having a faith framework that provides value in making sense of our lives and experiences, and that lets us function effectively within the larger reality.

What the scientific method can do is clarify our experiences around the soul and the afterlife, and help us theorize about how the experiences emerge in our consciousness and the evolutionary value they provide. We may be able to leverage that understanding to increase the quality of life. We may also see patterns that suggest characteristics of the reality in which we exist that we cannot yet study directly, much as we do with other areas of science. What many have identified as a spiritual dimension or alternative reality, may yet fit within a framework of emerging theories within physics and biology.

My Takeaways

As for my question about what my soul is like and what that means for my life after death, I have touched on a few of these points in this last chapter. I still am a dualist, but with that Judeo-Christian recognition that the soul's value is enhanced when paired with a body since it is in the pairing that we fulfill our creative, stewardship, and searcher-for-truth roles as individuals and as a species. I have concluded that the core of my soul is whatever it means to be in the "image of God," whether it evolved in us or appears in us as a seed that develops as we grow as individuals.

I recognize that there are identifiable areas of the brain associated with creating a sense of self and personhood, and that are associated with supporting relationships. Still, I cannot help but feel that what is being grown in the soul by its existence within the body is indeed some *higher-level* sense of selfness, personhood, and the fundamental essence of relationship with God and with others that will persist after death. I also am currently leaning towards the idea that the awareness of my soul's characteristics is like my consciousness of reality. It is probably a creation of my brain that suggests the reality that is "out there" and helps me function in this world (incl. a spiritual reality), but it doesn't fully encompass it. In essence, there is possibly more to my soul than just the *experience* of my soul. Eventually, part of the afterlife will be experiencing more of reality that includes the spiritual dimension, perhaps in a new body or bodies. In a Platonic sense, there is also something attractive about the idea of the soul understanding God's ultimate truths and the nature of God's creation.

It also seems clear to me that part of why we have bodies is to grow our ability to understand these more profound truths, bring heaven into being in the world in which we live, and prepare for graduate school in the afterlife. I suspect that the language that implies I will be literally resurrected in my current old body with my thinning hair and scraggy beard misses the intent of the promise. Instead, I think Philippians 3:21 "by the power that enables him to bring everything under his control, will transform our lowly bodies so that they will be like his glorious body" is probably closer to the mark. I think God will continue to leverage us as souls in bodies as active participants in the eternal creative process, which strikes me as part of God's fundamental nature. God will insert us into the bodies that we need. When we look at loved ones, we will not be limited by their physical form but will know and recognize their souls, as we may do when we embrace. The early Jewish view of eternity as being to the edge of what we know and beyond, also keeps more surprises as a possibility in our futures. Eternity I hope, is not one static note, one long "Ommm" or "Amennn." I envision it as an eternally growing set of stories and songs.

As you read this book, you hopefully looked at what I found along with the other sources that may have occurred to you, applied your filters, and perhaps have drawn conclusions about who you are and what your future will be. Still, in the great line of human history, most of us feel death after the lives we have had is not the end. For myself, I would agree with the many religious and spiritual traditions that there is undoubtedly an exciting afterlife awaiting us. Furthermore, as our species continues to mature, there will be moral and ethical challenges that we will have to wrestle with in light of whatever our beliefs are about the soul and the afterlife. I also believe the richness of living things that shine with the likeness of God will continue to grow. At the very least, as I promised in the Introduction, I can certify that many of the questions and speculations raised through this book make excellent dinner conversation!

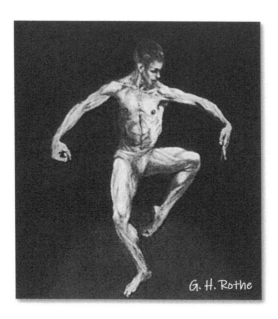

---

[145] I have to admit, my daughters, as they were starting to babble when they were little, certainly seemed like they might have their own personal languages.

[146] Do not try this at home.

[147] This number, used by Shakespeare and others, comes from Psalms 90 (KJV):

"The days of our years are threescore years and ten;
and if by reason of strength they be fourscore years,
yet is their strength labor and sorrow;
for it is soon cut off, and we fly away."

[148] Yet another reason to look at popular culture's explorations of the implications, for example, by watching *Gattaca* (1997).

[149] Among our ancestors, there was a sense of a parallel or alternate spiritual world. While this idea went through a time of being dismissed by materialist thinkers, physics has been postulating a universe that contains more dimensions than those which we physically occupy, and modes of existence that are alternatives to ours.

[150] The sense in the Hebrew here is probably not as much about control, as it is about being a kind of benevolent leader or steward for God. The sense of the Hebrew is we should be living among the rest of creation, and having a relationship with and caring for them as their lives contribute to ours and as we learn from them.

[151] This is with the exception of those views that see an eventual annihilation for those not spending eternity with God.

[152] There is irony in how earnestly some Americans yearn to be subjects in a kingdom, while taking particular pride in resisting centralized authority in the here and now. It reminds me of how I have cautioned employees and students to be careful when they escalate their disputes to upper management, because they may not be happy with what the supreme judge decides.

[153] An angel could even appear to Balaam's donkey, and not be seen by Balaam at all.

[154] Islam does say there will be marriage in heaven.

[155] I cover Mormons (a.k.a. the Church of Jesus Christ and Later Day Saints) and Muslim beliefs about the afterlife in more detail in the sections on their faiths.

[156] The idea of a "purpose" is an interesting one. During our lifetimes we may spend time thinking about our purpose during however many years we are allotted. When I was a manager, Human

Resources often reminded us that we do not hire for a project we hire for a career. When we think about our purpose, presumably God is thinking about the purpose of keeping us around for an eternity. My gut feeling is that somehow there must be more than simply existing in an adoring state. That would not be an ideal that we would recognize even in this world.

157 This does seem to acknowledge that there will exist a kind of spiritual sight, and that sight may be available in some sense now even if, as it says in 1 Corinthians 13:12, "For now we see only a reflection as in a mirror" (NIV) or "For now we see through a glass, darkly" (KJV).

158 One of the flaws that hopefully will be fixed is the musical talent that some of us lack.

159 Today, many recognize that a disability does not mean something is wrong with the person, but rather it is a problem with how the world itself is designed and we need to apply our creative talents and compassion to fix it.

160 It is worth remembering that some of our most meaningful moments and important steps in our growth are associated with experiencing and processing sadness.

161 Interestingly, in life, having everything we want reduces the value of the experiences and the opportunities for growth. Research shows even billionaires in the point one percent are not necessarily significantly more satisfied and happier than many of the rest of us.

162 I have never heard a sermon preached on this, but one interpretation of the "new heavens and the new Earth" is in parallel to Genesis 1:1. That would mean in Revelation 20:15 and 21:1 we might need to run through a Big Crunch to eliminate the old universe, and then a new Big Bang. Since God used almost fourteen billion years to create the current universe, a big chunk of the afterlife might be waiting for the next one to be ready for us. Perhaps this is more visionary than literal? Or, if we are freely speculating here, it may be a shift to an alternative universe predicted by the ten-dimensional string theory in physics.

163 One estimate of the total number of people who have lived on Earth is at fivethirtyeight.com/features/what-are-the-demographics-of-heaven/. Not everyone will have an equally good view of the throne room I suspect.

164 For some of us Scandinavians, we have already done a pretty good job of eliminating crying.

165 A place where there is no night, where everything is bright all the time, does not sound particularly pleasant either. As a metaphor, perhaps…

166 While it is harder to imagine a literal implementation of this vision, especially with billions of people in bodies arrayed around a throne, this is an area where it is easier to think about either the omniscient God being directly experienced everywhere rather than literally sitting on a throne, or where having a body might not be as useful as being one of billions of disembodied spirits.

167 One thing to note for those with a more libertarian or "Give me liberty or give me death" bent, is that heaven will not be a democracy. No "sin" means no one disobeys. Freedom is not one of the characteristics of heaven in the Abrahamic religions, as far as we know.

168 The focus, as elsewhere, really is we cannot know until we get there, so let's get on with exercising our being in the image of God to creatively fulfill the vision of making this world an expression of what it should be.

169 It should be recognized, for the literalists, that Adam and Eve eating of the tree violated God's command to not do it, but the act was not identified as a "sin" per se. Indeed, one of the key issues seemed to be "knowing good and evil" and as a result God said they "now became like one of us." In other words, they understood morality, and that implies they now shared a property of God that God had not given them. Christians, of course, believe that the plural form "us" refers to the Trinity, while others believe it reflected the early polytheistic roots of Judaism with God as above all others, or was more of a royal "we."

170 Assuming that babies before and after they are born, and children up to the age of accountability (usually assumed to be puberty) are admitted to heaven, there is a question about how that actually works in practice. Do the youngest enter heaven as fetuses and babies? Do they then grow for some time before settling into eternity? Do they ever have a chance to exercise free will even if they have to leave heaven? If they automatically accept salvation at that point, wouldn't that apply to others who have never heard the gospel? If they are given bodies, what kind of bodies would they be given? If we had to be alive for awhile to become what we are intended to be (which usually happens as a result of the pains and tears of life), how will that be made up in heaven?

171 While the general theme of aliens being essentially human, or having more intelligence or a higher (or lower) level of moral judgment than we do, is a common theme in science fiction, alien religion is less often explored. One series that comes close to the issues being discussed here is C. S. Lewis' *Space Trilogy*, and another that explores some of these of the questions is Orson Scott Card's *Speaker for the Dead*.

172 Given our history over the last two thousand years, we might have productive conversations looking for shared insights and common beliefs, we might try to convert one another, or we might go to war. It could be especially tense if we discovered they were doing a better job of living out their faith than we have done.

173 Nuclear transplantation is another procedure that is used today that raises the issue of what happens with the soul when the nucleus of an early stage embryo is transplanted into an unfertilized egg (if anything).

174 This is not unlike the computer called Deep Thought in *The Hitchhiker's Guide to the Galaxy*.

BIBLIOGRAPHY

Afterlife in Judaism (n.d.). Retrieved from *Jewish Virtual Library*: www.jewishvirtuallibrary.org/afterlife

Alcorta, C. S. (2005). Ritual, Emotion, and Sacred Symbols. *Human Nature*, 16(4), 323-359.

Aldhous, P. (2011). Elephants Know When They Need a Helping Trunk. Retrieved from *New Scientist*: www.newscientist.com/article/dn20212-elephants-know-when-they-need-a-helping-trunk/

Alex, B. (2018). Chimps Know Death When They See It. Retrieved from *Discover*: www.discovermagazine.com/planet-earth/chimps-know-death-when-they-see-it

Alex, B. (2021). Which Ancient City is Considered the Oldest in the World. Retrieved from *Discover*: www.discovermagazine.com/planet-earth/which-ancient-city-is-considered-the-oldest-in-the-world

Ancient Theories of the Soul (2009). Retrieved from *Stanford Encyclopedia of Philosophy*: plato.stanford.edu/entries/ancient-soul/

Anderson, J. R. (2018). Chimpanzees and Death. Retrieved from *Royal Society Publishing*: royalsocietypublishing.org/doi/10.1098/rstb.2017.0257

Andrei, M. (2015). Mankind and Its Relatives – Modern Homo Species. Retrieved from *ZME Science*: www.zmescience.com/science/archaeology/humanitys-relatives-modern-homo-species/

Archeology of the Hebrew Bible (2008). Retrieved from *NOVA Newsletter*: www.pbs.org/wgbh/nova/article/archeology-hebrew-bible/

Atkinson, Q. D. (2011). Beliefs About God, the Afterlife and Morality Support the Role of Supernatural Policing in Human Cooperation. *Evolution and Human Behavior*, 32(1), 41–49.

Ātman (Hinduism) (n.d.). Retrieved from *Wikipedia*: en.wikipedia.org/wiki/Atman_(Hinduism)

Attitudes Toward Spirituality and Religion (2018). Retrieved from *Gallup on Being Christian in Western Europe*: www.pewforum.org/2018/05/29/attitudes-toward-spirituality-and-religion/

Baker, C. F. (1972). *A Dispensational Theology*. Grand Rapids, MI: Grace Bible College Publications.

Bates, A. W. (2017). Have Animals Souls? The Late-Nineteenth Century Spiritual Revival and Animal Welfare. In A. W. Bates, *Anti-Vivisection and the Profession of Medicine in Britain: A Social History*. London, UK: Palgrave Macmillan. Retrieved from: www.ncbi.nlm.nih.gov/books/NBK513717/

Bayer, S. and Hettinger, A. (2019). Storytelling: A Natural Tool to Weave the Threads of Science and Community Together. *Bulletin of the Ecological Society of America*. Retrieved from: doi.org/10.1002/bes2.1542

BBC (2020). What Does Judaism Teach About Animal Rights? Retrieved from *Bitesize: Animal Rights*: www.bbc.co.uk/bitesize/guides/zsnv87h/revision/5

Becoming Like God (n.d.). Retrieved from *The Church of Jesus Christ of Latter-day Saints*: www.churchofjesuschrist.org/study/manual/gospel-topics-essays/becoming-like-god?lang=eng&_r=1

Being With Someone When They Die (n.d.). Retrieved from *Dying Matters*: www.dyingmatters.org/page/being-someone-when-they-die

Bell, G. and Gray, J. (1997). The Revolution Yet to Happen. In P. J. Denning (Ed.), *Beyond Calculation: The Next Fifty Years of Computing*. New York, NY: Springer-Verlag.

Benner, J. E. (n.d.). Eternity. Retrieved from *Ancient Hebrew Research Center*: www.ancient-hebrew.org/definition/eternity.htm

Bering, J. M. (2002). Intuitive Conceptions of Dead Agents' Minds: The Natural Foundations of Afterlife Beliefs as Phenomenological Boundary. *Journal of Cognition and Culture*, 2(4), 263-308.

Bethune, B. (2013). Why So Many People—Including Scientists—Suddenly Believe in an Afterlife. Retrieved from *Maclean's*: www.macleans.ca/society/life/the-heaven-boom/

Birch, J. S. (2020). Dimensions of Animal Consciousness. Retrieved from *Trends in Cognitive Sciences*: www.cell.com/trends/cognitive-sciences/fulltext/S1364-

6613(20)30192-3

Blake, A. (2021). The Rapid Decline of White Evangelical America? New Data Suggests a Bigger Decrease Then Previously Understood – Including in the GOP. *Washington Post*, July 8.

Bräuer, J., Hanus, D., Pika, S., Gray, R., and Uomini, N. (2020). Old and New Approaches to Animal Cognition: There Is Not "One Cognition." *Journal of Intelligence*, 8(3). Retrieved from: www.ncbi.nlm.nih.gov/pmc/articles/PMC7555673/

Brean, J. (2018). Millennials Are More Likely to Believe in an Afterlife Than are Older Generations. Retrieved from *National Post*: nationalpost.com/news/canada/millennials-do-you-believe-in-life-after-life#:~:text=It%20is%20a%20counterintuitive%20finding,project%20to%20track%20religious%20behaviour

Bruinius, H. (2017). Amid Evangelical Decline, Growing Split Between Young Christians and Church Elders. Retrieved from *The Christian Science Monitor*: www.csmonitor.com/USA/Politics/2017/1010/Amid-Evangelical-decline-growing-split-between-young-Christians-and-church-elders

Bryks, R. T. (2017). Life After Death. Retrieved from *The Rabbi with Answers*: rabbiwithanswers.com/life-after-death

Burton, N. (2012). The Origins of Heaven and Hell. Retrieved from *Psychology Today*: www.psychologytoday.com/us/blog/hide-and-seek/201206/the-origins-heaven-and-hell

Burton, T. I. (2017). "Spiritual but not religious": Inside America's Rapidly Growing Faith Group. Retrieved from *vox.com*: www.vox.com/identities/2017/11/10/16630178/study-spiritual-but-not-religious

Captive Killer Whales Share Personality Traits with Humans and Chimps (2018). Retrieved from *EarthSky*: earthsky.org/earth/killer-whales-personality-traits#:~:text=Killer%20whales%20share%20some%20personality,according%20to%20a%20new%20study

Carey, B. (2008). Standing in Someone Else's Shoes, Almost for Real. Retrieved from: www.nytimes.com/2008/12/02/health/02mind.html

Cartwright, M. (2017). Ancestor Worship in Ancient China. Retrieved from *Ancient History Encyclopedia*: www.ancient.eu/article/1132/ancestor-worship-in-ancient-china/

Catechism of the Catholic Church (n.d.). Retrieved from *Catechism of the Catholic Church*: www.vatican.va/archive/ENG0015/__P2M.HTM

Center, R. (2020). Paradise Polled: Americans and the Afterlife. Retrieved from *RoperCenter.Cornell.edu*: ropercenter.cornell.edu/paradise-polled-americans-and-afterlife

Chow, D. (2014). Killer Whale Populations Took Deep Dive During Ice Age. Retrieved from *NBC News*: www.nbcnews.com/science/science-news/killer-whale-populations-took-deep-dive-during-ice-age-wbna54280475

Clark, R. S. (2014). Reformed Basics on Dichotomy and Trichotomy. Retrieved from *Recovering the Reformed Confessions*: heidelblog.net/2014/03/reformed-basics-on-dichotomy-and-trichotomy/

Clegg, C. S. (2019). The Undiscovered Countries: Shakespeare and the Afterlife. *Religions*, 10, 174. Retrieved from: www.mdpi.com/2077-1444/10/3/174

Clottes, J. and Lewis-Williams, D. (1998). *The Shamans of Prehistory: Trance and Magic in the Painted Caves*. New York, NY: Harry N. Abrams Publishers.

Conservatives (2020). Retrieved from *Religious Landscape Study*: www.pewforum.org/religious-landscape-study/political-ideology/conservative/

Cooper, J. (2000). *Body, Soul & Life Everlasting*. Grand Rapids, MI: Wm. B. Eerdmans-Lightning Source.

Cooper, M. (2017). Jewish Word | Golem. Retrieved from *Moment*: momentmag.com/jewish-word-golem/

Coren, S. (2013). The Truth About Cats and Dogs—by the Numbers. Retrieved from *Psychology Today: Canine Corner*: www.psychologytoday.com/us/blog/canine-corner/201305/the-truth-about-cats-and-dogs-the-numbers#:~:text=Approximately%205%20to%207%20million,and%2070%25%20of%20cats).&text=While%20the%20number%20of%20owned,of%20owned%20cats%20are%20female

Coyle, S. (2020). Death: Can Our Final Moment be Euphoric? Retrieved from *BBC Future*: www.bbc.com/future/article/20200205-death-can-our-final-moment-be-euphoric

Creating God (2018). Retrieved from *NPR: Hidden Brain*: www.npr.org/2018/07/16/628792048/creating-god

Daley, J. (2018). Study Suggests Dolphins and Some Whales Grieve Their Dead. Retrieved from *Smithsonian Magazine*: www.smithsonianmag.com/smart-news/study-suggests-dolphins-and-some-whales-grieve-their-dead-180969414/#:~:text=For%20years%2C%20there's%20been%20anecdotal,unwilling%20to%20abandon%20the%20body

Daley, J. (2018). We Haven't Been Zapped Out of Existence Yet, So Other Dimensions Are Probably Super Tiny. Retrieved from *Smithsonian Magazine*: www.smithsonianmag.com/

Dalrymple, T. (2020). Why Evangelicals Disagree on the President. Retrieved from *Christianity Today Editorial*: www.christianitytoday.com/ct/2020/november-web-only/trump-election-politics-church-kingdom.html

Davis, S. (2016). Most Distinctive Obituary Euphemism for 'Died' in Each State. Retrieved from *Mental Floss.com*: www.mentalfloss.com/article/77544/most-distinctive-obituary-euphemism-died-each-state

Delistraty, C. (2014). Why Do We Believe In Heaven? Retrieved from *Thought Catalog*: thoughtcatalog.com/cody-delistraty/2014/02/why-do-we-believe-in-heaven/

DeRitter, M. (2019). Do Animals Go to Heaven? Retrieved from *mlive.com*: www.mlive.com/living/kalamazoo/2010/07/do_animals_go_to_heaven.html

Donovan, J. M. (2006). *Anthropology and Law*. New York, NY: Berghahn Books.

Duin, J. (2018). A Native American Tribe Demands the Return of Its Spiritual Relative — an Orca. Retrieved from *Religion News Service*: religionnews.com/2018/12/10/a-native-american-tribe-demands-the-return-of-its-spiritual-relative-an-orca/

Early Human Migrations (n.d.). Retrieved from *Wikipedia*: en.wikipedia.org/wiki/Early_human_migrations

Europe (2015). Retrieved from *The Future of World Religions: Population Growth Projections, 2010-2050*: www.pewforum.org/2015/04/02/europe/

Facts and Details (n.d.). Islamic Views on Heaven, Hell, Death and Judgement. Retrieved from: factsanddetails.com/world/cat55/sub358/item1449.html

Fallio, V. W. (2006). *New Developments in Consciousness Research*. New York, NY: Nova Publishers.

Father Saunders, W. P. (n.d.). Retrieved from *Straight Answers about the Catholic Faith*: catholicstraightanswers.com/

Feldman, D. (1994). Jewish Views on Abortion. In Bayme S., and Rosen, G. (Eds.). *The Jewish Family and Jewish Continuity.* ISBN 978-0-88125-495-2.

Fern, R. L. (2002). *Nature, God and Humanity: Envisioning an Ethics of Nature.* Cambridge, UK: Cambridge University Press.

Figula, M. S. (n.d.). The Afterlife. Retrieved from *Roman Pagan*: romanpagan.wordpress.com/the-afterlife/

Fischer, C. (2013). Boo! Americans and the Occult. Retrieved from: blogs.berkeley.edu/2013/10/29/boo-americans-and-the-occult/

Flaman, P. (2008). The Human Soul: A Catholic Theological Response to Non-Reductive Physicalism. Retrieved from *metanexus*: metanexus.net/human-soul-catholic-theological-response-non-reductive-physicalism/

Fogarty, G. G. (2018). Does Your Language Influence How You Think? Retrieved from *scientificamerican.com*: www.scientificamerican.com/article/does-your-language-influence-how-you-think/

George, J. J. (2020). The Soul's Journey Through the Ancient Egyptian Afterlife. Retrieved from *Owlcation*: owlcation.com/humanities/Journey-of-the-Soul-in-the-Ancient-Egyptian-Afterlife

Gervis, Z. (2018). 60 Percent of Americans Claim to Have Seen Ghosts. Retrieved from *Fox News Channel*: www.foxnews.com/lifestyle/60-percent-of-americans-claim-to-have-seen-ghosts

Goetz, S. and Taliaferro, C. (2011). *A Brief History of the Soul.* Hoboken, NJ: Wiley-Blackwell.

Goldingay, J. E. (2006). *Old Testament Theology (Vol. 2)*, 640.

Graham, B. (2011). We Will Be Given New Bodies in Heaven. Retrieved from *SeattlePI.com*: www.seattlepi.com/news/article/We-will-be-given-new-bodies-in-heaven-1182877.php

Grantham-Philips, W. (2020). This Orca Carried Her Dead Calf for 17 Days and 1,000 Miles. Now, She's Pregnant Again. Retrieved from *USA Today*: www.usatoday.com/story/news/nation/2020/07/28/orca-killer-whale-who-carried-dead-calf-miles-pregnant-again/5524797002/

Gray, H. T. (2008). Will Your Pets be Waiting for You in the Afterlife? Retrieved from *chicagotribune.com*: www.chicagotribune.com/news/ct-xpm-2008-08-27-

0808250353-story.html

Hamm, R. B. (2009). Hamlet and Horace Walpole's The Castle of Otranto. *Studies in English Literature 1500-1900*, 49(3), 667-692.

Harner, M. (1982). *The Way of the Shaman*. New York, NY: Bantam.

Harner, M. (1985). Comments. *Current Anthropology*, 26, 452.

Heaven, Hell, and the Afterlife in Jewish Thought (n.d.). Retrieved from *jewishideas.org*: www.jewishideas.org/heaven-hell-and-afterlife-jewish-thought?gclid=Cj0KCQiAvP6ABhCjARIsAH37rbQqua0SeDt-YAWAdpPUv3grVzmXnJkGI0xIXDhDCAgLMTXu_mCXmCMaAmLUEALw_wcB

Herzog, H. (2016). What Kinds of People Believe Animals Go To Heaven? Retrieved from *psychologytoday.com*: www.psychologytoday.com/us/blog/animals-and-us/201608/what-kinds-people-believe-animals-go-heaven

Heyes, C. (2012). New Thinking: the Evolution of Human Cognition. *Philosophical Transactions of the Royal Society of London, 2091-2096*. Retrieved from: www.ncbi.nlm.nih.gov/pmc/articles/PMC3385676/

Hirst, K. K. (2019). Ochre - The Oldest Known Natural Pigment in the World. Retrieved from *Thought Co.*: www.thoughtco.com/ochre-the-oldest-known-natural-pigment-172032

History.com Editors (n.d.). Buddhism - Definition, Founder & Origins. Retrieved from *History.com*: www.history.com/topics/religion/buddhism

Hoffmann, D. L. (2018). U-Th Dating of Carbonate Crusts Reveals Neandertal Origin of Iberian Cave Art. *Science*. Retrieved from: science.sciencemag.org/content/359/6378/912.full?_ga=2.151659641.1567133246.1519029579-924051890.1506085357

Hogenboom, M. (2015). Humans Are Nowhere as Special as We Like to Think. Retrieved from *BBC: Earth*: www.bbc.com/earth/story/20150706-humans-are-not-unique-or-special

Hollander, L. E. (2001). Unexplained Weight Gain Transients at the Moment of Death. *Journal of Scientific Exploration*, 495-500.

Holzer, H. (2012). *Ghosts*. New York, NY: Open Road Media.

Hullinger, J. (2017). 7 Behaviors That Prove Elephants Are Incredibly Smart. Retrieved from *mentalfloss.com*: www.mentalfloss.com/article/55640/7-behaviors-prove-elephants-are-incredibly-smart

In Search of Self (2002). *Nature Neuroscience*, 5(11), 1099. Retrieved from: www.nature.com/natureneuroscience

Irons, W. (2001). Religion as a Hard-to-Fake Sign of Commitment. In R. Nesse (Ed.), *Evolution and the Capacity for Commitment*. New York, NY: Russell Sage.

Jabr, F. (2019). The Story of Storytelling. Retrieved from *Harper's Magazine*: harpers.org/archive/2019/03/the-story-of-storytelling

Jackson, A. V. (1906). Zoroastrianism and the Resemblances Between It and Christianity. *The Biblical World*, 27(5), 335-343. Retrieved from: www.jstor.org/stable/pdf/3140852.pdf

James, W. (1890). *Principles of Psychology*. New York, NY: Henry Holt and Company.

James, W. (1898). Human Immortality: Two Supposed Objections to the Doctrine. Retrieved from: www.uky.edu/~eushe2/Pajares/jimmortal.html

James, W. (1902). *The Varieties of Religious Experience: A Study in Human Nature*. Harvard, MA: Harvard University Press.

Jenn. (2016). SDSU Study: Religion Down, Afterlife Belief Up Among Millennials; Reason? Feeling "Entitled" to get "Something for Nothing." Retrieved from *The Search for Life After Death*: thesearchforlifeafterdeath.com/2016/03/22/sdsu-study-religion-down-afterlife-belief-up-among-millennials-reason-feeling-entitled-to-get-something-for-nothing/

Jonas, E. and Fischer, P. (2006). Terror Management and Religion - Evidence That Intrinsic Religiousness Mitigates Worldview Defense Following Mortality Salience. *Journal of Personality and Social Psychology*, 91(3), 553-567.

Jones, J. (2018). So Neanderthals Made Abstract Art? This Astounding Discovery Humbles Every Human. Retrieved from *The Guardian*: www.theguardian.com/artanddesign/2018/feb/23/neanderthals-cave-art-spain-astounding-discovery-humbles-every-human

Judaism (n.d.). Retrieved from *Britannica.com*: www.britannica.com/science/death/Mesopotamia#ref38508 2

Kelley, T. (2001). *The Art of Innovation*. New York, NY: Doubleday.

Kennedy, L. (2019). The Prehistoric Ages: How Humans Lived Before Written Records. Retrieved from *history.com*:

www.history.com/news/prehistoric-ages-timeline

Kitchener, C. (2018). What It Means to be Spiritual but Not Religious. Retrieved from *theatlantic.com*: www.theatlantic.com/membership/archive/2018/01/what-it-means-to-be-spiritual-but-not-religious/550337/

Koch, C. (2019). Is Death Reversible? Retrieved from *Scientific American*: www.scientificamerican.com/article/is-death-reversibl/

Kübler-Ross, E. (1969). *On Death and Dying: What the Dying Have to Teach Doctors, Nurses, Clergy & Their Own Families*. New York, NY: Scribner.

Landen, K. (n.d.). The Common Ground of Elephants and Humans. Retrieved from *zambezi.chobe*: elephantswithoutborders.org/downloadspapers/Common_grounds_elephants_humans.pdf

Lester, D. (2005). *Is There Life After Death? An Examination of the Empirical Evidence*. Jefferson, NC: McFarland & Company, Inc.

Lewis, M. E. (2010). *The Early Chinese Empires*. Cambridge, MA: Harvard University Press.

Lichfield, G. (2015). The Science of Near-Death Experiences. Retrieved from *The Atlantic*: www.theatlantic.com/magazine/archive/2015/04/the-science-of-near-death-experiences/386231/

Lieberman, P. (1991). *Uniquely Human*. Cambridge, MA: Harvard University Press.

Lindberg, T. (2007). What the Beatitudes Teach. Retrieved from *Hoover Institution Policy Review*: www.hoover.org/research/what-beatitudes-teach

Lipka, M. (2015). 18% of Americans Say They've Seen a Ghost. Retrieved from *Pew Research Center: Fact Tank*: www.pewresearch.org/fact-tank/2015/10/30/18-of-americans-say-theyve-seen-a-ghost/

Lorenz, H. (2009). Ancient Theories of Soul, In Edward N. Zalta (Ed.), *The Stanford Encyclopedia of Philosophy (Summer 2009 Edition)*. Retrieved from: plato.stanford.edu/archives/sum2009/entries/ancient-soul/

MacDougall, D. (1907). The Soul: Hypothesis Concerning Soul Substance Together with Experimental Evidence of the Existence of Such Substance. *American Medicine*. Retrieved from: books.google.com/books?id=sQAKAwAAQBAJ

Madison, P. (2018). Who First Buried the Dead? Retrieved from *Sapiens*: www.sapiens.org/culture/hominin-burial/

Mark, J. J. (2011). Mesopotamian Religion. Retrieved from *Ancient History Encyclopedia*: www.ancient.eu/Mesopotamian_Religion/

Martin, A. (2020). The History of Funeral Rites and Rituals of the Ancient World. Retrieved from *Choice Mutual*: choicemutual.com/funeral-rituals-ancient-world/

Martin, R. and Barresi, J. (2006). *The Rise and Fall of Soul and Self: An Intellectual History of Personal Identity*. Cambridge, MA: Cambridge University Press.

Martone, R. (2019). New Clues Found in Understanding Near-Death Experiences. Retrieved from *Scientific American*: www.scientificamerican.com/article/new-clues-found-in-understanding-near-death-experiences/

McAndrew, F. T. (2015). Why Some People See Ghosts and Other Apparitions. Retrieved from *PsychologyToday.com*: www.psychologytoday.com/us/blog/out-the-ooze/201507/why-some-people-see-ghosts-and-other-apparitions

McDonald, S. (2014). Dogs Love Us, Says Science – So We Have to Love Them Back. Retrieved from *The Guardian*: www.theguardian.com/commentisfree/2014/mar/17/dogs-rights-canine-sentience-research

McGraw, C. (1985). Gorilla's Pets: Koko Mourns Kitten's Death. *Los Angeles Times*.

Meinch, T. (2021). The Future of Psychotherapy? *Discover*, July/August.

Menendez, D. H. (2020). Children's Emerging Understanding of Death. *Child Development Perspectives*, 1-6.

Merriam-Webster (n.d.). Soul. Retrieved from *Merriam-Webster.com Dictionary*: www.merriam-webster.com/dictionary/soul

Michel, A. (2017). Humans Are Animals, Too: A Whirlwind Tour of Cognitive Biology. Retrieved from *Association for Psychological Science*: www.psychologicalscience.org/observer/humans-are-animals-too-a-whirlwind-tour-of-cognitive-biology

Mithen, S. J. (1996). *The Prehistory of the Mind*. London, UK: Thames and Hudson.

MJL (n.d.). Body and Soul. Retrieved from *My Jewish Learning*: www.myjewishlearning.com/article/body-soul/

Monyak, S. (2018). When the Law Recognizes Animals as People. Retrieved from *newrepublic.com*: newrepublic.com/article/146870/law-recognizes-animals-people

Moody, R. A. (1975). *Life After Life*. New York, NY: Bantam

Books.

Morgan, T. J.-T. (2015). Experimental Evidence for the Co-evolution of Hominin Tool-making Teaching and Language. *Nature Communications*, 6, 6029. Retrieved from: doi.org/10.1038/ncomms7029

Morin, R. (2015). A Conversation with Koko the Gorilla. Retrieved from *The Atlantic*: www.theatlantic.com/technology/archive/2015/08/koko-the-talking-gorilla-sign-language-francine-patterson/402307/

Mysteries of Egypt: The Creation Myth (n.d.). Retrieved from *Canadian Museum of History*: www.historymuseum.ca/cmc/exhibitions/civil/egypt/egcr09e.html

Native American Religion and Spirituality – Common Threads, Unique Beliefs, and Too Many Misconceptions (2019). Retrieved from *powwows.com*: www.powwows.com/native-american-religion-and-spirituality-common-threads-unique-beliefs-and-too-many-misconceptions/

Newport, F. (2011). More Than 9 in 10 Americans Continue to Believe in God. Retrieved from *gallup.com*: news.gallup.com/poll/147887/americans-continue-believe-god.aspx

Newport, F. (2016). Most Americans Still Believe in God. Retrieved from *gallup.com*: news.gallup.com/poll/193271/americans-believe-god.aspx

Oxford English Dictionary (OED, 2020). Soul. Retrieved from *OED Online*: www-oed-com.offcampus.lib.washington.edu/view/Entry/185084?rskey=Sff2AA&result=2 (accessed February 13, 2021)

Olson, K. R. (2013). Children's Understanding of Death and the Afterlife. Retrieved from *Psychology Today*: www.psychologytoday.com/us/blog/developing-minds/201312/children-s-understanding-death-and-the-afterlife?amp

Pappas, N. (2017). Retrieved from *askphilosophers.org*: www.askphilosophers.org/question/26180

Paradise Polled: Americans and the Afterlife (2020). Retrieved from *Roper Center*: ropercenter.cornell.edu/paradise-polled-americans-and-afterlife

Peoples, H. C., Duda, P, and Marlowe, F. W. (2016). Hunter-Gatherers and the Origins of Religion. *Human Nature*, 27(3), 261-82. Retrieved from:

pubmed.ncbi.nlm.nih.gov/27154194/#:~:text=Results%20in dicate%20that%20the%20oldest,by%20shamanism%20and% 20ancestor%20worship.

Pew Research Center (2021). Religious Landscape Study. Retrieved from: www.pewforum.org/religious-landscape-study/

Pfeifer, J. H., Lieberman, M. D., and Dapretto, M. (2007). "I Know You Are But What Am I?!": Neural Bases of Self- and Social-Knowledge Retrieval in Children and Adults. *Journal of Cognitive Neuroscience*, 19(3), 1323-1337.

Physical and Emotional Changes as Death Approaches. (n.d.). Retrieved from *Frankel Cardiovascular Center: Michigan Medicine*: www.umcvc.org/health-library/aa150174

Progress and Plans (2020). Retrieved from *koko.org*: www.koko.org/about/programs/project-koko/progress-and-plans/

Rabbi Schulweis, H. (n.d.). Afterlife: What Happens After I Die. Retrieved and used with permission from *Valley Beth Shalom*: www.vbs.org/worship/meet-our-clergy/rabbi-harold-schulweis/sermons/afterlife-what-happens-after-i-die

Rabbis Brawer, N. and Romain, J. (2017). Does our dog have a soul? An Orthodox and a Reform Rabbi Tackle Issues in Contemporary Jewish life. Retrieved from *thejc.com*: www.thejc.com/judaism/rabbi-i-have-a-problem/does-our-dog-have-a-soul-1.441160

Ransome, A. (1909). *A History of Story-Telling*. London, UK: Scholar Select.

Redmon, T. (2020). Does the Greek Word Aion Mean Eternity? Retrieved from *Mercy on All*: www.mercyonall.org/posts/does-the-greek-word-aion-mean-eternity

Regalado, A. (2014). What It Will Take for Computers to Be Conscious. Retrieved from *MIT Technology Review*: www.technologyreview.com/2014/10/02/171077/what-it-will-take-for-computers-to-be-conscious/

Researchers Study Elephants' Unique Interactions with Their Dead (2020). Retrieved from *San Diego Zoo Institute for Conservation Research*: institute.sandiegozoo.org/news/researchers-study-elephants%E2%80%99-unique-interactions-their-dead

Roach, M. (2005). A Soul's Weight. Retrieved from: lostmag.matthewbrian.com/issue1/soulsweight.php

Russell, H. S. (2014). *Indian New England Before the Mayflower*. Lebanon, NH: University Press of New England.

Rutman, J. Y. (2016). In Search of the Soul: Between Torah and Science. Retrieved from *TheTorah.com*: www.thetorah.com/article/in-search-of-the-soul-between-torah-and-science

Safina, C. (2015). The Depths of Animal Grief. Retrieved from *Nova*: www.pbs.org/wgbh/nova/article/animal-grief/

Sahgal, N. (2018). 10 Key Findings about Religion in Western Europe. Retrieved from *Fact Tank: News in the Numbers*: www.pewresearch.org/fact-tank/2018/05/29/10-key-findings-about-religion-in-western-europe/

Sapir-Whorf Hypothesis. (n.d.). Retrieved from *ScienceDirect.com*: www.sciencedirect.com/topics/psychology/sapir-whorf-hypothesis

Schmidt, M. (2020). The Empathetic Reader. *Discover*.

Segal, E. (2002). Afterlife for Animals? Jewish Authorities Disagree as to Whether All Cows Go to Heaven. Retrieved from *myjewishlearning.com*: www.myjewishlearning.com/article/afterlife-for-animals/

Seth, A. K. (2020). Our Inner Universes: Reality is Constructed by the Brain, and No Two Brains Are Exactly Alike. *Scientific American*, Fall, 6-11.

Shermer, M. (2008). Patternicity: Finding Meaningful Patterns in Meaningless Noise. Retrieved from *Scientific American*: www.scientificamerican.com/article/patternicity-finding-meaningful-patterns/

Smith, S. B. (1901). Primitive Customs and Religious Beliefs of the Indians of the Pacific Northwest Coast. *The Quarterly of the Oregon Historical Society*, 2(3), 255-265. Retrieved from: www.jstor.org/stable/pdf/20609504.pdf

Society (n.d.). St. Francis of Assisi. Retrieved from: www.humanesociety.org/resources/st-francis-assisi

Sohn, E. (2019). Decoding Consciousness. *Nature*. Retrieved from: www.nature.com/articles/d41586-019-02207-1

Some American Indian Beliefs About an Afterlife (2015). Retrieved from *NativeAmericanRoots.net*: nativeamericannetroots.net/diary/1936

Sorlini, G. B. (1985). The Megalithic Temples of Malta. In P. A. Bonanno (Ed.), *Archaeology and Fertility Cult in the Ancient Mediterranean: Papers Presented at the First International Conference on Archeology of the Ancient Mediterranean*. Msida, Malta: University of Malta.

Spoon, M. (2018). A Video Game Can Change the Brain, May

Improve Empathy in Middle Schoolers. Retrieved from *sciencedaily.com*: www.sciencedaily.com/releases/2018/08/180809175051.htm

Standish, C. and Pike, A. (2018). It's Official: Neanderthals Created Art. Retrieved from *Sapiens*: www.sapiens.org/archaeology/neanderthal-art-discovery/

Stanghini, J. (2013). The History of Shamanism: A Brief Overview of Shamanism. Retrieved from *Jeremiah Stanghini*: jeremiahstanghini.com/2013/08/05/the-history-of-shamanism-a-brief-overview-of-shamanism-part-1/

Stavrianos, L. S. (1991). *A Global History: From Prehistory to the Present*. Hoboken, NJ: Prentice-Hall.

Steiner, R. (2015). Disembodied Souls: The Nefesh in Israel and Kindred Spirits in the Ancient Near East, with an Appendix on the Katemuwa Inscription. *Ancient Near East Monographs*, 11, 127.

Stewart, D. (n.d.).What Does Islam Believe About Resurrection, Judgment, and the Afterlife? (Heaven and Hell). Retrieved from *Blue Letter Bible*: www.blueletterbible.org/Comm/stewart_don/faq/islam/15-what-does-islam-believe-about-resurrection-judgement-and-the-afterlife.cfm

Stewart-Williams, S. (2018). Afterlife Beliefs: An Evolutionary Perspective. Retrieved from *OSF*: osf.io/rtmyk/

Strauss, M. (2016). The Campaign to Eliminate Hell. Retrieved from *National Geographic*: www.nationalgeographic.com/news/2016/05/1680513-theology-hell-history-christianity/

Sussman, D. (2005). Poll: Elbow Room No Problem in Heaven. Retrieved from *ABC News*: abcnews.go.com/US/Beliefs/story?id=1422658

Szczesniak, D. (2019). Usursonline.com. Retrieved from *Euphemisms for Death: 200+ Ways to Describe Death & Dying*: www.usurnsonline.com/oddbits/euphemisms-for-death/

Talor, A. E. (1955). *Aristotle*. Mineola, NY: Dover Publications.

Tarlach, G. (2018). What the Ancient Pigment Ochre Tells Us About the Human Mind. Retrieved from *Discover*: www.discovermagazine.com/planet-earth/prehistoric-use-of-ochre-can-tell-us-about-the-evolution-of-humans

Taylor, H. (1998). Large Majority of People Believe They Will Go to Heaven. Retrieved from *The Harris Poll*: theharrispoll.com/wp-content/uploads/2017/12/Harris-

Interactive-Poll-Research-LARGE-MAJORITY-OF-
PEOPLE-BELIEVE-THEY-WILL-GO-TO-H-1998-
08.pdf?fbclid=IwAR3NDg5A1AanMEBckNUrfO3OmPZm
WNnEP3vrtLdgiBshAMCvwLlAvWXMxE4#:~:text=Fully%
2084%25%20of%20all%20ad

Taylor, S. (2018). Near-Death Experiences and DMT. Retrieved
from *Psychology Today*:
www.psychologytoday.com/us/blog/out-the-
darkness/201810/near-death-experiences-and-dmt

The Global Religious Landscape (2012). Retrieved from
pewforum.org: www.pewforum.org/2012/12/18/global-
religious-landscape-exec/

The History of Dualism (n.d.). Retrieved from *The Basics of
Philosophy*: www.philosophybasics.com/branch_dualism.html

The Social Intelligence of Orcas and Communication – Orca Series
II (n.d.). Retrieved from *Orca Nation*:
www.orcanation.org/2019/10/10/the-social-intelligence-of-
orcas/#:~:text=Conclusion,they%20are%20highly%20intellig
ent%20animals.&text=The%20size%20and%20structure%20
of,sophisticated%20animal%20on%20the%20planet.

The Soul (2011). Retrieved from *NativeAmericanRoots.net*:
nativeamericannetroots.net/diary/1148

Twenge, J. M. (2016). *Declines in American Adults' Religious
Participation and Beliefs, 1972-2014*. Thousand Oaks, CA: Sage
Open. Retrieved from:
journals.sagepub.com/doi/10.1177/2158244016638133

University of British Columbia (2020). Hearing Persists at End of
Life. Retrieved from *Science Daily*:
www.sciencedaily.com/releases/2020/07/200708105935.htm
#:~:text=Now%20UBC%20researchers%20have%20evidenc
e,they%20are%20close%20to%20death.

University of Colorado Denver (2013). Early Human Burials
Varied Widely but Most Were Simple. Retrieved from
ScienceDaily:
www.sciencedaily.com/releases/2013/02/130221084747.htm

Walsh, R. (1989). What is a Shaman? Definition, Origin, and
Distribution. *Journal of Transpersonal Psychology*, 21(1).

Whetstine, L. M. (1996). The History of the Definition(s) of Death:
From the 18th Century to the 20th Century. *The Lancet*.
Retrieved from: doi:doi.org/10.1016/S0140-6736(96)04015-9

Whorf, B. L. (1949). Science and Linguistics. Retrieved from
web.mit.edu:

web.mit.edu/allanmc/www/whorf.scienceandlinguistics.pdf

Willis, M. (1995). Frankenstein and the Soul. Retrieved from *Essays in Criticism*: knarf.english.upenn.edu/Articles/willis.html

Wolff, P. and Holmes, K. J. (2011). Linguistic Relativity. Retrieved from: doi.org/10.1002/wcs.104

Wreschner, E. E.-W. (1980). Red Ochre and Human Evolution: A Case for Discussion [and Comments and Reply]. *Current Anthropology*, 21(5), 631-644. Retrieved from: www.jstor.org/stable/2741829?seq=1

Wuethrich, B. (1995). Elephants Lead the Way Out of Africa. Retrieved from *New Scientist*: www.newscientist.com/article/mg14619822-900-elephants-lead-the-way-out-of-africa/

Žabkar, L. V. (1968). Study of the Ba Concept in Ancient Egyptian Texts. Retrieved from *University of Chicago Press*: oi.uchicago.edu/sites/oi.uchicago.edu/files/uploads/shared/docs/saoc34.pdf

ABOUT THE AUTHOR

Arnold (Arnie) Lund, PhD, is a Professor of Practice at the University of Washington, Bothell, in the Computing & Software Systems Division of the School of Science, Technology, Engineering & Mathematics. His focus areas are artificial intelligence systems, adaptive and natural user interfaces, and interactive media design. He received his BA in Chemistry from the University of Chicago, with an emphasis on philosophy and psychology, and attended seminary at Trinity Evangelical Divinity School. He earned his MA in Experimental Psychology from California State University, Fullerton, and then returned to Chicago for his PhD in Experimental Psychology: Human Learning and Memory from Northwestern University.

He began his career at Bell Telephone Laboratories. Dr. Lund then moved to Ameritech in Chicago to help build their science and technology organization as a Senior Director of Human Factors and Emerging Technologies. After that, he and his family continued their migration to US West Advanced Technologies, and during the dot-com bubble, he joined the new Sapient office in Denver, Colorado. The next stop was as a Director of User Experience at Microsoft in Redmond, WA. Eventually, Dr. Lund joined GE Global Research at its new software center in the San Francisco Bay Area. He became the

Technology Leader for two labs working on a vision of a fully accessible, intelligent, and adaptive digital world. Finally, he moved back to Seattle to manage user research for Amazon's Alexa product before ending up as a professor at the University of Washington.

Dr. Lund has received thirty patents; and has published more than eighty articles on popular culture, emerging technologies, human-computer interaction, and management topics. He has written chapters in various books, and in 2011 published *User Experience Management: Essential Skills for Leading Effective UX Teams*. Dr. Lund is a member of the Association of Computing Machinery SIGCHI's Academy and is a Fellow of the Human Factors and Ergonomics Society. He is currently on the Board of Directors for the Foundation for Professional Ergonomics. He has also been on the Board of Directors for INFINITEC (an assistive technology center) and was President of the Board of Directors for the Board of Certification in Professional Ergonomics.

> *"Let knowledge grow from more to more and*
> *so be human life enriched."*
> – University of Chicago Motto